Criminology Throughout History

Critical Readings

CONTENTS

PREFACE	IX

PART I
Historical Development of Criminological Thought — 1

Part I Timeline — 1
Editor's Introduction — 8

READING 1
The Enlightenment's Philosophical Contributions to the Study of Crime and Justice — 12
Rosalva Resendiz, Ph.D. and Lucas E. Espinoza Ph.D.

READING 2
Classical Criminology — 20
Roger Hopkins Burke

READING 3
The Origins of Modern Criminology — 29
Rob Watts, Judith Bessant, and Richard Hil

READING 4
Born to Be Bad: Biological, Physiological, and Biosocial Theories of Crime — 53
Mark M. Lanier, Stuart Henry, and Desiré Anastasia

READING 5
Sociological Positivism — 70
Roger Hopkins Burke

READING 6
Capitalism as a Criminogenic Society: Conflict and Radical Theories of Crime — 102
Mark M. Lanier, Stuart Henry, and Desiré Anastasia

PART II
Early Theories of Causation 123

Part II Timeline 123
Editor's Introduction 126

READING 7
Anomie-Strain Theory 130
Timothy Brezina

READING 8
Learning Criminal Behavior: Social Process Theories 138
Mark M. Lanier, Stuart Henry, and Desiré Anastasia

READING 9
Labelling Theories 158
Roger Hopkins Burke

READING 10
Social Control Theories 172
Roger Hopkins Burke

PART III
New Directions in Criminology: In the Pursuit of Equality, Freedom, and Justice 187

Part III Timeline 187
Editor's Introduction 189

SECTION A
Feminist Criminology 195

READING 11
Feminist Criminology 196
Tim Newburn

READING 12
At the Intersections: Race, Gender and Violence 224
Nikki Jones and Jerry Flores

READING 13

Identities and Intersectionalities: Structured Action Theory, Left Realism, Postmodern Feminism, and Black/Multiracial Feminist Criminology   240
Claire M. Renzetti

SECTION B
Critical Criminology   **267**

READING 14

The History of Critical Criminology in the United States   268
Raymond Michalowski

READING 15

Keynote Address: Critical Criminology for a Global Age   284
Raymond Michalowski

READING 16

Crimes of the State   297
Richard Quinney

READING 17

A Suitable Amount of Street Crime and a Suitable Amount of White-collar Crime: Inconvenient Truths about Inequality, Crime and Criminal Justice   317
Paul Leighton and Jeffrey Reiman

PREFACE

This textbook arose out of a need to provide our students a way to situate themselves within the historical production of knowledge. Criminology has been traditionally taught as schools of thought. However, students who learn in this manner fail to gain a full understanding of the impact of history on the development of knowledge and theory. Students learn *about* criminology but are not immersed in criminology. In order to facilitate their learning, we have incorporated historical timelines to help students understand the historical forces that shaped their perspectives as theorists. In the spirit of C. W. Mills, we hope the student will be able to consider the theory within its historical period and critically analyze and compare the development of traditional criminology to critical and feminist perspectives. We begin the timeline with European history, and as we proceed, we begin to narrow our focus to events which have impacted the history of the United States.

According to C. W. Mills, in order to understand the social structure, we must develop a "quality of mind," or what he labels the sociological imagination. We must situate ourselves at the intersection of our biography and history to truly understand the forces that shape us and our society. In analyzing the social structure, we invite our students to consider Patricia Hill Collins's intersectionality, or the "matrix of domination," which uses concepts such as race, ethnicity, gender, sex, sexuality, etc., as an integrative, intersecting framework of analysis. The "matrix of domination" provides another level of analysis that helps us analyze systemic oppressions and the evolution of liberal philosophy, the social sciences, and criminology.

This book is to be used by undergraduate and graduate students of criminology and criminal justice programs. The textbook is divided into three parts. Part 1 focuses on the historical development of criminological thought, beginning with an overview of the impact of liberal philosophy. Part II takes a closer look at the early theories of causation. Part III provides new directions in criminology, embracing the ideals set by the liberal philosophers: equality, freedom, and justice.

PART I

Historical Development of Criminological Thought

Part I Timeline

1492	The beginning of conquest, colonization, and genocide of the Americas by Spain, Portugal, Britain, France, and the Netherlands
1642–1651	English Civil War
1650s–1810s	**The Enlightenment: Age of Reason**
1650	Spain forcibly kidnaps 300,000 Africans to be used as slaves in the Americas
1650–1726	Age of Piracy: Bands of pirates threaten military and commercial shipping in the Caribbean and along the North American Eastern Seaboard, the West African coast, and the Indian Ocean
1652	The Fronde: French aristocratic revolt against Cardinal Mazarin by members of Parliament.
1652	Anglo-Dutch War: England fights over control of trade and colonization
1654	Portugal signs the Treaty of Hague and keeps control of Brazil in South America
1659	Portugal gains their independence from Spain in the Battle of Elvas
1660	England establishes the Royal Society to promote scientific study
1660	The monarchy is restored in the Commonwealth of England, Scotland, and Ireland

1661	Louis XIV begins his rule of France with the death of regent Cardinal Mazarin
1661	French colonizers exile the Indigenous Caribs from their homeland, Martinique
1661	Barbados slave codes are established to maintain slavery in the Caribbean and the southern English colonies
1675–1676	King Philip's War: The Wampanoag Indians fight against English colonial settlers in New England for their land; the English settlers destroy the Wampanoag's villages and their chief, King Philip
1681	Religious persecution of Protestants (Huguenots) by King Louis XIV of France; almost 400,000 Huguenots convert to Catholicism
1682	King Louis XIV of France builds the lavish Versailles
1688	English Revolution/Glorious Revolution: War for the throne of James II of England
1689	English Constitution and Bill of Rights are signed by the Parliament
1692–1693	Salem Witch Trials, Massachusetts Bay Colony
1696	British establish the Navigation Acts to control trade, resulting in maritime piracy and smuggling in the colonies
1701–1714	War of the Spanish Succession: France and Austria fight for the Spanish throne
1703	Spain authorizes colonies to confer public offices to mestizos
1713	Britain exports African slaves to Spanish America
1718–1776	Under the Transportation Act, 30,000 British convicts are forcibly sent to the English colonies in America and Australia
1719	English stock market crashes due to fraud by King George I and the chancellor of the exchequer
1723	Peter the Great of Russia converts all household slaves into serfs
1727–1729	Anglo-Spanish War: War between Britain and Spain over the Netherlands
1733	France declares war on Austria in War of Polish Succession
1739–1748	War of Jenkins' Ear: Britain declares war on Spain over the land between South Carolina and Florida
1740	South Carolina introduces basic slave laws prohibiting the congregation of more than seven slaves
1740–1786	Fredrick II rules Prussia
1744–1748	King George's War: North American military operations of the War of Austrian Succession between Britain and France

1750–1917	**Age of Revolution: The Rise of Democratic Republics**
1754–1763	French and Indian War/The Seven Years' War: Britain and France fought over land boundaries in the New World; the Indians created alliances on both sides
1755	First Indian Department established as a wing of the British military to oversee relations between Britain and the indigenous people (disbanded in 1965)
1758–1761	Anglo-Cherokee War: English militia in Virginia attack and kill several Cherokee warriors, to which the Cherokee retaliate
1759	The Cherokee Nation declares open war against the British
1761	The Cherokee sign a peace treaty in Charleston, South Carolina, with Virginia
1761	Slavery is abolished in Portugal
1762–1796	Catherine the Great rules Russia with an iron fist after murdering her husband
1763–1766	Pontiac's War: Indians fight against the British in a series of attacks
1767	Jesuits are expelled from Spanish America
1773	Boston Tea Party: 342 chests of tea belonging to the British East India Company are thrown into the Boston Harbor by English colonists, disguised as Mohawk Indians, in protest of a tax on tea
1774	First Continental Congress is formed in Philadelphia, with representatives from all the English colonies except Georgia
1775–1783	American Revolution: War of independence between the English colonists in America and the British Empire
1776–1794	Cherokee-American Wars: Cherokees fight for control of their homelands in the frontier West
1776	Second Continental Congress issues the Declaration of Independence
1780–1790	Joseph II rules Austria
1783	Treaty of Paris recognizes American independence and ends the American Revolution
1785–1795	Northwest Indian War: War between the United States and a confederation of the Indian tribes, supported by the British
1786	Shay's Rebellion: Armed uprising in Massachusetts due to tax increases in the newly formed United States
1787	United States Constitution and Bill of Rights are signed
1787–1803	Spanish crown authorizes a botanical expedition to South America: Colombia, Ecuador, Panama, Venezuela, Peru, Brazil, and Western Guyana

1789	George Washington is inaugurated as first United States president
1789–1799	The French Revolution deposes the throne to establish a constitutional government
1789	Women's March on Versailles: The people riot over the high price of bread and the scarcity of it
1790s–1850s	**The Romantic Era: European Reaction to the Enlightenment and Industrial Revolution**
1790–1860s	Underground Railroad conducts slaves to freedom
1790	Pennsylvania limits the flogging of slaves to no more than a hundred lashes to avoid killing them
1792	September Massacre: King Louis XVI is arrested by insurgents in Paris, France, resulting in the death of nobles and priests
1793	France becomes a constitutional monarchy
1793	France's King Louis XVI and Queen Marie Antoinette are executed by guillotine
1793	Reign of Terror: Maximilien Robespierre, under the French Republic's Committee of Public Safety, arrests 300,000 and executes 17,000 enemies of the state
1794	Robespierre and his allies are arrested and executed as traitors to the Republic
1794	Slave Trade Act of 1794: Slave trade is banned between the United States and other foreign countries, leading to the increase of forced breeding of slaves
1794	Slavery is abolished in the French colonies
1796	Catherine the Great from Russia dies and is succeeded by Paul I
1796	Napoleon Bonaparte becomes commander of the French forces in Italy
1797	Treaty of Campo Formio: France gains territories from Austria
1799	Napoleon overthrows the Directory of France through a *coup d'état*
1802	Slavery is reintroduced in the French colonies
1803–1815	Napoleonic Wars: Bonaparte attempts to conquer Europe and Russia
1803	President Thomas Jefferson purchases the Louisiana territory from France and expands the boundary of the republic to the Rocky Mountains
1804	Napoleon crowns himself emperor of France
1805	Battle of Trafalgar: Britain defeats Spain, establishing British naval supremacy for more than 100 years
1810	Mexico begins fight for independence from Spain

1812–1815	War of 1812: The United States and the British fight over trade
1812–1814	Spain establishes a constitutional monarchy and in 1814 King Ferdinand VII replaces it with an absolute monarchy
1813–1814	Creek War: Creek Indians kill 250 white settlers in Alabama and are defeated by the military
1814–1815	Congress of Vienna: European states meet to provide a long-term peace plan after the French Revolutionary wars and the Napoleonic wars
1815	Napoleon Bonaparte is defeated by the British at the Battle of Waterloo and is exiled
1815–1824	Louis XVIII regains the French throne
1819	Onís-Adams Treaty: Spain sells Florida to the United States
1820	King Ferdinand VII is ousted from the Spanish throne
1820–1875	Texas Indian Wars: Conflict between white settlers and the Indigenous peoples of the Tejas region
1821	Agustín de Iturbide proclaims Mexico's independence
1821–1870	Comanche-Mexico Wars: Large-scale raids of Northern Mexico by Comanches
1822	End of the Spanish caste system in Mexico
1822–1823	Iturbide rules as constitutional emperor of Mexico
1823	Mexico allows Anglo settlers to colonize their northern territories
1823	The United States establishes the Monroe Doctrine, or Manifest Destiny, calling for nonintervention from European countries as it expands west and continues the genocide of the Indigenous peoples
1830	Indian Removal Act: United States President Andrew Jackson begins removal of Indigenous people from their homelands in order to give the land to white settlers
1831–1877	Trail of Tears: 16,000 Cherokee Indians are forcibly removed from their ancestral homes to areas of the west; 4,000 die as they make the trek
1833	Abolition of slavery in Britain
1835–1836	Texas Revolution: Anglo settlers fight for independence from Mexico in order to maintain slavery and establish the Republic of Texas
1836	Texas becomes a republic, with Sam Houston as their first president
1837	Queen Victoria becomes the British monarch and empress of India
1838–1839	The French Pastry War: Mexico ousts the French, with many leaving for New Orleans

1840	In Canada, Indigenous children are forcibly removed from their families and placed in the Wikwemikong Indian Residential School (closed in 1963)
1845–1849	Potato famine: Ireland suffers mass starvation, disease, and emigration to the New World
1846	Texas becomes the 28th state of the United States
1846–1848	Mexican-American War: United States attacks Mexico in order to expand the United States boundary to the Rio Bravo/Rio Grande River. The United States defeats Mexico and gains the territories of California, New Mexico, Arizona, Utah, and Nevada
1846	Treaty with Great Britain gives United States part of the Oregon territory
1848–1850	Gold Rush in California leads to an increase of white settlers and discrimination against Mexican Americans and Indians
1850	Fugitive Slave Act: Federal laws allow the capture and return of runaway slaves within the territory of the United States
1850–1880	California Indian War: United States military is sent to remove the Indians
1852	Indian Appropriation Act: Five military reservations are created for the removal of the Indigenous people
1853	Gadsden Purchase: Mexico sells portions of New Mexico and Arizona to the United States for the Southern Pacific Railroad
1859	Abolitionist John Brown leads an unsuccessful slave rebellion in Virginia
1861	Abraham Lincoln takes office as United States president
1861–1864	The French invade Mexico and install Maximilian of Austria as emperor on behalf of Napoleon III
1861–1865	American Civil War: Fought between the Union (the northern states of the United States) against the Confederate States of America (the southern states); the Confederacy wants to secede from the United States in order to maintain their system of slavery; the Union is victorious
1863	The Emancipation Proclamation is signed by Abraham Lincoln, freeing all slaves
1863	New York City Draft Riots: Violence arises from working-class discontent with military draft laws for the ongoing American Civil War
1865	Assassination of Abraham Lincoln by White supremacist John Wilkes Booth
1865	Black Codes: Laws passed by Southern states in the United States after the American Civil War to restrict African Americans' freedoms
1866	United States Congress passes another resolution to forcibly remove land from Indians in order to complete the railroad

1866	The 9th and 10th Cavalry and the 24th and 25th Infantry units are created by Congress; these cavalry and infantry units are composed of Black soldiers (Buffalo soldiers) with white officers
1866	Ku Klux Klan is founded in Tennessee
1867	Mexico gains independence from Emperor Maximilian I, Maximilian I is court-martialed and executed, and Benito Juarez, an indigenous leader, becomes president of Mexico
1869	Transcontinental railroad is completed in the United States
1870s	Bison are slaughtered to starve the Apaches and force them onto reservations; it is estimated that almost three million buffalo were killed
1873	Spain becomes a republic
1873	Slavery is abolished in Puerto Rico
1875	Comanches are defeated and forced onto reservations
1876	Black Hills War: The United States military fights and defeats the indigenous Lakota Sioux and Northern Cheyenne; Crazy Horse and Sitting Bull Surrender; the Lakota are moved to Great Sioux Reservation
1877	Chief Crazy Horse of Oglala Sioux surrenders to the United States Army and later is killed in custody
1877–1911	Porfirio Diaz is dictator of Mexico for 35 years; under his rule, European investment grows and class warfare increases
1879	The Women's National Indian Association is founded by white reformers to promote assimilation and Christianization of Indians in the United States
1879	Carlisle Indian Industrial School is established in Pennsylvania; Indigenous children are forcibly taken in an effort to "civilize" them
1880–1930	European migration wave to the United States
1881	The last of the Lipan Apache warriors are captured in Texas under the false promises of food; over 200 Apaches are taken, and their chiefs are killed
1886	Geronimo surrenders, ending the American Indian Wars
1890	Wounded Knee Massacre: 300 unarmed Sioux Indians are massacred by the United States military while being relocated to a reservation
1897	Cuba becomes autonomous but not fully independent from Spain
1898	United States acquires Puerto Rico from Spain
1898–1902	United States invades Cuba

Editor's Introduction

Part I establishes the historical development of criminological thought, which has been influenced by multiple histories and philosophies. By the time the Age of Reason rises, the world has seen the conquering of indigenous peoples, who resisted violent colonization and genocide by the great European powers of Spain, Portugal, Britain, France, and the Netherlands. The Westernization of the Americas began in 1492 with the arrival of Christopher Columbus, who eradicated and enslaved Indigenous peoples from the Americas and Africa (Beck et al., 2014; Jalata, 2016; World Digital Library, n.d.-a).

The Enlightenment, or the Age of Reason, began as the English Civil War (1642–1651) was ending. This period was an intellectual and cultural movement emphasizing reason over superstition by using the rational standards of observation and empiricism. The philosophers of the period highlighted freedom, equality, and justice. Meanwhile, in 1650, Spain was kidnapping 300,000 Africans to be sent to the Americas as forced labor (Beck et al., 2014; Jalata, 2016). By 1713, Britain had entered the slave trade with the Treaty of Utrecht, which granted maritime, commercial, and financial supremacy to Britain (Sorsby, 1975). In 1718, following the Transportation Act, 30,000 convicts were forcibly sent to the English colonies. In the English colony of South Carolina, the Negro Act of 1740 was enacted to prohibit the congregation of more than seven slaves in an attempt to restrict the upheaval and revolt of slaves. Any slave that attempted to rebel was permitted by the law to be killed (Education Broadcasting Corporation, 2004; Library of Congress, n.d.-b).

As we move into the Age of Revolution in 1750, Beck et al. (2014) highlight that the advent of revolutionary action occurred in Europe and colonial America. In other words, the movement from absolute monarchies to representative democracies began. In 1775, the War of Independence between the disgruntled English colonists in America and the British Empire began. The excessive taxation of the colonies led to the Declaration of Independence in 1776 (World Digital Library, n.d.-b). The fight for independence ended with the Treaty of Paris in 1783. The treaty ended the conflict between the English colonies and the British Empire. As a result, the US Constitution with the Bill of Rights, largely written by Thomas Jefferson and the other members of the Second Continental Congress, was adopted in 1787, espousing the liberal ideals of the right to life, liberty, and property, which only applied to white wealthy males (Historical Association, 2018; World Digital Library, n.d.-a; World Digital Library, n.d.-b). Yet as these ideals were espoused in the constitution, the Indigenous peoples of North America were stripped of their land, their freedom, and their way of life. African slaves in the United States were also exploited for the sake of the economy and suffered brutal acts of abuse by their masters. Thomas Jefferson is an example of this hypocrisy, taking a 14-year-old slave girl as his lover (Library of Congress, n.d.-b).

Meanwhile, in France in 1789, the people were upset with the way King Louis XVI and his wife, Queen Marie Antoinette, were running the country into financial ruin due to their extravagant spending and excessive taxation. Protests of the high price and scarcity of bread resulted in rioting and social upheaval (Beck et al., 2014; World Digital Library, n.d.-a). In 1792, the September Massacre arose, with King Louis XVI getting arrested by insurgents in Paris. As a result, both King Louis XVI and Queen Marie Antoinette were executed by guillotine. Under the new government, which was overseen by the Committee on Public Safety, a new Reign of Terror arises with Maximilien Robespierre arresting 300,000 and executing 17,000 enemies of the state. By 1799, Napoleon Bonaparte overthrew the Directory, who are the five directors who oversaw the government, through a coup. He held some victories that allowed him to get a foothold in Europe. During this time, Napoleon attempted to conquer Europe and Russia beginning in 1803 (Library of Congress, n.d.-a).

Beck et al. (2014) state that as Napoleon Bonaparte set out to conquer Europe, the people of Mexico made a call for revolution against their Spanish oppressors. In 1810, the declaration of war against colonial Spain by Miguel Hidalgo y Costilla ignited the spark, calling for the mestizos and Indigenous people to take up arms. Though the revolt was a failure, it touched the people, and an armed insurgency occurred for over 11 years, with 500,000 casualties. The war would not be over until 1821, under the Treaty of Cordoba, which liberated the Mexican people from Spanish rule (Brady, 2018; World Digital Library, n.d.-a).

Moreover, in the United States, the government continued their attacks on the Indigenous peoples, breaking every single treaty of peace and taking Indigenous lands. In 1813, the Treaty of Fort Jackson forced the Creek Federation to surrender 21 million acres, the area now known as Georgia and Alabama. By 1830, the Indian Removal Act was passed (Wang, 2015). President Andrew Jackson mandated the removal of Indigenous people from their ancestral homelands through the act we know as the Trail of Tears (1831–1877). More than 16,000 Cherokee Indians were forcibly removed, and 4,000 died as they made the trek and their land was given to white settlers (Beck et al., 2014).The development of the United States continued under the premise of Manifest Destiny.

Also, Henson (2010) has found that Mexico allowed Anglo settlers in the region known as Tejas, north of the Nueces River, to get rid of the Indians. By 1835, the Anglo settlers were fighting against Mexico for their independence. Mexico had outlawed slavery, and these Anglo colonizers wanted to maintain the slave system and therefore fought to become the Republic of Texas, although it was never recognized by the Mexican government. The United States saw this opportunity for their continued expansion of Manifest Destiny, leading to the Mexican-American War of 1846–1848, in which they stripped Mexico of their territories, and the annexation of Texas as the 28th state. The 1848 Treaty of Guadalupe Hidalgo ended the war, with Mexico losing its northern territories of Alta California and Santa Fe de Nuevo México. Mexico was forced to acknowledge the loss of the area that would become Texas and accept the Rio Grande River as their northern boundary (Barker et al., 2010).

The issue of slavery would eventually lead to the American Civil War (1861–1865) between the Union, the northern states, and the Confederate States of America, the southern states (WGBH Educational Foundation, n.d.; World Digital Library, n.d.-a; World Digital Library, n.d.-b). In 1863, the Emancipation Proclamation was signed by Abraham Lincoln, freeing all slaves. Over four million

Black slaves were freed into poverty, while former slave owners were provided compensation. The freedom of the slaves led to the implementation of Black Codes or Jim Crow Laws in the South, which was to continue the exploitation and oppression of the newly formed group of African Americans (Constitutional Rights Foundation, n.d.; Library of Congress, n.d.-b). In other parts of the United States, Indians continued to fight for their lives as the U.S. Army forcibly removed them from their lands and into reservations. Over three million buffalo were killed to starve the Indians and force them to reservations. Their children were forcibly removed from the care of their parents and put into schools such as the Carlisle Indian Industrial School, which was to "civilize" and Christianize the children into assimilation (Juneau et al., 2001). By 1890, the Indigenous peoples were defeated. The Sioux Indians gave up their arms to secure food for their people in what resulted in the Wounded Knee Massacre. Three hundred unarmed warriors, women, and children were killed by the U.S. Army. The American Indian Wars ended with the Apaches' surrender that same year under the leadership of Geronimo (Nelson, 2009).

References

Barker, E., Pohl, J., & Scheer, M. (2010). Texas revolution. *Texas State Historical Association.* https://tshaonline.org/handbook/online/articles/qdt01

Beck, R. B., Black, L., Krieger, L. S., Naylor, P. C., & Shabaka, D. I. (Eds.). (2014). *World history: Patterns of interaction.* Holt McDougal/Houghton Mifflin Harcourt.

Brady, H. (2018, September 14). Mexico Independence Day: What you need to know. *National Geographic.* https://www.nationalgeographic.com/culture/2018/09/mexico-independence-day-confusion-cinco-de-mayo

Constitutional Rights Foundation. (n.d.). Southern Black Codes. https://www.crf-usa.org/brown-v-board-50th-anniversary/southern-black-codes.html

Education Broadcasting Corporation. (2004). Slavery and the making of America. *Timeline: Time & Place.* https://www.thirteen.org/wnet/slavery/timeline/1739.html

Henson, M. S. (2010) Anglo-American colonization. *Texas State Historical Association.* https://tshaonline.org/handbook/online/articles/uma01

Historical Association. (2018). Age of Revolutions resources. https://www.history.org.uk/secondary/categories/514/info/3637/age-of-revolutions-resources

Jalata, A. (2016). Colonial terrorism and the incorporation of Africa into the capitalist world system. *Phases of Terrorism in the Age of Globalization*, 87–113. https://doi.org/10.1057/9781137552341_6

Juneau, S., Fleming, W. C., & Foster, L. M. (2001). *History and foundation of American Indian education.* Montana Office of Public Instruction.

Library of Congress. (n.d.-a). Creating French Culture The Rise and Fall of the Absolute Monarchy. https://www.loc.gov/exhibits/bnf/bnf0005.html

Library of Congress. (n.d.-b). From slavery to freedom: The African-American pamphlet collection, 1822–1909. Classroom Materials. http://www.loc.gov/teachers/classroommaterials/connections/slavery/file.html

Nelson, S. (2009). We shall remain: America through Native eyes part V Wounded Knee. Public Broadcasting System. https://www.pbs.org/wgbh/americanexperience/films/weshallremain

Sorsby, V. (1975). *British trade with Spanism American under the asiento (1713–1740)*. University College, London.

Wang, H. S. (2015, January 18). Broken promises on display at Native American treaties exhibit. National Public Radio. https://www.npr.org/sections/codeswitch/2015/01/18/368559990/broken-promises-on-display-at-native-american-treaties-exhibit

WGBH Educational Foundation. (n.d.). Civil War and Reconstruction (1850–1877). Public Broadcasting Service. https://www.pbslearningmedia.org/collection/kenburnsclassroom/era/civil-war-and-reconstruction-1850-1877

World Digital Library. (n.d.-a). World history timelines. Library of Congress with support from United Nations Educational Scientific and Cultural Organization. https://www.wdl.org/en/sets/world-history/timeline/

World Digital Library. (n.d.-b). United States history timelines. Library of Congress with support from United Nations Educational Scientific and Cultural Organization. https://www.wdl.org/en/sets/us-history/timeline/n/sets/us-history/timeline/

READING 1

The Enlightenment's Philosophical Contributions to the Study of Crime and Justice

Rosalva Resendiz, Ph.D. and Lucas E. Espinoza Ph.D.

The period of the Enlightenment, also known as the Age of Reason, was crucial toward the institutionalization of liberal philosophy in Western civilization and the development of the social sciences in the university system. The intellectuals of that period were concerned with human nature and the origins of civil society. In exploring the origins of society, they had to consider the elements that would drive a free individual to seek a contract with other individuals. They concluded that having unlimited freedom in the state of nature also meant that one's self-preservation would continuously be under attack, vulnerable to violence and theft. In an attempt to understand the progress from the state of nature to a state of laws, philosophers contemplated the types of systems that would provide its citizens legal protections yet maintain the freedom and equality purported by nature.

The writers of the Enlightenment wrote in support of social, economic, and political reforms, advocating for the right to liberty and freedom as it combated ideas of superstition, bigotry, and intolerance (Zeitlin, 2001). Liberal philosophy was an ideology of social change and progress, with the ultimate goal the perfectibility of humankind through the empirical study of the natural laws. Social change would be guided by reason and would be expressed harmoniously in a society of equals. Through the pursuit of knowledge, individuals would be enlightened. These beliefs impacted the development of the social sciences, including sociology, as they set a method for uncovering the natural laws of our society (Collins, 1994; Westby, 1991; Zeitlin, 2001). The revolution of the Enlightenment further set a framework for the rise of democratic societies based on the ideas that "no one ought to harm another in life, health, liberty, or possessions" (Locke, 1952, p. 5).

Locke (1632–1704)

One of the leading political philosophers of the Enlightenment was John Locke (1632–1704). John Locke's works influenced European scholars, as well as the British colonies in the Americas. The establishment of the United States of America was founded on the ideals expounded by John Locke, and they were written into the Declaration of Independence by Thomas Jefferson. John Locke not only influenced the American Revolution of 1776, he was also considered "the theorist of the English Revolution of 1688" (Locke, 1952, p. vii).

Two of the most critical works that influenced and contributed to the development of the social sciences were the "*Essay Concerning Human Understanding*" and *Second Treatise of Government* (Locke, 1952; Parsons et al., 1961; Westby, 1991; Zeitlin, 2001). Locke (1952) believed that human nature was governed by reason and inevitably led individuals to civil society. John Locke concluded that in the state of nature, humans were gifted by nature the rights to "life, liberty, and property," but they did not have security and were therefore inclined to submit to a social contract. The social contract as an agreement between free individuals would create civil law based on majority rule.

Locke explained that the state of nature is governed by the law of nature, which is guided by reason. This law or reason "teaches all mankind who will but consult it that, being all equal and independent, no one ought to harm another in his life, health, liberty, or possessions" (Locke, 1952, p. 5). Locke further noted that the same laws that govern nature also govern civil law, because they are the expression of reason. Therefore, the same considerations must be taken when dealing with offenses, which should be punished according to their severity and as a form of deterrence. And the laws of punishment in the state of nature carry over to civil society. Locke (1952) further added,

> Each transgression may be punished to that degree and with so much severity as will suffice to make it an ill bargain to the offender. ... Every offense that can be committed in the state of nature may in the state of nature be also punished equally and as far forth as it may in a commonwealth. (p. 9)

Additionally, Locke (1952) acknowledged that besides having the power to preserve one's life and property, one has the power to judge and punish, "even with death itself in crimes where the heinousness of the fact in his opinion requires it" (p. 48).

These ideas are explored in the state of nature; the laws give the individual the power to preserve his or her life, as well as to be judge and punisher to any person who has caused injury to him or her. But under the social contract, the individual no longer is the judge. Locke (1952) emphasized that the power to punish becomes the duty of the commonwealth and must "set down what punishment shall belong to the several transgressions" (p. 49). Therefore, it falls on the commonwealth to protect its citizens and their property, as well as "the power to punish any injury done unto any of its members" (Locke, 1952, p. 49). The state is then vested to create standing laws through its legislative and executive powers to regulate "how far offenses are to be punished when committed within the commonwealth" (Locke, 1952, p. 49).

Montesquieu (1689–1755)

Montesquieu is another philosopher of the period whose major contribution to the social sciences is *The Spirit of the Laws*, which inspired the work of Cesare Beccaria, as well as penal law (Richter, 1990). For Montesquieu, "spirit … refers to the distinctive character of a system of laws" (Zeitlin, 2001, p. 11). He further suggested that "law in general is human reason, to the extent that it governs all the peoples of the earth. The political and civil laws of each nation ought to be only particular cases of the application of human reason" (Richter, 1990, p. 114).

In *The Spirit of the Laws*, Montesquieu does a historical comparative study, using ideal types to classify societies by describing the laws, customs, and characteristics of each. Richter (1990) noted that Montesquieu viewed all institutions that make up society to have an "interdependent and correlative relationship to one another and as [] depending on the form of the whole" (p. 8). The institutions of education, justice, marriage, family, and politics develop their form from the customs of their people and their environment. Society then develops into a republic, monarchy, or despotic government.

Montesquieu further describes two types of laws: laws of nature and positive laws. The laws of nature are derived from our being. When individuals enter society, they succumb to positive laws, losing some freedom and equality from the natural state in order to increase their strength through solidarity. The society is governed by public laws, which govern the relationships between ruler and citizen, and civil laws, which govern the relationships of citizen to citizen. And each state is subject to a law of nations or international law (Richter, 1990).

Additionally, Montesquieu pointed out the characteristics of a republican government and the laws that uphold a democracy (Richter, 1990). In such a government, all citizens are equal, and its priority is the common welfare of its citizens. For Montesquieu, a successful republic must be characterized by political virtue. He described political virtue as the love toward one's nation and the love for equality, resulting in love for the nation's laws. In order for a republican government to succeed, laws governing education are necessary to prepare individuals to be citizens. Political virtue must be instilled through education so that its citizens love their country above their own self-interest. Therefore, a good citizen "loves the laws of his land and is moved to act by them" (Richter, 1990, p. 106). As part of a democracy, the good citizen is able to act through his or her right to vote. Laws are set to regulate citizens' participation as voters and provide its people the power to enact laws. Montesquieu also acknowledged, "In republics, everything depends upon establishing such love. To inspire it ought to be the concern of education. The surest means of instilling love of country among children is for their fathers themselves to possess it" (Richter, 1990, p. 34).

From this, the duty of the state is to provide political liberty, which Montesquieu defines as the "tranquility of mind which derives from [a] sense of security" (Richter, 1990, p. 82). The citizen must be able to not fear other citizens. In order to ensure political liberty, a system of checks and balances is needed to prevent the abuse of power. A republican government should have three powers: legislative, executive, and judicial. The judicial power is responsible for punishing crime or settling disputes among parties in order to ensure fairness; "judgements ... should be determined only by the precise text of the law" (Richter, 1990, p. 184).

Rousseau (1712–1778)

Jean-Jacques Rousseau, as a philosopher of the Enlightenment, was concerned with freedom, equality, the perfectibility of man, the laws of nature, and the social contract. "Rousseau's chief objective ... was to find a social order whose laws were in greatest harmony with the fundamental laws of nature" (Zeitlin, 2001, p. 18). Two of his most notable publications are the *Discourse on the Origin of Inequality* and *The Social Contract or Principles of Political Right*.

According to Rousseau (1974), individuals have two conditions: the natural and the social. In the state of nature, individuals live in a perfect balance of their needs and available resources but lack security. In order to protect one's life, freedom, equality, and property, individuals will willingly choose to enter a social contract guided by the general will of the people or the will of the majority. In submitting to the general will, humans lose their natural freedom but gain civil freedom and the right to their possessions. Rousseau argues that the civil state also provides moral freedom, because humans need civil law to curb their natural appetites, which can make them slaves to those desires. Rousseau (1974) noted, "Another gain can be added to those that come with the civil state: moral freedom, which alone makes man truly his own master, for impulsion by appetite alone is slavery, and obedience to self-imposed law is freedom" (pp. 20–21).

In Book 2, Rousseau (1974) addresses the two types of laws that guide humans: the laws of nature and the laws of the state. The laws of the state are a declaration of the general will, which are needed to "join rights to duties and direct justice toward its object" (p. 33). Like the laws of nature, the laws of the state must be guided by reason. Like Montesquieu, Rousseau agreed that the development of the state occurred through its social interaction with the environment. The environmental and social characteristics of a people develop laws in the spirit of their needs. Those civil laws are an expression of its people and can only be enforced with the agreement of the people. Rousseau indicated,

> Laws are, properly speaking, only the terms of the civil association. A people bound by laws should be the author of them; only those who come together to form a society are entitled to specify the conditions under which they do so. (p. 35)

Rousseau further discusses the various systems of laws, of which, in order to provide the greatest good, their goals should be freedom and equality. Rousseau (1974) noted, "If we seek to determine precisely what constitutes the greatest good of all, which should be the goal of every system of law, we find that it can be reduced to these two main elements: [civil] freedom and equality" (p. 45). Moreover, Rousseau's concept of equality was based on the idea of moderation and balance, which would have to be upheld by the force of law. The citizens in high positions were to restrain from abusing their influence and wealth, while the citizens in humbler positions were to restrain from "avarice and covetousness" (Rousseau, 1974, p. 45). Additionally, Rousseau (1974) explained,

> As for equality, the word must not be taken to imply that power and wealth are to be exactly the same for everyone, but rather that power shall not reach the point of violence and never be exercised except by virtue of rank and law, and that, so far as wealth is concerned, no citizen shall be rich enough to be able to buy another, and none poor enough to be forced to sell himself. (p. 45)

And in order for the constitution of the state to be "strong and durable," there must be a "close observance of what is proper that natural relations are in harmony with the law on every point and law serves only … to assure, accompany and rectify them" (Rousseau, 1974, p. 46). Order is brought to the state by addressing the various relations existing in a commonwealth.

Rousseau (1974) further classifies three types of laws: political, civil, and criminal. Political laws are fundamental laws that establish the government as an intermediate body responsible for the execution of the laws and for maintaining civil and political freedom. Civil laws govern the citizens, while criminal laws govern the relations between the individual and the law. Criminal laws also include sanctions and punishment for violations against property, individuals, and the state. Rousseau (1974) mentions a fourth law, which is not a law, but it is "in the hearts of the citizens [and] it forms the true constitution of the state" (p. 47). Rousseau (1974) believes that morals, customs, and public opinion are the most important, keeping "the people in the spirit of the institutions" (p. 47).

Wollstonecraft (1759–1797)

Mary Wollstonecraft was the first liberal philosopher to advocate for the equality of the sexes. Her call for equality and education made her a contributor to the ideological development of the social sciences (Zeitlin, 2001). She believed that both men and women were innately rational beings that through the acquisition of knowledge could perfect themselves. She was influenced by Rousseau, yet she criticized his thoughts on the education of women, which were based on religious prejudices and ideas from classical Greece. In response to Rousseau, as well as to other contemporaries who ignored the plight of women, she wrote the *Vindication of the Rights of Woman* (1985). She was the first female to declare that women deserved equal rights, basing her ideas on the principles of the Enlightenment and against the principle of natural subordination.

Her work, according to Zeitlin (2001), was heavily influenced by Catherine Macauley, the English author of *Letters on Education*. Wollstonecraft believed that education could provide the foundation for establishing women's rights. Moreover, she believed that women had the right to the same social and political equality given to men and it was achievable through the education of both sexes. The social inferiority of women was the result of their subjugation and the lack of educational opportunities in developing their physical and intellectual capabilities. She recommended a national education that would challenge both boys and girls to think for themselves. It would be the goal of a public education to form rational citizens. Wollstonecraft (1985) suggested,

> Let an enlightened nation then try what effect reason would have to bring them back to nature, and their duty; and allowing them to share the advantages of an education and government with man, see whether they will become better, as they grow wiser and become free. (p. 286)

As part of their instruction, Wollstonecraft (1985) explained that students would be taught "humanity by the exercise of compassion to every living creature" (p. 291). She also believed that children needed to be taught compassion to animals and noted that civilization, with its class systems, had taught boys "habitual cruelty" toward the less fortunate. This early education, void of compassion for all beings, would eventually result in "domestic tyranny over wives, children, and servants" (Wollstonecraft, 1985, p. 292).

Condorcet (1743–1794)

Collins (1994) points out that the modern disciplines grew from the intellectual activity of the Enlightenment period. From 1780 to 1820, there was an intellectual revolution instituting philosophy as one of the leading sciences. The religious wars and the church-state conflicts in Europe affected intellectual life, as governments tried to cut ties with the Papacy and their attention increasingly turned toward mercantilism. The socioeconomic political climate of the period demanded civil servants, and hence more students turned to the universities for training. With the renewed interest in intellectual life, there was a demand for liberal arts faculty. Reason and empiricism as the new tools of theintellectuals were then utilized to fulfill the needs of the state. The institutionalization of liberal thought and method was facilitated by scholars such as Condorcet (1795), who contributed to the development of concepts such as social facts, comparative studies, and the belief that through careful analysis we could discover and master natural laws.

As a late Enlightenment thinker, Condorcet helped bridge liberal philosophy to the social sciences by using historical comparative methods and noting causal relationships (Collins, 1994; Westby, 1991). A key element in the continued advancement of liberal philosophy was Condorcet's notion that humans were perfectible. It was this line of thought that gave rise to the need to study the past in order to understand and master human nature. By studying the history of civilization, many scholars agreed that humans were slowly progressing toward an ideal state of order and peace (Condorcet, 1795; Rousseau, 1974; Gordon, 2011; Wollstonecraft, 1985). It was believed that inequality in society could be remedied using reason and science by revealing the natural laws in order to guide humanity. Condorcet noted that inequality of wealth and education were aspects that could be eliminated through reforms. It was his belief that the progress of ideas would "culminate in complete material security and equality, international peace, and individual liberty for everyone" (Westby, 1991, p. 9).

The ideas of historical progress toward the perfectibility of the human race were first introduced by Anne-Robert Jacques Turgot (1727–1781) and further developed by Marquis de Condorcet (1743–1794) in his *Sketch for a Historical Picture of the Progress of the Human Mind*, which was published after his death. Condorcet is credited with developing the first theory of progress, in which he analyzed history comparatively into 10 eras. Condorcet finds in the ninth epoch, from Descartes to the French Republic, that human reason has slowly formed from the natural progression of civilization to reveal our true state of nature—equality (Condorcet, 1795). Condorcet (1795) further noted,

> After ages of error ... writers upon politics and the law of nations at length arrived at the knowledge of the true rights of man, which they deduced from this simple principle: that *he is being endowed with sensation, capable of reasoning upon and understanding his interests, and of acquiring moral ideas.* (p. 185, emphasis in original)

Condorcet also argued that through the analysis of pain and pleasure, humans develop morality and the principles of the laws of justice. By knowing such principles, society is able to educate its citizens to conduct themselves in a lawful manner. Condorcet (1795) acknowledged,

> In the same manner, by analyzing the faculty of experiencing pain and pleasure, men arrived at the origin of their notions of morality, and the foundation of those general principles which form the necessary and immutable laws of justice; and consequently discovered the proper motives of conforming their conduct to those laws, which, being deduced from nature of our feeling, may not improperly be called our moral constitution. (p. 194)

Conclusion

Overall, the ideals set forth by the liberal philosophers of the Enlightenment contributed to the establishment of democracies and the institutionalization of the social sciences in education. Liberal philosophy influenced the direction of knowledge production through the use of reason as a method. Liberal philosophers assisted in removing religion from education, focusing on the study of society as a means to understand our natures. As European society distanced themselves from the Papacy, universities opened their doors to philosophy and the objective study of social phenomena. Although the liberal philosophers had influenced the republican government of the United States, liberal ideals trickled slowly into the country. In the United States, universities and colleges were traditional and dominated by religion. In 1876, Johns Hopkins University was the first to break from traditional curriculums and imitated the German models. The German university model stood as one of the leaders in Western civilization, having developed the first social science in economics. Curriculum reforms in the United States helped establish institutions such as the University of Chicago in 1892, which would go on to lead in sociological and criminological research and thought (Collins, 1994).

References

Collins, R. (1994). *Four sociological traditions* (Vol. 1). Oxford University Press.

Condorcet, M. (1795). *Outlines of an historical view of the progress of the human mind.* Liberty Fund.

Locke, J. (1952). *Second treatise of government* (T. Peardon, Ed.). Liberal Arts Press.

Parsons, T., Shils, E., Naegele, K., & Pitts, J. (Eds.). (1961). *Theories of society: Foundations of modern sociological theory* (Vol. 1). Free Press of Glencoe.

Richter, M. (Ed.). (1990). *Montesquieu: Selected political writings.* Hackett.

Rousseau, J. (1974). *The essential Rousseau* (L. Bair, Trans.). Meridian.

Gordon, D. (Ed.). (2011). *The Turgot collection: Writings, speeches, and letters of Anne-Robert Jacques Turgot, Baron de Laune.* Ludwig von Mises Institute.

Westby, D. L. (1991). *The growth of sociological theory: Human nature, knowledge, and social change.* Prentice-Hall.

Wollstonecraft, M. (1985). *Vindication of the rights of woman.* Penguin. (Original work published 1792)

Zeitlin, I. M. (2001). *Ideology and the development of sociological theory* (2nd ed.). Prentice Hall.

READING 2

Classical Criminology
Roger Hopkins Burke

Classical criminology emerged at a time when the naturalistic approach of the social contract theorists we encountered above was challenging the previously dominant spiritualist approach to explaining crime and criminal behaviour and it was Cesare Beccaria in Italy and Jeremy Bentham in Britain writing in the late eighteenth century who established the essential components of the rational actor model.

The Classical Theorists

Cesare Beccaria (1738–1794) was an Italian mathematician and the author of *Dei delitti e delle pene (On Crimes and Punishment)* (1963, originally 1767), a highly influential book which was translated into 22 languages and had an enormous impact on European and US legal thought. In common with many of his contemporary intellectuals—and inspired by social contract theories—Beccaria was strongly opposed to the many inconsistencies that existed in government and public affairs, and his major text was essentially the first attempt at presenting a systematic, consistent and logical penal system.

Beccaria considered that criminals owe a 'debt' to society and proposed that punishments should be fixed strictly in proportion to the seriousness of the crime. Torture was considered a useless method of criminal investigation, as well as being barbaric. Moreover, capital punishment was considered to be unnecessary with a life sentence of hard labour preferable, both as a punishment and deterrent. The use of imprisonment should thus be greatly extended, the conditions of prisons improved with better physical care provided and inmates should be segregated on the basis of gender, age and degree of criminality.

Beccaria was a very strong supporter of 'social contract' theory with its emphasis on the notion that individuals can only be legitimately bound to society if they have given their consent to the societal arrangements. It is nevertheless the law that provides the necessary conditions for the social contract and punishment exists only to defend the liberties of individuals against those who would interfere with them. Beccaria's theory of criminal behaviour is based on the concepts of free will and hedonism where it is proposed that all human behaviour is essentially purposive and based on

Roger Hopkins Burke, "Classical Criminology," *An Introduction to Criminological Theory*, pp. 27-35, 351-393. Copyright © 2009 by Taylor & Francis Group. Reprinted with permission.

the pleasure-pain principle. Beccaria argues that punishment should reflect that principle and thus fixed sanctions for all offences must be written into the law and not be open to the interpretation, or the discretion, of judges. The law must apply equally to all citizens while the sole function of the court is to determine guilt. No mitigation of guilt should be considered and all that are guilty of a particular offence should suffer the same prescribed penalty. This extremely influential essay can be summarised in the following thirteen propositions:

1. In order to escape social chaos, each member of society must sacrifice part of their liberty to the sovereignty of the nation-state.
2. To prevent individuals from infringing the liberty of others by breaking the law, it is necessary to introduce punishments for such breaches.
3. 'The despotic spirit'—or the tendency to offend— is in everyone.
4. Punishments should be decided by the legislature not by the courts.
5. Judges should only impose punishment established by the law in order to preserve consistency and the certainty of punishment.
6. The seriousness of the crime should be judged not by the intentions of the offender but by the harm that it does to society.
7. Punishment must be administered in proportion to the crime that has been committed and should be set on a scale—or a tariff—with the most severe penalties corresponding to offences which caused the most harm to society. The most serious crimes are considered to be those that threaten the stability of society.
8. Punishment which follows promptly after a crime is committed will be more just and effective.
9. Punishment has to be certain to be effective.
10. Laws and punishments have to be well publicised so that people are well aware of them.
11. Punishment is imposed for the purpose of deterrence and therefore capital punishment is unnecessary and should not be used.
12. The prevention of crime is better than punishment.
13. Activities which are not expressly prohibited by law therefore not illegal and thus permissible.

It is important to recognise that Beccaria's ideas have had a profound effect on the establishment of the modern criminal law and, while they may not be expressed in quite the same way, it is easy to detect resonances of his views in any popular discussion on crime. The doctrine of free will is built into many legal codes and has strongly influenced popular conceptions of justice.

Jeremy Bentham was a leading disciple of Beccaria. As a philosopher—as we saw above—he is classed as a utilitarian, or a *hedonistic utilitarian*, due to his emphasis on the human pursuit of pleasure. He was very much influenced by the philosophical materialism of John Locke which had denied the existence of innate ideas and traditional, established religious notions of original sin. He consequently ascribed criminal behaviour to incorrect upbringing or socialisation rather than innate propensities to offend. For Bentham, criminals were not incorrigible monsters but 'forward children', 'persons of unsound mind', who lacked the self-discipline to control their passions according to the dictates of reason.

Bentham's ideas are very similar to those of Beccaria and his most famous principle—'the greatest happiness for the greatest number'—is the fundamental axiom of all utilitarian philosophy. People are rational creatures who will seek pleasure while trying to avoid pain. Thus, punishment must outweigh any pleasure derived from criminal behaviour, but the law must not be as harsh and severe as to reduce the greatest happiness. Moreover, the law should not be used to regulate morality but only to control acts harmful to society which reduce the happiness of the majority. He agreed with Beccaria about capital punishment, that it was barbaric and unnecessary, but disagreed about torture, allowing that on occasion it might be 'necessary' and thus have utility. This is a significant point worth reflecting on. If the intention is to get someone—anyone—to admit to having committed a criminal act then the use of torture will be useful but if the purpose is to ensure that you have found the right offender then it is of no use. This seems to be the point being made by Beccaria. If, on the other hand, you wish to obtain urgently some *important* information from someone who you have good reason to believe is withholding this—as for example, in the case of a planned terrorist atrocity—then the rationale for torture is rather different. This seems to be the utilitarian point being made by Bentham. Moreover, we might note that although Bentham believed in the doctrine of free will, there is a strong hint in his work that suggests criminality might be learned behaviour.

Bentham spent a considerable amount of time and energy designing a prison, an institution to reflect and operationalise his ideas on criminal justice. Prisons were not much used as a form of punishment in pre-modern times, being reserved for holding people awaiting trial, transportation or some other punishment. They were usually privately administered, chronically short of money, undisciplined and insanitary places.

In 1791 Bentham published his design for a new model prison called a Panoptican. The physical structure of this edifice was a circular tiered honeycomb of cells, ranged round a central inspection tower from which each could be seen by the gaolers. He proposed that the constant surveillance would make chains and other restraints superfluous. The prisoners would work sixteen hours a day in their cells and the profits of their labour would go to the owner of the Panoptican. Bentham described the prison as a 'mill for grinding rogues honest' and it was to be placed near the centre of the city so that it would be a visible reminder to all of the 'fruits of crime'. Furthermore, said Bentham, such an institution should act as a model for schools, asylums, workhouses, factories and hospitals that could all be run on the 'inspection principle' to ensure internal regulation, discipline and efficiency.

Underpinning all of these institutions of social control was a shared regime and common view of discipline and regimentation as mechanisms for changing the behaviour of the inmates. The rigorous regime proposed as the basis of these institutions was itself part of a more general discipline imposed on the working class in the factories and mills:

> [The prison] took its place within a structure of institutions so interrelated in function, so similar in design, discipline and language of command that together the sheer massiveness of their presence in the Victorian landscape inhibited further challenge to their logic.
>
> It was no accident that the penitentiaries, asylums, workhouses, monitorial schools, night refuges and reformatories looked alike or that their charges marched to the same disciplinary cadence. Since they made up a complementary and independent structure of control, it was essential that their diets and deprivations be calibrated in an ascending scale, school-workhouse-asylum-prison, with the pain of the last serving to undergird the pain of the first.
>
> Nor was it accidental that these state institutions so closely resembled the factory … the creators of the new factory discipline drew inspiration from the same discourse in authority as the makers of the prison: nonconformist asceticism, faith in human improvability through discipline, and the liberal theory of the state.
>
> (Ignatieff, 1978: 214–15)

The Panoptican, in its strict interpretation, was never built in England but two American prisons were built based on such a model but these institutions did not prove to be a success in terms of the original intentions of the builders and they had to be taken down and rebuilt. A variation on the theme, London's Millbank Prison, built in 1812, was also poorly conceived, built and administered, and was eventually turned into a holding prison rather than a penitentiary. Bentham's proposal also called for the provision of industrial and religious training and pre-release schemes, and suggested the segregation and classification of prisoners in order to avoid 'criminal contamination'.

Michel Foucault (1977) and Michael Ignatieff (1978) have both traced the development of the prison as a concept and as a physical institution observing that it was one of many 'carceral' institutions developed around the time in order to rationalise and discipline human activity along the lines of early modern thought. Foucault provides the following extract from rules drawn up for the House of Young Prisoners in Paris:

> At the first drum-roll, the prisoners must rise and dress in silence, as the supervisor opens the cell doors. At the second drum-roll, they must be dressed and make their bed. At the third, they must line and proceed to the chapel for Morning Prayer. There is a five-minute interval between each drum-roll. …
>
> (Foucault, 1977: 6)

These imposing new penal institutions soon competed for domination of the new urban skylines with the great palaces, cathedrals and churches which had long provided the symbols of the concerns of an earlier age. While the original Panoptican idea was not widely implemented, a variation on the theme developed and built from the early part of the nineteenth century still forms a substantial part of the prison estate in many countries. After a number of aborted experimental institutions had failed, a new model prison was built in North London, inspired by the Quaker prison reformer John Howard. Pentonville prison provided a template for over fifty similar prisons in Britain and for many others throughout the world.

While his writings focused on reform of the penal system, Bentham was also concerned to see crime prevented rather than punished, and to this end made suggestions that alcoholism should be combated and that those with no means of sustenance should be cared for by the state.

The Limitations of Classicism

The philosophy of the Classical theorists was reflected in the *Declaration of the Rights of Man* in 1789 and the *French Penal Code* of 1791, the body of criminal law introduced in the aftermath of the French Revolution. The authors of these documents had themselves been inspired by the writings of the major Enlightenment philosophers, notably Rousseau. It was nevertheless attempts such as these to put these ideas of the Classical School into practice that exposed the inherent problems of its philosophy of criminal justice. The Classical theorists had deliberately and completely ignored differences between individuals. First offenders and recidivists were treated exactly alike and solely on the basis of the particular act that had been committed. Children, the 'feeble-minded' and the insane were all treated as if they were fully rational and competent.

This appearance in court of people who were unable to comprehend the proceedings against them did little to legitimise the new French post-revolutionary criminal code and consequently, this was revised in 1810, and again in 1819, to allow judges some latitude in deciding sentences. It was thus in this way that the strict, formal, philosophical elegance of the Classical model was to be breached. It was to become increasingly recognised that people are not equally responsible for their actions and as a result a whole range of experts gradually came to be invited into the courts to pass opinion on the degree of reason that could be expected of the accused. Judges were now able to vary sentences in accordance with the degree of individual culpability argued by these expert witnesses and it was this theoretical compromise that was to lead to the emergence of a modified criminological perspective that came to be termed the *neo-Classical School*.

The Neo-Classical Compromise

Neo-Classicists such as Rossi (1787-1848), Garraud (1849–1930) and Joly (1839–1925) modified the rigorous doctrines of pure Classical theory by revising the doctrine of free will. In this modified form of the rational actor model, ordinary sane adults were still considered fully responsible for their actions and all equally capable of either criminal or non-criminal behaviour. It was nevertheless now recognised that children—and in some circumstances, the elderly—were less capable of exercising free choice and were thus less responsible for their actions. Moreover, the insane and 'feeble-minded' might be even less responsible. We can thus observe here the beginnings of the recognition that various innate predisposing factors may actually determine human behaviour which is a significant perception that was to provide the fundamental theoretical foundation of the predestined actor model that is the focus of the second part of this book.

It was these revisions to the penal code that admitted into the courts for the first time, non-legal 'experts' including doctors, psychiatrists and, later, social workers. They were gradually introduced into the criminal justice system in order to identify the impact of individual biological, psychological and social differences with the purpose of deciding the extent to which offenders should be held responsible for their actions. The outcome of this encroachment was that sentences became more individualised, dependent on the perceived degree of responsibility of the offender and on mitigating circumstances.

It was now recognised that a particular punishment would have a differential effect on different people and as a result punishment came increasingly to be expressed in terms of punishment appropriate to rehabilitation. Though, as those eminent proponents of the more radical variant of the victimised actor model, Taylor, Walton and Young (1973: 10) were later to observe:

> There was however, no radical departure from the free will model of man involved in the earlier Classical premises. The criminal had to be punished in an environment conducive to his making the correct moral decisions. Choice was (and still is) seen to be a characteristic of the individual actor—but there is now recognition that certain structures are more conducive to free choice than others.

The neo-Classicists thus retained the central rational choice actor model notion of free will, but with the modification that certain circumstances may be less conducive to the unfettered exercise of free choice than others. Indeed, it can be convincingly argued that most modern criminal justice systems are founded on this somewhat awkward theoretical compromise between the rational actor model of criminal behaviour and the predestined actor model that we will encounter in the second part of the book. This debate between free will and determinism is perhaps one of the most enduring in the human and social sciences.

In summary, it is possible to identify the following central attributes of the Classical and neo-Classical Schools that provide the central foundations of the rational actor model:

1. There is a fundamental focus on the criminal law and the simple adoption of a legal definition of crime. This leaves the perspective crucially exposed to the criticism that legal definitions of crime are social constructions which change over time and with geographical location.

2. There is the central concept that the punishment should fit the crime rather than the criminal. This leaves it exposed to the criticism that it fails to appreciate the impact of individual differences in terms of culpability and prospects for rehabilitation.

3. There is the doctrine of free will according to which all people are free to choose their actions and this notion is often allied to the hedonistic utilitarian philosophy that all people will seek to optimise pleasure but avoid pain. From this perspective, it is assumed that there is nothing 'different' or 'special' about a criminal that differentiates them from other people. It is a doctrine thus exposed to the criticism that it fails to appreciate that the exercise of free will may be constrained by biological, psychological or social circumstances.

4. There is the use of non-scientific 'armchair' methodology based on anecdote and imaginary illustrations in place of empirical research and it was thus an administrative and legal criminology, concerned more with the uniformity of laws and punishment rather than really trying to explain criminal behaviour.

The rational actor model was to go out of fashion as an explanatory model of crime and criminal behaviour at the end of the nineteenth century and was to be replaced predominantly by the new orthodoxy of the predestined actor model in its various guises. It nevertheless continued to inform criminal justice systems throughout the world.

The Enduring Influence of Classicism

The enduring influence of the Classical school is evident in the legal doctrine that emphasises conscious intent or choice, for example, the notion of *mens rea* or the guilty mind. In sentencing principles, for example, the idea of culpability or responsibility; and in the structure of punishment, for example, the progression of penalties according to the seriousness of the offence or what is more commonly known as the 'sentencing tariff'.

Philosophically, the ideas of the Classical school are reflected in the contemporary 'just deserts' approach to sentencing. This involves four basic principles. First, only a person found guilty by a court of law can be punished for a crime. Second, anyone found to be guilty of a crime must be punished. Third, punishment *must not be more* than a degree commensurate to—or proportional to—the nature or gravity of the offence and culpability of the offender. Fourth, punishment *must not be less* than a degree commensurate to—or proportional to—the nature or gravity of the offence and culpability of the criminal (von Hirsch, 1976).

Such principles have clear foundations in the theoretical tradition established by Beccaria and Bentham. There is an emphasis on notions of free will and rationality, as well as proportionality and equality, with an emphasis on criminal behaviour that focuses on the offence not the offender, in accordance with the pleasure-pain principle, and to ensure that justice is served by equal punishment for the same crime. 'Just deserts' philosophy eschews individual discretion and rehabilitation as legitimate aims of the justice system. Justice must be both done and seen to be done and is an approach which is closely linked with the traditional Classical school notion of 'due process'.

Packer (1968) observes that the whole contemporary criminal justice system is founded on a balance between the competing value systems of *due process* and *crime control*. The former maintains that it is the purpose of the criminal justice system to prove the guilt of a defendant beyond a reasonable doubt in a public trial as a condition for the imposition of a sentence. It is based on an idealised form of the rule of law where the state has a duty to seek out and punish the guilty but must prove the guilt of the accused (King, 1981). Central to this idea is the presumption of innocence until guilt is proved.

A due process model requires and enforces rules governing the powers of the police and the admissibility and utility of evidence. There is recognition of the power of the state in the application of the criminal law but there is a requirement for checks and balances to be in place to protect the interests of suspects and defendants. The use of informal or discretionary powers is seen to be contrary to this tradition.

A strict due process system acknowledges that some guilty people will go free and unpunished but this is considered acceptable in order to prevent wrongful conviction and punishment while the arbitrary or excessive use of state power is seen to be a worse evil. Problematically, a high acquittal rate gives the impression that the criminal justice agencies are performing inadequately and the outcome could be a failure to deter others from indulging in criminal behaviour.

A crime control model, in contrast, prioritises efficiency and getting results with the emphasis on catching, convicting and punishing the offender. There is almost an inherent 'presumption of guilt' (King, 1981) and less respect for legal controls that exist to protect the individual defendant. These are seen as practical obstacles that need to be overcome in order to get on with the control of crime and punishment. If occasionally some innocent individuals are sacrificed to the ultimate aim of crime control then that is acceptable. Such errors should nevertheless be kept to a minimum and agents of the law should ensure through their professionalism that they apprehend the guilty and allow the innocent to go free.

In the crime control model the interests of victims and society are given priority over those of the accused and the justification for this stance is that swifter processing makes the system appear more efficient and that it is this that will deter greater criminality. In other words, if you offend you are likely to be caught and punished and it is therefore not worth becoming involved in criminality. The primary aim of crime control is thus to punish the guilty and deter criminals as a means of reducing crime and creating a safer society.

It was observed above that the rational actor model had gone out of fashion as an explanatory model of criminal behaviour with the rise of the predestined actor tradition at the end of the nineteenth century. It was nevertheless to return very much to favour with the rise of the 'new' political right—or populist conservatism—during the last quarter of the twentieth century. It was however a revival where the purist Classical tradition of 'due process' promoted in particular by Beccaria was to be very much superseded by the interests of the proponents of the crime control model of criminal justice.

References

Beccaria, C. (1963, first English edition 1767). *On Crimes and Punishment*, translated by H. Paolucci. Indianapolis, IN: Bobbs-Merrill Educational.

Foucault, M. (1977). *Discipline and Punish—the Birth of the Prison*. London: Allen Lane.

Ignatieff, M. (1978). *A Just Measure of Pain: The Penitentiary and the Industrial Revolution*. London: Macmillan.

King, M. (1981). *The Framework of Criminal Justice*. London: Croom Helm.

Packer, H. (1968). *The Limits of the Criminal Sanction*. Stanford, CA: Stanford University Press.

Taylor, I., Walton, P. and Young, J. (1973). *The New Criminology: For a Social Theory of Deviance*. London: Routledge & Kegan Paul.

Von Hirsch, A. (1976). *Doing Justice: The Choice of Punishments. Report of the Committee for the Study of Incarceration*. New York: Hill and Wang.

READING 3

The Origins of Modern Criminology
Rob Watts, Judith Bessant, and Richard Hil

It can seem that the only question about memory worth asking these days is how much you have in your computer. At least this makes the point that a computer without a memory is just a piece of junk. Russell Jacoby (1974) made the same point about people without a memory. Drawing on the work of Sigmund Freud, Jacoby argued that people who cannot remember their past are unable to think or act rationally in the present. Just as the accident victim with amnesia is totally disoriented, so too people without a memory are disoriented and unsure about what to do or where to go. As Harald Weinrich (2004: 136) notes, Freud's point was that the capacity to think well, and so to live well, depends on us having a good memory.

Criminologists produce research, develop theory, teach, give their expert views to the media, and advise governments, the courts and police forces. To do all these things they rely on a vocabulary and a tradition of ideas and concepts assembled into complex criminological arguments. These ideas and this vocabulary have a history which is worth rehearsing.

Many people may well think history is a yawn, and that being interested in the past means you are intellectually 'old fashioned' or some kind of 'fuddy-duddy'. After all, the future is always a far more interesting place. Yet understanding contemporary criminology requires an understanding of how and why it has taken the shape it has. This chapter explores the development of certain ideas in the eighteenth and nineteenth centuries that came to characterize criminology as a social science.

A history of criminology assists us in seeing the partly accidental and evolutionary development of certain ways of thinking about crime, criminal activity and the criminal justice system. We are especially interested in the ways people who identify themselves as criminologists, along with the sociologists, psychologists and anthropologists interested in crime, thought about, inquired into, researched and defined crime, criminal activity and the criminal justice system. Martha Nussbaum (2001), writing a history of ancient Greek philosophy, argues this is just another way of doing philosophy. Writing a history of criminology is likewise best understood as another way of doing criminology. Recalling the history of criminology helps in a fundamental way to answer the question: 'What is modern criminology?'

Rob Watts, Judith Bessant, and Richard Hil, "The Origins of Modern Criminology," *International Criminology: A Critical Introduction*, pp. 31-50, 239-259. Copyright © 2008 by Taylor & Francis Group. Reprinted with permission.

What kind of history?

If history is important, how do we tell that story or write that history? One way of doing it has been to write what David Garland calls a 'standard textbook history'. This works by telling a story of the 'stages' in the history of criminology, a story which emphasizes the progress made as 'primitive criminology' evolves into 'modern', 'advanced' and 'scientific' criminology. As Garland (1994: 20) puts it:

> The received wisdom of the discipline [can be] simplified into a tale of icons and demons (Beccaria, Lombroso, Burt, Radzinowicz ...), a few key distinctions (classicism, positivism, radicalism ...) and an overarching narrative in which ideological error is gradually displaced by the findings of science ...

This is the kind of history of criminology written by Mannheim (1960), Radzinowicz (1966), or Quinney (1974, 1979). These writers began with a story about how a primitive kind of criminology developed in the eighteenth century. This history suggests that the early attempt to do criminology—mostly by 'amateurs', like philosophers and journalists, who did not understand the 'scientific method'—fortunately evolved into 'modern criminology' characterized by the use of the 'scientific method' to support a rigorous empirical social science (Mason 1996). This is 'whig history' with a vengeance, a history that, as Steve Fuller (2000: 22) says, is 'history written about the past to vindicate the present'.

This is a history that talks of stages such as 'classical criminology' which was created by philosophers and reformers such as Jeremy Bentham in the eighteenth century. This 'stage' gave way to 'positivist criminology', associated with Cesare Lombroso in the 1870s. In turn 'neo-classical criminology', associated with Gabriel Tarde or Cyril Burt, set the stage for a new kind of criminology between the 1890s and the 1920s. These stages in turn made it possible for 'modern criminology' to emerge in the second half of the twentieth century.

Is there anything wrong with writing a history of criminology as a story of progress or of developmental stages? According to Garland (1994: 21): 'The standard textbook history is, of course, broadly accurate—it would be very surprising if it were not. But the broad sweep of its narrative and the resounding simplicity of its generic terms can be profoundly misleading if they are taken as real history, rather than as a kind of heuristic ...'. (The word 'heuristic' here means any framework for making sense of things.)

Contemporary criminologists like David Garland say that the actual story is not quite so simple. A more accurate history of criminology might point to a far messier, or *contingent*, approach to thinking about and researching crime, the criminal and the law. The 'radically simple' story of stages and progress mistakenly asserts that there was something recognizable as 'criminology' in the eighteenth century—or earlier. Some historians of criminology have claimed that, for as long as there have been 'states', 'theorists' and writing, there have been people who think about these issues who could be called 'criminologists'.

It is more useful to think about contemporary criminology as a set of distinctive intellectual activities and practices that comes to be organized into a recognizable discipline or 'profession' only in the second half of the nineteenth century.

Further, a thoughtful approach to this history also implies that we might stop trying to use a radically simplified chronology of criminology which talks of certain 'progressive' and sequential stages or phases, such as 'classical criminology', 'positivist criminology', 'neo-classical criminology', 'modern criminology' and now 'post-modern criminology'. The idea that the history of criminology is a history of stages ignores the possibility that the way people have done criminology is messier than metaphors of 'progress' or 'stages' allow for. For example, it is clear that most contemporary criminologists do not define themselves as 'post-modern criminologists'. In many respects the work of many contemporary statistically inclined criminologists is not all that different from the pioneering work done by statistical pioneers like Adolphe Quételet in the 1840s or by Cyril Burt in the 1920s. This consideration suggests that there are important continuities between allegedly discrete stages in the way people did criminology.

The simplifying approach at work in the 'whig histories' of criminology also mistakenly asserts that there has been a progressive increase in the 'rational' or 'scientific' treatment of 'reality' as criminology 'matured' or 'progressed'. How for example would those who accept the 'whig' idea of constant progress in criminological knowledge and theory validate such a claim? Do we now actually have better explanations for why people do criminal things than were on offer a century ago?

In a way the kind of history that might better grasp what happened is closer to what Steve Fuller (2000: 24) calls a 'tory history'. This is a history that allows that the figures of the past being written about either got it 'more right' than is now commonly allowed for, or to put this idea more pungently, that what is being done now is simply recycling old ideas using new words to do so.

A Revised History of Criminology

David Garland (1994) offers another approach to the history of criminology. Garland argues that his 'revisionist' history of criminology reveals two traditions, or what he calls 'projects', operating over the past few centuries, projects which continue to co-exist even now. Garland refers to these respectively as the 'governmental project' and the 'science of causes'. What does Garland mean by this?

As Garland (1994: 18) says: 'By a "governmental project" I mean … the long series of empirical inquiries that since the eighteenth century have sought to enhance the efficient and equitable administration of justice by charting the patterns of crime and monitoring the practice of police and prisons.' (The word 'empirical' here refers to the theory that what we know of the world is based on our senses like sight or sound.)

Garland's idea of 'government' is not just about the activities of governments but refers also to institutions like the family, churches and schools as they seek to regulate (or govern) the lives of people by passing laws, making policies or disciplining conduct. This idea of 'government' comes from the work of Michel Foucault (1991), the French philosopher–historian who died in 1984. Families, for example, engage in 'government' by regulating the behaviour of children in activities like cleaning, telling the truth or eating at the table instead of in front of the TV. Governments likewise employ police and health-care workers to control behaviour in the streets or teachers to educate people with approved ideas, values and information.

Garland suggests that across the nineteenth century Western governments increasingly used fact-gathering techniques like censuses and other social statistics to describe the essential features of a range of 'problem populations' like 'the poor', 'the mad' or the 'criminal classes'. Foucault (1991) called this kind of knowledge 'governmentality', making a play on the 'mentality' part of the word. The reference to 'mentality' points to the role of ideas and evidence gathered by experts using techniques like the census. 'Governmentality' includes the variety of *scientific* and statistical surveillance techniques and statistical information used to inform a system of expert administration designed to regulate human behaviour. On this interpretation, gathering crime statistics is just one part of the project of government.

This kind of research work is a central preoccupation of contemporary criminology. It is the kind of criminology produced by in-house police and civil service research units, as well as academic research centres that regularly produce statistics on crime and justice. Much of this work is designed to help governments and police to work out where to put police resources by, for example, identifying areas in cities with high crime rates.

However, Garland says that alongside this activity, criminology also became an academic discipline based in universities, with academics developing an interest in *explaining* why crime occurs. This is what Garland means when he says criminology has also aspired to be a 'science of causes'. According to Garland the 'science of causes' like any science has to make certain assumptions. In this case criminologists who pursue a 'science of causes' promote a 'form of inquiry which aims to develop an etiological, explanatory science based on the premise that criminals can somehow be differentiated from non-criminals' (1994: 18). Garland also refers to this as the Lombrosian project, after the work of the Italian Cesare Lombroso (1911) who published his famous study *Criminal Man* (or *L'Uomo Delinquente*) in 1876. Lombroso was a nineteenth-century 'positivist' who did much to promote criminology as a 'science of causes'. (We will discuss what Lombroso thought and some of the issues with it later in this chapter.)

Garland's main point is that, far from being a history of discrete stages, the history of criminology is better understood as a kind of parallel process in which the 'governmental project' evolved alongside the pursuit of a 'science of causes'. Garland says that the result is 'modern criminology', a tension-filled field of study, teaching and research caught between an 'ambitious science of causes' and a more pragmatic, policy-oriented, administrative project seeking to use science in the service of management and social control. It is tension-filled partly because these two projects operate with different assumptions about the nature of human beings and their conduct, as well as different assumptions about what kinds of knowledge are credible.

Garland's account of modern criminology as a combination of a 'governmental project' evolving alongside a 'science of causes' is a very useful starting point. However, he overstates the point when he suggests that most criminologists today work within either a broadly defined *positivist* tradition or an *empiricist* approach to their research. (The meanings of and debates about these complex and controversial concepts are discussed later.) We will qualify that point by showing that there have always been other criminologists working against those conventions of empiricism and positivism. There are criminologists who have developed an approach to understanding human activity by developing *interpretive* methods. To compound the complexity, another tradition is to be found at work in the history of criminology, best referred to as a *critical*, or *sceptical*, style of criminology. A giant figure in American criminology like Edwin Sutherland (1924 and 1947) was critical early on about the conservative character of conventional criminology. Sutherland (1947) thought this kind of criminology was socially conservative because it focused on the crimes of the poor as opposed to the crimes of the rich and powerful—or what he called 'white-collar crime'. Likewise other early US criminologists associated with the Chicago School of Sociology were heavily influenced by the anti-positivist philosophy of US pragmatists like C. S. Peirce and William James. As we show in Chapter 3 what became an ethnographic approach to criminology, firstly at the University of Chicago, was based on a scepticism about the possibility of ever producing a 'science of crime'. Though sceptical and critical criminologists have never provided anything more than a counterbalance to mainstream criminologists, they have been an important part of the history of modern criminology.

In short we need to modify Garland's account. Contemporary criminology is certainly a tension-filled field of study, teaching and research. There are criminologists who pursue a policy-oriented administrative project seeking to use science in the service of management and social control. There are criminologists like Gottfredson and Hirschi (1990) who relentlessly pursue a 'science of causes'. Finally, as the careers of writers like Stanley Cohen (1997, 2001) and David Garland (1990, 1997, 2001) suggest, a more critical, sceptical style of criminology continues to find a readership.

Nonetheless Garland's idea of a 'governmental project' and a 'science of causes project' at work in criminology provides a good starting point.

Bentham and the Governmental Project

The first half of the nineteenth century in many countries, including Britain and America, saw the flowering of some of the key institutions that mark out the 'governmental project'. These institutions include the development of the modern penitentiary, the growth of police forces, and the systematic collection of statistical data designed to assist the discovery and regulation of social problems among certain sections of the population. How did this come about?

In countries like France, the UK and the USA the eighteenth century had seen the development of networks of lawyers, journalists, intellectuals and self-declared 'social reformers'. These groups constituted a 'public sphere' based on newspapers, journals and intellectual societies whose members met in coffee-shops, universities and salons run by wealthy and powerful aristocrats. These intellectuals and professionals—or *philosophes* as they were called in France—were committed to a programme of 'enlightened' and critical thought. They promoted the kind of natural science associated with Isaac Newton, the political programme grounded in the liberalism of John Locke, the sceptical empiricism of David Hume and the utilitarian ethics of writers like Jeremy Bentham.

Collectively these writers believed in the promise of a new social and intellectual order based on a broadly defined commitment to *Reason*, or rationality. They advocated the scientific investigation of the social and natural world. They believed profoundly in the capacity of Reason to change human beings and in the power of education and science to make the 'good society'. Indeed all were part of that process which led to what some historians have said is the greatest invention of the eighteenth century, the idea that every human being has a right both to happiness and to freedom.

Their ideas helped to shape a wide-ranging programme of political and intellectual change across Europe and in the American colonies, and played their part in what has been called 'the democratic revolution' that saw Britain lose its American colonies in 1785 and France engage in revolutionary change after 1789.

This was a time when writers and academics were generalists rather than experts in a narrow field. There was no particular special knowledge or response to crime of the kind that marks out the *modern* criminological project, just a preoccupation with the *social problem*.

The 'social problem' referred to the existence of millions of poor, exploited, politically disenfranchised and potentially revolutionary urban, working-class people. The existence of these people, and their perceived potential for trouble, triggered off traditional responses like military repression, political trials and secret police surveillance. It would also sponsor numerous exercises in social scientific research, social policy and democratic reform, especially in the second half of the eighteenth and throughout the nineteenth century. Though no one person can be held responsible for this, one figure stands out.

Jeremy Bentham (1748–1832) was a wealthy gentleman–lawyer, lobbyist and *philosophe* who tirelessly promoted a rational programme of law reform and rational social change designed to increase the sum total of human happiness, or what he called 'utility'. To use Foucault's and Garland's word 'governmentality' we can say that Bentham played a central role in developing a revolution in 'governmentality' that took off in the nineteenth century and was to directly sponsor the development of the twentieth-century idea that governments have an obligation to promote human welfare. Bentham was extremely influential throughout the nineteenth century and continues to be an invisible but significant presence into our own time. Bentham stands as the 'father' of so many distinctively 'common-sense' modern views and practices that we can easily miss his impact.

Bentham is also important because he linked his utilitarianism to his advocacy of the use of scientific evidence as a basis for policy-making, and for a systematic approach to law reform enacted by governments using statutory law.

Bentham was one of the first great modern advocates of treating the law as an agency of social reform. Bentham tirelessly pursued law reform as an instrument for larger social transformation. He was an early advocate of evidence-based law reform. He was an inexhaustible promoter of ideas like privatizing prisons, putting 'the poor' to work, and was ever ready to write constitutions for any country willing to pay him as a consultant. Among his ideas was that precisely designed buildings could be used as schools, prisons or hospitals to regulate the behaviour of almost anyone needing to be educated, imprisoned or cured of disease. He called his design idea a 'Panopticon': the idea that required putting a group of people under surveillance by teachers, doctors or wardens situated in a central point or space in a building, and thereby enabling them to regulate the inmates' behaviour. This idea was to inform the building of prisons like Alcatraz in the nineteenth and twentieth centuries.

His influence, however, runs more deeply than as the promoter of bright ideas. As a rationalist he believed in the power of evidence to persuade people to make necessary social change. Bentham took the proposition from Helvétius, an eighteenth-century *philosophe*, that all valid knowledge is empirical. Bentham believed that all knowledge is based on sensations—like sight or hearing. Grounded in this philosophy of knowledge Bentham sponsored a process of rational social change administered by an expert bureaucracy responsible for an efficient *scientific* system of administration and relying on the systematic gathering of societal facts and statistics. His ideas mattered especially in Britain. Bentham through his social and political networks and his protégés had a tremendous practical and intellectual influence. He was an early advocate for systematic empirical enquiry that ushered in the age of Select Committees and Royal Commissions in Britain. His influence is evident in legislation such as the *Metropolitan Police Act 1828*, the *Poor Law Act 1834* and the *Public Health Act 1848*.

Bentham's promotion of the systematic collection and use of descriptive social statistics to better inform government has led some historians, following Foucault, to suggest that his idea of the 'Panopticon', originally intended as a design principle to construct buildings that could keep the inmates under constant surveillance, should also be seen as a metaphor for governments' collection of social statistics to keep a close watch on social problems or certain groups of problematic people.

Yet Bentham was more than the caricature of Gradgrind, the Benthamite reformer Dickens satirized in his novel *Hard Times* for wanting only 'the facts'. Bentham's passion for change was grounded also in an ethical idea that has proved his greatest legacy: governments, he thought, had an obligation to promote the greatest happiness of the greatest number of their citizens.

Bentham is one of the key figures in modern philosophy and public policy because of his advocacy of the ethical system called 'utilitarianism' ('utility' is another word for happiness or welfare). Bentham was a key advocate of the idea that all humans have a right to happiness. This idea is embedded in the American Declaration of Independence which refers to the pursuit of liberty and happiness. Bentham did not invent the system of ethics called utilitarianism. He drew on the work of writers like Hutcheson and Beccaria (1963), an Italian philosopher of punishment, to develop the principle of utility into the ethical system we now refer to as 'utilitarianism'.

Bentham was a rationalist and a utilitarian. He held that all human action is driven by rational self-interest. Bentham argued that as human beings we naturally and rationally seek to maximize our happiness and minimize or avoid things that give us pain. Utilitarians like Bentham claim that the way we judge something to be good is by asking whether it will make us happy. If the answer is 'yes', then it is 'good'. As individuals we are driven to do only what will maximize our happiness or minimize pain. He drew on this idea to argue that governments ought to promote the greatest happiness of the greatest number of people. At the societal level Bentham argued that any ethical judgement or political process should be judged only against the principle of whether an action or policy will advance 'the greatest happiness of the greatest number'.

Utilitarianism is the belief or value system that has supplied the dominant ethical framework to the cultures of the Anglo-American world. That framework is alive and well in the twenty-first century as evidenced by the thriving state of a neo-classical economics of 'rational selfishness' which informs contemporary neo-liberal policies, as well as Animal Liberation philosophers like Peter Singer. In spite of powerful critiques by philosophers from Kant to Finnis (2005: 112–18), showing precisely why this doctrine is senseless, it retains an extraordinary status in the contemporary Anglo-American world.

This is so probably because of the elective affinity between utilitarianism and any society with an ethic of individualism and a market-based economy: happiness in such societies is readily equated with consuming more goods or having more money. Bentham himself had sponsored the increasingly important belief that it was both possible and desirable to *measure* any increase or decrease in happiness—or utility. Bentham proposed using money as an index of happiness, but votes, public opinion polls or any equivalent metric would do as well. Bentham was one major proponent of the idea that we can quantify our ethical preferences, using what he called the 'felicific calculus'. It has also allowed economists like Becker (1978) to develop an economic theory of crime.

The Revolution in Government

Bentham stands behind all those attempts to give effect to the 'governmental project' that took off in the nineteenth century. The utilitarian ethic and the practice of a rational, empirically based, efficient legal and administrative system which Bentham promoted was central to the increase in the range and scope of state interventions in Britain from the 1830s on. Given his premise that it was the duty of government to advance 'the greatest happiness of the greatest number', Bentham helped to unleash the 'Victorian revolution in government' that gathered speed in the 1830s and 1840s.

At the urging of his disciples, utilitarian reformers like Edwin Chadwick, James Mill, Nassau Senior and John Stuart Mill, British governments after 1832 increasingly undertook a range of interventionist, regulatory and information-gathering activities. The 'Victorian revolution in government' involved a reform project designed to make the law more rational and government more efficient by developing an expert-based administrative system which made increasing use of statistics to guide policy-making.

The 'revolution in government' involved a programme of systematic surveillance of social problems, the systematic collection of statistics and the use of inspectors to report on the progress of reform. By the 1850s British governments were relying on an army of inspectors and experts to collect facts about a large number of social problems, including crime, poverty, homelessness, prostitution and 'street children'. The revolution in government also saw Bentham's disciples build and manage the archetypal 'industrial' institutions of the nineteenth century, beginning with workhouses for the poor. Subsequently governments undertook the construction of schools, prisons and hospitals. These institutions treated people as so much raw material to be regulated and re-educated. They relied less on the threat of punishment or pain and more on the efficient management and regulation of the inmates' behaviour.

Garland (1994: 35) explains why this mattered for the development of criminology:

> The various forms of charitable and social work with the poor, the societies for the care of discharged convicts, the management of workhouses, inquiries about the causes and extent of inebriety, investigations into the labour market, the employment and education of children, education, the housing of the poor, the settlements and boys' club movements, could all be identified as the roots of ... the modern criminological mix.

Why did this happen? There is little doubt that this 'reform' agenda was driven by elite and middle-class business and professional fears that the 'lower classes' would maintain the momentum for democratic change, one that might lead even to socialist revolution (Hobsbawm 1975). Memories of the revolutions in America (1776–84) and France (1789–1814) nourished these fears. The middle-class impulse to reform and regulate was also fed by the unrelenting revelation by reformers, investigators and lobbyists of a plethora of social problems crying out for action. The development of what we call 'social sciences' was implicated in this process.

The Statistical Movement and a Science of Causes

Until the mid-nineteenth century, the collection of social statistics had been at best rudimentary and sporadic. The development of statistics flowered in the nineteenth century and was the work of men like Edwin Chadwick and Adolphe Quételet, who possessed of a deep interest in, and passion for, social reform drawing on *scientific* techniques (Stigler 1987: 162–82 and 263–300). In this way the 'governmental project' itself sponsored the development of a 'science of causes' that was to shape the development of modern criminology.

Benthamite reformers who promoted the emergent governmental project relied on an ever-increasing volume of social statistics designed to describe the social, cultural and economic lives of the people by focusing on such things as death rates and suicide rates, as well as crime rates. The architects of the 'revolution in government' required more and more information about more and more of the population, and the development of social statistics played a central role in this process. The need for social facts that led to an explosion in social statistics was well advanced by the 1840s and supported by the growth of groups such as the London and Manchester Societies for Social Statistics. Investigations like Henry Mayhew and his multi-volume studies of London's poor (1861–62) added more colourful kinds of evidence.

It is in this respect then that Garland's distinction between criminology approached as a 'governmental project' and as a 'science of causes' implies a clear-cut set of boundaries between the two than is the case. This becomes apparent as we trace out the development of social statistics and the contribution this made to a 'science of causes'.

The Belgian statistician Adolphe Quételet (1796–1874) made an enormous contribution to the modern 'empirical' social sciences. Quételet's innovations in statistics provided some of the technical basis for the development of criminology as a 'science of causes' based on what can be called a 'broad church' kind of positivism.

Quételet's primary achievement was to develop and apply statistical ideas about averages to many social phenomena, showing how deviations from the average were determined and not a random phenomenon. (He did this by using the curve of normal distribution or a Gaussian distribution.)

Quételet (1842) developed a number of basic ideas about social problems like crime which have persisted into our own time. His data showed that most crimes were committed by younger people aged 15 to 21 and that most serious crimes were performed by males. He claimed to show that many social phenomena were persistent and stable over time, making it possible to talk about an 'average' person by drawing on observations about thousands or tens of thousands of people in each group. He demonstrated that the rates at which various crimes were committed, discovered and punished were likewise regular and varied very little over time. And if crime rates were constant, this suggested to Quételet, that the 'causes' of such phenomena were likewise regular and must be operating according to some 'laws of causality' that could be discovered.

All of this led him to an early version of a sociological model of crime: individuals may commit crimes but they are merely the agent of societal pressures and causes. As Quételet (1842: 6, 108) put it: 'Every social state presupposes, then, a certain number and a certain order of crimes, these merely being the necessary consequences of its organization ... Society prepares crime, and the guilty are only the instruments by which it is executed.' At some point in the 1840s, Quételet came to see a clear distinction between 'normal distributions' and 'unusual deviations' from this statistical norm.

Like modern criminologists, Quételet found it difficult to resist giving expression to his own class- and gender-bound prejudices, something which sooner or later overwhelms even the most cautious of empirical social scientists. Using techniques for ascertaining a normal distribution, Quételet concluded that while every 'normal' man had a certain tendency to commit crime, this rarely happened. Of more concern was the criminality of the 'statistically' unusual kind manifested by people he thought were degenerates, vagrants, 'gypsies', the 'inferior classes' and people of 'low moral character'. By the late 1840s Quételet, in clear anticipation of Lombroso and Galton, concluded that crime was likely to be a consequence of hereditary and biological defects. In France followers of Quételet, like Guerry, promoted the development of social statistics into recognizably 'modern' forms. In the last decades of the nineteenth century Quételet's work offered the statistical basis for the distinctively 'positivist' idea that the social sciences could and should emulate the physical sciences.

There is no evidence that British social researchers and 'reformers' took much immediate notice of Quételet's work. This was in spite of the fact that by the late 1840s in Britain John Stuart Mill, the dominant philosopher of his age who had been raised by Bentham as a utilitarian and social reformer, was also one of the leading advocates for a statistically based social science and for French 'positivism'. By the 1870s, however, in Britain social researchers like Rawson, Fletcher and Glyde began using the techniques of Quételet.

The word 'positivism' needs some brief consideration here.

Positivism

'Positivism' is a controversial word with a considerable history. Auguste Comte (1798–1857) coined the word 'positivism' (he also coined the word 'sociology'). Like many other key ideas it can be used either as a weapon to insult someone we disapprove of or to help us to talk or think clearly. There is continuing controversy about what the word refers to. This lack of clarity or consensus about its meaning has long been a feature of this word throughout its career. Needless to say there is no single, neat definition of what it means (see Hacking 1983: 42–57).

For contemporary criminologists 'positivism' involves a commitment to a 'commonsense' reliance on scientific method. The practice of this kind of positivism is based on 'operationalizing' a concept so as to render it amenable to measurement, carrying out some data collection and then doing statistical analysis—like regression analysis—on that data. This apparently 'common-sense' approach is often taught in university 'empirical research methods' or 'quantitative research methods' courses and incorrectly assumes or asserts that because it is based on 'common sense' it has nothing to do with theories or philosophy. For those criminologists who are aware of the history of philosophy, 'positivism' will be understood to refer to what a group of mostly Austrian philosophers, who belonged to the Vienna Circle in the 1920s, promoted (Ayer 1959). For other criminologists 'positivism' is what nineteenth-century criminologists like Lombroso stood for. We can see here fruitful grounds for confusion.

An examination of what Auguste Comte meant by 'positivism' helps identify some of the main claims and assumptions still made by many criminologists.

Comte was violently opposed to religious ideas and what he called 'metaphysics'. (In this respect Comte was heavily indebted to the work of eighteenth-century French *philosophes* like Voltaire, Condillac and Montesquieu.) Comte's deep antagonism to religious belief was fed by his faith in empiricism: if something had no material qualities enabling it to be seen, smelled, heard or touched then it did not exist and could not be the proper object of scientific knowledge. 'God' on this account was just a quaint and irrational hangover from the Middle Ages and had no part to play in the development of scientific reason. Comte preferred to put his faith in the achievements of modern sciences like chemistry, physics and medical research. In broad terms Comte thought that the methods of the natural sciences could and should be applied to all forms of knowledge and to what we now refer to as the 'social sciences'. (Unlike twentieth-century positivists, Comte did not believe it either possible or wise to establish definitively that there was a single scientific method: Comte allowed that each science could and should have its own special methods and laws.)

As twentieth-century French scholars like Canguilhem (1990) have shown, Comte and his followers were heavily reliant on biological and medical metaphors and explanations. This biological model fed the development of a new science of society in the 1840s that Comte called 'sociology'. Comte's 'science of society' spoke increasingly of 'social health' and identified 'antisocial' factors using medical metaphors which would come to identify crime as a 'social pathology'. Comte's advocacy of the idea of a science of the societal rested on a number of basic propositions.

1. As an empiricist Comte believed that the only secure knowledge about the world was knowledge based on what was observable. If an idea was not observable or measurable, it could never become the substance of knowledge. (This had serious consequences for many ideas apart from 'God', like 'justice', 'democracy' or 'love'.) Comte relied on one early version of what became known as the verifiability criterion of meaning. This is the philosophical claim that our knowledge of the world ought properly to consist of 'ideas' which are traces of sense data emitted by 'real objects' in the world. In short any word, in order to be meaningful, had to refer to something that was 'real' or observable. Using this criterion, for example, the word 'unicorn' has no meaning and cannot be regarded as playing any part in any scientific claim about the world.

2. Positivism in Comte's hands became a *method of research* based on observation and measurement. Comte argued that any claims wishing to be 'scientific' had to be based on careful observation and precise measurement.

3. Comte further argued that the positivist scientist's goal was explanation: success in explaining anything would be verified when it became the basis of prediction. According to Comte, explaining anything successfully required successful prediction. He did not favour older notions of

causality as much as a model of explanation based on the laws of succession. (Laws of succession work by relating events that occur across time, like the claim that 'swallowing cyanide causes death'.) Like Hume and Kant, Comte accepted that *causality* was simply a *metaphysical* idea because causality is not strictly speaking an observable relationship, although in one sense his reliance on the 'laws of succession' was a way of reinstating causality.

4. Finally, Comte adopted *a spectator model of knowledge.* Pierre Manent (1998: 50–85) argues that nineteenth-century social sciences introduced a deterministic logic into its 'science of man' with paradoxical effects. One of these effects was to obscure any real interest in the nature of human conduct. Manent begins by noting that whereas classical political philosophy had adopted the viewpoint of the practical actor—that is a citizen or statesman who participates in the world—sociology early took the 'viewpoint of the spectator'. The viewpoint of the spectator is 'pure and scientific' and accords no real initiative to the agent or agents, but considers their actions or works 'as the necessary effects of necessary causes'. Objectivity on the part of the social scientist implied that the writer–expert was committed not only to eliminating *bias* but also to eliminating the psychological dimensions of experience and even of 'the feeling and willing self' (Bannister 1987: 40).

In short, being a 'positivist' meant for Comte that it was desirable and possible to use what he thought were the methods of the 'natural sciences'—like physics, chemistry or physiology—to do research into social matters like crime. Many of us will doubtless think that this is just common sense.

Yet there are many issues with taking this common sense seriously. Take the idea that scientists just look at the facts and develop theories from those facts. Gerald Holton (1988) has shown how all so-called 'hard sciences' like physics or chemistry rely on 'themata'. (What Holton called 'themata' Gadamer 1994 described as simply rock-solid prejudices without which we cannot think or do science.) 'Themata', or prejudices, are beliefs that we either cannot find facts to support or else refuse to think about, but simply assume to be true. Holton shows, for example, how Newton's famous mathematical account of the laws of the universe in *Principia Mathematica* (1687) relied on a 'thematum' called 'God'.

Notwithstanding these and similar problems with positivism, it matters only that Comte's ideas were enthusiastically, if selectively, taken up in both Britain and America by key figures like John Stuart Mill and Herbert Spencer, each of whom was a key point of transmission of the aggressive and 'irreligious' positivism of Auguste Comte into both Britain and America. Even so, both of these nineteenth-century philosophers were sceptical about the very systemic and rationalist quality of Comte's work, perhaps seeing this as a consequence of Comte's being a Frenchman.

It is important to note that both Mill and Spencer helped to promote and consolidate some of the elements of what 'a proper social science' should look like. In almost every respect their advocacy of a social science was 'positivist', except for one key point. Neither Mill nor Spencer let go of the Benthamite idea that people are individuals pursuing their self-interest and maximizing their happiness by some kind of rational calculation. To this extent they resisted the properly positivist idea that people are driven by factors or causes outside their control.

From the 1840s on, utilitarians like J. S. Mill (1806–73) (himself a pupil of Bentham), arguably the most influential British philosopher of the nineteenth century, constructed a powerful synthesis of liberal individualism, ethical utilitarianism and an empiricist–positivist approach to scientific knowledge. Mill's *System of Logic* (1843) provided a detailed and systematic outline of a *proper* 'positivist' social science. In effect Mill succeeded in codifying the elements of an inductive model of the social sciences. In America, Comte's ideas and vocabulary were spread by Herbert Spencer (1820–1903) on his lecturing tours. Spencer had a major intellectual impact on American academics. His advocacy of a science of 'social physics', or 'sociology', was influential in promoting the development of both sociology and criminology in the USA, as was his commitment to spreading his version of Darwinism which became known as social Darwinism.

Charles Darwin's book *The Origin of Species* (1859) and his subversive assault on the biblical idea that every species of animal and plant was created by God in either one day or seven days (there are two accounts of the creation in Genesis) added further weight to the status of scientific biology in helping to shape the social sciences. Darwin's account of 'racial types', or what he also called 'species', was to have a major impact on the evolution of modern criminology and the idea that criminology should aim to become a 'science of causes'.

Granted the somewhat complex development of European positivism, it is still the case that it was only with the publication in 1876 of Cesare Lombroso's *Criminal Man* that an explicitly positivist criminology was made available to a wide audience. In this book a strong positivist claim was made that factors outside our personal control make some of us criminals. Lombroso's fame rested on his claim that he could *explain* crime through the medium of scientific analysis, because he had discovered that there was a specific type of man—'criminal man'—whose behaviour was something over which he had little if any control. In effect 'criminal man' was a Darwinian 'throwback'.

Lombroso and the 'Science of Causes'

Many histories of criminology (Jeffrey 1972) treat the publication of Cesare Lombroso's *Criminal Man* in 1876 as a benchmark event. For these writers, Lombroso's book marks the installation of a determinist 'science of criminality'. In an intellectual context already influenced by Darwin's biology and soon to be shaped by Galton's development of a biologically based sociology, Lombroso's *Criminal Man* (1911) represents one version of a biologically determinist shift towards the *scientific* treatment of the crime problem.

According to Lombroso's account, criminal activity was an example of a 'predictable' and 'habitual' form of conduct which was best understood as something causally determined by 'forces' beyond any person's control. As Cohen notes, the 'positivist revolution' in criminology popularly ascribed to Lombroso's *Criminal Man* (1876) assumed

... not rationality, free will and choice but determinism (biological, psychic or social) ... the subsequent structure and logic of criminological explanation remained largely within the positivist paradigm. Whether the level of explanation was biological, psychological, sociological or a combination of these ('multi-factorial' as some versions were dignified) the Holy Grail was a general causal theory: why do people commit crime? This quest gave the subject its collective self-definition: 'the scientific study of crime'.

(Cohen 1992: 4)

For Lombroso, individual free will was a myth because 'individual behaviours', including criminal activity, were largely beyond people's control.

From 1876 when Lombroso's book *Criminal Man* appeared, extraordinary interest and acclaim greeted his work. His vivid writing style perhaps explains part of the impact. Lombroso's study of Italian army recruits and prison inmates used both craniometry (measuring skull size) and anthropometry (measuring body shape) in an attempt to identify different *racial types* and subject them to scientific scrutiny and categorization.

In this respect Lombroso's work seemed—and seems—eminently scientific. To this day *real* science is marked by the measurement of things. Lombroso played a part in legitimating the enthusiasm for physical and psychological measurement that has continued down to this day. The mania for measurement would lead to the measurement of schoolchildren beginning with their skull size and routine measurement of their 'intelligence', reading age and mathematical abilities. It was to sponsor the mass testing of soldiers' IQs and the IQs of other groups in the population after 1914. It also encouraged the collection and measurement of the skulls of natives in North America and Australasia, to say nothing of murdered Jews and gypsies in the Institutes of Racial Science that flourished in Nazi Germany after 1939.

Lombroso recalls his 'eureka' moment when opening up the skull of a 'criminal' named Vilella:

I found on the occipital part ... a distinct depression which I named median *occipital fossa* because of its situation precisely in the middle of the occiput, *as in inferior animals, especially rodents*... at the sight of that skull, I seemed to see all of a sudden, lighted up as a vast plain under a flaming sky, the problem of the nature of the criminal, an atavistic being who reproduces in his person the ferocious instincts of primitive humanity and the inferior animals.

(Ferri-Lombroso in Lombroso 1911: xxiv–xxv; our emphasis)

Here we see the effect of Lombroso's assumption that it was necessary to treat criminals as different from the rest of us. He felt confident in this assumption because it seemed to derive from the dramatic biological revolution unleashed by Darwin's *The Origin of Species* (1859). Lombroso's talk of 'causes' implies a deterministic view of human conduct in which our conduct is caused by factors outside our control. Lombroso believed that some people were 'biologically' disposed to commit crime and that they had no choice. (Some of us now use the language of genetics to say the same thing.) On Lombroso's account of a 'science of causes', certain people were inherently 'criminals' and belonged to a 'criminal class'. They could not help themselves in regard to their 'criminal conduct'.

Lombroso's research was based on the principle that criminals were biological throwbacks to a more primitive version of *homo sapiens*. Lombroso drew on an idea shared by Darwin, Galton and Freud, that the development of each human from embryo to adult recapitulates the evolutionary process of the human species. For Lombroso, 'criminal man' was a poor unfortunate, 'an atavistic being who reproduces in his person the ferocious instincts of primitive humanity'. His work contributed to what became a veritable tidal wave of psychological and physical measurements that went on at least into the 1950s.

Lombroso advanced the project of a 'science of causes' in criminology firstly by his insistence on studying 'the criminal' as a type. He sought to establish a modern science of the criminal by virtue of his attempt to delineate a definitive anthropological entity: 'the natural-born criminal'. That is, Lombroso insisted that 'the criminal' was a *type* different from the rest of us, and was worthy of scientific study. At a stroke Lombroso constituted the conceptual entity (*the criminal*) that could sustain a discursive and disciplinary enterprise in terms that were recognizably *modern* and *criminological*, while reassuring his middle-class readers that they were largely safe from producing or being such throwbacks themselves.

Lombroso left his readers with the impression that here was a genuine 'criminological science of causes'. The *criminal* was now being constituted as a conceptual object worthy of a criminology, defined as a science of causes. And though he should not be given sole credit for this, by 1890 'criminology' was a word in common use.

Yet in many ways Lombroso's central claim that he had developed a genuine 'criminological science of causes' was the least credible aspect of his work. From the start when European criminologists met at a series of international conferences beginning in 1883, French, Italian and German criminologists subjected Lombroso's work to damaging criticism. (British experts deigned to attend the Geneva Congress of Criminal Anthropology only from 1896 onwards.) Lombroso's work was frequently and vigorously criticized as crude nonsense. It is to his credit that Lombroso himself later accepted this criticism, leading him to radically rethink his position.

This criticism reflects the point that nothing is ever quite simple or straightforward. For even as Lombroso was propounding his ideas about the causes of criminality, a newer model of scientific explanation took over in the second half of the nineteenth century. This owed much to the statistical revolution in nineteenth-century astronomy and physics. As Ian Hacking (1990) has shown, more and more scientists stopped talking about *causality* and began talking about the *probability* of something causing something else to happen. Natural scientists came increasingly to accept that many factors could explain why something happened. This idea of multi-causality informed the increasing use by social scientists of statistical techniques like regression and correlation analysis pioneered by Francis Galton and Karl Pearson in the last decades of the nineteenth century. Ultimately this model of causality triumphed in most of the social sciences. In the twentieth century a good deal of academic criminology has been done that involves gathering information and analysing it statistically so as to construct elaborate explanations of crime that point to many factors at work.

Lombroso's work proved to be important in the long run because of the reactions it provoked. Among the many criticisms of Lombroso, Gabriel Tarde's critique stands out. Tarde's intervention proved to be quite influential and his work is often referred to as the 'neo-classical synthesis'. Equally in Britain Lombroso's work stimulated Francis Galton to refine the biological and statistical explanation of social behaviour.

Responses to Lombroso: Tarde and the Neo-Classical Synthesis

Before the end of the nineteenth century, the French criminologist Gabriel Tarde (1843–1904) produced his 'neo-classical synthesis'. This was the result of his criticizing both 'classicism' and Lombroso's 'positivism'.

Tarde (1886) argued that neither Bentham nor Lombroso provided the right kind of basic principles and assumptions that might inform a 'modern philosophy of punishment'. In 1890 Tarde, in *Penal Philosophy*, accused 'classicists'—like Bentham—of over-emphasizing the free-will and rationality of the human actor. Equally Tarde accused the 'positivists' of over-emphasizing the machine-like, determined and causal explanations of criminality. In a way he echoes Marx's insight that humans were indeed the makers of their own history, but not of the circumstances in which they found themselves.

Tarde developed a much more sociological idea of crime. That is, Tarde emphasized the distinctively social or collective aspects of human conduct. Tarde argued that 'imitation' was the core social and psychological phenomenon that explained most social phenomena, including crime. As Tarde (1890: 322) put it: 'Imitation is that powerful, generally unconscious, always partly mysterious action by means of which we account for all the phenomena of society.' In terms that later criminologists have found useful, Tarde also argued that another key sociological factor predisposing some people to crime was living in cities. Living in large cities exposed people to what Tarde called an 'agitation of the spirit' that came from being exposed to mass or collective existence which effectively detached people from traditional moral codes. (Here we see one instance of Tarde's ideas anticipating a tradition of sociological criminology promoted by the Chicago School.)

As Tarde was producing his sociological account of crime, in Britain Francis Galton was refining both the statistical basis of the social sciences and providing an influential biological account of human activity.

Responses to Lombroso: Galton and Eugenics

Sir Francis Galton (1822–1911) did much to develop a sophisticated and highly credible *programme* of statistically based scientific research that helped to define the modern social sciences evolving between 1880 and 1940. Galton, who was first cousin to the biologist Charles Darwin, was an extremely wealthy, psychologically driven gentleman–scholar (Gould 1989). He gave the world scientific meteorology while he made a major practical contribution to criminal investigations by police with his discovery that fingerprints were unique to each individual. Following Quételet, Galton pioneered the collection of large-scale physical anthropometric measurements in Britain and initiated the first *scientific measurement* of intelligence. He also sponsored the growth of modern empirical psychology and the study of what he called 'individual differences'. To do all this Galton revolutionized statistics with his pioneering work on those key techniques of modern social statistics, regression analysis and the determination of correlation coefficients (Stigler 1987: 290–9). In this last respect Galton quietly re-landscaped the very ground on which social science had stood, moving it away from a simple idea of causal determinism to those very modern ideas of probability and multi-factorial analysis.

Like Bentham, Galton was more than just a man interested in scientific facts: he was also obsessed with the idea that it was possible to use science to improve human well-being. Galton devoted the last decades of his long life to the development of a form of scientific racism. While it is now customary to treat *racism* as reactionary and unscientific, for the first forty years of the twentieth century it was deemed by many to be both scientific and *progressive*. Indeed it is not going too far to say that social sciences like psychology, sociology and criminology were shaped by Galton's ideas about *racial improvement*.

Galton believed devoutly that intelligence and moral commitments to things like hard work and self-improvement were factors that made some people, and even an entire *race*, equipped to succeed in the great Darwinian struggle for survival. And he believed that these kinds of factors were inherited. 'Racial fitness' was the Darwinian notion that people with characteristics such as high intelligence would secure long-term species survival. Conversely 'racial unfitness' referred to all of those characteristics that doomed a race—or a species—to extinction.

Galton was obsessed by the idea that the 'superior races'—naturally the white races—were under threat internationally from the 'coloured races'. Equally he held that the 'racially superior' upper classes—to which he belonged—were under threat from the expansion of 'racially unfit' elements chiefly found essentially among 'the poor' and the working classes. To counter these threats Galton promoted an international movement called *eugenics* (meaning 'well-born'), committed to scientific research, policy-making and education.

In the last decades of the nineteenth century the Darwinian revolution began to feed increasing public anxiety about the mounting evidence of 'racial unfitness'. Everything, from homosexuality and prostitution, alcoholism, poverty, mental deficiency, stupidity, laziness and crime, was treated as a sign of 'racial unfitness'. All were understood to be natural in their manifestations and to be biologically transmissible. (Versions of this idea have returned since the 1990s to inform aspects of the social sciences including criminology, to say nothing of the way the popular understanding of the human genome project has been constituted.)

Eugenicists argued that only by adopting what they called 'racial hygienic' measures would the 'racially fit' survive. Racial hygiene meant encouraging the 'racially fit' to breed, while discouraging the 'unfit' by sex education, or preventing them from reproducing by contraception (called 'racial hygiene'), or, when all else failed, using compulsory sterilization.

Galton's preoccupation with collecting and analysing the results of his preoccupation with the size of people's skulls or their body shape and later their intelligence were to have fateful consequences. To make sense of his measurements, Galton sponsored the development of regression analysis. Subsequently Galton's disciples, especially William Cattell (at Columbia University) and Karl Pearson and George Yule (at London University), elaborated and refined most of the basic statistical techniques (including regression analysis and chi-square) to make them the indisputable methodological core of modern empirical social sciences.

From the start the highly sophisticated statistical techniques developed by Galton were oriented to practical policy outcomes. These statistical innovations were all part of a project to identify those in the community who were *unfit* as a prelude to state intervention.

It is important to note that there were, especially after 1920, two kinds of eugenicists (Kevles 1985). 'Negative eugenicists' took a strong biologically determinist line and were inclined to emphasize coercive policies like compulsory sterilization. In terms of practical policy measures, the *negative eugenic* project designed to identify and prevent unfit people from breeding achieved only partial success. Numerous states in North America, and several European countries, including Nazi Germany, passed compulsory sterilization legislation. (Virginia compulsorily sterilized its last victim, an Afro-American woman, in 1969.) It is also the case that under its medical killing programme, the Third Reich killed around 200,000 psychiatric patients and children with intellectual and physical disabilities.

The more numerous *positive eugenicists* saw biological, social and cultural factors as all playing a part in a much wider range of policy interventions aimed at enhancing the welfare and health of the whole population (Burleigh 1994). This refusal to explain everything in terms of biology also provided a research programme in which researchers could argue about the relative weight of biological *and* social factors in causing crime or poverty or whatever. Among the numerous practical interventions sponsored by eugenicists were:

- systematic IQ tests, and the study and normalizing of children's educational development, including age-based norms for reading, writing, etc.;
- professional training of teachers, social workers and prison workers;
- state provision of maternal and child welfare programmes;
- epidemiological studies of disease patterns as well as mass inoculation campaigns;
- mental hygiene movements to medicalize the treatment both of mental illness and physical and intellectual disability;
- medical testing of children;
- the study, diagnosis and treatment of juvenile delinquency;
- birth control and sex education clinics usually called 'racial hygiene' centres;
- sexually transmitted disease clinics;
- national nutritional research and campaigns to improve diets;
- campaigns to abolish slums and provide quality welfare housing;
- promotion of physical education, kindergartens, free playgrounds, national parks, urban planning and other preventive projects.

Eugenicist thinking provided the dominant progressive social scientific paradigm up to 1940. Most significant, progressive and rationalist intellectuals and academics in the Anglo-American and European world espoused variations of eugenicist ideas. Those who directly or indirectly supported such ideas included economists (Keynes and Pareto), psychologists (Freud, Pearson, Stanley Hall, Burt, Spearman and Thorndike) and many first-rank educators, doctors and physiologists, social workers, urban planners and leading policymakers.

Moreover, it helped establish a technical–statistical basis for social and epidemiological research, able to compute and analyse large data sets. In 1929 a British Parliamentary Joint Committee on Mental Deficiency estimated that there were at least 350,000 'mental defectives' in the UK. The committee claimed that this represented a doubling of 'defectives' since 1908; three-quarters of these came from families 'persistently below the average in income and social character'. The defectives included 'insane persons, epileptics, paupers, criminals (especially recidivists), unemployables, habitual slum dwellers, prostitutes, inebriates and other social inefficients' (quoted in Kevles 1985: 112). Even so, confronted with this 'evidence' the British government on this occasion did not pursue the favoured eugenicist policy of compulsory sterilization of the defectives. The reliance on large-scale statistical analysis has achieved an unquestioned and canonical status within the empirical social sciences of sociology, psychology and criminology into our own time.

By the start of the twentieth century some of the characteristics of criminology as a distinctive modern social science were either emerging or in place. Out of the eugenic impulse to know more and do more about social problems came an increasingly scientific and highly technical interest in the causes of crime. Garland (1994: 39–40) says this involved

> an avowedly scientific approach to crime, concerned to develop a 'positive', factual knowledge of individual offenders, based upon observation, measurement and inductive reasoning [where scientific explanation amounted to causal explanation] … identifying in particular the characteristics which appeared to mark the criminal off from normal law-abiding citizens …

The practical interest in managing crime and criminals, or what Garland (1994) has called the 'governmental project', was helping to identify the kinds of questions with which criminology in the twentieth century would be preoccupied. Equally by the start of the twentieth century, and courtesy of the pioneering work of Galton, the methodological and technical basis for a science of causes had been laid down. This would enable later mainstream criminologists to pursue the elusive search for the explanatory factors that produced both *crime* as well as explain the conduct of *the criminal*.

Like most of their American colleagues, British criminologists, for example Charles Goring, rejected the narrow mono-causal version of 'positivist' research represented by Lombroso. One of the chief consequences of Galton and Pearson's style of statistical analysis was that it emphasized the idea of probability rather than strictly mono-causal explanations and insisted on identifying the many factors, or 'variables', involved in a given social problem like crime.

Those of Galton's followers interested in crime initially called themselves criminal anthropologists. Havelock Ellis, an early British eugenicist, produced *The Criminal* (1914), a landmark in criminal anthropology based essentially on the works of writers like Marro, Von Baer, Nacke, Laurent and Perrier. Like so many other eugenicists, Ellis distanced himself from Lombroso-style explanations. He concluded:

> The criminal … in some of his most characteristic manifestations, is a congenitally weak-minded person whose abnormality, while by no means leaving the mental aptitudes absolutely unimpaired, chiefly affects the feelings and volition so influencing conduct and rendering him an anti-social element in society.
>
> (1914: xv)

This approach was evident in other early modern British criminological research like Charles Goring's *The English Convict* (1913). Goring did his empirical data analysis at Karl Pearson's Biometric Laboratory at London University, the nerve centre of the British eugenics movement and sophisticated statistical analysis. Heavily reliant on a mass of social statistics, Goring refuted Lombroso's biological 'throwback' thesis, and the idea that there was a distinct 'criminal type'. Far from assuming that there was a distinct 'criminal type', Goring argued that criminality was an extreme version of characteristics all normal people share. He argued that the specification of causes must be central to any objective science of crime but that this must be based on very large data sets carefully interrogated with techniques like regression analysis. As a eugenicist, Goring found that genetic factors were operating in the development of criminal behavioural traits in certain persons. He believed, for instance, that 'low intelligence' and 'poor physique' correlated highly with criminal conduct. He argued that crime would flourish as long as 'we allow criminals to propagate' and that government must 'regulate the reproduction of those constitutional qualities—feeble mindedness, epilepsy, inebriety, deficient social instincts, insanity—which are conducive to the committing of crime' (Goring 1913: 14).

Conclusion

An historical account of the rise of modern criminology points to a number of factors. Fear of social disorder posed by large numbers of poor, urban, working-class people led reformers influenced by Bentham to document and to try to regulate problems like poverty and crime. This 'governmental project' led to persistent exercises in gathering social statistics in the interests of social order. In 1876 Lombroso's famous biological account *Criminal Man* showcased a more ambitious if controversial attempt to develop a 'science of causes'. More influential in the long run and less rigidly determinist was Francis Galton's sponsorship of a statistically informed model of the social sciences. Galton's use of statistical techniques like regression analysis was ultimately to sustain a more successful though no less 'positivist' account of human behaviour than Lombroso's.

References

Ayer, A.J., 1959, *Language, Truth and Logic*, Penguin, Harmondsworth.

Bannister, R., 1987, *Sociology and Scientism: The American Quest for Objectivity 1880–1949*, University of North Carolina Press, Chapel Hill.

Beccaria, C., 1963, *On Crimes and Punishments* (trans. Paolucci, H.), Bobbs Merrill, New York.

Becker, G., 1978, *The Economic Approach to Human Behavior*, University of Chicago Press, Chicago, IL.

Burleigh, M., 1994, *Death and Deliverance: 'Euthanasia' in Germany c.1900–1945*, Oxford University Press, Oxford.

Canguilhem, G., 1990, *The Normal and the Pathological*, Zone Books, New York.

Cohen, S., 1992, 'Footprints in the Sand: A Further Report on Criminology and the Sociology of Deviance in Britain', in Cohen, S., *Against Criminology*, Transaction, New Brunswick, NJ.

Cohen, S., 1997, 'Intellectual Scepticism and Political Commitment: The Case of Radical Criminology', in Walton, P. and Young, J. (eds), *The New Criminology Revisited*, Macmillan, London.

Cohen, S., 2001, *States of Denial*, Polity Press, Cambridge.

Ellis, H., 1914, *The Criminal* (3rd edition), Walter Scott, London.

Finnis, J., 2005, *Natural Law and Natural Rights*, Clarendon Press, Oxford.

Foucault, M., 1991, 'Governmentality', in Burchell, G., Gordon, C. and Miller, P. (eds), *The Foucault Effect: Studies in Governmentality*, Harvester-Wheatsheaf, London.

Fuller, S., 2000, *Thomas Kuhn: A Philosophical History of Our Times*, University of Chicago Press, Chicago, IL.

Gadamer, H.-G., 1994, *Truth and Method* (4th edition), Plenum, New York.

Garland, D., 1990, *Punishment and Modern Society: A Study in Social Theory*, Oxford University Press, Oxford.

Garland, D., 1994, 'Of Crimes and Criminals: The Development of Criminology in Britain', in Maguire, M., Morgan, R. and Reiner, R. (eds), *The Oxford Handbook of Criminology*, Clarendon Press, Oxford.

Garland, D., 1997, 'Of Crimes and Criminals: The Development of Criminology in Britain', in Maguire, M., Morgan, R. and Reiner, R. (eds), *The Oxford Handbook of Criminology* (2nd edition), Oxford University Press, Oxford.

Garland, D., 2001, *The Culture of Control*, Cambridge University Press, Cambridge.

Goring, C., 1913, *The English Convict: A Statistical Study*, HMSO, London.

Gould, S.J., 1989, *The Mismeasure of Man*, Penguin, Harmondsworth.

Hacking, I., 1983, *Representing and Intervening*, Cambridge University Press, Cambridge.

Hacking, I., 1990, *The Taming of Chance*, Cambridge University Press, Cambridge.

Hobsbawm, E., 1975, *The Age of Revolution, 1815–1848*, Collins, London.

Holton, G., 1988, *Thematic Origins of Scientific Thought: Kepler to Einstein* (2nd edition), Harvard University Press, Cambridge, MA.

Jacoby, R., 1974, *Social Amnesia*, Basic Books, New York.

Jeffrey, C., 1972, 'The Historical Development of Criminology', in Mannheim, H. (ed.), *Pioneers in Criminology* (2nd edition), Patterson Smith, Montclair, NJ.

Kevles, D., 1985, *In the Name of Eugenics*, University of California Press, Berkeley.

Lombroso, C., 1911, *Criminal Man: According to the Classification of Cesare Lombroso* (1876), Putnam, New York.

Manent, P., 1998, *The City of Man* (trans. LePain, M.), Princeton University Press, Princeton, NJ.

Mannheim, H. (ed.), 1960, *Pioneers in Criminology*, Stevens, London.

Mason, B., 1996, 'From Shamans to Shaming: A History of Criminological Thought', in Hazlehurst, K. (ed.), *Crime and Justice: An Australian Textbook in Criminology*, Law Book Co., Sydney.

Nussbaum, M., 2001, *The Fragility of Goodness* (2nd edition), Cambridge University Press, Cambridge.

Quételet, A., 1842, *A Treatise on Man* (trans. Knox, R. and Smibert, T.), Chambers, Edinburgh, online: www.cimm.jcu.edu.au/hist/stats.quet/qbkfour5.htm.

Quinney, R., 1974, *Criminal Justice in America*, Little, Brown, Boston, MA.

Quinney, R., 1979, *Criminology*, Little, Brown, Boston, MA.

Radzinowicz, L., 1966, *Ideology and Crime*, Stevens, London.

Stigler, S., 1987, *The History of Statistics*, Belknap Press at Harvard, Cambridge, MA.

Sutherland, E., 1924, *Criminology*, J.B. Lippincott, Philadelphia, PA.

Sutherland, E., 1947, *Criminology*, J.B. Lippincott, Philadelphia, PA.

Tarde, G., 1886, *La criminalité comparée*, Alcan, Paris.

Tarde, G., 1890, *Penal Philosophy*, Green & Co, London.

Weinrich, H., 2004, *Lethe: The Art and Critique of Forgetting*, Cornell University Press, Ithaca, NY.

READING 4

Born to Be Bad

Biological, Physiological, and Biosocial Theories of Crime

Mark M. Lanier, Stuart Henry, and Desiré Anastasia

Biological and Positivistic Assumptions

To comprehend biological theories, it is necessary to grasp the underlying assumptions about humans that biological criminologists make. The major emphasis of this applied science of criminology is that humans have unique characteristics, or predispositions, that, under certain conditions, lead some to commit criminal acts. In other words, something within the individual strongly influences his or her behavior, but this will occur only under certain environmental conditions. For example, some people seem to behave perfectly normally most of the time, but when they get behind the wheel of a car the slightest inconvenience sends them into an angry rage (James and Nahl 2000). Without the automotive environment, they do not manifest anger. According to biological theory, the same can be true for other offenders. For some, the setting and act together provide a thrill that, according to biological theorists, might satisfy an abnormal need for excitement. For others, the environmental trigger to crime might be alcohol, drugs, or being subjected to authority.

For early biological criminologists, the classical theory of crime was intuitive and unscientific speculation. Any significant examination of criminal behavior cannot assume that humans are essentially all the same. Rather, they contended that looking at individuals' unique characteristics and differences would reveal the underlying causes of criminal tendencies. Early biological criminologists believed that the key to understanding crime was to study the criminal actor, not the criminal act. Criminologists should study the nature of criminals as "kinds of people" who would commit such acts (A. Cohen 1966).

Of central importance to these founding biological criminologists was how to study the criminal. Accurate investigation of human features demands both rigorous methods and careful observation. The approach adopted by these pioneers of scientific criminology is called the "positivist" method, which argues that social relations and events (including crime) can be studied scientifically using methods derived from the natural sciences. "Its aim is to search for, explain and predict future patterns

Mark M. Lanier, Stuart Henry, and Desiré Anastasia, Selection from "'Born to Be Bad': Biological, Physiological and Biosocial Theories of Crime," *Essential Criminology*, pp. 73-84, 88, 341-396. Copyright © 2014 by Taylor & Francis Group. Reprinted with permission.

of social behaviour" (McLaughlin and Muncie 2012, 325). Positivism "has generally involved the search for cause and effect relations that can be measured in a way that is similar to how natural scientists observe and analyse relations between objects in the physical world" (ibid.). As Rafter (1992, 1998) points out, however, unlike contemporary positivists, early positivists also accepted folk wisdom, anecdotes, and analogies to lower forms of life as part of their empirical data.

Those first interested in this approach were criminal anthropologists. They believed that criminals could be explained by physical laws that denied any free will (ibid.). They claimed it was possible to distinguish types of criminals by their physical appearance. The physical features most often studied were body type, shape of the head, genes, eyes, and physiological imbalances. Although their methods were crude and later shown to be flawed, an understanding of these founding ideas is instructive.

The Social Context of Criminal Anthropology

Evolutionary biology heralded a different way of looking at human development. In 1859, Englishman Charles Darwin (1809–1882) presented his theory of evolution, *On the Origin of Species* ([1859] 1968), in which he argued that the development of any species proceeds through natural variations among offspring. The weakest strains fail to adapt to their environment and die off or fail to reproduce, whereas the strong survive, flourish, and come to dominate the species at a more advanced state. Cesare Lombroso (1835–1909), a professor of forensic medicine, psychiatry, and later criminal anthropology, and his students, Enrico Ferri and Raffaele Garofalo, applied these ideas to the study of crime. This "holy three of criminology" became known as the Italian School (Schafer 1976, 41). Their position was radically opposed to Italian classicists such as Beccaria, whom they saw as overemphasizing free will at the expense of determinism. Rather than seeing humans as self-interested, rational individuals who possess similar capacities to reason, the Italian School criminologists believed humans differ and that some are more crime-prone than others. As Jock Young has pointed out, their approach was the mirror image of classicism: "Free-will disappears under determinacy, equality bows before natural differences and expert knowledge, and human laws that are created become scientific laws that are discovered" (1981, 267). If classicism was the language of logical deduction, traditional opinion, and abstract reasoning, then, wrote Ferri, "We speak two different languages" (1901, 244).

The new scientific criminology, founded on positivist assumptions, valued the "experimental method" as the key to knowledge based on empirically discovered facts and their examination. This knowledge was to be achieved carefully, over years of systematic observation and scientific analysis. The task of the criminologist was to apply the appropriate scientific apparatuses, the calipers, dynamometer, and aesthesiometer, to measure and chart the offender's deformities (Rafter 1992). Only then would we discover the explanation for crime and for what would become known as the "born criminal."

The Born Criminal

To both realize and value the revolutionary nature of these early biological and physiological theories, it is necessary to recall that in the late nineteenth century, science was viewed as a sort of "new religion," a source of knowledge, and a solution to problems such as disease, starvation, unemployment, and—of interest to us—crime. Lombroso is widely recognized as the most influential founding scholar to rely on the scientific method to study crime and is often called the "father of modern criminology." With Ferri and Garofalo, and later with his daughter Gina Lombroso-Ferraro he explored the differences between ordinary "noncriminal" people and those who committed criminal offenses; therein, he argued, would be found the secret to the causes of crime.

Lombroso's theory of "atavism," explained in his 1876 book *The Criminal Man*, was founded on Darwinian ideas about humanity's "worst dispositions," which were "reversions to a savage state" (Darwin 1871, 137). Atavism (or reversion) is a "condition in which characteristics that have previously disappeared in the course of evolution suddenly recur" (Faller and Schuenke 2004, 61). According to this theory, criminals were hereditary throwbacks to less developed evolutionary forms. Since criminals were less developed, Lombroso believed they could be identified by physical stigmata, or visible physical abnormalities, which he called "atavistic features": "For Lombroso, these anomalies resembled the traits of primitive peoples, animals and even plants, 'proving' that the most dangerous criminals were atavistic throwbacks on the evolutionary scale" (Gibson and Rafter 2006, 1). These anomalies or signs included such characteristics as asymmetry of the face; supernumerary nipples, toes, or fingers; enormous jaws; handle-shaped or sensile ears; insensitivity to pain; acute sight; and so on. Possessing five of the eighteen stigmata indicated atavism and could explain "the irresistible craving for evil for its own sake, the desire not only to extinguish life in the victim, but to mutilate the corpse, tear its flesh and drink its blood" (Lombroso 1911, xiv). Because these anomalies could be examined, counted, and classified, Lombroso "promised to turn the study of criminality into an empirical science … called … 'criminal anthropology,' reflecting his desire to reorient legal thinking from philosophical debate about the nature of crime to an analysis of the characteristics of the criminal" (Gibson and Rafter 2006, 1). As he says in the first 1876 edition of his classic work, "Most criminals really do lack free will" (quoted in ibid., 43).

Not all criminals, however, fell into the atavistic category. By the fifth edition of his book, Lombroso recognized four main classes of criminals. The first group, referred to as "born criminals," was atavistic, responsible for the most serious offenses, and recidivist. This group made up about a third of the criminal population and was considered by Lombroso to be the most dangerous and incorrigible. The second class, "criminals by passion," commits crime to correct the emotional pain of an injustice. Third was the "insane criminal," who could be an imbecile or have an affected brain and is unable to distinguish right from wrong. Fourth, the "occasional criminal" included four subtypes: (a) the "criminaloid," who is of weak nature and easily swayed by others; (b) the "epileptoid," who suffers from epilepsy; (c) the habitual criminal, whose occupation is crime; and (d) the pseudocriminal, who commits crime by accident (Martin, Mutchnick, and Austin 1990, 29–32).

Eventually, Lombroso conceded that socioenvironmental factors, such as religion, gender, marriage, criminal law, climate, rainfall, taxation, banking, and even the price of grain, influence crime. By the time his last book, *Crime: Its Causes and Remedies* ([1912] 1968), was published in 1896, he had shifted from being a biological theorist to being an environmental theorist, but not without forcefully establishing the idea that criminals were different from ordinary people and especially different from the powerful members of society. Even though his main ideas were disproved and his research found to be methodologically unsound, the search for the biological cause of crime was inspired by his work (Goring [1913] 1972).

It is important to note that Lombroso's progression of work, though possessing some serious flaws, has been seriously distorted by translators until recently. Even his daughter, Gina Lombroso-Ferraro, was thought to considerably simplify the complexity of her father's original ideas in his original work, *Criminal Man*. One example is his "biological determinism," which always recognized multiple causes, and eventually included social causes, which allowed him to "continue denying free will by conceptualizing environmental and biological forces as equally determinate" (Gibson and Rafter 2006, 12). Often neglected, too, is that he proposed humanitarian reforms as alternatives to incarceration to prevent crimes by "occasional criminals," especially children, whose occasional criminality was a temporary phase, advocated institutions for the criminally insane, and urged that the severity of punishment match the dangerousness of the criminal (ibid., 2). However, Lombroso did advocate the death penalty, abolished in Italy in 1889, for the born criminal, arguing in the Darwinian fashion that "progress in the animal world, and therefore the human world, is based on a struggle for existence that involves hideous massacres." Society need have no pity for born criminals who were "programmed to do harm" and are "atavistic reproductions not only of savage men but also the most ferocious carnivores and rodents." Capital punishment in this view would simply accelerate natural selection, ridding society of the unfit (Gibson and Rafter 2006, 15).

Lombroso's student at the University of Turin, Enrico Ferri (1856–1929), was even more receptive to environmental and social influences that cause crime, but he still relied on biological factors, and in fact coined the term *criminal man*, later used by Lombroso, and the term *criminal sociology*. Ferri, who studied statistics at the University of Bologna, and later, in Paris, was influenced by the ideas of French lawyer and statistician A. M. Guerry (1802–1866) and Belgian mathematician and astronomer Lambert Adolphe Jacques Quételet (1796–1874). Ferri used his statistical training to analyze crime in France from 1826 to 1878. Ferri's studies (1901) suggested that the causes of crime were physical (race, climate, geographic location, and so forth), anthropological (age, gender, psychology, and so on), and social (population density, religion, customs, economic conditions, and others). This view was much more encompassing than Lombroso's original ideas, was accepted by Lombroso as furthering his theory, and is not dissimilar from modern theorists' ideas about multiple causality.

However, Ferri's anticlassicist ideas, and his Marxist leanings, cost him his university position. They also affected his views on criminal justice and policy, which he was invited to implement in Mussolini's fascist regime (and which were eventually rejected for being too radical). He argued that because causes needed scientific discovery, juries of laypeople were irrelevant and should be replaced by panels of scientific experts, including doctors and psychiatrists. Not surprisingly, since he rejected the idea that crime was a free choice, Ferri also believed it was pointless to retributively punish offenders, preferring instead the idea of prevention through alternatives (which he called substitutions). His idea was to remove or minimize the causes of crime while protecting the state. He advocated "hygienic measures" such as social and environmental changes and, consistent with his socialist politics, favored the state provision of human services. He also advocated "therapeutic remedies" that were designed to be both reparative and repressive and "surgical operations," including death, to eliminate the cause of the problem (Schafer 1976, 45). Ferri's primary contribution was to offer a more balanced, complete picture of crime relying on scientific methods.

Raffaele Garofalo (1851–1934), also a student of Lombroso, trained in the law and was of Spanish noble ancestry, although he was born in Naples. He saw crime as rooted in an organic flaw that results in a failure to develop both altruistic sensibilities and a moral sentiment for others. Garofalo presented a principle called "adaptation" which was based on Darwin's work. He argued that criminals who were unable to adapt to society, and who thereby felt morally free to offend, should be eliminated, consistent with nature's evolutionary process. This should be accomplished through one of three methods: death, long-term or life imprisonment, or "enforced reparation" (Bernard, Snipes, and Gerould 2009). Indeed, echoing Lombroso's Darwinist thinking on the state-administered death penalty, he stated: "In this way, the social power will effect an artificial selection similar to that which nature effects by death of individuals unassimilable to the particular conditions of the environment in which they are born or to which they have been removed. Herein the state will be simply following nature" (Garofalo 1914, 219–220, cited in Morrison 1995, 126).

These three theories have been relegated to the status of historical artifacts, and subject to some distortion, although each contains some resonance of truth. The research methods employed were simplistic or flawed, revealed a racist and even sexist bias, and have not stood up to empirical verification. But the theories are important because they chart the course of later theories and also point out the importance of using scientific principles. Many of the research methods associated with the perspective of the Italian School persist into the twenty-first century.

Early US Family-Type and Body-Type Theories

Shortly after the conclusion of the American Civil War in 1865, it was widely believed that there were basic differences between individuals and among ethnic groups and that certain families could be mentally degenerate and "socially bankrupt." This notion has to be understood in historical context.

Society in the United States was undergoing rapid transformation with the abolition of slavery and massive immigration of Europeans of various ethnic groups, who, like the freed slaves, were largely poor and unskilled. These immigrants moved into the rapidly urbanizing cities, where, living in crowded conditions, they presented a threat of poverty and disease to established Americans. In fact, since the 1870s some Americans had been calling for eugenics measures, according to which a nation could save its stock from degeneration by rejecting the unfit, preventing their reproduction, and encouraging the fit to procreate (McKim 1900; Rafter 1992).

Richard Louis Dugdale's work, which fascinated Lombroso, was consistent with these views. In his book *The Jukes: A Study in Crime, Pauperism, Disease, and Heredity* ([1877] 1895), Dugdale found that the Juke family (from the name of the family of illegitimate girls that a Dutch immigrant's sons had married) had criminals in it for six generations. Dugdale concluded that "the burden of crime" is found in illegitimate (non-married) family lines, that the eldest child has a tendency to be criminal, and that males are more likely than females to be criminal. Obviously, his conclusions are subject to varying interpretations.

Following Dugdale's degenerative theory, European criminal anthropology became available in the United States through a variety of works (e.g., MacDonald 1893; Boies 1893; Henderson 1893; Drahms [1900] 1971; and Lydston 1904; see Rafter 1998 for an overview). These authors were the first US criminal anthropologists to claim that their approach was a new science studying the criminal rather than the crime, just as medicine studies disease. Rafter (1998) states that the central assumption of this new science was that the physical body mirrors moral capacity, and criminals were, as Boies argued, "the imperfect, knotty, knurly, worm-eaten, half-rotten fruit of the human race" (1893, 265–266).

After the turn of the nineteenth century, science was still viewed as being the solution to most human problems. Social science research became more rigorous, and improved research methods, such as larger sample sizes and control groups, became important. For example, in 1939 E. A. Hooton, a Harvard anthropologist, published *The American Criminal: An Anthropological Study* based on his research comparing 14,000 prisoners to 3,000 noncriminals. His results indicated that "criminals were organically inferior" and that this inferiority is probably due to inherited features, including physical differences such as low foreheads, compressed faces, and so on.

Hooton's methods have been criticized on several grounds. First, his control or comparison group included a large percentage of firefighters and police officers who were selected for their jobs based on their large physical size. Second, the differences he found were very small, and furthermore there was more variation between prisoners than between prisoners and civilians. Finally, his methods have been called "tautological," meaning that they involved circular reasoning. For example, some people are violent so there must be something wrong with them; find out how they are different, and this explains their violent behavior.

Ten years later, in spite of a general decline in the idea of a correspondence between the human body and moral behavior, physician William Sheldon and his colleagues sought to explain the relationship between the shape of the human body and temperament. The most complete statement on this typology and crime was *Varieties of Delinquent Youth* (Sheldon, Hastl, and McDermott 1949). Using "somatotyping" (classifying human bodies), Sheldon observed three distinct human body types. The first, endomorphs, were of medium height with round, soft bodies and thick necks. Mesomorphs were muscular, strong-boned people with wide shoulders and a tapering trunk. The final group, ectomorphs, had thin bodies and were fragile, with large brains and developed nervous systems. Sheldon recognized that no "pure" type existed and that each person shares some of all the features. Each type had a different personality and favored a different kind of criminal activity. Endomorphs, motivated by their gut, were tolerant, extroverted, sociable, and inclined to delinquency and occasional fraud. Ectomorphs had sensitive dispositions and were tense, thoughtful, and inhibited. They could become occasional thieves. Mesomorphs lacked sensitivity and were assertive, aggressive, and prone to habitual violence, robbery, and even homicide. Some of these results were confirmed in the 1950s studies on delinquency by Sheldon Glueck and Eleanor Glueck (1956), whose study of five hundred incarcerated, persistently delinquent boys compared with five hundred nondelinquent boys found that although only 31 percent of the noncriminal comparison group were mesomorphs, 60 percent of the delinquents had a mesomorphic body type. However, when other factors were considered, such as parenting practices, Glueck and Glueck found that body type was only one of several factors contributing to delinquency. Other controlled studies claim stronger correlations, one finding that 57 percent of delinquents were mesomorphic compared to 19 percent of nondelinquent controls (Cortes and Gatti 1972).

Fishbein pointed out "early 'biological criminology' was eventually discredited for being unscientific, simplistic and monocausal" (1998, 92). The early studies suffered critical methodological weaknesses, including poor sample selection, inadequate measurement criteria, and the failure to control for factors such as unreported delinquency, social class, and criminal justice agency bias. In addition, one cannot avoid the observation that they tend to reinforce class, gender, and especially racial stereotypes. By excluding hidden crime, crimes by women, occupational crimes, and crimes of the powerful, and by often relying on samples of convicted offenders, body-type theories tell us more about who is likely to be processed through criminal justice agencies than about what causes crime. However, these theories were sufficiently provocative to stimulate a new generation of inquiry into the nature of what was inheritable. This new era of biosocial criminological theory is more sophisticated and deserves serious consideration, not least because it is built on new knowledge about the human brain and the multidisciplinary insights gained from "genetics, biochemistry, endocrinology, neuroscience, immunology and psychophysiology" (Fishbein 1998, 92).

Contemporary Biological Perspectives

In spite of its earlier methodological shortcomings, biological theory and the use of scientific methods remain popular in criminology in the twenty-first century. Indeed, "a growing literature base has served to substantiate that genetic factors are as important to the development of some forms of criminal activity as are environmental factors" (Ishikawa and Raine 2002, 81). Rather than determining crime, "multiple genes—acting in combination—result in varying degrees of genetic disposition to criminal behavior ... through heritable physiological processes such as neurotransmitter and autonomic nervous system functioning, which, in turn, predispose some individuals toward crime" (ibid., 82). Improved technology, computerization, and software design and advanced statistical techniques have allowed more precise measurement and improved data collection, especially with regard to detailing the genetic process and mapping genes.

Genes, called the "atoms of heredity," were discovered by Gregor Mendel in 1865 and reinvigorated again in the 1920s as essential elements in chromosomes. The 1952 discovery of the chemical constitution of genes as an explanation of how "like begets like" fueled the new genetic era of biology. By 1959, genes were being used to explain every aspect of individuals, every variation of their personality, yet, as Fishbein pointed out, although "numerous studies have attempted to estimate the genetic contribution to the development of criminality, delinquency, aggression and anti-social behavior ... it is difficult to isolate genetic factors from developmental events, cultural influences and housing conditions" (1998, 95). First among the contemporary approaches were twin and adoption studies.

Twin Studies and Adoption Studies

A major boost to the genetic theory of crime came with evidence from twin studies and adoption studies. Put simply, if crime is the outcome of some genetically conveyed heritable factor (e.g., impulsivity, low arousal to pain, sensation seeking, or minimal brain dysfunction), then we would expect to find more crime in the twin partners of identical twins—where one twin is criminal—than in fraternal twins or between siblings. This is because monozygotic (MZ) twins are identical, with 100 percent of their genes in common, since they result from fertilization of a single egg. In contrast, fraternal, or dizygotic (DZ), twins occur when two separate eggs are fertilized at the same time (and as a result share around 50 percent of the same genes). Genetically, they are no different from two separate eggs being fertilized at different times, as with other siblings. This explains why MZ twins are always of the same sex, whereas DZ twins may be of opposing sexes. Researchers have compared twins of each type and claim to find that there are greater similarities in criminal convictions between identical (MZ) twins than between fraternal (DZ) twins, which lends support to the genetic basis for crime.

The most comprehensive study of this type was conducted by Karl Christiansen (1977; Mednick and Christiansen 1977), who studied 3,568 pairs of Danish twins born between 1881 and 1910. He found that 52 percent of the identical twins (MZ) had the same degree of officially recorded criminal activity, whereas only 22 percent of the fraternal twins (DZ) had similar degrees of criminality. These findings persisted even among twins who were separated at birth and raised in different social environments. Numerous twin studies have since found the same basic relationship, with identical twin pairs being up to two and a half times more likely to have similar criminal records when one of the pair is criminal than are fraternal twin pairs.

This apparently consistent finding has been criticized for its methodological inadequacy. Factors criticized include dependence on official crime statistics, especially conviction records; unreliable processes for classifying twins such as inaccurate determinations of monozygosity; errors resulting from small samples or biases in sample selection; failure to take into account the similar environmental upbringing of identical twins compared with fraternal twins; and the inability of genetics to explain "why the majority of twin partners of criminal twins are not themselves criminal" (Einstadter and Henry 2006, 97). And although some studies based on self-reports (rather than official crime statistics) found both greater criminality and greater criminal association among identical twins where one twin admitted delinquency compared with fraternal twins, several others argue that the higher-quality twin studies are less clear about the genetic contribution (Hurwitz and Christiansen 1983; Walters 1992).

Adoption studies seem to offer a way out of some of the environmental confusion plaguing twin studies by examining rates of criminality in children who are adopted away from their birth families (Rafter 2008, 229). If some biologically predispositional factor is involved in criminality, we would expect that the biological children of convicted criminals would have criminal records more consistent with those of their natural parents than with their adoptive parents. In fact, several studies "indicate that some relationship exists between biological parents' behavior and the behavior of their children, even when their contact has been nonexistent" (Siegel 2012, 154). Barry Hutchings and Sarnoff Mednick (1975) studied adoptees born between 1927 and 1941 in Denmark. They found that if boys had adoptive parents with a criminal record but their natural parents had no criminal record, then just fewer than 15 percent of the adoptive sons were convicted of criminal activity (Rafter 2008, 230). This was little different from cases where neither natural nor adoptive parents had a criminal record (13.5 percent). But where boys had noncriminal adoptive parents but criminal natural parents, 20 percent of the adoptive sons were found to be criminal. Moreover, these effects seem additive, such that where both adoptive and biological fathers were criminal, 25 percent of adoptive sons were found to be criminal (ibid.). Reporting more recent studies with larger samples and looking at both parents, the authors found similar though less pronounced results (Mednick, Gabrielli, and Hutchings 1987, 79). This finding was confirmed between adoptive girls and their mothers (Baker et al. 1989) and has been supported by other studies (Crowe 1975; Cadoret 1978). In spite of proponents' claims, critics have raised several questions about adoption studies. A major problem is "selective placement," whereby the adoption agency may match the adoptive home with the natural home in terms of social class and physical characteristics (Kamin 1985; Walters and White 1989; Walters 1992; Rydenour 2000). Another problem is whether the effects being measured reflect prenatal or perinatal factors (Denno, 1985, 1989). Overall, then, what at first seemed to offer solid and consistent scientific evidence of a heritable genetic predisposition to crime turns out to raise more questions than it answers. This has not stopped various processes from being identified as causal candidates for explaining crime.

Biosocial Criminology: A Developmental Explanation of Crime

Since the 1950s, researchers have received media attention for various "discoveries" that they claim may explain the biological causes of crime (Nelkin 1993; Nelkin and Tancredi 1994). The April 21, 1997, cover of *U.S. News & World Report* carried a similar title to that of this chapter—"Born Bad?"—and dealt with the biological causes of crime.

Before examining illustrative examples of these processes, it is important to understand the logic used by the biosocial criminologists to explain crime. Biosocial criminology was founded on the ideas of E. O. Wilson (1975), whose book *Sociobiology* marked a resurrection of the role of biological thinking in social science. The basic premise is that the "gene is the ultimate unit of life that controls all human destiny" (Siegel 2012, 143). Although sociobiologists believe that environment and experience also have an impact on behavior, their main assertion is that "most actions are controlled by a person's 'biological machine'. Most important, people are controlled by the innate need to have their genetic material survive and dominate others," which is more commonly known as "the selfish gene" (ibid.). All advocates of genetic explanations for crime agree that they are not claiming that genes alone determine behavior or that there is a "crime gene" (ibid.; Ishikawa and Raine 2002, 82). Rather, as stated above, criminal behavior is believed to result from the combination of hereditary factors interacting with environmental ones. Together, these factors affect the brain and cognitive processes that in turn control behavior (Jeffery 1994; Ellis 1988; Ellis and Walsh 1997; Fishbein and Thatcher 1986; Raine 2002; Wilson and Herrnstein 1985; Hurwitz and Christiansen 1983; Ishikawa and Raine 2002, 98–99). More recently, though, researchers have found a region of the chromosome where there are variants of a gene that "regulates the production of the enzyme monamine oxidase (MAOA), which has been proposed as a possible mechanism for a genetic theory of violence. ... In this theory a variant of a gene either overexpresses or underexpresses a chemical that affects a region of the brain" (Krimsky and Simoncelli 2011, 266). A study that looked at the genotypes of 1,155 females and 1,041 males who participated in a long-term analysis of adolescent health from 1994 to 2002 found that individuals with the gene that results in low MAOA activity were twice as likely to join a gang as those with the high-activity form (Calloway 2009).

In addition to the interaction between genetic predispositions and environment, contemporary biological theorists do not abandon the notion of free will, as their predecessors did. Instead, they prefer the concept of "conditional free will." In this approach, various factors restrict and channel an individual's decision to act, and each "collaborates internally (physically) and externally (environmentally) to produce a final action: The principle of conditional free will postulates that individuals choose a course of action within a preset, yet changeable, range of possibilities and that, assuming the conditions are suitable for rational thought, we are accountable for our actions. ... This theory ... predicts that if one or more conditions to which the individual is exposed are disturbed or irregular, the individual is more likely to choose a disturbed or irregular course of action. Thus, the risk of such a response increases as a function of the number of deleterious conditions" (Ishikawa and Raine 2002, 104–105).

The research on biosocial criminology and behavior has empirical support. For one example, Raine conducted a review and semi-meta-analysis of thirty-nine studies and concluded, "When biological and social factors are grouping variables and when antisocial behavior is the outcome, then the presence of both risk factors exponentially increases the rates of antisocial and violent behavior" (2002, 311).

Chromosomes, Nervous System, Attention Deficit Disorder, Hormones, and the Brain

The list of causal candidates for the predispositional side of this interactive equation is long, and growing. None have captured the imagination more than those based on aspects of genetic theory. For example, in the 1960s, a chromosomal theory of crime attributed violent male criminality to an extra Y chromosome. This extra chromosome created what was termed a "supermale," one who was excessively violent. This theory was initially supported by the finding that 1 to 3 percent of male inmates had an extra Y chromosome compared to less than 1 percent of the general population of males (P. Jacobs et al. 1965; Telfer, Baker, and Clark 1968). Further research revealed, however, that incarcerated inmates with an extra Y chromosome were less likely to be serving a sentence for a violent crime. Moreover, the XYY chromosome pattern was more prevalent among prison officers than prisoners (Sarbin and Miller 1970; R. Fox 1971). However, "recent research has failed to support a relationship between the XYY chromosomal complement and criminal behavior; some studies even suggesting that XYY males are less likely to exhibit aggressive behavior than those with an XY chromosomal pattern" (Flowers 2003, 9).

Another candidate used to explain the intergenerational transmission of criminality is the autonomic nervous system (ANS), which is the "regulatory sector of the central nervous system and is largely responsible for controlling arousal and one's ability to adapt to the surrounding environment" (Bowman, 2010, 602). The argument here is that "law-abiding behavior is a learned trait. ... Individuals learn to act in a social manner through proper primary caregiver interaction in childhood, most often through their rearing parents" (ibid.). Despite criticisms, there has been some support garnered for ANS theory through adoption studies, brain wave analyses, and delayed response experiments.

Attention deficit disorder (ADD) and attention deficit hyperactivity disorder (ADHD) have also been targeted as possibly heritable factors in criminality (Moffitt and Silva 1988; S. Young and Gudjonsson 2008). According to epidemiological data, approximately 4 to 6 percent of the US population has ADHD. That is about eight to nine million adults. ADHD usually persists throughout a person's lifetime. It is not limited to children. Approximately one-half to two-thirds of children with ADHD will continue to have significant problems with ADHD symptoms and behaviors as adults, which impacts their lives on the job, within the family, and in social relationships (Jaska 1998). Studies conducted in the United States, Canada, Sweden, Germany, Finland, and Norway indicated that two-thirds of institutionalized young offenders and about one-half of the adult prison population screened positively for ADHD (Cole, Daniels, and Visser 2013, 3).

Children and adults with ADHD are "less likely than others to succeed in school, form healthy and lasting social and family relationships, or find and sustain productive work in order to contribute to their societies" (ibid.). Johnson and Kercher (2007) studied ADHD, strain, and criminal behavior and concluded that people with ADHD are less able to cope with strain in legitimate ways. According to recent research, "Post-traumatic stress disorder caused by child abuse produces symptoms similar to ADHD symptoms, and ... these disorders frequently coexist and overlap" (Matsumoto and Imamura 2007). Weinstein, Staffelbach, and Biaggio supported this observation in the case of victims of child sexual abuse (2000).

Hormones have also been claimed as causal agents in criminality. Hormones are "a group of molecules that are responsible for carrying messages to cells throughout the body." Higher than normal levels of testosterone in men have been linked to aggression and violence (Ferguson 2010, 88). Some researchers have also found that abnormal levels of androgens (male sex hormones) produce aggressive behavior (Siegel 2012, 146). But reviews of the evidence suggest that neither of the hormonal explanations has adequate research support, and some have even argued that hormonal changes "may be the product rather than the cause of aggression" (Curran and Renzetti 1994, 73; see also Janet Katz and Chambliss 1991; and Horney 1978).

As we are increasingly seeing, the relationship between biology and crime is not simple, and probably not linear but more likely reciprocal, with both biological and environmental factors feeding into and enhancing each other.

The Importance of Neurotransmitters in Relation to Depression and Aggression

The role of neurochemical processes, particularly neurotransmitters, is increasingly seen as important. These are chemicals, such as serotonin and dopamine, released by electrical signals given off by nerves that transmit information to receptors in the brain. The brain then instructs the body to adjust various behaviors, including aggression, in relation to the human organism's environment. Serotonin in humans or animals inhibits aggression, and having relatively low levels of this substance released by neurotransmitters results in a failure to inhibit violent and impulsive behavior (Virkkunen et al. 1987, 1989; Fishbein 1990, 1998; Coccaro and Kavoussi 1996). A review of studies found that overall the low-serotonin relationship to antisocial behavior is significant (Moore, Scarpa, and Raine 2002).

In contrast, dopamine is an excitatory transmitter that offsets the effects of low serotonin. As Fishbein says, dopamine "operates as the 'fuel' while serotonin provides the 'brakes' for behavioral responses" (1998, 99). Dopamine "operates by setting into motion a biological process that gives rise to an emotional response that motivates behavior. It affects a person's ability to respond to environmental 'cues' that are associated with some sort of reward or stimulus that satisfies some drive" (Fishbein 2002, 111). When the dopamine system is stimulated, "novelty-seeking and self-stimulation behaviors increase." When this system goes awry, behavior may be stimulated "in the absence of a reward, a threat, or other appropriate stimulus" (ibid.).

As with hormones, however, it is uncertain whether changes in serotonin and dopamine are the outcome of changes in environment or the reverse (W. Gibbs 1995). For example, Miczek showed that "an increase in serotonin can occur at the time of aggression and can continue to increase throughout a potential attack demonstrating that an environment or situation or social context can trigger appropriate serotonin production to help deal with it" (Einstadter and Henry 2006, 89). Indeed, as Miczek said, "Instead of only looking at biology as the cause of behavior, we also need to consider the reverse—that being the aggressor or victim of aggression is the event that sets the neurobiological processes in motion" (cited in Niehoff 1999, 116). Put simply, recent analyses of the relationship between the human brain, its environment, and behavior challenge notions of predisposition and suggest, rather, that the relationship might be reciprocal; that is, not only might biological factors result from behavioral and environmental ones, but the biological factors are not immutable and can be altered by changes in behavior and environment.

References

Baker, Laura A., Wendy Mack, Terry E. Moffitt, and Sarnoff A. Mednick. 1989. "Sex Differences in Property Crime in a Danish Adoption Cohort." *Behavior Genetics* 19: 355–370.

Bernard, Thomas J., Jeffrey B. Snipes and Alexander L. Gerould. 2009. *Vold's Theoretical Criminology.* 6th ed. New York: Oxford University Press.

Boies, Henry M. 1893. *Prisoners and Paupers.* New York: G. P. Putnam.

Bowman, John. 2010. "Mednick, Sarnoff A.: Autonomic Nervous System (ANS) Theory." In *Encyclopedia of Criminological Theory* Cullen, Francis T. and Pamela Wilcox, eds., 602–605. Thousand Oaks, CA: Sage Publications.

Cadoret, R. J. 1978. "Psychopathology in Adopted-Away Offspring of Biologic Parents with Antisocial Behavior." *Archives of General Psychiatry* 35: 176–184.

Callaway, Ewen. 2009. "'Gangsta Gene' Identified in US teens." *New Scientist.* www.newscientist.com/article/dn17337-gangsta-gene-identified-in-us-teens.html (accessed February 13, 2013).

Christiansen, Karl O. 1977. "A Preliminary Study of Criminality Among Twins." In *Biological Basis of Criminal Behavior,* edited by Sarnoff A. Mednick and Karl O. Christiansen. New York: Gardner.

Coccaro, E. F., and R. J. Kavoussi. 1996. Neurotransmitter Correlates of Impulsive Aggression. In *Aggression and Violence: Genetic, Neurobiological, and Biosocial Perspectives,* edited by D. M. Stoff and R. B. Cairns, 67–99. Mahwah, New Jersey: Lawrence Erlbaum Associates.

———. 1966. *Deviance and Control.* Englewood Cliffs, NJ: Prentice Hall.

Cole, Ted, Harry Daniels, and John Visser. 2013. *The Routledge International Companion to Emotional and Behavioural Difficulties.* New York: Routledge.

Cortes, J. B., and F. M. Gatti. 1972. *Delinquency and Crime: A Biopsychosocial Approach.* New York: Seminar Press.

Crowe, R. R. 1975. "An Adoptive Study of Psychopathy: Preliminary Results from Arrest Records and Psychiatric Hospital Records." In *Genetic Research in Psychiatry,* edited by R. R. Fieve, D. Rosenthal, and H. Brill. Baltimore: Johns Hopkins University Press.

Curran, Daniel J., and Claire M. Renzetti. 1994. *Theories of Crime.* Boston: Allyn & Bacon.

Darwin, Charles R. [1859] 1968. *On the Origin of Species.* New York: Penguin.

———. 1871. *Descent of Man: Selection in Relation to Sex.* London: John Murray.

Denno, Deborah. 1985. "Sociological and Human Developmental Explanations of Crime: Conflict or Consensus." *Criminology* 23: 711–741.

———. 1989. *Biology, Crime, and Violence: New Evidence.* Cambridge: Cambridge University Press.

Drahms, August. [1900] 1971. *The Criminal: His Personnel and Environment—a Scientific Study.* Introduction by Cesare Lombroso. Montclair, NJ: Patterson Smith.

Dugdale, Richard Louis. [1877] 1895. *The Jukes: A Study in Crime, Pauperism, Disease, and Heredity.* 3d ed. New York: G. P. Putnam.

———. 2006. *Criminological Theory: An Analysis of Its Underlying Assumptions.* 2d ed. Boulder, CO: Rowman & Littlefield.

———. 1988. "Neurohormonal Bases of Varying Tendencies to Learn Delinquent and Criminal Behavior." In *Behavioral Approaches to Crime and Delinquency,* edited by E. K. Morris and C. J. Braukmann. New York: Plenum.

Ellis, Lee, and Anthony Walsh. 1997. "Gene Based Evolutionary Theories in Criminology." *Criminology* 35: 229–267.

Faller, Adolf, and Michael Schuenke. 2004. *The Human Body: An Introduction to Structure and Function.* New York: Thieme.

Ferguson, Christopher J. 2010. *Violent Crime: Clinical and Social Implications.* Thousand Oaks, CA: Sage Publications.

Ferri, Enrico. 1901. *Criminal Sociology.* New York: D. Appleton.

Fishbein, Diana H. 1990. "Biological Perspectives in Criminology." *Criminology* 28: 27–72.

———. 1998. "Biological Perspectives in Criminology." In *The Criminology Theory Reader,* edited by Stuart Henry and Werner Einstadter. New York: New York University Press.

———. 2002. "Biocriminology" In *Encyclopedia of Crime and Punishment* edited by David Levinson, 109–117. Thousand Oaks, CA: Sage Publications.

Fishbein, Diana H., and Robert W. Thatcher. 1986. "New Diagnostic Methods in Criminology: Assessing Organic Sources of Behavioral Disorders." *Journal of Research in Crime and Delinquency* 23: 240–267.

Flowers, R. Barri. 2003. *Male Crime and Deviance: Exploring Its Causes, Dynamics, and Nature.* Springfield, IL: Charles C. Thomas Publisher.

Garofalo, Raffaele. 1914. *Criminology.* Translated by Robert Wyness Millar. Boston: Little, Brown.

Gibbs, W. Wayt. 1995. "Seeking the Criminal Element." *Scientific American* 272: 100–107.

Gibson, Mary, and Nicole Hahn Rafter. 2006. Introduction to *Criminal Man,* by Cesare Lombroso. Durham, NC: Duke University Press.

Glueck, Sheldon. 1956. "Theory and Fact in Criminology: A Criticism of Differential Association." *British Journal of Delinquency* 7: 92–109.

Glueck, Sheldon, and Eleanor Glueck. 1950. *Unraveling Juvenile Delinquency.* New York: Commonwealth Fund.

Goring, Charles. [1913] 1972. *The English Convict: A Statistical Study, 1913.* Montclair, NJ: Patterson Smith.

Henderson, Charles R. 1893. *An Introduction to the Study of the Dependent, Defective and Delinquent Classes.* Boston: D. C. Heath.

Hooton, Ernest A. 1939. *The American Criminal: An Anthropological Study.* Cambridge, MA: Harvard University Press.

Horney, Julie. 1978. "Menstrual Cycles and Criminal Responsibility." *Law and Human Nature* 2: 25–36.

Hurwitz, Stephan, and Karl O. Christiansen. 1983. *Criminology.* London: George Allen & Unwin.

Hutchings, Barry, and Sarnoff A. Mednick. 1975. "Registered Criminality in the Adoptive and Biological Parents of Registered Male Criminal Adoptees." In *Genetic Research in Psychiatry,* edited by R. R. Fieve, D. Rosenthal, and H. Brill. Baltimore: Johns Hopkins University Press.

Ishikawa, Sharon S., and Adrian Raine. 2002. "Behavioral Genetics and Crime." In *The Neurobiology of Criminal Behavior,* edited by J. Glicksohn, 4: 81–110. Norwell, MA: Kluwer Academic Publishing.

Jacobs, Patricia A., M. Brunton, M. M. Melville, R. P. Brittain, and W. McClemont. 1965. "Aggressive Behavior Mental Subnormality and the XYY Male." *Nature* 208: 1351–1352.

James, Leon, and Diane Nahl. 2000. *Road Rage and Aggressive Driving: Steering Clear of Highway Warfare.* New York: Prometheus Books.

Jaska, Peter. 1998. *ADHD Fact Sheet.* Attention Deficit Disorder Association. Accessed November 8, 2012. www.add.org.

———. 1994. "Biological and Neuropsychiatric Approaches to Criminal Behavior." In *Varieties of Criminology: Readings from a Dynamic Discipline*, edited by Gregg Barak: 15–28. Westport, CT: Praeger.

Johnson, M. C., and G. A. Kercher. 2007. "ADHD, Strain, and Criminal Behavior: A Test of General Strain Theory." *Deviant Behavior* 28, no. 2: 131–152.

Kamin, L. J. 1985. "Criminality and Adoption." *Science* 227: 982.

Katz, Janet, and William J. Chambliss. 1991. "Biology and Crime." In *Criminology: A Contemporary Handbook,* edited by Joseph F. Sheley. Belmont, CA: Wadsworth.

Krimsky, Sheldon, and Tania Simoncelli. 2011. *Genetic Justice: DNA Data Banks, Criminal Investigations, and Civil Liberties.* New York: Columbia University Press.

———. 1911. Introduction to *Criminal Man According to the Classification of Cesare Lombroso,* edited by Gina Lombroso-Ferrero. New York: Putnam.

———. [1912] 1968. *Crime: Its Causes and Remedies.* Montclair, NJ: Patterson Smith.

Lydston, George F. 1904. *The Diseases of Society (The Vice and Crime Problem).* Philadelphia: J. B. Lippincott.

MacDonald, Arthur. 1893. *Criminology,* with an introduction by Dr. Cesare Lombroso. New York: Funk & Wagnalls.

Martin, Randy, Robert J. Mutchnick, and Timothy W. Austin. 1990. *Criminological Thought: Pioneers Past and Present.* New York: Macmillan.

Matsumoto, Toshihiko and Fumi Imamura. 2007. "Association Between Childhood Attention-Deficit-Hyperactivity Symptoms and Adulthood Dissociation in Male Inmates: Preliminary Report." *Psychiatry and Clinical Neurosciences* 61: 444–446.

McKim, W. Duncan. 1900. *Heredity and Human Progress.* New York: G. P. Putnam.

McLaughlin, Eugene, and John Muncie. 2012. *The SAGE Dictionary of Criminology,* 3rd ed. Thousand Oaks, CA: Sage Publications.

Mednick, Sarnoff A., and Karl O. Christiansen. 1977. *Biosocial Bases of Criminal Behavior.* New York: Gardiner.

———. 1987. "Genetic Factors in the Etiology of Criminal Behavior." In *The Causes of Crime: New Biological Approaches,* edited by Sarnoff A. Mednick, Terrie Moffitt, and Susan Stack. Cambridge: Cambridge University Press.

Moffitt, Terrie, and Phil Silva. 1988. "Self-Reported Delinquency, Neuropsychological Deficit, and History of Attention Deficit Disorder." *Journal of Abnormal Psychology* 16: 553–569.

Moore, Todd M., Angela Scarpa, and Adrian Raine. 2002. "A Meta-analysis of Serotonin Metabolite 5-HIAA and Antisocial Behavior." *Aggressive Behavior* 28, no. 4: 299–316.

Morrison, Wayne. 1995. *Theoretical Criminology: From Modernity to Post-Modernism.* London: Routledge.

Nelkin, Dorothy. 1993. "The Grandiose Claims of Geneticists." *Chronicle of Higher Education* (March 3): B1–B3.

Nelkin, Dorothy, and Lawrence Tancredi. 1994. "Dangerous Diagnostics and Their Social Consequences." *Scientist* 12: 12.

Niehoff, Debra. 1999. *The Biology of Violence.* New York: Free Press.

Rafter, Nicole Hahn. 1992. "Criminal Anthropology in the United States." *Criminology* 30: 525–545.

———. 1998. *Creating Born Criminals.* Champaign, IL: University of Illinois Press.

———. 2008. *The Criminal Brain: Understanding Biological Theories of Crime.* New York: New York University Press.

Raine, Adrian. 2002. "Annotation: The Role of Prefrontal Deficits, Low Autonomie Arousal, and Early Health Factors in the Development of Antisocial and Aggressive Behavior in Children." *Journal of Child Psychology and Psychiatry* 43: 417–434.

Rydenour, T. A. 2000. "Genetic Epidemiology of Antisocial Behavior." In *The Science, Treatment, and Prevention of Anti-social Behaviors,* edited by Diana H. Fishbein, Kingston, NJ: Civic Research Institute.

Sarbin, T. R., and L. E. Miller. 1970. "Demonism Revisited: The XYY Chromosome Anomaly." *Issues in Criminology* 5: 195–207.

———. 1976. *Introduction to Criminology.* Reston, VA: Reston.

Sheldon, William H., Emil M. Hastl, and Eugene McDermott. 1949. *Varieties of Delinquent Youth.* New York: Harper and Brothers.

———. 2012. *Criminology: Theories, Patterns and Typologies.* 11th ed. Belmont, CA: Wadsworth.

Telfer, Mary A., David Baker, and Gerald R. Clark. 1968. "Incidence of Gross Chromosomal Errors Among Tall Criminal American Males." *Science* 159: 1249–1250.

Virkkunen, M., A. Nuutila, DeJong, F. K. Goodwin and M. Linnoila. 1987. "Cerbrospinal Fluid Monoamine Metabolic Levels in Male Arsonists." *Neuropsychobiology* 17: 19–23.

Virkkunen, M., J. DeJong, J. Bartko, F. K. Goodwin, and M. Linnoila. 1989. "Relationship of Psychobiological Variables to Recidivism in Violent Offenders and Impulsive Fire Setters." *Archives of General Psychiatry* 46: 600–603.

Walters, Glenn. 1992. "A Meta-Analysis of the Gene-Crime Relationship." *Criminology* 30: 595–613.

Walters, Glenn, and Thomas White. 1989. "Heredity and Crime: Bad Genes or Bad Research." *Criminology* 27: 455–486.

Weinstein Dan, Darlene Staffelbach, and Maryka Biaggio. 2000. "Attention-Deficit Hyperactivity Disorder and Posttraumatic Stress Disorder: Differential Diagnosis in Childhood Sexual Abuse." *Clinical Psychology Review* 20: 359–378.

Wilson, Edmund O. 1975. *Sociobiology: The New Synthesis.* Cambridge: Harvard University Press.

Wilson, James Q., and Richard Herrnstein. 1985. *Crime and Human Nature.* New York: Simon and Schuster.

———. 1981. "Thinking Seriously About Crime: Some Models of Criminology." In *Crime and Society: Readings in History and Society,* edited by Mike Fitzgerald, Gregor McLennan, and Jennie Pawson. London: Routledge and Kegan Paul.

———. 2008. "Growing Out of ADHD: The Relationship Between Functioning and Symptoms" *Journal of Attention Disorders* 12 no, 2: 162–169.

READING 5

Sociological Positivism
Roger Hopkins Burke

We have seen that both the biological and psychological variants of the predestined actor model of crime and criminal behaviour locate the primary impulse for criminal behaviour in the individual. The sociological version rejects these individualist explanations and proposes those behaviours defined as criminal behaviour are simply those that deviate from the norms acceptable to the consensus of opinion in society. This perspective should not be confused with that of the victimised actor model, which proposes that it is the weak and powerless who are defined as criminal and targeted by the rich and powerful in an inherently unequal and unfair society. Sociological *positivists* recognise that crime is a socially constructed entity but at the same time acknowledge that it poses a real threat to the continuance of that society and thus needs to be controlled in some way.

The sociological variant of the predestined actor model involves the 'scientific' measurement of indicators of 'social disorganisation'—such as rates of crime, drunkenness and suicide—in specified urban areas. Proponents recommend that once the whereabouts of existing and potential 'trouble spots' are identified, these must be 'treated', controlled or, in future, 'prevented', if serious social disorder is to be avoided. It is a long-established tradition with its roots in the work of the nineteenth century 'moral statisticians', Quételet (in Belgium) and Guerry (in France) and their social campaigning counterparts in England—Mayhew, Colquhoun, Fletcher and others—who used early empirical methods to investigate the urban slums where crime and deviance flourished. It is an enduring tradition that owes much to the important contribution to sociology established by Emile Durkheim.

Emile Durkheim and Social Disorganisation Theory

Emile Durkheim was the founding father of academic sociology in France and a major social theorist working at the turn of the twentieth century. It was because of the strength and rigour of his large and complex sociological theory that he was able to assert powerfully the merits of social factors in explaining individual and group action. For Durkheim it was not just the psychological and

Roger Hopkins Burke, "Sociological Positivism," *An Introduction to Criminological Theory*, pp. 110-141, 351-393. Copyright © 2009 by Taylor & Francis Group. Reprinted with permission.

biological versions of the predestined actor model that were unable to provide an adequate explanation of social action, he was also strongly opposed to those theoretical ideas—social contract theory and utilitarianism—that had provided the foundations of the rational actor model. In short, a society that is divided into different interest groups on an unequal basis is not one in which 'just contracts between individuals and society could be made' (Durkheim, 1933 originally 1893: 202).

At this point a few words of caution should be indicated. Durkheim is often misrepresented as a conservative indistinguishable from his French predecessor Auguste Comte. Taylor, Walton and Young (1973)—the eminent radical criminologists discussed fully in the third part of this book—and the present author (Hopkins Burke, 1998b, 1999b) consider this orthodox interpretation to be a gross simplification of a significant, radical, social and criminological theorist. Indeed, much of what has been said about Durkheim is more appropriate to the work of his French predecessor Auguste Comte.

Comte had argued that the process whereby with the development of industrialised society people have become increasingly separated into different places of residence and employment has subverted the moral authority of a previously united society. Thus, from this perspective, people are seen to commit criminal acts not because it is in their material interests to do so, but because there is no strong moral authority influencing them to do otherwise. For Comte, it is the purpose of positivist social science to create this higher moral authority.

The essential difference between Comte and Durkheim lies in their differing views of human nature. For the former, the human being has a natural and inherent desire to reach perfection and it is the creation of a moral authority by social scientists that can create the ordered society that will bring about that state of being. Durkheim simply rejects this view. It is utopian and idealistic to argue that a higher moral authority could restrain human desires at all times in history. Thus, Durkheim, in contrast to Comte, proposes a 'dualistic' view of human nature: a duality between the needs of the body and the soul. Human instincts are biologically given, while it is the task of the social world to develop through the human 'soul' an adherence to a *moral consensus* that is the basis of social order and control. With the changing nature of complex modern society that consensus is a shifting and adaptable entity.

It is possible to observe here a similarity between Durkheim and Freud for both argue that an increased repression of the individual conscience is the basis of the development of a civilised society but there are nevertheless substantial differences in their positions. For Durkheim, individual desires have to be regulated not simply because they have certain biological needs and predispositions, but because the failure to control this aspect of the person can lead to a situation of disharmony and despair, culminating in what he terms egoism and anomie. Durkheim did agree with Freud that individuals were not really human until they had been socialised. Freud, however, saw socialisation and the development of a conscience as necessary for individual well-being. For Durkheim, the lack of socialisation and a conscience leads to conflict between the individual and society.

Durkheim was opposed to the utilitarians—because he considered them to be idealists rather than social scientists—and argued that moral authority can only be acceptable to men and women if it is relevant to their particular position in a changing society. If people are caught up in occupations that are unsuitable to their talents—and they recognise this underachievement—they can have little enthusiasm for moral authority. Central to his social theory is a concern with social change and his enthusiasm to eradicate the 'forced division of labour'.

It was in *The Division of Labour in Society*, first published in 1893, that Durkheim described the processes of social change that accompanies the industrial development of society, arguing that earlier forms of society had high levels of mechanical solidarity, while the more developed industrial societies are characterised by an advanced stage of 'organic' solidarity. However, a further note of caution needs to be indicated here: no society is entirely mechanical or organic with any social formation being in a state of development between the two extremes. Indeed, there may well be many pockets of intense mechanical solidarity in highly developed organic societies and this is an important point well worth remembering and which is discussed further below.

For Durkheim societies with high levels of mechanical solidarity are characterised by the conformity of the group. There is thus a likeness and a similarity between individuals and they hold common attitudes and beliefs that bind one person to another. Now this is a form of social solidarity that may at first sight appear attractive—suggesting popular notions of the close-knit community—but at the same time severe restrictions are placed on the ability of an individual to develop a sense of personal identity or uniqueness. Thus, co-operation between individual members of the group is restricted to what can be achieved through the close conformity of each member to a single stereotype.

Durkheim argues that such societies can further be identified by a very intense and rigid collective conscience where members hold very precise shared ideas of what is right and wrong. There are, however, individuals within that group who differ from the uniform ideal and in these cases the law is used as an instrument to maintain that uniformity. Moreover, repressive and summary punishments are used against individuals and minority groups that transgress against the collective conscience of the majority. This punishment of dissenters usefully emphasises their inferiority while at the same time encouraging commitment to the majority viewpoint. In this sense crime is a normal feature of a society with high levels of mechanical solidarity. Punishment performs a necessary function by reinforcing the moral consensus—or world view—of the group where a reduction in behaviour designated as criminal would as a necessity lead to other previously non-criminal activities becoming criminalised. Indeed, Durkheim takes this argument a step further and claims that a society with no crime would be abnormal. The imposition of tight controls that make crime impossible would seriously restrict the potential for innovation and social progress.

Durkheim argues that with greater industrialisation societies develop greater levels of organic solidarity where there is a more developed division of labour and different groups become dependent on each other. Social solidarity now relies less on the maintenance of uniformity between individuals, and more on the management of the diverse functions of different groups. Nevertheless, a certain degree of uniformity remains essential.

It is time to indicate a further cautionary note. There has been a tendency—encouraged by some influential introductory sociology textbooks—for students to confuse the arguments presented by Durkheim on the increasing development of organic society, with those put forward by nineteenth century conservatives, and the German sociologist Ferdinand Tönnies. For those writers, it was precisely this increasing fragmentation of communal beliefs and values that was the problem and the proposed solution thus lies in reestablishing the moral certainties of a society with high levels of mechanical solidarity. This is not the argument presented by Durkheim.

For Durkheim, the division of labour is a progressive phenomenon. Its appearance signals not the inevitable collapse of morality, but the emergence of a new *content* for the collective conscience. In societies dominated by mechanical solidarity the emphasis is on the obligation of the individual to society: with organic formations, the focus is increasingly on the obligation of society to the individual person. Now to give the maximum possible encouragement to individual rights does not mean that altruism—that is, self-sacrifice for others—will disappear; on the contrary, moral individualism is *not* unregulated self-interest but the imposition of a set of reciprocal obligations that binds together individuals (Durkheim, 1933 originally 1893). Here lies the essential originality of Durkheim's interpretation of the division of labour.

For Adam Smith (1910, originally 1776), the founder of free-market economics, and the utilitarians, the specialisation of economic exchange is simply an effect of the growth of wealth and the free play of economic self-interest. For Durkheim, the true significance of the division of labour lies in its *moral* role. It is a source of restraint upon self-interest and thereby renders society cohesive. The idea that unbridled *egoism*—or competitive individualism—could ever become the basis of a civilised order is for Durkheim quite absurd. In short, Durkheim regarded the cohesion of nineteenth century *laissez-faire* society, with its wholly unregulated markets, its arbitrary inequalities, and its restrictions on social mobility and its 'class' wars, as a dangerous condition. Such imperfect social regulation leads to a variety of different social problems, including crime and deviance.

Durkheim provided a threefold typology of deviants. The first typology is the biological deviant who is explained by the physiological or psychological malfunctioning we encountered in the previous two chapters and who can be present in a normal division of labour. The other two typologies are linked to the nature and condition of the social system and are present in those societies which are characterised by an abnormal or forced division of labour. Thus, the second typology, the functional rebel is, therefore, a 'normal' person who is reacting to a pathological society, rebelling against the existing, inappropriate and unfair division of society and indicating the existence of strains in the social system. For Durkheim, such a person expresses the true 'spontaneous' or 'normal' collective consciousness as opposed to the artificial 'forced' or 'pathological' one currently in operation (Taylor,

Walton and Young, 1973). The third typology, skewed deviants involves those who have been socialised into a disorganised pathological society and are the usual focus of the student of deviance and criminal behaviour.

Durkheim proposed two central arguments to explain the growth of crime and criminal behaviour in modern industrial societies. First, such societies encourage a state of unbridled 'egoism' that is contrary to the maintenance of social solidarity and conformity to the law. Second, the likelihood of inefficient regulation is greater at a time of rapid modernisation, because new forms of control have not evolved sufficiently to replace the older and now less appropriate means of maintaining solidarity. In such a period, society is in a state of normlessness or 'anomie', a condition characterised by a breakdown in norms and common understandings.

Durkheim claimed that without external controls, a human being has unlimited needs and society thus has a right to regulate these by indicating the appropriate rewards that should accrue to the individual. Except in times of crisis, everyone has at least a vague perception of what they can expect to earn for their endeavours but at a time of economic upheaval, society cannot exert controls on the aspirations of individuals. During a depression, people are forced to lower their sights, a situation which some will find intolerable but, on the other hand, when there is a sudden improvement in economic conditions, social equilibrium will also break down and there is now no limit on aspirations.

A fundamental recurring criticism of Durkheim emphasised in virtually any introductory sociology text refers to his apparently unassailable methodological collectivism or over-determinism as it is usually termed. Individuals, apparently seem to have little, indeed no, choice in their actions, or in terms of the terminology used in this text their lives appear predestined because of the social conditions in which they live. It is without doubt this interpretation of Durkheim—where it appears impossible to locate any acceptable mechanism to explain social change—that has led to his work being almost universally dismissed as methodologically and politically conservative. A more recent methodological individualist reinterpretation of Durkheim contained in the work of his French compatriot Raymond Boudon (1980) recognises that individuals do have choices, come together with others and form coalitions of interest on which they act and that it is in this way that social change can and does occur. Opportunities for conceiving of, and carrying out, that action are nonetheless invariably *constrained* by—sometimes overwhelmingly—structural constraints, not least the more strongly asserted, believed and enforced *conscience collectives* that are the products of the ultra, or intense, mechanical solidarities that dominate not only simple societies but also pockets of varying size within more complex contemporary societies. In short, individual choice—or acceptance or rejection of a particular way of life or apparent destiny—is possible, from this perspective, but the choices available may be limited, or, in some cases, virtually non-existent (Hopkins Burke and Pollock, 2004: 9).

Hopkins Burke and Pollock (2004) adopt this methodological individualist interpretation of Durkheim in their discussion of hate crime motivation—hate crimes being criminal acts motivated by hatred, bias or prejudice against a person or property based on the actual or perceived race, ethnicity, gender, religion or sexual orientation of the victim—and observe that even in a complex post-industrial society characterised by high levels of organic solidarity, and multifarious interdependencies, the concept of mechanical solidarity retains considerable explanatory power. The authors observe that even within complex and diverse societies, mechanical solidarities continue to significantly exist at three levels in the social world. First, there is the *macro* societal level of national identities that may be particularly strong in those societies where the collective conscience is rigidly enforced by reference to a fundamentalist religious or political belief system. Second, there is the *mezzo* or intermediate level of the organisation and institution, for example, organised hate groups. Third, there is the *micro* level of the small group or gang, such as a 'football firm' in Britain or Europe or localised less organised hate groupings.

Hopkins Burke and Pollock (2004) observe that many contemporary hate groups have philosophies based on the notion of a collective society, consisting of common values, culture, identity, attitude and homogeneity. Those who deviate—or are in some way different from the perceived norm—are defined and labelled as being deviant and outsiders. Deviance, is a necessary function of any mechanical solidarity—whether it be at the macro, mezzo or micro level—inhabited by hate groups because its existence and endurance tests the boundaries of tolerance leading to an ongoing evaluation of prevailing norms and values. Transgressors against the dominant world view—'subaltern' (Perry, 2001) or subordinate groups, those whose sexual, racial, gendered, or ethnic, identities are different to the traditional white, male, heterosexual identity that exist in a 'normal' society—are perceived to have contravened the mechanical solidarity and are consequently censured.

Hopkins Burke and Pollock (2004) observe that this situation whereby a number of mezzo and micro mechanical solidarities co-exist alongside each other in the same geographical space provides a fertile enabling environment for racist hate as a sense of insecurity and uncertainty can arise among at least certain sections of the traditional white majority. Both Enoch Powell (in Britain) and Jean Marie Le Penn (in France) have successfully taken advantage of the political opportunities proffered by this insecurity and dissent during the latter decades of the twentieth century by claiming that non-white immigration would pose a threat to tradition, culture and opportunity for the traditional 'white' community (Heywood: 1992). Thus, hate crime perpetrators motivated by fears of cultural change, construct themselves as victims and demand first class preferential citizenship as they feel alienated from their traditional community or mechanical solidarity.

In concluding this section we might note that although there continues to be controversy about the accuracy of Durkheim's disorganisation theory taken as a whole, his notion that crime is linked to a breakdown in social controls has been a major inspiration to different sociologists in the twentieth century. In particular, his concept of anomie had a marked influence on the later work of Robert Merton discussed below. Moreover, the twin notions of anomie and egoism are extremely useful in helping to explain the nature of crime and criminal behaviour that occurred in the UK during the 1980s and the early 1990s, a more recent period of severe economic and social disruption. The aftermath of that period is still with us and will be examined in later chapters of this book. In the meantime, we will consider the more readily recognised influence that is apparent in the work of the Chicago School.

The Chicago School

In the early part of the twentieth century, the USA underwent a major transition from a predominantly rural and agricultural society to one based on industrial and metropolitan centres. Chicago, for example, grew from a town of 10,000 inhabitants in 1860 to a large city with a population of over two million by 1910. Life was nevertheless hard; wages were low; hours were long; factory conditions were appalling; and living in slum tenements created serious health problems (see Lilly, Cullen and Ball, 1986).

Sociologists working at the University of Chicago reached the conclusion that growing up and living in such negative conditions undoubtedly influenced the outcome of people's lives. Moreover, crime and criminal behaviour in such an environment could not simply be explained in the individualist terms proposed by the biological and psychological versions of the predestined actor model. It made more 'sense' when viewed as a social problem and it was argued that the poor are not simply born into a life of crime but are driven by the conditions of their social environment. Thus, by changing their surroundings it would be possible to reverse the negative effects of the city and transform these people into law-abiding citizens.

Robert Park (1921) contributed two central ideas to the work of the Chicago School. First, he proposed that like any ecological system, the development and organisation of the city is neither random nor idiosyncratic but patterned, human communities, like plants, live together symbiotically. In other words, different kinds of human beings share the same environment and are mutually dependent on each other. At the same time, patterns of change in the city are comparable to changes in the balance of nature, the human population in US cities was migratory, rather than fixed with new immigrants moving into the poor areas and replacing the previous inhabitants as they moved out to the suburbs. Second, Park observed that the nature of these social processes had their impact on human behaviours like crime, and these could be ascertained only through the careful study of city life. It was a research agenda that several researchers were to embrace.

Ernest Burgess (1928) produced a model of the city that provided a framework for understanding the social roots of crime and argued that as cities expand in size, the development is patterned socially. They grow radially in a series of concentric zones or rings. Burgess outlined five different zones and proposed that a competitive process decided how people were distributed spatially amongst these: commercial enterprises were located in the central business district (or loop) in close proximity to the transport systems; the most expensive residential areas were in the outer commuter zones or suburbs, away from the bustle of the city centre, the pollution of the factories and the homes of the poor.

It was the 'zone in transition'—containing rows of deteriorating tenements and often built in the shadow of ageing factories—that was the particular focus of study. The outward expansion of the business district led to the constant displacement of residents. As the least desirable living area, the zone was the focus for the influx of waves of immigrants who were too poor to reside elsewhere. Burgess observed that these social patterns weakened family and communal ties and resulted in 'social disorganisation'. It was this disorganisation thesis that was influentially presented as the primary explanation of criminal behaviour.

Clifford Shaw and Henry McKay (1972, originally 1931) set out to empirically test concentric zone theory, collating juvenile court statistics in order to map the spatial distribution of juvenile offending throughout the city and their analysis confirmed the hypothesis that offending behaviour flourished in the zone in transition and was inversely related to the affluence of the area and corresponding distance from the central business district. They studied court records over several decades and were able to show that crime levels were highest in slum neighbourhoods regardless of which racial or ethnic group resided there and, moreover, as these groups moved to other zones, their offending rates correspondingly decreased. It was this observation that led Shaw and McKay to conclude that it was the nature of the neighbourhoods—not the nature of the individuals who lived within them—that regulated involvement in crime.

Shaw and McKay emphasised the importance of neighbourhood organisation in allowing or preventing offending behaviour by children and young people. In more affluent communities, parents fulfilled the needs of their offspring and carefully supervised their activities but in the zone of transition families and other conventional institutions—schools, churches, and voluntary associations—were strained, if not destroyed, by rapid urban growth, migration and poverty. Left to their own devices, young people in this zone were not subject to the social constraints placed on their contemporaries in the more affluent areas and were more likely to seek excitement and friends in the streets of the city.

Shaw actively promoted appreciative studies of the deviant, using the criminal's 'own story' by means of participant observation in their particular deviant world which became known as the ethnographic or 'life-history' method and led to the publication of titles like *The Jack Roller: A Delinquent Boy's Own Story, The Natural History of a Delinquent Career* and *Brothers in Crime* (Shaw, 1930, 1931, 1938). These studies showed that young people were often recruited into offending behaviour through their association with older siblings or gang members.

Shaw and McKay concluded that disorganised neighbourhoods help produce and sustain 'criminal traditions' that compete with conventional values and can be 'transmitted down through successive generations of boys, much the same way that language and other social forms are transmitted' (Shaw and McKay, 1972: 174). Thus, young people growing up in socially disorganised inner city slum areas characterised by the existence of a value system that condones criminal behaviour could readily learn these values in their daily interactions with older adolescents. On the other hand, youths in organised areas—where the dominance of conventional institutions had precluded the development of criminal traditions—remains insulated from deviant values and peers. Thus, for them, an offending career is an unlikely option.

Shaw and McKay fundamentally argued that juvenile offending can only be understood by reference to the social context in which young people live and, in turn, this context itself is a product of major societal transformations brought about by rapid urbanisation and massive population shifts. Young people born and brought up in the socially disorganised zone of transition are particularly vulnerable to the temptations of crime, as conventional institutions disintegrate around them they are given little supervision and are free to roam the streets where they were likely to become the next generation of carriers of the area's criminal tradition. It was this aspect of their work that provided crucial theoretical foundations for Edwin Sutherland's theory of 'differential association' which was discussed in the previous chapter.

The work of the Chicago School has been criticised from a number of standpoints. First, it has been observed that while the deterministic importance of the transmission of a 'criminal culture' is emphasised there is substantially less detail provided on the origins of that culture. Second, there have been criticisms of a tendency to see the spatial distribution of groups in the city as a 'natural' social process. The role that power and class domination can play in the creation and perpetuation of slums and the enormous economic inequality that permeates such areas is ignored. Third, it has been proposed that they provide only a partial explanation of criminality that seems best able to explain involvement in stable criminal roles and in group-based offending behaviour.

The Chicago School criminologists have nevertheless rightly had a substantial influence on the development of sociological explanations of crime and criminal behaviour. Particularly influential has been the recognition that where people grow up—and the people with whom they associate—is closely linked to a propensity for involvement in criminal activity.

The Chicago School has also had a further practical influence. In the 1930s Clifford Shaw established the 'Chicago Area Project' (CAP). The intention was to allow local residents in socially deprived areas the autonomy to organise neighbourhood committees in the fight against crime and the project encompassed several approaches to crime prevention. First, a strong emphasis was placed on the creation of recreational programmes that would divert young people from criminal activity. Second, efforts were made to have residents take pride in their community by improving the physical appearance of the area. Third, CAP staff members would attempt to mediate on behalf of young people in trouble with those in authority, such as schoolteachers. Fourth, local people were employed as 'street credible' workers in an attempt to persuade youths that education and a conventional lifestyle was in their best interest. Schlossman, Zellman and Shavelson (1984) conducted an evaluation of 50 years of the CAP project and reached the conclusion that it had long been effective in reducing rates of reported juvenile offending.

In summary, social disorganisation theory—as developed by Shaw and McKay—called for efforts to reorganise communities. The emphasis on cultural learning suggests that treatment programmes that attempt to reverse the criminal learning of offenders can counteract involvement in crime. Young offenders should thus be placed in settings where they will receive pro-social reinforcement, for example, through the use of positive-peer-counselling.

Robert Merton and Anomie Theory

Robert Merton's anomie—or strain—theory attempts to explain the occurrence of not only crime but also wider deviance and disorder and in this sense it is a wide-ranging, essentially sociological explanation that promises a comprehensive account of crime and deviance causation, but—while it provides a major contribution to this endeavour—ultimately fails to fulfil this ambition.

Merton borrowed the term anomie from Emile Durkheim in an attempt to explain the social upheaval that accompanied the Great Depression of the 1930s and later the social conflicts that occurred in the USA during the 1960s. His writings are particularly significant because they challenged the orthodoxy of the time that saw the USA as being characterised by the term, 'the American Dream', a vision of a meritocratic society in which hard work and endeavour—in the context of conservative values—would supposedly distribute social and economic rewards equitably.

Merton essentially followed the Chicago School sociologists in rejecting individualistic explanations of crime and criminal behaviour but at the same time took his sociological argument a step further than Durkheim had done previously. Whereas his predecessor had considered human aspirations to be natural, Merton argued significantly that they are usually socially learned. Moreover, there are—and this is the central component of his argument—social structural limitations imposed on access to the means to achieve these goals. His work therefore focuses upon the position of the individual within the social structure rather than on personality characteristics and in his words, 'our primary aim lies in discovering how some social structures exert a definite pressure upon certain persons in the society to engage in nonconformist conduct' (Merton, 1938: 672).

Merton proposed that this central aim could be achieved by distinguishing between *cultural goals* and *institutionalised means*. The former are those material possessions, symbols of status, accomplishment and esteem that established norms and values encourage us to aspire to, and are, therefore, socially learned; the latter are the distribution of opportunities to achieve these goals in socially acceptable ways. Merton observes that it is possible to overemphasise either the goals or the means to achieve them and that it is this that leads to social strains, or 'anomie'.

Merton was mainly concerned with the application of his theory to the USA and proposed that in that society there is an overemphasis on the achievement of goals such as monetary success and material goods, without sufficient attention paid to the institutional means of achievement and it is this cultural imbalance that leads to people being prepared to use any means, regardless of their legality, to achieve that goal (Merton, 1938: 674). The ideal situation would be where there is a balance between goals and means and in such circumstances individuals who conform will feel that they are justly rewarded.

Deviant, especially criminal, behaviour results when cultural goals are accepted, for example, and people would generally like to be financially successful, but where access to the means to achieve that goal is limited by the position of a person in the social structure. Merton outlined five possible reactions—or adaptations—that can occur when people are not in a position to legitimately attain internalised social goals.

Conformity

Conformity is a largely self-explanatory adaptation whereupon people tend to accept both the cultural goals of society and the means of achieving them. Even if they find their social ascent to be limited, they still tend not to 'deviate'. Merton claimed that in most societies this is the standard form of adaptation, for if this were not the case society would be extremely unstable. He did nevertheless note that for many people, whose access to the socially dictated 'good things in life' through established institutionalised means is in some way more difficult than conventionally portrayed, the 'strain' to achieve might well become intolerable. People could alleviate the strain in such instances by either changing their cultural goal and/or by withdrawing their allegiance to the institutionalised means. In following either or both courses, people would be deviating from norms prescribing what should be desired (success) or how this should be achieved (legitimate means such as education, approved entrepreneurship or conscientious employment). The following four 'modes of adaptation' describe various ways of alleviating 'strain' generated by social inequalities.

Retreatism

Merton considered retreatism to be the least common adaptation. Retreatists are those who reject both social goals *and* the means of obtaining them and these are true 'aliens', they are 'in the society but not *of* it' (Merton, 1938: 677). It is a category of social 'dropouts' that includes among others drug addicts, psychotics, vagrants, tramps and chronic alcoholics.

Ritualism

Merton identifies many similarities between 'ritualists' and 'conformists' with an example of the former a person who adheres to rules for their own sake. Bureaucrats who accept and observe the rules of their organisations uncritically provide the classic example. Those in rule-bound positions in the armed services, social control institutions or the public service may be particularly susceptible to this form of adaptation where the emphasis is on the means of achievement rather than the goals. These people, or groups, need not of course be particularly successful in attaining their conventional goals but their overemphasis on the 'means' clouds their judgement on the desirability of appreciating the goals.

Innovation

The innovator—the usual focus for the student of crime and criminal behaviour—is keen to achieve the standard goals of society, wealth, fame or admiration, but, probably due to blocked opportunities to obtain these by socially approved means, embarks on novel, or innovative, routes. Many 'innovative' routes exist in complex organic societies, so much so that some innovators may be seen to overlap with 'conformists'. For example, the sports, arts and entertainment industries frequently attract, develop and absorb 'innovators', celebrating their novelty in contrast to the conformist or ritualist, and providing opportunities for those whose circumstances may frustrate their social ascent through conventionally prescribed and approved routes.

The innovator may be exceptionally talented, or may develop talents, in a field that is restricted or unusual and conventionally deemed worthy of celebration for its novelty but these individuals are relatively unthreatening to conventional views of the acceptable means of social achievement. There are others, on the other hand, who appear to pose a distinctly destabilising influence on conventional definitions of socially acceptable means of achievement and it is, therefore, one of the strengths of anomie—or strain theories—that they appreciate that some of these 'innovations' are merely 'deviant', and subjectable to informal social controls and censure, while others are proscribed by the criminal law of the relevant jurisdiction.

Some activities are usually seen as 'criminally' censurable in most societies, although they may be excusable in certain circumstances. Robbery is usually seen as an offence when committed against an individual or an institution such as a bank. However, this might not be the case when committed in wartime against the persons or institutions of an 'enemy' state. Homicide is regarded as a serious offence in most jurisdictions, yet it is acceptable when promoted by socially or politically powerful interests in times of war. Similarly, where does the financial 'entrepreneur' stretch the bounds of legality or previously established 'acceptable' business means to the achievement of previously determined goals? Lilly, Cullen and Ball (1986) provide the example of stock exchange regulation abusers in the 1980s as an example of innovative business deviants. At a time when business deregulation had generated many fortunes, some people were encouraged by the prevailing economic circumstances to take opportunities to shorten the means to the social goal of wealth through 'insider dealing' and similar practices.

In short, the innovator may be seen to overemphasise the goals of achievement over the means. Conventionally regarded success may be achieved by any means that seem appropriate to the innovator, who strives to overcome barriers to achievement by adopting any available strategies for achieving established goals.

Rebellion

For Merton rebellious people are those who not merely reject but also wish to change the existing social system and its goals. Rebels thus reject both the socially approved means and goals of their society. The emergence of popular images of the potential of both innovative and rebellious modes of adaptation to the standard social and economic patterns of Western life in the 1960s did much to renew an interest in Merton's approach to crime and deviance.

Three main criticisms have been made of anomie theory. First, it has been observed to be a self-acknowledged 'theory of the middle range' that does little to trace the origins of criminogenic circumstances. Merton is thus accused of being a 'cautious rebel' who fails to explain neither the initial existence of inequality, nor the exaggerated emphasis in society on making money (Taylor, Walton and Young, 1973). Indeed, it was criticisms of this kind that instigated the search for a more totalising, historically and politically aware criminology—or 'sociology of deviance'—in the late 1960s and 1970s. The rise—and indeed fall—of this mode of explaining criminal behaviour is the central focus of the third part of this book.

Anomie theory is not as comprehensive an account of crime and deviance as it may at first look for it fails to explain certain behaviours that are commonly labelled 'deviant'—such as recreational drug use—and which are often undertaken by people who otherwise accept the standard cultural goals and the institutionalised means of achieving them.

The second criticism is targeted at Merton's assumption that cultural goals and values are known and shared by all members of society. Lemert (1972), for example, argued that society is more accurately characterised by the notion of a plurality of values and if this is the case, then Merton's 'ends–means' approach becomes problematic and generally insufficient in explaining crime and deviance. He can be partially defended in that he did state that different goals are possible within his scheme, but he does not give sufficient emphasis to different groups and different values. Moreover, the assumption that it is the 'lower classes' who are most likely to suffer from frustrated aspirations and who are subject to strain and commit criminal or deviant acts may not be accurate. Later criminological studies reveal that there is a great deal more deviant behaviour in society than Merton's formula suggests. Anomie theory—we are told—is hard-pressed to account for business fraud and other 'white-collar' crimes, and also for 'lower-class' conformity. Thus, anomie theory predicts both too few deviant activities among the more privileged members of society and too much among those potentially most subject to strain.

In defence of Merton, it would seem that he was motivated to explain those forms of highly visible and immediately apparent crime that have traditionally been committed by the poorer sections of society and which have been of immediate concern to the public and hence politicians and inevitably criminologists. Indeed, later researchers—predominantly working in the victimised actor tradition, which is the focus of the third part of this book—have sought to use the concept of anomie in an attempt to explain corporate crime. From this perspective, it has been argued that explanations based on individual motivations are inadequate and that it is necessary to consider these in the context of corporate goals, the essential one of which is to maximise profit over a long period (Etzioni, 1961; Box, 1983). Box thus identifies five potential sources of 'environmental uncertainty' for the corporation that represent obstacles to the lawful attainment of its main goal; these are: competitors; the government;

employees; consumers; and the public, especially as represented by protectionists. Box observes that confronted with such obstacles, the corporation adopts tactics that frequently involve breaking the law, in order to achieve its goal.

Staw and Szwajkowski (1975) compared the financial performance of 105 large firms subject to litigation involving illegal competition with those of 395 similar firms not so involved and concluded that environmental scarcity did appear linked to a whole range of trade violations. Box (1983) goes further and argues that adherence to the profit motive renders the corporation inherently criminogenic with the bulk of corporate crime initiated by high-ranking officials and he suggests, moreover, that the very factors connected with career success in corporations—and the consequences of such success—are themselves criminogenic.

Gross (1978) conducted a survey of several studies of corporate career mobility and noted the relevance of personality differences. He thus found senior managers to be ambitious, easily accepting of a non-demanding moral code, and to regard their own success at goal attainment as being linked to the success of the organisation. Box (1983) took this notion a step further and argued that the very nature of the corporate promotion system means that those who reach the top are likely to have the very personal characteristics required to commit business crime, the greater success they achieve, the more free they feel from the bind of conventional values. In this way, we might observe that Box's interpretation of anomie seems to be closer to that of Durkheim than Merton.

Financial profit is not the only goal relevant to anomie. Braithwaite (1984: 94) has described fraud as 'an illegitimate means to achieving any one of a wide range of organisational and personal goals when legitimate means … are blocked', for example, he found a widespread willingness among pharmacologists to fabricate the results of safety tests. This behaviour could sometimes be attributed to financial greed but there were other explanations. Some scientists, for example, have an intense commitment to their work and when the value of this is threatened by test results there could be considerable temptation to cover this up in order to defend professional prestige.

Levin and McDevitt (1993) and Perry (2001) have observed the tendency for hate crime offenders to blame their economic instability or lack of job opportunities on the immigration of 'foreigners', while Hopkins Burke and Pollock (2004) argue that it is the actual adaptation of conformity that is problematic in this context. Central to the whole notion of conformity is the sense that adherents in some way buy into the legitimacy of the whole social order and exactly why they do this is not questioned by Merton but adherence to the law, the influence of macro or localised 'correct' thinking, perhaps in the work context in the case of the latter, and a lack of opportunity could all be legitimate reasons why a person with latent—hidden or suppressed—hate crime motivation keeps this under control. It could well be that as an outcome of a change in structural circumstances—for example, the arrival of a group of immigrants or asylum seekers in the locality, the chance meeting of a new friend or colleague with similar latent views, perhaps while on holiday or after the consumption of a few 'social' drinks, or as the outcome of surfing the Internet—that latent hate crime motivation could well be transformed into something more insidious.

These observations suggest a fundamental premise that hate crime motivation is essentially a pathological deviation from societal norms. Hopkins Burke and Pollock (2004) nevertheless argue the converse and observe that hate crime motivation is simply normal and unremarkable in society as currently constituted. The powerful macro, mezzo and micro mechanical solidarities that exist in even the most complex contemporary organic societies—absorbed and internalised during a socialisation process that may well have prioritised notions of hard work, law-abiding behaviour and indeed conformity to the group—legitimate hate motivation as normal. Given the opportunity in the right venue among 'our own kind' where such views are very much the norm it is possible that latent hate motivation might well be actualised, where the at least tacit approval of the (perhaps) silent majority of conformists might provide succour, support and legitimisation for those prepared to act upon their hate motivation.

The third criticism of Merton is that he made no attempt to apply his typology to women and, at first sight it seems totally inapplicable to them. Leonard (1983) proposes that the main goal of US women is to achieve successful relationships with others not the attainment of material wealth and this is an argument to which we return in the following chapter.

Anomie theory has been subjected to many criticisms but is generally sympathetically regarded in the fields of sociology and criminology. Merton did a great deal to broaden the study of crime and criminal behaviour and to introduce the importance of social structure in shaping the life choices of individuals. Some have argued that he did not go far enough with this endeavour; however, it would seem that Merton—along with many liberal or social democratic critics of unrestrained egoism and conservative values both in his native USA and Britain—had no inclination to see a socialist transformation of society. The latter tends to be the ultimate goal of his critics working at the more radical end of the spectrum in the victimised actor model tradition. To criticise the substantial elements of his theoretical concerns on that basis is therefore rather unfair, particularly as many of those critics have since radically modified their views and come themselves to accept the explanatory potential of Merton's notion of anomie. In short, his work has provided a useful starting point for subsequent researchers.

Messner and Rosenfeld (1994) have developed an institutional anomie theory where they observe that the 'American Dream' is a broad, cultural ethos that entails a commitment to the goal of material success, to be pursued by everyone, in a mass society dominated by huge multinational corporations. They argue that not only has economics come to dominate our culture but the non-economic institutions in society have become subservient to the economy, for example, the entire educational system appears to have become driven by the employment market (nobody wants to go to college just for the sake of education anymore), politicians get elected on the strength of the economy, and despite widespread political discourses promoting the sanctity of family values, executives are expected to uproot their families at the behest of the corporation. Goals other than material success (such as parenting, teaching, and serving the community) are simply secondary to the needs of the economy.

Messner and Rosenfeld (1994) argue that the dominant cause of crime is anomie which is promoted and endorsed by the American Dream and where the emphasis is on seeking the most efficient way to achieve economic success. In this context, crime is invariably the most effective and efficient way to achieve immediate monetary gain. Beliefs, values, and commitments are the causal variables, and the closer they are linked to those of the marketplace, the more likely the logic of the economy (competitive, individualistic, and materialistic) will dictate a powerful social force that motivates the pursuit of money 'by any means necessary'. Moreover, since this lawlessness-producing emphasis is caught up in the structural emphasis society places on the economy (and little else), none of the many 'wars' on crime (for example, the war against drugs) will ever be successful (since they indirectly attack the economy).

Messner and Rosenfeld (1994) observe that while commitment to the goal of material success is the main causal variable there are significant others such as values and beliefs. The two values that constitute the American Dream are those of achievement and individualism. Achievement involves the use of material success to measure self-worth with individualism referring to the notion of intense personal competition to achieve material success. Other beliefs related to the American Dream include universalism—the idea that chances for success are open to everyone—and this belief creates an intense fear of failure. While another belief, the 'fetishism' of money refers, in this instance, to the notion that there are no rules for establishing when one has enough money (Messner and Rosenfeld, 1994). An area where the enduring influence of anomie theories is most apparent is in the discussion of deviant subcultures below.

Deviant Subculture Theories

There are different deviant subculture explanations of crime and criminal behaviour but all share a common perception that certain social groups have values and attitudes that enable or encourage delinquency. The highly influential US subcultural tradition was at its peak during the 1940s and 1950s and incorporated five main explanatory inputs.

First, there was Merton's concept of anomie with its proposition that people may either turn to various kinds of deviant conduct in order to gain otherwise unobtainable material rewards or, failing that, seek alternative goals.

Second, there were the case studies conducted by the Chicago School that had suggested that young males living in socially 'disorganised' areas had different moral standards from other people and these helped facilitate their willingness to become involved in offending behaviour. Moreover, some of these patterns of conduct were passed on—or 'culturally transmitted'—from one generation to the next.

Third, there was the 'masculine identity crisis theory' outlined by the then highly influential functionalist sociologist Talcott Parsons (1937) during a period when his work was highly influenced by Freud. Parsons argued that the primary social role of the adult male is job-centred while that of the adult female is home-centred. Consequently the father is absent from the family home for much of the time and is unable therefore to function as a masculine role model for his children. The outcome is that children of both sexes identify with their mother to the exclusion of their father and this is particularly problematic for the male child who encounters strong cultural expectations that he adopt a masculine role but has no real concept of what this involves. But he has, during his childhood, discovered that stealing, violence and destruction provoke the disapproval of his mother and hence identifies these as non-feminine and therefore masculine characteristics. Offending behaviour satisfies these criteria of masculinity.

Fourth, there was the 'differential association theory' that Edwin Sutherland had developed from the social disorganisation thesis of the Chicago School—discussed in the previous chapter—and which proposed that a person was more likely to offend if they had frequent and consistent contact with others involved in such activities. Offending behaviour was likely to occur when individuals acquired sufficient inclinations towards law breaking which came to eclipse their associations with non-criminal tendencies.

Fifth, there were the early sociological studies of adolescent gangs carried out in the social disorganisation–cultural transmission tradition developed by the Chicago School. Thrasher (1947) thus argued that the adolescent gang emerged out of spontaneous street playgroups of young children in relatively permissive and socially disorganised slum areas but the young males involved were neither 'disturbed' or 'psychopathic' nor 'driven' by socio-economic forces beyond their control, they were simply looking for excitement, adventure and fun. This could be found on the streets but not at school or home.

Later studies of adolescent gangs followed in the tradition established by Thrasher and all argued that involvement in the young male gang was a natural response to a socially disorganised environment and deviant behaviour when it did occur had been learned from previous generations of adolescents (see for example, Yablonsky, 1962). These studies continued throughout the 1930s, 1940s and 1950s in the USA with a few minor examples in the UK. At the same time, the concept of the 'delinquent subculture' was emerging in the USA.

Early US Deviant Subculture Theories

Albert Cohen (1955) observed that previous research had tended to focus on the process through which individual young males had come to adopt deviant values and had either ignored—or taken for granted—the existence of deviant subcultures or gangs. By analysing the structure of such subcultures, Cohen argued that juvenile offending was rarely motivated by the striving for financial success proposed by Merton. In contrast, he argued that adolescent gang members in fact stole for the fun of it and took pride in their acquired reputations for being tough and 'hard'. The gang—or subculture—offers possibilities for *status* and the acquisition of respect that are denied elsewhere. Involvement in gang culture is to use contemporary terminology simply cool.

Cohen noted that although society is stratified into socio-economic classes it is the norms and values of the middle class that are dominant and employed to judge the success and status of everybody in society. The young working-class male nevertheless experiences a different form of upbringing and is unlikely to internalise these norms and values. He is thrust into a competitive social system founded on alien and incomprehensible middle-class norms and values with the outcome that he experiences a deficit of respect and *status frustration.*

Since the young male is involved in a process of interaction with others who are faced with the same difficulties, a mutually agreed solution may be reached and a separate subculture with alternative norms and values with which young males can relate is formed. In this way he can achieve status and respect for involvement in all the things the official culture rejects: hedonism, aggression, dishonesty and vandalism. In short, there is a conscious and *active* rejection of middle-class norms and values.

Cohen's delinquent subculture theory has attracted its share of criticism not least because he failed to base his theoretical formulation on empirical data and, indeed, all attempts to test it have failed and it can be argued that it is inherently untestable. Kitsuse and Dietrick (1959) showed there was no real basis for the assertion that the young working-class male experiences 'problems of adjustment' to middle-class values. They observe that middle-class norms and values are simply *irrelevant* to young working-class men because they have absolutely no interest in acquiring status within the dominant social system. Their aspirations are thus *not frustrated*. They simply resent the intrusion of middle-class outsiders who try to impose their irrelevant way of life upon them and offending behaviour should therefore be considered rational and utilitarian in the context of working-class culture.

Walter Miller (1958) develops this theme and argues that offending is simply the product of long-established traditions of working-class life and it is the very structure of that culture that generates offending behaviour not conflicts with middle-class values. The *focal concerns* of working-class society—toughness, smartness, excitement, fate and autonomy—combine in several ways to produce criminality. Those who respond to such concerns automatically violate the law through their behaviour and, thus, the very fact of being working class places the individual in a situation that contains a variety of direct incitements towards deviant conduct. Implicit in this formulation is a significant attack on the notion that subcultures originate as a response to lack of status or thwarted aspirations. On the contrary, delinquency is simply a way of life and a response to the realities of their particular lives.

Miller himself problematically offers no explanation for the origins of these highly deterministic working-class values from which there appears to be no escape. All he does is note their existence and explain that conforming to them will lead to criminal behaviour. His work was strongly influenced by Parson's masculinity identity crisis (Parsons, 1937) where it had been noted that it is common in lower-class households for the father to be absent, often because he has transgressed against the criminal law. The home life is thus a female-dominated environment that leads working-class males to look for 'suitable' role models outside the home and these could be readily found in the street gangs—termed by Miller 'one-sex peer units'—where the adolescent male could take part in activities that uphold working class 'focal concerns' and give him a sense of belonging, status and respect.

Richard Cloward and Lloyd Ohlin's *Delinquency and Opportunity* (1960) was a major development in deviant subculture theory and provided one of the central foundations of labelling theory which itself is a central element of the victimised actor tradition we will encounter in the third part of this book. They essentially argue that it is necessary to have two theories in order to fully explain adolescent criminal behaviour: first, there is a need for a 'push' theory to explain why it is that large numbers of young people offend and second, a 'pull' theory to explain the continuance of this behaviour and how it becomes passed on to others. The originality of their work lies in their use of a combination of Merton's anomie theory to explain the 'push' and Sutherland's differential association theory to explain the 'pull'.

Cloward and Ohlin observe that there is a discrepancy between the aspirations of working-class adolescent males and the opportunities available to them. When an individual recognises that membership of a particular ethnic group or social class and/or lack of a suitable education has seriously restricted his access to legitimate opportunities he will blame an unfair society for his failure and withdraw his belief in the legitimacy of the social order. It is this awareness that leads to a rejection of conventional codes of behaviour.

Cloward and Ohlin followed Cohen in stressing that individuals have to actively seek out and join with others who face the same problems and together these young males will devise a collective solution to their predicament for surrounded by hostile adults they need all the support that they can get from each other. Moreover, they need to develop techniques to neutralise the guilt they feel and this is easier to achieve as the member of a like-minded group.

Underlying this reformulation of anomie theory is the assumption that illegitimate routes to success are freely available to those individuals who 'need' them. Cloward and Ohlin combine the cultural transmission theory of Shaw with the differential association theory of Sutherland to create an 'illegitimate opportunity structure' concept that parallels the 'legitimate opportunity structure' of Merton. From this theory the existence of three separate delinquent subcultures were predicted. First, *criminal* delinquent subcultures are said to exist where there are available illegitimate opportunities for learning the motivations, attitudes and techniques necessary in order to commit crimes. Second, a *conflict* subculture exists where adolescent males—denied access to the legitimate opportunity structure because of their social class, ethnic origin, etc.—have no available criminal opportunity structure and in this scenario, young males work off their frustrations by attacking people (assault), property (vandalism) and each other (gang fights). Third, *retreatist* subcultures tend to exist where drugs are freely available and membership is composed of those who have failed to gain access to either the legitimate or criminal subcultures. These young males retreat into drug misuse and alcoholism and are considered to be 'double failures'.

Cloward and Ohlin predicted—and this was 1960—that because the organisation within poor inner cities was collapsing and adult crime was becoming too sophisticated for adolescent males to learn easily, the criminal delinquent subculture would decline. The conflict or retreatist subcultures would on the other hand expand, with increased adolescent violence, 'muggings', vandalism and drug addiction.

Three main criticisms have been made of Cloward and Ohlin's work. First, it is observed that their notion of the criminal subculture is modelled on the fairly stable and structured adolescent gangs of the Chicago slum areas of the 1920s and 1930s and which had long since ceased to exist (Jacobs, 1961). Second, there is an inherent assumption that the working class is a relatively homogeneous group and this is simply not the case. Third, they, like their predecessors, provide a grossly simplistic explanation of drug misuse, which is, in reality, fairly common among successful middle-class professional people, particularly, if alcohol consumption is included under the generic term 'drugs'.

Coward and Ohlin's theory was nevertheless the focus of considerable academic debate with a major issue being the extent to which the actions of young males in delinquent gangs are determined by their socialisation and the extent to which they are committed to the delinquent norms of the group.

Ivan Spergel (1964) provided at least a partial answer to these questions, identifying an 'anomie gap' between aspirations measured in terms of aspired to and expected occupation and weekly wage, finding that the size of this gap differed significantly between offenders and non-offenders and between one subculture and another. Spergel consequently rejected Cloward and Ohlin's subculture categories and replaced them with his own three-part typology: first, *a racket subculture* is said to develop in areas where organised adult criminality is already in existence and highly visible; second, *a theft subculture*—involving offences such as burglary, shoplifting, taking and driving away cars—would develop where a criminal subculture was already in existence but not very well established and third, *conflict subcultures*—involving gang fighting and 'rep'utation would develop where there is limited or no access to either criminal or conventional activities.

Spergel significantly found that drug misuse was common to all subcultures as part of the transition from adolescent delinquent activity to either conventional or fully developed criminal activity among older adolescents and young adults while people involved in drug misuse do not in themselves constitute a subculture. Moreover, the common form of deviant behaviour specific to a particular area depends on the idiosyncratic features of that particular district and not, as Merton—and Cloward and Ohlin—imply, on *national* characteristics.

The general conclusion reached by critics of early US deviant subculture theories is that they fail to provide an adequate explanation of adolescent offending behaviour while a number of more specific criticisms can also be identified. First, descriptions of the 'typical' offender where they are portrayed as being in some way different from non-offenders and driven into offending behaviour by grim social and economic forces beyond their control make little sense. There is simply no attempt to explain why it is that many if not most young males faced with the same 'problems of adjustment' *do not* join delinquent gangs. Second, virtually all-deviant subculture explanations consider adolescent offending to be a gang phenomenon where in reality this is a very doubtful proposition. A lot of adolescent offending behaviour is a solitary activity or involves, at the most, two or three young males together. The fairly stable gangs identified by the deviant subculture theorists were certainly at that time very difficult to find. Third, none of these explanations takes into account the roles of authority figures—the police, parents, social workers and teachers—in labelling these young people as offenders. Fourth, no adequate explanations are provided of how it is that many young males appear to simply outgrow offending behaviour. Fifth, no explanation is provided for the offending behaviour of adolescent females. Sixth, there is an inherent assumption that offending is the preserve of the young male lower working classes and this is clearly not the case.

The deviant subculture concept has nevertheless been subsequently successfully applied elsewhere in the study of deviant and criminal behaviour with some researchers usefully utilising it to explain corporate—or business—crime. Aubert (1952) examined the attitudes of certain Swedish citizens towards violation of wartime rationing regulations and found that two sorts of obligation influenced the behaviour of each research subject. First, 'universalistic' obligations affected their behaviour as a law-abiding citizen and these should have provided sufficient motivation to obey the law, but sanctions against those who transgressed were found to be invariably weak. Second, 'particularistic' obligations were considered to be due to business colleagues, and these were supported by a philosophy that demanded only avoidance of certain 'blatant offences'. The groups to which white-collar criminals belong were described as having 'an elaborate and widely accepted ideological rationalisation for the offences and ... great social significance outside the sphere of criminal activity' (Aubert, 1952: 177). Corporate crimes were found to be sometimes acceptable and endorsed by group norms with certain types of illegal activity seen as normal. Braithwaite (1984) similarly found that bribing health inspectors was normal and acceptable business practice in the pharmaceutical industry.

These subcultural influences are nevertheless not fully deterministic. Executives who violate laws are not pressured into action by irresistible forces beyond their control. Deviance may be encouraged and condoned but it is not automatic or uncontested destiny. Both Geis (1967) and Faberman (1975) found that even within industries where criminal practices are common, some employees were not prepared to get involved in spite of often quite extensive pressure from senior managers. It seems that individual characteristics, variations between groups within a subculture and the degree of exposure to subcultural values seem to be relevant in this context.

Hopkins Burke and Pollock (2004) note the value of the deviant subculture concept in helping to account for hate crime motivation, for being part of a particular ethnic group with its additional transmitted traditions and mechanical solidarities can undoubtedly act as a particular focus for collective belonging and can undoubtedly provide both the fulcrum for the actualisation of hate crime behaviour and protection against it. The authors also note that it is a particularly useful theoretical tool for helping to explain the kind of institutional racist police behaviour identified in the London Metropolitan Constabulary by the Macpherson Report 1999.

There has long been a tough working class police culture—'canteen culture' as it has been termed (see Holdaway, 1983; Fielding, 1988; Reiner, 2000)—that has been transmitted and adapted to changing circumstances across the generations. Working in a hard, tough environment, invariably at risk of serious violence, notions of always looking after your colleagues in the face of external censure and senior management, has made considerable sense to serving officers brought together in a perceived shared adversity and has rather inevitably led to them looking inwards to the group for a supportive shared world view. The outcome has been a 'stereotyping', separating and labelling of the public into categories deemed worthy of police assistance—the community or 'those like us'—and the 'others', the 'toe-rags', 'slags', 'scrotes', 'scum' and 'animals'. Some have argued that these stereotypes drive the day-to-day nature and pattern of police work (Smith and Gray, 1986; Young, 1991, 1993) and the Macpherson Report 1999 clearly identified a significant issue of institutional racism within the Metropolitan police where young black males were apparently not deemed worthy of victim status even when murdered.

Hopkins Burke (2004b) observes that this subculture was undoubtedly *relatively* non problematic during an era when police intervention against the rougher elements of a predominantly white monocultural working class had undoubted support from most elements of society including the socially aspiring respectable elements within that class who lived cheek-by-jowl with the roughs and sought protection from them. It was with the fragmentation of that society and the emergence of the ethnic and sexual preference diversity discussed in the final part of this book that this macho-police subculture became increasingly problematic.

This early US deviant subcultural tradition has been widely accused of being overly determinist in its apparent rejection of free will and in this variant of the predestined actor model deviants are seen to be not only different from non deviants but in some way committed to an alternative 'ethical' code that makes involvement in deviant activity appear somewhat mandatory. While it is extremely likely that some young people, or police officers and business personnel, for that matter, are so strongly socialised into the mores of a particular world view—or mechanical solidarity—through membership of a particular ethnic group, the upbringing of their parents and the reinforcing influences of neighbourhood groups or gangs that they do not challenge this heritage in any way, it also likely that many others have less consistent socialisation experiences and have a far more tangential relationship to such deviant behaviour, although they may be at considerable risk of being drawn into a far deeper involvement.

David Matza and the Anti-Determinist Critique

The best and most comprehensive critique of the highly determinist early deviant subculture tradition is provided by David Matza and in doing so he provides an influential and crucial link with the later non-determinist explanations discussed in the third part of this book. Matza (1964) observed that all criminologists working in the predestined actor tradition—from Lombroso onwards—have made three basic assumptions about crime which although they have some validity have simply been taken too far. First, there has been a focus on the criminal and their behaviour while the role of the criminal justice system—a significant part of the environment of the criminal—is ignored. Second, the predestined actor model is overly determinist in its rejection of the notion of rational free will and simply fails to recognise that human beings *are* capable of making rational choices but these are limited by structural constraints. Third, the predestined actor model considers criminals to be fundamentally different types of people from non-criminals, although there are, of course, substantial variations on this theme. Lombroso, for example, considered the criminal to have been 'born bad' while the deviant subculture theorist, on the other hand, considered the actions of the offender to be determined by a commitment to an alternative 'ethical' code that makes involvement in delinquent activity seem mandatory.

Matza notes that those working in the predestined actor tradition have simply failed to explain why it is that most young offenders 'grow out' of offending behaviour. From that determinist perspective, offenders would presumably continue to offend all the time, except of course when they have been incarcerated. This is clearly not the case but it is the logical deduction that can be made from the position taken by such writers as Cohen, and Cloward and Ohlin. In response, Matza proposes that delinquency is a *status* and delinquents are *role players* who intermittently act out a delinquent role. These young men are perfectly capable of engaging in conventional activity and, therefore, the alleged forces that compel them to be delinquent are somehow rendered inactive for most of their lives. They simply 'drift' between delinquent and conventional behaviour. The young person is neither compelled nor committed to delinquent activity but freely chooses it sometimes and on other occasions does not do so.

Matza accepted the existence of subcultures whose members engage in delinquency but, on the other hand, denied the existence of a specific deviant subculture. Theories that propose the existence of such a subculture assume that this involves a contra culture, one that deliberately runs counter to the values of the dominant culture. Matza argued that this position is problematic for the following reasons. First, there is the implication that the young person does not experience feelings of guilt and this is not the case. Second, there is an assumption that young offenders have no respect for conventional morality whereas, in reality, most young people involved in offending behaviour recognise the legitimacy of the dominant social order and the validity of its moral standards. Third, it is argued that young offenders define all people outside their 'delinquent subculture' as potential victims whereas they distinguish special groups—mostly other delinquents—as legitimate targets to victimise. Fourth, it is proposed that delinquents are immune from the demands of the larger culture whereas, in reality, the members of these supposed 'delinquent subcultures' are *children* and cannot escape from disapproving adults and their condemnation of delinquent behaviour must therefore be taken into consideration with the strong probability that their demands for conformity will be internalised.

Matza found that young males could moreover remain within the 'subculture of delinquency' *without* actually taking part in offending behaviour. Thus, when he showed a sample of photographs of various criminal acts to a group of delinquents—some of which they themselves had committed—their reactions ranged from mild disapproval to righteous indignation.

Matza argued that adolescents go through three stages in a process of becoming deviant. The first stage is the nearest the young male comes to being part of an oppositional subculture and such a situation arises when he is in the company of other young males and where there appears to be an 'ideology of delinquency' implicit in their actions and remarks. In these circumstances he is motivated by his anxiety to be accepted as a member of the group and his concerns about his own masculinity and 'grown-up' status. In this condition of anxiety he reaches conclusions, in his own mind, about what will be the 'correct' form of behaviour to adopt, the 'correct' attitude to present and the 'correct' motives for engaging in a particular form of behaviour from the remarks, gestures and behaviour of the other adolescents. He hears and perhaps sees others in the group approving of or doing daring, but illegal, acts and assumes that, to be accepted, he must join in and show that he is just as good (or bad), if not better than, all the others. So he steals things, vandalises things, hits people not because he 'really' wants to but because he feels he 'ought' to want to, because that is what being 'grown up' is all about.

Matza observes that what this young man fails to realise is that the other members of the group feel exactly the same as he does. The others are also plagued by doubts about acceptance, masculinity and adulthood and, indeed, may be taking *their* cues from him. In other words, all the members of the group are trapped in a vicious circle of mutual misunderstandings. This circle can be broken when two young men confess to each other that they do not like offending or when the particular individual is sufficiently old to stop feeling anxieties about masculinity and adult status. At this stage of maturity a young man can decide to leave the group and cease involvement in deviant activity or to continue.

The second stage thus occurs when the young man, having overcome his original anxieties about masculinity, is faced with another problem, he must overcome his initial socialisation that has taught him not to be deviant and hence protect himself from feelings of guilt. He must find extenuating circumstances that will release him from conventional control and leave him free to choose to drift into deviancy and thus, in this way, young males utilise 'techniques of neutralisation' to justify their behaviour. Matza identifies five major types of neutralisation:

- denial of responsibility (I didn't mean it);
- denial of injury (I didn't really harm him);
- denial of the victim (he deserved it);
- condemnation of the condemners (they always pick on us); and

- appeals to higher loyalties (you've got to help your mates).

These techniques are by themselves merely excuses and not explanations of deviant behaviour. Matza argued that at a deeper level there is a commitment to 'subterranean values', which—like Miller's 'focal concerns' which they resemble—exist in the wider culture of normal society. The most important of these values is what psychologists refer to as the 'need for stimulation', which means, in this context, the search for excitement. Young males commit deliberate criminal acts because they *are* criminal, quite simply, being deviant is better than being bored, deviancy is fun, it is exciting.

Matza argued that the operation of the criminal justice system and the actions of social workers might actually convince young people that deviant behaviour does not really matter. Deviant young males are not stupid, they are aware that many social workers, police officers, teachers and magistrates think that the young person is not fully responsible for their actions but will go ahead and punish—or rather 'treat'—them just the same. Deviant children are as quick as—or even quicker than—non-deviants to recognise this contradiction and to exploit it to their own advantage.

The third stage in a deviant career has now been reached with the young male now in a situation of 'drift' where he knows what is required of him and has learned the techniques of neutralisation which justify his deviant behaviour. On the other hand, he is not automatically *committed* to deviant behaviour and he *could* just boast about previous and unverifiable exploits, much as other young people boast about imaginary sexual encounters.

The missing impetus that makes actual deviant behaviour possible is 'free will' and it is this recognition that distinguishes Matza completely from those working in the predestined actor tradition. The deviant is *responsible* for their behaviour. They *know* that their activities are against the law. They *know* that they may be caught and they *know* that they may be punished. They probably accept that they *should* be punished. It is one of the rules of the game. If this is the case the question that remains to be asked is why the young person should continue to be involved in criminal behaviour.

In the first place, the young person has acquired certain skills partly from their older friends and partly from the mass media, for example television, which has made involvement in criminal behaviour possible. They will have learned from their friends how to manage guilt and discount the possibility of capture. They assume that they will not be caught and criminal statistics suggest that they are likely to be correct in this supposition. This state of *preparation* allows the young person to repeat an offence that they have committed before. Less frequently, the young person falls into a condition of *desperation* derived from a mood of *fatalism*, a feeling of being 'pushed around'. This feeling of being pushed around is sufficient for them to lose their precarious concept of their self as a 'real man' and, at that point, they need to 'make something happen' in order to prove that they are a *cause* not merely an effect and it is this feeling that leads them directly to become involved in more serious, previously untried, delinquent behaviour where even if caught they have still made something happen. The whole apparatus of police, juvenile court and social work department is concerned with them and has been activated by what *they them self* did. In a state of desperation the young person needs to do more than simply repeat an old offence. After all, as his or her peers would say, 'anyone can do that'. In the state of desperation, they need to do something that they have not tried before.

Matza's theoretical schema has also been usefully applied to the study of business crime. Corporate executives have thus been found to use 'techniques of neutralisation' to rationalise deviant acts and violate the law without feeling guilty (Box, 1983). Officials can deny responsibility by pleading ignorance, accident, or that they were acting under orders. Vague laws that rest on ambiguous definitions and permit meanings and interpretation to fluctuate help facilitate this and as a result it is difficult to distinguish praiseworthy corporate behaviour from illegal actions. Box (1983: 55) observes that in these circumstances, 'it is convenient for corporate officials to pull the cloak of honest ignorance over their heads and proceed under its darkness to stumble blindly and unwittingly over the thin line between what is condoned and what is condemned'.

Bandura (1973: 13) found that shared decision making in an organisation allows people to contribute 'to cruel practices ... without feeling personally responsible'. 'Denial of the victim' may also be used. The nature of much corporate crime permits an illusion that there is no real person suffering, particularly when the victims are other corporations or people in far off countries, especially if they are less developed countries (Braithwaite, 1984). Swartz (1975) has noted that company spokespersons have been prepared to blame industrial accidents on 'careless and lazy' workers or the development of brown lung in black workers on their 'racial inferiority'. The corporate criminal often denies that any harm has been caused. Geis (1968: 108) quotes an executive who described his activities as 'illegal ... but not criminal ... I assumed that criminal action meant damaging someone, and we did not do that'. Moreover, the corporate employee can 'condemn the condemners', by pointing to political corruption, or describing laws as unwarranted constraints on free enterprise. Acting for the good of the company—or following widespread but illegal business practices—is seen as more important than obeying the law.

Hopkins Burke and Pollock (2004: 31) discuss how techniques of neutralisation can be used by hate crime offenders to excuse, justify and legitimate their actions and use the following all inclusive and somewhat 'upmarket' illustration to make their point:

> Well I know it is rather unpleasant and one doesn't really like getting involved in these things, but they are different from us. They have a different way of life and it is not really what we want here. You really wouldn't want your children to mix with them now would you? I don't really approve of this sort of thing but something has to be done.

The authors note that having absorbed experiences and knowledge at each stage of their socialisation from parents and friends and having had these values reinforced by access to media—however self selecting this might be—provides the race hate perpetrator with choices which for them are very much rational. In a study conducted for the British Home Office, Rae Sibbitt (1999) found that the views held by all kinds of race hate perpetrators are shared very much by the communities to which they belong and perpetrators very much see this as legitimising their actions. In turn, the wider community not only spawn such perpetrators, but fails to condemn them and thus actively reinforce their behaviour. Hate crime perpetrators are invariably very much part of their local deviant subculture or mechanical solidarity.

Early British Deviant Subcultural Studies

Early British deviant subcultural studies tended to follow the lead of the US theories discussed above. The main influences were the work of Miller and Cohen with the work of Cloward and Ohlin appearing to have had little or no application in Britain, well at least at that time.

John Mays (1954) argued that in certain—particularly older urban—areas, the residents share a number of attitudes and ways of behaving that predispose them to criminality. These attitudes have existed for years and are passed on to newcomers. Working-class culture is not intentionally criminal. It is just a different socialisation, which, at times, happens to be contrary to the legal rules. Criminal behaviour—particularly adolescent criminal behaviour—is not therefore a conscious rebellion against middle-class values but arises from an alternative working-class subculture that has been adopted over the years in a haphazard sort of way.

Terence Morris (1957) argued that social deviants are common among the working classes and that it is the actual characteristics of that class that creates the criminality. Forms of antisocial behaviour exist throughout society and in all classes, but the way in which the behaviour is expressed differs. He considered criminal behaviour to be largely a working-class expression. The family controls middle-class socialisation, it is very ordered and almost all activities are centred on the home and the family. In the working classes, in contrast, the socialisation of the child tends to be divided between family, peer group and street acquaintances with the outcome that the latter child is likely to have a less ordered and regulated upbringing. The peer group is a much stronger influence from a much earlier age and they encounter controls only after they commit a crime and when they are processed by the criminal justice system. The whole ethos of the working class, according to Morris, is oriented towards antisocial and criminal, rather than 'conventional', behaviour.

David Downes (1966) conducted a study among young offenders in the East End of London and found that a considerable amount of offending behaviour took place, but this mostly happened in street corner groups, rather than organised gangs. Status frustration did not occur to a significant degree among these young males and their typical response to a lack of success at school or work was one of 'dissociation', a process of opting out rather than reaction formation. The emphasis was on leisure activities—not on school or work—with commercial forms of entertainment the main focus of interest not youth clubs with their middle-class orientation. Access to leisure pursuits was nevertheless restricted by a lack of money and as an alternative means of entertainment youths would take part in offending. Peter Wilmott (1966) also conducted a study of teenagers in the East End of London and reached much the same conclusions as Miller finding that adolescent offending behaviour was simply part of a general lower working-class subculture. Teenagers became involved in petty crime simply for the fun and 'togetherness' of the shared activity experience.

Howard Parker (1974) conducted a survey of unskilled adolescents in an area of Liverpool that official statistics suggested had a high rate of adolescent offending and found that there was a pattern of loosely knit peer groups, not one of tightly structured gangs. Offending behaviour was not a central activity. Young males shared common problems, such as unemployment and leisure opportunities were limited. Some youths had developed a temporary solution in the form of stealing car radios. Furthermore, the community in which the young males lived was one that largely condoned theft, as long as the victims were from outside the area.

Ken Pryce (1979) studied African-Caribbean youngsters in the St Paul's area of Bristol and suggested that the first African-Caribbeans to arrive in the 1950s came to Britain with high aspirations but found on arrival that they were relegated to a force of cheap labour while they and their children were subject to racism and discrimination, which contributed to a pattern of 'endless pressure'. Pryce suggested there were two types of adaptation to this pressure: one was to be stable, conformist and law-abiding while the other was to adopt an expressive, disreputable rebellious attitude. Second and third generation African-Caribbeans were more likely—but not bound—to adopt the second response.

These earlier British deviant subculture studies were important because they drew our attention to specific historical factors, in particular the level of economic activity, and to the importance of a structural class analysis in the explanation of subcultural delinquency (Hopkins Burke and Sunley, 1996, 1998). They also demonstrated that different groups within the working class had identified distinct problems in terms of negative status and had developed their own solutions to their perceived problems. They moreover tended to neglect the involvement of young women in offending behaviour. Thus, where young women are discussed, they tended to be dismissed as 'sex objects' or adjuncts to male offending behaviour, merely 'hangers-on'.

Studies of deviant youth subcultures carried out in the USA since the late 1960s have predominantly focused on issues of violence, ethnicity, poverty and the close links between all three. Wolfgang and Ferracuti (1967) identified 40 years ago a 'sub-culture of violence' where there was an expectation that the receipt of a trivial insult should be met with violence. Failure to respond in this way—and thus walk away from trouble—was greeted with social censure from the peer group. Curtis (1975) adapted this theory to explain violence among American Blacks and found that the maintenance of a manly image was found to be most important in the subculture with individuals unable to resolve conflicts verbally and more likely to resort to violence in order to assert their masculinity. Behaviour is seen to be partly a response to social conditions, and partly the result of an individual's acceptance of the ideas and values that he has absorbed from the subculture of violence. Maxson and

Klein (1990) more recently recognised that certain youth groups, for example, racist 'skinheads' and neo-Nazi organisations, engage in group related violent behaviour for ideological-including political and religious-ends.

Recent research in the USA has proposed that poverty is basically the root cause of gangs and the violence they produce. Miller (1958) had argued that lower-class delinquency was a normal response to sociocultural demands but in his later writings he essentially adopts a 'culture of poverty' view to explain the self-perpetuation of gang life, a view that emphasises the adaptational aspects of the gang to changing socio-economic circumstances (Miller, 1990). However, the most popular current theory to explain criminal behaviour among poor young people in the US inner city is William Julius Wilson's 'underclass theory' where it is suggested that groups in socially isolated neighbourhoods have few legitimate employment opportunities. Inadequate job information networks and poor schools not only lead to weak labour force attachment but also significantly increases the likelihood that people will turn to illegal or deviant activities for income (Wilson, 1991).

Wilson has been accused of failing to address the issues of gang formation and explain the development of specific types of gang problems (Hagedorn, 1992) but a number of other observers assume a close correlation between gangs, gang violence and the development of a socially excluded underclass (Krisberg, 1974; Anderson, 1990; Taylor, 1990). Poverty is central to the underclass thesis and various writers recognise that the absence of economic resources leads to compensatory efforts to achieve some form of economic and successful social adjustment (Williams, 1989; Moore, 1991; Hopkins Burke, 1999a). It is in this context that Spergel (1995: 149) argues that, 'a subculture arises out of efforts of people to solve social, economic, psychological, developmental, and even political problems'.

References

Anderson, E. (1990). *Street Wise*. Chicago, IL: University of Chicago Press.
Aubert, W. (1952). 'White Collar Crime and Social Structure', *American Journal of Sociology*, 58: 263–71.
Bandura, A. (1973). *Aggression: A Social Learning Analysis*. Englewood Cliffs, NJ: Prentice Hall.
Boudon, R. (1980). *The Crisis in Sociology: Problems of Sociological Epistemology*. London: Macmillan.
Box, S. (1983). *Crime, Power and Mystification*. London: Sage.
Braithwaite, J. (1984). *Corporate Crime in the Pharmaceutical Industry*. London: Routledge.
Burgess, E.W. (1928). 'The Growth of the City', in R. Park, E.W. Burgess and R.D. McKenzie (eds) *The City*. Chicago, IL: University of Chicago Press.
Cloward, R.A. and Ohlin, L.E. (1960). *Delinquency and Opportunity: A Theory of Delinquent Gangs*. New York: Free Press.
Cohen, A.K. (1955). *Delinquent Boys: The Culture of the Gang*. New York: Free Press.
Curtis, L.A. (1975). *Violence, Race and Culture*. Lexington, MA: Heath.

Downes, D. (1966). *The Delinquent Solution*. London: Routledge & Kegan Paul.

Durkheim, E. (1933 originally 1893). *The Division of Labour in Society*. Glencoe, IL: Free Press.

Etzioni, A. (1961). *A Comparative Analysis of Complex Organisations*. Glencoe, IL: Free Press.

Faberman, H.A. (1975). 'A Criminogenic Market Structure: The Automobile Industry', *Sociological Quarterly*, 16: 438–57.

Fielding, N. (1988). *Joining Forces*. London: Routledge.

Geis, G. (1967). 'The Heavy Electrical Equipment Anti-trust Cases of 1961', in M.B. Clinard and R. Quinney (eds) *Criminal Behaviour Systems*. New York: Holt, Rinehart & Winston.

Geis, G. (1968). *White-collar Crime: The Offender in Business and the Professions*. New York: Atherton.

Gross, E. (1978). 'Organisations as Criminal Actors', in J. Braithwaite and P. Wilson (eds) *Two Faces of Deviance: Crimes of the Powerless and the Powerful*. Brisbane: University of Queensland Press.

Hagedorn, J. (1992). 'Gangs, Neighbourhoods, and Public Policy', *Social Problems*, 38(4): 529–42.

Heywood, A. (1992). *Political Ideologies*. London: McMillan Press.

Holdaway, S. (1983). *Inside the British Police: A Force at Work*. Oxford: Blackwell.

Hopkins Burke, R.D. (1998b) 'The Contextualisation of Zero Tolerance Policing Strategies', in R.D. Hopkins Burke (ed.) *Zero Tolerance Policing*. Leicester: Perpetuity Press.

Hopkins Burke, R.D. (1999a) *Youth Justice and the Fragmentation of Modernity*. Scarman Centre for the Study of Public Order Occasional Paper Series, The University of Leicester.

Hopkins Burke, R.D. (1999b) 'The Socio-Political Context of Zero Tolerance Policing Strategies', *Policing: An International Journal of Police Strategies & Management,* 21(4): 666–82.

Hopkins Burke, R.D. (2004b) 'Policing Contemporary Society' in R.D. Hopkins Burke, *'Hard Cop/Soft Cop': Dilemmas and Debates in Contemporary Policing*. Cullompton: Willan Publishing.

Hopkins Burke, R.D. and Pollock, E. (2004). 'A Tale of Two Anomies: Some Observations on the Contribution of (Sociological) Criminological Theory to Explaining Hate Crime Motivation', *Internet Journal of Criminology*.

Hopkins Burke, R.D. and Sunley, R. (1996).. *'Hanging Out' in the 1990s: Young People and the Postmodern Condition,* Occasional Paper 11, COP Series. Scarman Centre for the Study of Public Order, University of Leicester.

Hopkins Burke, R.D. and Sunley R. (1998). 'Youth Subcultures in Contemporary Britain', in K. Hazelhurst and C. Hazlehurst (eds) *Gangs and Youth Subcultures: International Explorations*. New Brunswick, NJ: Transaction Press.

Jacobs, J. (1961). *The Death and Life of Great American Cities*. New York: Vintage.

Kitsuse, J.I. and Dietrick, D.C. (1959). 'Delinquent Boys: A Critique', *American Sociological Review,* 24: 208–15.

Krisberg, B. (1974). 'Gang Youth and Hustling: The Psychology of Survival', *Issues in Criminology*, 9: 115–31.

Lemert, E. (1972). *Human Deviance, Social Problems and Social Control, 2nd edition*. Englewood Cliffs, NJ: Prentice-Hall.

Leonard, E. (1983). *Women, Crime and Society*. London: Longmans.

Levin, J. and McDevitt, J. (1993). *Hate Crimes: The Rising Tide of Bigotry and Bloodshed*. Boston, MA: Plenum.

Lilly, J.R., Cullen, F.T. and Ball, R.A. (1986). *Criminological Theory: Context and Consequences*. London: Sage.

Matza, D.M. (1964). *Delinquency and Drift*. New York: Wiley.

Maxson, C.L. and Klein, M.W. (1990). 'Street Gang Violence: Twice as Great or Half as Great?' in C.R. Huff (ed.) *Gangs in America*. Newbury Park, CA: Sage.

Mays, J.B. (1954). *Growing Up in the City: A Study of Juvenile Delinquency in an Urban Neighbourhood*. Liverpool: Liverpool University Press.

Merton, R.K. (1938). 'Social Structure and Anomie', *American Sociological Review*, 3: 672–82.

Messner, S. and Rosenfeld, R. (1994). *Crime and the American Dream*. Belmont, CA: Wadsworth.

Miller, W.B. (1958). 'Lower Class Culture as a Generalising Milieu of Gang Delinquency', *Journal of Social Issues*, 14: 5–19.

Miller, W.B. (1990). 'When the United States Has Failed to Solve its Youth Gang Problem', in C.R. Huff (ed.) *Gangs in America*. Newbury Park, CA: Sage.

Moore, J.W. (1991). *Going Down to the Barrio*. Philadelphia, PA: Temple University Press.

Morris, T.P. (1957). *The Criminal Area: A Study in Social Ecology*. London: Routledge & Kegan Paul.

Park, R.E. (1921). *Introduction to the Study of Sociology*. Chicago, IL: University of Chicago Press.

Parker, H. (1974). *View From the Boys*. Newton Abbot: David and Charles.

Parsons, T. (1937). *The Structure of Social Action*. New York: McGraw-Hill.

Perry, B (2001). *In the Name of Hate*. London: Routledge.

Pryce, K. (1979). *Endless Pressure: A Study of West Indian Life-styles in Bristol*. Harmondsworth: Penguin.

Reiner, R. (2000). 'Crime and Control in Britain', *Sociology*, 34(1): 71–94.

Schlossman, S., Zellman, G. and Shavelson, R. (1984). *Delinquency Prevention in South Chicago: A Fifty-Year Assessment of the Chicago Area Project*. Santa Monica, CA: Rand.

Shaw, C.R. (1930). *The Jack-Roller: A Delinquent Boy's Own Story*. Chicago, IL: University of Chicago Press.

Shaw, C.R. (1931). *The Natural History of a Delinquent Career*. Chicago, IL: University of Chicago Press.

Shaw, C.R. (1938). *Brothers in Crime*. Chicago, IL: University of Chicago Press.

Shaw, C.R. and McKay, H.D. (1972 originally 1931) *Juvenile Delinquency and Urban Areas*. Chicago, IL: University of Chicago Press.

Sibbitt, R (1999). *The Perpetrators of Racial Harassment and Racial Violence*, Home Office Research Study 176. London: Home Office.

Smith, A. (1910). *The Wealth of Nations*. London: Dent.

Smith, D. and Gray, J. (1986). *Police and People in London*. London: Policy Studies Institute.

Spergel, I.A. (1964). *Racketsville, Slumtown, Haulburg*. Chicago, IL: University of Chicago Press.

Spergel, I.A. (1995). *The Youth Gang Problem: A Community Approach*. Oxford: Oxford University Press.

Staw, B.M. and Szwajkowski, E. (1975). 'The Scarcity-Munificence Component of Organizational Environments and the Commission of Illegal Acts', *Administrative Science Quarterly*, 20: 345–54.

Swartz, J. (1975). 'Silent Killers at Work', *Crime and Social Justice*, 3: 15–20.

Taylor, C.S. (1990). *Dangerous Society*. East Lansing, MI: Michigan State University Press.

Taylor, I., Walton, P. and Young, J. (1973). *The New Criminology: For a Social Theory of Deviance*. London: Routledge & Kegan Paul.

Thrasher, F. (1947). *The Gang*. Chicago, IL: University of Chicago Press.

Williams, T. (1989). *The Cocaine Kids: The Inside Story of a Teenage Drug Ring*. Reading, MA: Addison-Wesley Publishing Co.

Wilmott, P. (1966). *Adolescent Boys in East London*. London: Routledge & Kegan Paul.

Wilson, W.J. (1991). 'Public Policy Research and the Truly Disadvantaged', in C. Jencks and P.E. Peterson (eds) *The Urban Underclass*. Washington, DC: The Brookings Institution.

Wolfgang, M.E. and Ferracuti, F. (1967). *The Sub-culture of Violence: Towards an Integrated Theory in Criminology*. Beverly Hills, CA: Sage.

Yablonsky, L. (1962). *The Violent Gang*. New York: Macmillan.

Young, M. (1991). *An Inside Job: Policing and Police Culture in Britain*. Oxford: Oxford University Press.

Young, M. (1993). *In the Sticks*. Oxford: Oxford University Press.

READING 6

Capitalism as a Criminogenic Society
Conflict and Radical Theories of Crime

Mark M. Lanier, Stuart Henry, and Desiré Anastasia

"For the powerful, crimes are those that others commit."

—Noam Chomsky, *Imperial Ambitions:
Conversations on the Post-9/11 World*

In the last four years Earl Sampson, 28, has been questioned by police 258 times, searched more than 100 times, jailed 56 times, and arrested for trespassing 62 times. The majority of these citations occurred at his place of work, a Miami Gardens convenience store where the owner says police are racially profiling" (*New York Daily News*, 2013).

> Strongly identified with violent criminality by skin color alone, the anonymous young black male in public is often viewed first and foremost with fear and suspicion, his counterclaims to propriety, decency, and law-abidingness notwithstanding. Others typically don't want to know him, and in public seek distance from him and those who resemble him. ... Because the young black male is essentially disenfranchised and considered a troublemaker, or at best a person of no account, his is a provisional status. Every black male is eligible for skeptical scrutiny, which renders him vulnerable to harassment for any infraction, real or imagined. His credibility is always shaky. The constant confusion between the street-oriented and the law-abiding black male means that all are subject to suspicion in white eyes, and such public reception then encourages many

---

Mark M. Lanier, Stuart Henry, and Desiré Anastasia, Selections from "Capitalism as a Criminogenic Society: Conflct and Radical Theories of Crime," *Essential Criminology*, pp. 243-266, 269, 270, 341-396. Copyright © 2014 by Taylor & Francis Group. Reprinted with permission.

blacks not to trust whites. Thus, both blacks and whites assign provisional status to the other, deepening the racial divide. (E. Anderson 2008, 3, 21)

Racial profiling is at the forefront of serious examination of police practices (Barkley 2006). Racial profiling has been defined as the use of racial or ethnic stereotypes in the decision to take a law-enforcement action, and even can include cases where race is one of the factors in that decision process (Ramirez, McDevitt, Farrell 2010). Traditionally, profiling has been a frowned-upon, ignored, denied, and vilified practice. This is particularly true of the racial profiling of African Americans while driving. Many people of color still feel victimized by this practice and have coined the term DWB, Driving While Black (Meehan and Ponder 2002, 400; Anderson and Callahan 2001). "Blacks and white liberals have been decrying the situation for several years. Many conservatives, on the other hand, dismiss such complaints as the exaggerations of hypersensitive minorities. Or they say that if traffic cops do in fact pull over and search the vehicles of African Americans disproportionately, then such 'racial profiling' is an unfortunate but necessary component of modern crime fighting" (Anderson and Callahan 2001).

Clearly, racial profiling is nothing new in America. It began to receive attention following the Civil War when African Americans were the target of increased police attention. This is not just a perception. As Michael Smith and Matthew Petrocelli noted, "Historically, minorities, particularly African Americans, have had physical force used against them or have been arrested or stopped by police at rates exceeding their percentage in the population" (2001, 5). Recent research also shows that while African Americans and Hispanics are stopped about the same amount as others, African American and Hispanic drivers are more than twice as likely to be searched and are issued more tickets than whites (E. Robinson 2007; Dixon, Schell, Giles, and Drogos 2008). The practice that flourished with the profiles of drug couriers in the 1980s and 1990s has now shifted toward those suspected of terrorist threats (John Jay College of Criminal Justice 2001).

Although African Americans make up less that 13 percent of the total US population, they are arrested for nearly a third of all crimes. Hispanics are stopped by police even more often than African Americans (M. Smith and Petrocelli 2001; "Our Opinion" 2009). Law enforcement officials often counter, "Well, they commit more crime!" In fact, "many law enforcement officers view racial profiling as an appropriate form of law enforcement" (Barlow and Barlow 2002, 337). The issue is not so clear-cut, however. Social standing may also play a role. Meehan and Ponder noted that "disparate treatment by the police may not be the product of race alone—the racial and class composition of a neighborhood influences police behavior" (2002, 400).

The crimes and laws resulting from the conflict between different racial and ethnic groups in a society, and the political and legal struggle surrounding how this is played out, are not easily explained by the theories that we have examined so far (with the exception of social constructionist and labeling theories). Radical and conflict theorists, however, provide a theoretical explanation for this and other similar collective struggles, as we illustrate in this chapter and as Engel, Calnon, and Bernard (2002) noted. Radical and conflict theorists are centrally concerned with social inequity, with class differences, and with the power used by the ruling class to define what counts as crime and what does not (Schwendinger and Schwendinger 2001).

Conflict and radical theorists consider how social structure and the agencies of government, referred to as "the State," impact human behavior. As well as conflict over race, ethnicity, and gender issues, conflict and radical theorists are also very interested in crimes involving economic power, including corporate and government crimes, because they bring out features of the structural causes that are not immediately apparent when criminologists look at conventional street crime. Conflict and radical theorists suggest that crime is not simply an individual but also a societal phenomenon. They argue that law, crime, and law enforcement are often political acts rooted in the conflict between groups or classes in society and see the source of crime in the conflict that stems from the inequalities produced by capitalist society (Schwendinger and Schwendinger 2001; Turk 2006).

Although some theorists use the terms *conflict* and *radical* interchangeably, others (ourselves included) make a clear distinction. There is no one "radical" or "conflict" view of crime, and "no firm consensus or precise definition of radical criminology, either with respect to its key concepts or its primary theoretical emphasis" (Lynch and Groves 1986, 4). But it is useful to differentiate between conflict and radical theories based on their different conceptions of inequality (Vold, Bernard, and Snipes [1998] 2001; Bernard, Snipes and Gerould 2009; Einstadter and Henry 2006).

In general, conflict criminologists draw their analysis from the ideas of the nineteenth-century German sociologists Max Weber and Georg Simmel: "Conflict theorists emphasize that the needs and interests of different people and different groups are often incompatible and contradictory, especially with regard to the distribution of scarce material or financial resources" (D. Johnson 2008, 367). Conflict theorists see inequality based on differences in wealth, status, ideas, religious beliefs, and so forth. These differences result in the formation of interest groups that struggle with each other for power. Radical criminologists, who instead draw on the ideas of the German social theorist Karl Marx, believe that the fundamental conflict is economic. This conflict is between capitalists, or propertied classes (the bourgeois), who own the "means of production" (i.e., wealth and the capital used to make it), and wage earners, or nonpropertied classes, who own only their labor, which they sell to make a living. The result is a class-divided society, with those in the lower classes being exploited by those in the upper classes. Radical theorists argue that the conflict over economic inequality is at the root of all of the conflicts that the conflict theorists identify.

Not only does capitalist society generate vast inequalities of wealth, but those who own the wealth, who head large corporations, and financial and commercial institutions, influence the decisions of those who hold political power. Both conflict and radical theorists reject the restricted legal definitions of crime because they take power for granted. Indeed, "the role of power in the definition of crime is the central focus of conflict criminology" (Vold and Bernard 1986, 267).

Moreover, "In discussions of legalism/illegalism the state and its corporate backers set the terms of debate. Against statist definitions of ill/legality radical criminologists must assert the needs of people and their environments (including natural environments and their non-human occupants)" (Shantz 2012).

In the first half of this chapter, we look briefly at the roots of conflict theory in the sociology of Max Weber and Georg Simmel and the resulting "conservative" view of conflict theory found in Ralf Dahrendorf (1959). Then we discuss its criminological application through the ideas of George Vold ([1958] 1979), who explored group conflict; Austin Turk (1964, 1966, 1969), who questioned authority and subject roles and their relationship to legal norms; and the early ideas of Richard Quinney (1970), who analyzed societal constructions of crime by powerful segments of society.

In the second half of the chapter we explore the ideas of radical theorists, beginning with Marx and Engels, and the first application of radical theory to crime by Dutch criminologist Willem Bonger. Among contemporary radical theorists, we look at the ideas of William Chambliss (1975, 1988), the later works of Richard Quinney (1974, 1977), and the radical criminology of Ian Taylor, Paul Walton, and Jock Young (1973, 1975). Before we focus on these particular theorists, however, let us see what ideas conflict and radical theorists contribute to our understanding of crime.

Common Themes and Assumptions and Some Key Differences

Conflict and radical theorists share a view that humans are active, creative agents who invest their energy to build the social structure. Conflict theorists see individuals cooperating with like-minded others to form groups, which then compete in the struggle over resources, ideas, ideologies, and beliefs. There are also similarities between conflict and radical theories over the cause of crime. Each views crime as being the result of the way society is organized. Furthermore, both conflict and radical views share a macrolevel perspective. Thus, each looks to structural causes of crime in the conflict within society; most crime is seen as the result of large forces (e.g., economic, form of government, and so forth) and not individual pathologies.

Conflict and radical perspectives also share a concern with the possession of power and closely examine law creation, and how laws are interpreted and enforced. Consistent with their ideas about society, however, conflict theorists see law as a social-control mechanism, a resource and weapon in the struggle for power intended to help those who capture it to maintain or increase that power (Turk 1969). Conflict theorists recognize that law has a symbolic role, publicly representing the social standing of the ideas of those in power (Gusfield 1963). They argue that groups who have power over others (whether it is economic, social, ideological, moral, or religious) typically define which behaviors are criminal and which are not. Thus, laws reflect the values and interest of the dominant group(s). As a result, laws mainly criminalize crimes of the powerless, leaving harms caused by the powerful (such as corporations and government) as lesser administrative or regulative offenses. Similarly, the powerful organize the system of criminal justice to benefit those with money (Barkley 2006). Any sanctions given to powerful offenders are typically civil or restitutive in nature. Consequently, although severe prison sentences are given on rare occasions to the powerful who commit exceptional crimes, and corporations are sometimes given large fines, the majority of such offenders receive relatively little punishment. Economic differences are also only one point of concern. Radical and conflict theorists agree that there are other types of limited resources, both material and social.

Despite these important similarities, there are some important differences. Conflict theorists view human nature as amoral rather than good or bad. Radicals view human nature in a more positive light: people are born with a "perfectible" nature, but forces serve to shape them in imperfect, deviant, and criminal ways. If humans behave badly, therefore, it is not their doing alone but how their nature is shaped by the social structure. Humankind is assumed to be basically good, and the structure of society is what creates or causes evil people. Marx thus believed human nature is "perfectible," but perfection requires a society that celebrates social and communal connections over individuality. Radical theorists also see humans as social beings who use their energies to transform the world. They are thus purposeful. In the course of transforming the world, they are themselves shaped and formed. As Marx insightfully observed, "Humans are both the producers and products of history" (J. Young 1981, 295; Marx [1859] 1975). Marx also believed people are shaped more by their society's economic organization than by their own individuality.

Although both versions see the idea of consensus as a myth, their ideas about the nature of conflict differ. Conflict theorists recognize that society is composed of many different groups that have differing, and often competing, interests, values, and norms. Since there are also limited resources (both material and social) available in any given society, competition between these different groups for resources inevitably results in conflict—don't you compete with the other students for used textbooks until those are gone and then those who lose have to buy their books new at full price? In California, students have to compete with each other to get into classes; those who don't succeed have then to compete with other students to get an override, known as "crashing," and once the room is at capacity, those who don't get in have to wait until another semester to take the class. This sets up a conflict between students with "priority registration" and those who register late. As a result, some students will resort to a variety of competitive resource manipulations, such as registering for more classes than they are actually going to take (hoarding) or kissing up to an instructor to outcompete their fellow students.

Although more conservative conflict theorists (Simmel [1908] 1955; Coser 1956; Dahrendorf 1959) believe the competition among interest groups produces a balance and compromise that can actually prove functional to society, others believe that some groups emerge as dominant and that such domination can be destructive (Vold [1958] 1979). In particular, those who control the resources and those who have authority positions also have power in society (Turk 1966, 1969). This is because over time humans in subordinate positions learn to follow those who dominate them.

Based on Marx's analysis, radical theorists offer a more dichotomous view of the source of conflict and see this rooted in economic inequalities: those who own and control the "means of production" (capitalists) are in conflict with and control the lives of those who do not, the labor providers (workers). The radical analysis, therefore, is primarily focused on economic structure and class stratification (I. Taylor, Walton, and Young 1973; Quinney 1974), with all other conflicts being an outcome of the basic economic struggle between the capitalist and working classes. Radical theorists believe either that the law represents the machinery of capitalist repression, directly controlling those who challenge the economically powerful (instrumentalists) (Quinney 1975b, 1977), or that the law is an ideological device that mystifies, or renders opaque, the power of the dominant classes by pretending to be neutral in its protection of individuals, regardless of their power (structuralists) (J. Young 1981). Radical criminologists define crime much more broadly than do legal definitions to include all acts that create harm, including those that violate human rights. Consequently, crimes of domination such as "imperialism, racism, capitalism, sexism and other systems of exploitation" are defined as criminal by those sharing a radical perspective (Platt 1974, 6; Schwendinger and Schwendinger 1970, 2001; Quinney and Wildeman 1991).

There are also other differences. Methodologically, "radical criminologists are more specific than conflict theorists in their identification of the explanatory variables that presumably account for crime" (Bohm 1982, 566). Radicals look to the political and economic structure of society, whereas conflict theorists consider stratification as the culprit. Radicals see the capitalist structure as forcing humans into competitive hostility with one another rather than helping people to be cooperative partners. Crime is the outcome of this competition and an expression of the anguish that exploitation imposes on the powerless (Engels [1845] 1958; Bonger [1905] 1916). As a result, some crime is also an expression of political protest at the capitalist system (I. Taylor, Walton, and Young 1973).

The Roots of Conflict Criminology

Social conflict is present in all societies and occurs at all levels, from individuals to groups. It has been defined as "a struggle over values or claims to status, power, and scarce resources, in which the aims of the conflicting parties are not only to gain the desired values but also to neutralize, injure, or eliminate their rivals" (Coser 1968, 232). We discussed Sellin's ideas of culture conflict (1938) and will not reiterate these, except to say that culture conflict is an integral part of conflict theory's intellectual roots. Here, we are concerned with the ideas of those who look at crime as resulting from structural rather than cultural differences, although the two are clearly interrelated, as we have just seen. Early ideas about broad notions of structural conflict can be found in the work of Max Weber.

Weber's Class, Status, and Party

Max Weber (1864–1920), a German lawyer and sociologist, is considered one of the three founders of sociology and a major contributor to the understanding of the sources of conflict. At age thirty-four, he suffered acute depression and did not recover to resume his academic writing until he was thirty-nine, when he made major contributions. Weber did not present a theory of crime causation, but he did lay the basis for others to do so by explicating sources of conflict.

Weber's discussion of conflict emerges in his analysis of the role played by charismatic leaders in the transition from traditional society to modern capitalist society ([1922] 1966). Weber identified three important dimensions of inequality: (1) power, represented by party; (2) wealth, which relates to economic position, represented by class; and (3) prestige, which is attached to those in high-status groups. Conflict, according to Weber, is most likely to occur when these three major kinds of stratification coincide—when those who have wealth also have status and power. Conflict is also likely when only a few are allowed access to the privileged positions or when social mobility to these positions is highly restricted. Such a merger produces tensions and resentment among those without power, prestige, and wealth who engage in conflict with the privileged group. Those excluded also become receptive to charismatic leaders who organize conflict groups to challenge traditional authority (Turner 1986, 146–149).

Simmel's Functions of Group Conflict

Like his friend Max Weber, Georg Simmel (1858–1918) was a German sociologist, but he was far more optimistic about the nature of modern society and the role of conflict. For most of his life, he taught at the University of Berlin, becoming a professor only four years before his death. Simmel was one of the first sociologists to explain conflict as a common and stable form of interaction. Conflict to Simmel was one of several patterns of reciprocal relations, along with competition and cooperation, that underpin complex social behavior. Indeed, for him "conflict and competition are often interwoven in subtle and complex ways with processes of cooperation and social integration" (D. Johnson 2008, 367). Unlike Weber, Simmel looked at the interrelationships between individual meanings attributed to social action and the transpersonal meanings that people construct. His major contribution to conflict theory was a short but influential essay in which he argued that conflict is both inevitable and functional in its ability to resolve contradictions and leads to a unity of the systemic whole ([1908] 1955). Simmel believed that biological differences are natural, and he believed they are exacerbated by differences of interest but could also be placated by harmonious relations. He believed that conflict is a variable phenomenon and that some levels of less violent conflict serve a functional "tension-reducing" process that "promoted the solidarity, integration and orderly change of systems" (Turner 1986, 140). Simmel saw violent conflict occurring where different groups have a high degree of harmony, emotional involvement, and solidarity among their members and where the nature of conflict is beyond the members' individual interests.

Dahrendorf's Dialectical Conflict Perspective

Ralf Dahrendorf (1929–2009), a sociologist who taught at the University of Hamburg and Stanford University and later became director of the London School of Economics, went into politics when he was appointed as a life peer in the British House of Lords. In a critique of functionalism, which he saw as utopian and unrealistic, Dahrendorf (1959) presented a "pluralistic" version of conflict in which he showed two faces of society, both consensus and conflict, existing in a dialectical relationship. This was based on Hegel's notion that a society produces contradictions (seen here as conflicts between opposing forces) whose resolution results in a new organization different from its original (seen here as consensus) (Balkan, Berger, and Schmidt 1980, 336).

By examining conflict between economic interest groups and a variety of groups that compete for authority, Dahrendorf incorporated Weberian ideas, although some say as a result he ultimately reproduced a conservative-consensus perspective (I. Taylor, Walton, and Young 1973, 238; Turner 1986). Dahrendorf described groups as having an organization of social roles whereby some people exercise power over others whom they can coerce to conform. Thus, people exist in relations of domination and subordination. But these relations of domination and subjugation need not mean people are totally dominated; they may hold different positions in different groups or organizations: "Since domination in industry does not necessarily involve domination in the State or a church, or other associations, total societies can present a picture of a plurality of dominant (and conversely, subjected) aggregates" (1959, 171). Dahrendorf argued that such power relationships become accepted by members as legitimate authority (1958, 1959). Simultaneously, power and authority are seen as resources to be won and over which subgroups within the organization fight. Those who acquire power coerce groups without power to conform. This creates two basic types of social groups, each contesting authority: the rulers and the ruled, the former trying to preserve their power, the latter trying to redistribute it. Should those who are dominated take control, the whole cycle repeats, resulting in further polarization around new interests, followed by further conflict and resolution (Dahrendorf's dialectical process of social change). Thus, conflict is continually coming and going as conflicting groups first win control and then stabilize before again reverting into conflictual relations.

For Dahrendorf, conflict is not a matter of a particular underlying inequality of economic interests but can be based on any kind of difference. For him, the existence of inequality is inevitable because humans evaluate each other as different rather than equal. Therefore, some will always be dominant over others in terms of a rank-ordered social status. Inequality, then, is a function of organizational processes that produce legitimate authority roles of domination and subordination. Like some other founding conflict theorists, Dahrendorf did not specifically address crime, but his ideas greatly influenced later conflict criminologists, particularly Austin Turk, as we shall see later.

Vold's Group Conflict Theory

George Vold (1896–1967) was one of the first criminologists to systematically apply the conflict ideas presented by Weber, Simmel, and Dahrendorf to the study of crime. Vold, who taught at the University of Minnesota and was a contemporary of Dahrendorf, published his highly respected *Theoretical Criminology* in 1958. Later editions of this book are still much in use today, and the work has become a standard text on criminological theory ([1958] 1979; Vold and Bernard 1986; Vold, Bernard, and Snipes 2001, Bernard, Snipes, and Gerould, 2009). Vold was especially influenced by the work of Simmel. He presented a view of certain crimes being caused by conflict and argued that it was absurd to explain these acts using individual-level theories. He pointed out that humans are group-involved beings and that society is a continuity of group interaction "of moves and countermoves, of checks and cross-checks" ([1958] 1979, 283). Society exists in a state of equilibrium and relative stability, not because of consensus among all its members but because of "the adjustment, one to another of the many groups of varying strengths and of different interests" (ibid., 284). However, Vold argued that groups come into conflict because of overlapping interests and encroachments over territory that lead to competition. Group members must protect against the danger of being taken over or replaced. Members of groups are invested in defensive activity, which they express through acts of identification, loyalty, and self-sacrifice, each intensified by conflict. In the conflict between groups, the weak are generally overwhelmed and absorbed, whereas the strong may either increase their power, be vanquished, or meet with compromise.

Applying these ideas to crime, Vold argued that in the conflict between groups, each seeks the support of the State to defend its rights and protect its interests, with the result that "the whole political process of law making, law breaking, and law enforcement directly reflects deep-seated and fundamental conflicts between interest groups and their more general struggles for the control of the police power of the state" (ibid., 288). Those who win dominate the policies that define crime. With regard to crime, Vold noted a prevalence of group involvement, from organized crime to delinquent gangs, each fighting for turf, markets, and social honor in ways that are in conflict with those of organized society. In a study of deviant driving behavior in South Africa, Khoza and Potgieter (2005) used Vold's theory to explain how the conflict of group interests is reflected in criminal traffic law.

The group also provides definitions of its members' behavior as acceptable, even honorable. Vold described how much criminal activity is a product of the clash of interests between groups and their members' attempts to defend against challenges to their control. Obvious examples are violence as a result of disrespect or turf infringements by members of different gangs, violence between rival organized drug-distribution networks, and violence protesting dominant systems of justice. Vold concluded, "There are many situations in which criminality is the normal, natural response of normal, natural human beings struggling in understandably normal situations for the maintenance of the way of life to which they stand committed" ([1958] 1979, 296).

Contemporary Conflict Criminology

Since Dahrendorf and Vold, others have sought to develop and extend the ideas of these founding conflict theorists to crime and the law (Box [1971] 1981; Hills 1971; Chambliss and Seidman [1971] 1982; Krisberg 1975; Pepinsky 1976; Reiman [1979] 1995; Schwendinger and Schwendinger 2001). Here, we focus on two illustrative contributors: Austin Turk (1969), whose ideas closely follow those of Dahrendorf, and Richard Quinney (1970), whose theory was more derived from Vold's approach.

Turk and the Criminalization of Resisting Subordinates

Austin Turk's major contribution to conflict criminology, *Criminality and the Legal Order* (1969), was deeply indebted to Dahrendorf's dialectical conflict theory of society. Turk (1966, 1969) attempted to show how people in subordinate positions of authority are subject to the values, standards, and laws of those in authority positions. Unless the subordinates learn to be deferential to authority, their behaviors will be defined as criminal and they will be given the status of criminals. Turk argued that people continually learn to interact with each other as holders of superior or inferior social status. The learning is never complete or stabilized but is in constant adjustment and conflict because of individual differences. Turk defined the norms learned in this process as "norms of domination" and "norms of deference." People who learn norms of domination believe they are superior to others and destined to command them. In Turk's view, the extent to which a person relates to norms of domination is related to sociocultural factors such as age, race, and gender. Most people, however, learn norms of deference, meaning that they see themselves as inferior, destined to obey others, and subject to their authority: "Criminality is a label imposed on subjects who resist the claims and impositions of authorities" (2006, 186). "Norm resisters" are found to be those relatively unsophisticated in the "knowledge of patterns in the behavior of others which is used in attempts to manipulate them" (1966, 348). In short, for Turk, crimes are the acts of those who have not been "conditioned to accept as a fact of life that authorities must be reckoned with," and it is such conditioning that underlies social order in all societies (1969, 44).

Turk went on to identify the conditions that make conflict between authorities and subjects over different norms and values more likely: (1) when cultural values and social actions of authorities are in close agreement and a similar congruence exists in the case of subjects, (2) when authorities and subjects are organized, and (3) when authorities or subjects are less sophisticated. He then described the conditions under which conflict will lead to subjects' being criminalized. Again three major factors are involved: (1) when law enforcers (police) and the courts (prosecutors and judges) agree on the serious nature of the offenses and are committed to enforcing the law, (2) when there is a large power differential between enforcers and resisters, and (3) the realism or lack of realism of each party's actions in relation to their chances of success, which for resisters is avoiding criminalization and for enforcers is imposing norms and stopping resistance (2006, 186). Turk suggested that over time the authority-subject relationship becomes less coercive and more automatic, as new generations of people are born into the existing set of laws, rules, and definitions of reality, which they are less likely to contest. Schwendinger and Schwendinger's (2001) analysis of student protest and the government's response is an excellent illustration of Turk's conflict-type analysis.

In his later work, Turk (1976, 1982) examined how legal orders generate or aggravate or alternatively resolve conflicts. Here he defines *law* as a form of power that is mobilized in five ways and combinations to shape legal institutions and processes, often fostering rather than preventing conflicts: "(1) violence (i.e., police or military power); (2) production, allocation, and use of material resources (i.e., economic power); (3) decision-making processes (i.e., political power); (4) definitions of and access to knowledge, beliefs, and values (i.e., ideological power); and (5) human attention and living time (i.e. diversionary power)." He continued: "Gaining law power becomes itself a goal of conflict insofar as the law facilitates defending or advancing the interests or values of some parties against those of others. ... Law may preclude or hinder the informal resolution of disputes by explicitly pitting contending parties against one another, legitimating inequalities, and producing symbolic rather than acceptable decisions on issues in dispute. In sum, law is, at best, a mixed blessing in its impact on the formation and sustenance of social order" (2006, 187). Unlike many conflict and radical criminologists who want revolutionary change to solve these problems, as we show in the policy section below, Turk believed that "conflict criminology's postulates imply the radical transformation of our current system through specific policy initiatives" (ibid., 188).

Importantly, in his recent work, Turk (2003, 2004) develops his analysis in relation to global political issues, not least to global political conflict and terrorism. He uses a model to explain the escalation and de-escalation of political violence that has a remarkable application to conflicts in the Middle East, Northern Ireland, and elsewhere. He sees these political conflicts escalating and de-escalating through three stages: (1) *coercive violence*, using coercion to try to send a persuasive message to those they oppose—where authorities through law enforcers suspend civil liberties, while norm resisters vandalize symbols of authority through riots and property destruction; (2) *injurious violence*, designed to punish the failure to learn from the messages and comply with the coercive violence—which can involve extreme torture and other physical brutality; and (3) *destructive violence*, intended to exterminate opponents—which for authorities is military search-and-destroy operations and for norm resisters involves terrorist attacks. As he says, "In the final analysis, my position is that criminology necessarily becomes embedded in political sociology as we deal with the increasingly murky distinctions between legal and illegal, crime and not-crime, authority and power" (2006, 189).

Quinney's Social Reality of Crime

As a contemporary of Austin Turk's, Richard Quinney has become one of the most prolific critical theorists in criminology. His contribution to conflict sociology came with his 1970 book, *The Social Reality of Crime*. Drawing on several of the conflict traditions discussed previously, particularly Simmel's and Vold's work, Quinney saw humans as rational, purposeful actors subject to an unequal distribution of power that produces inevitable conflict. This conflict is between competing groups or "segments" of society, whose members' actions are designed to maintain or advance their position (1970, 8–14).

Segments of society share norms, values, and ideology, but unlike Vold's interest groups, they need not be organized (Vold [1958] 1979, 302). Those who have the power to shape public policy act through authorized agents in society (such as legislators and judges) to formulate definitions of crime that contain, or control, the behaviors of members of those segments with whom they are in conflict. Recall the discussion of racial profiling. The conflict need not be organized political struggle but can consist of individual acts of resistance by members of powerless segments. Criminalization is done with a view to maintain the current balance of power or increase a segment's position of control.

Definitions of crime are not merely legislated but become part of the public psyche and popular culture as a result of their dissemination through the mass media. In other words, some rather than other meanings of a crime have "social reality" because they are defined, illustrated, elaborated, and sensationalized in the media. Quinney further argued that criminal definitions are then applied by the authorized agents (police, judges) of those segments of society having power. This is done in relation to the degree of threat that the powerful perceive from the powerless and in proportion to the degree of visibility of their crime(s). Thus, crimes most visible and most threatening to the powerful are those most subject to criminal processing. In response, those who are relatively powerless develop patterns of behavior in relation to the definitions imposed on them (Quinney 1970, 15–23). From this, Quinney concluded that the social reality of crime in a politically organized society is a political act designed to protect and perpetuate a particular set of interests over others. In support of Quinney's theory, Olaussen (2004) stated that crime is the result of societal agreements on moral behavior that are institutionalized and thus empower certain people.

The Roots of Radical Theory: Marx's Analysis of Capitalist Society

German Jewish philosopher, sociologist, and historian Karl Marx (1818–1883) is one of the most influential social thinkers of all times. Entire governments and social systems have been developed from his ideas and Marxist theory has also been one of the major frameworks of study in all the social sciences. It is therefore surprising for students to learn that Marx wrote very little about crime! What Marx and his colleague, cotton mill owner Friedrich Engels (1820–1895), did write about was the economic class conflict that exists in capitalist societies that they believed would ultimately result in those societies' downfall. Their analysis was based on the concept of *historical materialism*, which is a method of study and explanation for understanding how past empirical events shape future social systems. Unlike the German philosophical idealist Georg Hegel (1770–1831) (who believed humans created the world from their own thoughts and ideas), Marx and Engels adopted the opposite, materialist view that human consciousness was created by the concrete conditions of productive work (labor). But Marx's notion of materialism was not the traditional one that saw humans laboring as isolated individuals but a new "historical" materialism that recognized the social relations of productive activity in different historical eras (Carver 1987, 105). Thus, in one of Marx's most frequently quoted passages, he argued:

> In the social production of their existence, [humans] inevitably enter into definite relations, which are independent of their will, namely relations of production appropriate to a given stage of development of their material forces of production. The totality of these relations of production constitutes the economic structure of society, the real foundation, on which arises a legal and political superstructure and to which correspond definite forms of social consciousness. The mode of production of material life conditions the general character of the social, political, and intellectual life. It is not the consciousness of [humans] that determines their existence, but their social existence that determines their consciousness. At a certain stage of development, the material productive forces of society come into conflict with the existing relations of production. Then begins an era of social revolution. (Marx [1859] 1975, 425–426)

Marx believed that different historical periods typically have a dominant or characteristic mode of production (e.g., slavery, feudalism, capitalism, socialism). This is a particular combination of the forces or means of production (e.g., technology, resources, tools, energy, knowledge, skills) and the relations of production that compromise "the network of social roles encompassing the use and ownership of productive forces and of the products that emerge" (e.g., employer, worker, investor, dependent) (Carver 1987, 109). Curran and Renzetti helpfully translate this nineteenth-century terminology: people "make a living" through a productive process that we call the economy. Economies can be of different types in different periods of history depending on the resources, technology, and environment in which they operate and the relationships they enter into in order to do productive work. We are now shifting from a service-based economy to an information-based economy, just as we went from an agricultural to an industrial or manufacturing one, and this latest shift has been termed by some as the "postmodern era," which we look at in more detail in a later chapter. The important point Marx makes is that "people do not make their living in isolation, but rather in association with other people. The production process is not just physical or material, it is also social" (Curran and Renzetti 1994, 25).

According to Marx, throughout history the relations of production have been class relations, and the history of existing society is a history of class conflict. In capitalist society, these social relations exist between owners of the means of production and those who own only their labor. Conflict is rooted in the contradictions of the capitalist system, which at its heart is a system of economic exploitation. One simplistic, yet insightful, summary of this conflict is that it is "inherent in the nature of social arrangements under capitalism, for it was capitalism that generated the vast differences in interests and capitalism that gave the few at the top so much power over the many at the bottom" (Lilly, Cullen, and Ball [1989] 1995, 134). Class conflict is based on the inequality in the ownership of wealth whereby those capitalists who own the means of production (capital, plants, equipment, machinery) exploit workers who merely own their labor, which they must sell to capitalists for a wage in order to make a living. The providers of labor, whom Marx called the proletariat, sell their labor to the capitalists, who prosper through paying the laborers less than the value of their work and keep the difference as profit ("surplus value"; see Lynch 1988).

To enable profit to be made, it is necessary to keep wage levels low. This is achieved by retaining a "surplus population" of unemployed to be drawn on whenever the competition between employers increases the cost they have to pay for workers. This *lumpen proletariat*, as Marx put it, occupies the lowest strata of society: under employed or unemployed persons who do not contribute to society in any meaningful way other than as a reserve source of labor, should capitalist business require it (Lynch and Groves 1986, 10). Capitalism's need for keeping a reserve labor force that will gladly work for low, rather than no, wages also produces the contradiction of poverty, disease, and social problems as these people struggle to survive on very little (Lanier 2009). To live, some of the lumpen proletariat devise nefarious and tenuous means, including begging, prostitution, gambling, and theft. They thus form "criminal classes" that are seen as a danger and a threat to the capitalist system. From this point of view, crime is an inevitable product of the inherent contradictions of capitalism.

It may be asked, why do the masses of underemployed remain complacent? Why don't they riot against the capitalist system? For that matter, why don't exploited workers strike or revolt if they are so exploited? To Marx, one answer was ideology, which among other meanings "is a process whereby beliefs, deriving from real social relationships, hide or mask the precise nature of such relationships, masking from exploited classes the nature of their oppression and its precise source" (Beirne and Messerschmidt [1991] 1995, 342). Marx described this as "false consciousness" and said it results in part from capitalist society's superstructure. One's awareness or consciousness is shaped in a way that is consistent with one's class position. Institutions of society's superstructure (i.e., the political institutions, the legal institutions, the Church, the educational system) instill into people certain values and ideas. For example, most religions teach that it is good to be humble and accept your position in life since you will be rewarded in the afterlife. For this reason Marx called religion the "opiate of the masses." The actual quote is more expressive: "Religion is the sigh of the oppressed creature, the heart of a heartless world, and the soul of soulless conditions. It is the opium of the people" ([1844] 1975, 175). Education in capitalist societies stresses delayed gratification and hard work as the means to monetary and emotional reward. One of the most important ideological components of the superstructure is provided by law.

Marx's Paradox of Law and Capitalism as Crime Producing

The capitalist system of law, bourgeois legality, as a part of the superstructure, reflects the particular mode of production of capitalist society. Bourgeois law serves the capitalist power holders, or *bourgeoisie*, who use it and other means to retain or increase their power and control. This is done not simply as a coercive instrument of power but as ideological domination in which workers are both controlled and defined by law. People are simultaneously "protected" by law from the dangerous classes and from extreme excesses of exploitation created by the capitalist system. Law, therefore, controls by the assent of the majority. As Jock Young pointed out, state law under capitalism exists in a dual relation: it limits excessive exploitation but allows the system of exploitation to remain, it controls all of the population but exercises greater control over some classes than others, and it provides the freedom for the worker to sell his or her labor while preventing the worker from owning the means of production (1981, 299).

In addition to the crimes committed by the lowest strata, Marx and Engels also recognized that the capitalist system of production was "criminogenic" (crime-prone) overall because of the way it impoverished all those within it. One way it does this is through alienation. According to Marx ([1844] 1975), alienation refers to the way the capitalist system of production separates and isolates humans from their work, from its products, from themselves, and from each other. It estranges (separates) them from (1) the products of their labor since they contribute to only a part of the production process, the outcome or products over which they have no ownership or control (the Harley-Davidson company recognized the problems with this, and now has a group of three workers completely build each of its Sportster model motorcycles); (2) their own work process, which loses all personal ownership and intrinsic worth as it is sold to owners and carried out under their control; (3) their own unique creativity and intellectual possibilities, which are lost to the instrumental purpose of work; and (4) other workers and capitalists, with whom they are set in conflict and competition. Thus, workers in a capitalist society—"in their alienation from the product of their labor, from their capacity to freely direct their own activities, from their own interests and talents, from others and from human solidarity—are alienated from their deepest human needs, that is, their needs for self-determination and self-realization" (Bender 1986, 3). This impoverishment by capitalism renders humans "worthless." Through the alienated work process they learn to view one another as isolated individuals and potential enemies rather than social beings with mutual interests (Jaggar 1983, 58). This leads to a lack of human caring and concern for others. Alienation therefore makes the harm of crime more tolerable to the society and to those who may offend.

Engels ([1845] 1958) argued that crime also emerged as a reflection of the inherent strains and pressures that capitalism creates. One way the conditions of crime are created by the capitalist system is through its use of technology. As technology is improved and production is made more efficient, there is less need for workers and they are replaced by machines, a process that intensifies their feelings of worthlessness.

Another way criminogenic conditions are generated is from capitalist competition, which serves to further disempower members of the working class since they must "not only compete with the capitalist over working conditions, but are forced to compete with each other for a limited number of jobs and a limited livelihood. Consequently, Engels viewed crime as the result of competition over scarce resources" (Lynch and Groves 1986, 52). Engels viewed crime as a result of the brutalization, impoverishment, and dehumanization of workers by the capitalist system. They turn to crime because capitalism undermines their morality to resist temptation; crime is an expression of their contempt for the system that impoverishes them and an exercise in retaliatory justice. As Engels pointed out, when everyone looks to his or her own interests and fights only for him- or herself, whether "he [or she] injures declared enemies is simply a matter of selfish calculation as to whether such action would be to his [or her] advantage or not. In short, everyone sees in [his or her] neighbor a rival to be elbowed aside, or at best a victim to be exploited for [his or her] own ends" ([1845] 1958, 145–146).

Finally, Marx and Engels also saw crime, like any other activity, as sustained and exploited by the capitalist system while at the same time being a productive aspect of it. Marx pointed out that in addition to the ideological function, crime actually served those who live parasitically off the crime industry: "The criminal produces not only crime but also the criminal law, the professor who delivers lectures on this criminal law, and even the inevitable text-book in which the professor presents his lectures. The criminal produces the whole apparatus of the police and criminal justice, detectives, judges, executioners, juries, etc." ([1862] 1964, 158–160). The rapid increase of students majoring in criminal justice programs illustrates this, as do the huge numbers of people employed by the criminal justice system, especially in the United States.

Marx and Engels's criminological contribution was, as we have noted, tangential to their analysis of the capitalist system. The first systematic Marxist consideration of crime was attempted by Dutch criminologist Willem Bonger.

Bonger's Criminality and Economic Conditions

Willem Bonger (1876–1940) built on Marx's and particularly Engels's concern about the impoverishment that capitalism brings on society. This impoverishment sets the economic and social conditions for crime. But whereas Marx and Engels focused on the conditions conducive to working-class crime, Bonger extended the analysis to include crime at all levels of society. This included crime among the capitalist classes and a wide range of other crimes, including sex offenses, crimes of vengeance, and political crimes. Bonger saw crimes as the acting out of a "criminal thought." People are more likely to have criminal thoughts when a society promotes egoism rather than altruism. In a notion somewhat reminiscent of Durkheim's anomie theory, Bonger suggested that altruism was a predominant theme in traditional precapitalist societies where the simple productive process for consumption rather than exchange and shared conditions and problems of living promoted a sense of community among the people, "a uniformity of interest" that "obliged them to aid one another in the difficult and uninterrupted struggle for existence" ([1905] 1916, 35). The result of altruism was to suppress the criminal thought.

The change in the mode of production to capitalism brought with it the misery of impoverishment, a condition that was demoralizing and dehumanizing, but it also promoted egoism, which for Bonger meant individual greed, selfishness, and fervent excitement. The climate of egoism favors the criminal thought. The fragmentation of community brought by the capitalist system has a diminished capacity to curtail this destructive thought. The capitalist celebration of egoism is not reflected in official crime rates, argued Bonger, because the upper economic classes determine the shape of the criminal law to legalize the crimes of the rich and criminalize those of the poor, with the result reflected in the title of one radical's book, *The Rich Get Richer and the Poor Get Prison* (Reiman [1979] 1995; Reiman and Leighton 2012).

In spite of Bonger's attempt to bring Marx's work alive in criminology, his ideas and those of Marxism generally did little to stimulate criminologists until the advent of radical criminology some sixty-five years later.

References

———. 2008. *Against the Wall: Poor, Young, Black, and Male.* Philadelphia: University of Pennsylvania Press.

Anderson, William, and Gene Callahan. 2001. "The Roots of Racial Profiling: Why Are Police Targeting Minorities for Traffic Stops?" *Reason Magazine* (August–September). www.reason.com/news/show/28138.html (accessed January 4, 2009).

Balkan, Sheila, Ronald Berger, and Janet Schmidt. 1980. *Crime and Deviance in America: A Critical Approach.* Belmont, CA: Wadsworth.

Barkley, Charles. 2006. *Who's Afraid of a Large Black Man? Race, Power, Fame, Identity, and Why Everyone Should Read My Book.* New York: Riverhead Freestyle.

Barlow, David, and Melissa Hickman Barlow. 2002. "A Survey of African American Police Officers." *Police Quarterly* 5: 334–358.

Beirne, Piers, and James Messerschmidt. [1991] 1995. *Criminology.* 2d ed. Fort Worth: Harcourt Brace College Publishers.

Bender, Frederic. 1986. *Karl Marx: The Essential Writings.* Boulder, CO: Westview Press.

Bernard, Thomas J., Jeffrey B. Snipes and Alexander L. Gerould. 2009. *Vold's Theoretical Criminology.* 6th ed. New York: Oxford University Press.

Bohm, Robert. M. 1982. "Radical Criminology: An Explication." *Criminology* 19: 565–589.

Bonger, Willem. [1905] 1916. *Criminality and Economic Conditions.* Boston: Little, Brown.

Box, Steven. [1971] 1981. *Deviance, Reality, and Society.* New York: Holt, Rinehart, and Winston.

Carver, Terrell. 1987. *A Marx Dictionary.* Cambridge: Polity.

———. 1975. "Toward a Political Economy of Crime." *Theory and Society* 2: 149–170.

———. 1988. *Exploring Criminology*. New York: Macmillan.

Chambliss, William J., and Robert B. Seidman. [1971] 1982. *Law, Order, and Power*. 2d ed. Reading, MA: Addison-Wesley.

Coser, Lewis. 1956. *The Functions of Social Conflict*. New York: Macmillan.

———. 1968. "Conflict: Social Aspects." In *The International Encyclopedia of the Social Sciences,* edited by David L. Sills. Vol. 3. New York: Macmillan and the Free Press.

Curran, Daniel J., and Claire M. Renzetti. 1994. *Theories of Crime*. Boston: Allyn & Bacon.

Dahrendorf, Ralf. 1958. "Out of Utopia: Toward a Reconstruction of Sociological Analysis." *American Journal of Sociology* 67: 115–127.

———. 1959. *Class and Class Conflict in an Industrial Society*. London: Routledge and Kegan Paul.

Dixon, Travis L., Terry L. Schell, Howard Giles, and Kristin L. Drogos. 2008. "The Influence of Race in Police–Civilian Interactions: A Content Analysis of Videotaped Interactions Taken During Cincinnati Police Traffic Stops." *Journal of Communications* 58: 530–549.

———. 2006. *Criminological Theory: An Analysis of Its Underlying Assumptions*. 2d ed. Boulder, CO: Rowman & Littlefield.

Engel, Robin Shepard, Jennifer M. Calnon, and Thomas J. Bernard. 2002. "Theory and Racial Profiling: Shortcomings and Future Directions in Research." *Justice Quarterly* 19: 249–273.

Engels, Friedrich. [1845] 1958. *The Condition of the Working Class in England*. Oxford, UK: Blackwell.

Golgowski, Nina. 2013 November 22. "Florida police accused of racial profiling after stopping man 258 times, charging him with trespassing at work." *New York Daily News.* www.nydailynews.com/news/national/police-stop-man-258-times-charge-trespassing-work-article-1.1526422#ixzz2u6pie01Q (accessed March 21, 2014).

Gusfield, Joseph R. 1963. *Symbolic Crusade*. Urbana, IL: University of Illinois Press.

Hills, Stuart L. 1971. *Crime, Power, and Morality*. Scranton, PA: Chandler.

Jaggar, Alison. 1983. *Feminist Politics and Human Nature*. New Jersey: Rowman & Allanheld.

John Jay College of Criminal Justice. 2001. "Racial Profiling Is More Than a Black & White Issue." *Law Enforcement News*. 27, no. 568. (December 31). www.lib.jjay.cuny.edu/len/2001/12.31/facing.html (accessed March 22, 2009).

Johnson, Doyle P. 2008. *Contemporary Sociological Theory: An Integrated Multi-level Approach*. New York: Springer Science.

Khoza, V. and P.J. Potgieter, 2005. "Deviant Driving Behavior: An Epidemiological Study." *Acta Criminologica* 18, no. 2: 56–70.

Krisberg, Barry. 1975. *Crime and Privilege: Towards a New Criminology*. Englewood Cliffs, NJ: Prentice Hall.

Lanier, Mark M. (2009) "Epidemiological Criminology: A Critical Cross Cultural Analysis of HIV/AIDS." Acta Criminologica, 22, 2: 60–73.

Lilly, J. Robert, Francis T. Cullen, and Richard A. Ball. [1989] 1995. *Criminological Theory: Context and Consequences*. Thousand Oaks, CA: Sage.

Lynch, Michael. 1988. "Surplus Value, Crime, and Punishment." *Contemporary Crises* 12: 329–344.

Lynch, Michael J., and W. Byron Groves. 1986. *A Primer in Radical Criminology.* New York: Harrow and Heston.

Marx, Karl. [1844] 1975. *The Economic and Philosophical Manuscripts of 1844.* New York: International Publishers.

———. [1859] 1975. "'Preface' to a Contribution to the Critique of Political Economy." In *Karl Marx: Early Writings,* edited by Lucio Colletti. Harmondsworth, UK: Penguin.

———. [1862] 1964. "Theories of Surplus Value." In *Karl Marx: Selected Writings in Sociology and Social Philosophy,* edited by Thomas B. Bottomore and Maximilien Rubel. Vol. 1. New York: McGraw-Hill.

Meehan, Albert J., and Michael C. Ponder. 2002. "Race and Place: The Ecology of Racial Profiling African American Motorists." *Justice Quarterly* 19: 399–430.

Olaussen, Leif Petter. 2004. "Why Is Crime a Social Fact?" *Nordisk Tidsskrift for Kriminalvidenskab* 91, no. 1: 24–38.

"Our Opinion: DPS Revisions Cut Profiling, Searches in Traffic Stops." 2009. *Tucson Citizen,* January 2. www.tucsoncitizen.com/ss/border/106626.php (accessed January 4, 2009).

Pepinsky, Harold. 1976. *Crime and Conflict: A Study of Law and Society.* Oxford: Martin Robertson.

Platt, Tony. 1974. "Prospects for a Radical Criminology in the United States." *Crime and Social Justice* 1: 2–10.

Quinney, Richard. 1970. *The Social Reality of Crime.* Boston: Little, Brown.

———. 1974. *Critique of the Legal Order: Crime Control in a Capitalist Society.* Boston: Little, Brown.

———. 1975b. *Criminology.* Boston: Little, Brown.

———. 1977. *Class, State, and Crime.* New York: David McKay.

Quinney, Richard, and John Wildeman. 1991. *The Problem of Crime: A Peace and Social Justice Perspective.* 3d ed. London: Mayfield.

Ramirez, Deborah, Jack McDevitt, and Amy Farrell. 2010. *A Resource Guide on Racial Profiling Data Collection Systems.* Washington DC: US Department of Justice. www.ncjrs.gov/pdffiles1/bja/184768.pdf (accessed February 14, 2014).

Reiman, Jeffrey. [1979] 1995. 2007. *The Rich Get Richer and the Poor Get Prison.* New York: John Wiley.

Reiman, Jeffrey H., and Paul Leighton. 2012. *The Rich Get Richer and the Poor Get Prison.* New York: Pearson Education.

Robinson, Eugene. 2007. "Driving While Black or Brown." *Washington Post* (May 2).

Schwendinger, Herman, and Julia Schwendinger. 1970. "Defenders of Order or Guardians of Human Rights?" *Issues in Criminology* 5: 123–157.

———. 2001. "Defenders of Order or Guardians of Human Rights." In *What Is Crime?* edited by Stuart Henry and Mark M. Lanier, 65–100. Boulder, CO: Rowman & Littlefield.

Sellin, Thorsten. 1938. *Culture Conflict and Crime.* New York: Social Science Research Council.

Shantz, Jeff. 2012. "Radical Criminology: A Manifesto." *Radical Criminology* 1, no. 1: journal.radicalcriminology.org/index.php/rc/article/view/1/html (accessed February 22, 2012).

Simmel, Georg. [1908] 1955. *The Sociology of Conflict*, translated by Kurt H. Wolff, and *The Web of Group Affiliations,* translated by Reinhard Bendix. Glencoe, IL: Free Press.

Smith, Michael R., and Matthew Petrocelli. 2001. "Racial Profiling? A Multivariate Analysis of Police Traffic Stop Data." *Police Quarterly* 4: 4–27.

Taylor, Ian, Paul Walton, and Jock Young. 1973. *The New Criminology: For a Social Theory of Deviance.* London: Routledge and Kegan Paul.

———, eds. 1975. *Critical Criminology.* London: Routledge and Kegan Paul.

Turk, Austin T. 1964. "Prospects for Theories of Criminal Behavior." *Journal of Criminal Law, Criminology, and Police Science* 55: 454–461.

———. 1966. "Conflict and Criminality." *American Sociological Review* 31: 338–352.

———. 1969. *Criminality and the Legal Order.* Chicago: Rand McNally.

———. 1976. "Law as a Weapon in Social Conflict." *Social Problems* 23: 276–291.

———. 1982. *Political Criminality: The Defiance and Defense of Authority.* Beverly Hills, CA: Sage.

———. 2003. "Political Violence: Patterns and Trends," In *Crime and Justice at the Millennium: Essays by and in Honor of Marvin E. Wolfgang,* edited by Robert A. Silverman, Terence P. Thornberry, Bernard Cohen, and Barry Krisberg, 31–44. Norwell, MA: Kluwer Academic Publishers.

———. 2004. "The Sociology of Terrorism." *Annual Review of Sociology,* 271–286. Palo Alto, CA: Annual Reviews, Inc.

———. 2006. "Criminology and Conflict Theory." In *The Essential Criminology Reader*, edited by Stuart Henry and Mark M. Lanier, 185–190. Boulder, CO: Westview Press.

Turner, Jonathan H. 1986. *The Structure of Sociological Theory.* 4th ed. Chicago: Dorsey.

Vold, George B. [1958] 1979. *Theoretical Criminology.* New York: Oxford University Press.

Vold, George B., and Thomas J. Bernard. 1986. *Theoretical Criminology.* 3d ed. New York: Oxford University Press.

Vold, George B., Thomas J. Bernard, and J. B. Snipes. 1998 [2001]. *Theoretical Criminology.* 5th ed. New York: Oxford University Press.

Weber, Max. [1922] 1966. *The Theory of Social and Economic Organization.* New York: Free Press.

———. 1981. "Thinking Seriously About Crime: Some Models of Criminology." In *Crime and Society: Readings in History and Society,* edited by Mike Fitzgerald, Gregor McLennan, and Jennie Pawson. London: Routledge and Kegan Paul.

PART II

Early Theories of Causation

Part II Timeline

1880–1930	European migration wave to the United States
1890	Wounded Knee Massacre: 300 unarmed Sioux Indians are massacred by the United States military while being relocated to a reservation
1897	Cuba becomes autonomous but not fully independent from Spain
1898	United States acquires Puerto Rico from Spain
1898–1902	United States invades Cuba
1907–1908	United States recession results in the repatriation of Mexican workers
1910–1920	Mexican Revolution
1914–1918	World War I
1914	El Paso passes an ordinance banning the sale and possession of marijuana; local white citizens are afraid that Mexicans' smoking the "killer weed" would make them violent
1915	Resurgence of Ku Klux Klan
1915	The Bandit Wars: Texas Rangers unjustly persecute and kill Mexicans in south Texas
1917	Russian Revolution
1917	Abdication of Czar Nicholas II from the Russian throne, ending imperial rule

1918–1939	Inter-War Era: A period of peace in between the two world wars, characterized by economic boom and bust, as well as the growth of the polarizing ideologies of fascism and communism
1919	Chicago Race Riots
1920–1933	Prohibition Era: The United States bans the sale and drinking of alcohol under the 18th Amendment
1920	First Red Scare in the United States: Raids are conducted to capture and arrest suspected radical leftists, mostly Italian and Eastern European immigrants
1920	Women get the right to vote in the United States
1920s–1933	The rise of the Italian-American mafia
1921	Tulsa race riot: Mobs of whites attacked black residents and businesses of the Greenwood District in Tulsa, Oklahoma
1922	Union of Soviet Socialist Republics (USSR) is established
1925	Creation of the United States Border Patrol to police the Mexican border
1925–1945	Benito Mussolini rules as fascist dictator of Italy
1929–1939	Great Depression: New York Stock market crashes, and there is a period of economic global downturn in which unemployment and poverty is experienced; this leads to the rise of political extremism, the Nazi Party in Germany
1930–1932	Repatriation of Mexicans and illegal deportation of Mexican Americans
1931	Arrest of Scottsboro boys: Nine black teenagers are falsely accused of raping two white women aboard a train near Scottsboro, Alabama
1932	The Nazi Party gains control over the Republic of Germany
1933–1945	Franklin D. Roosevelt serves as United States president for four terms and establishes social welfare programs under the New Deal
1933	Hitler becomes chancellor of Germany
1936–1939	Spanish Civil War
1939–1975	General Francisco Franco rules Spain as a fascist dictator until his death
1939–1945	World War II: Hitler attempts to conquer the world; the war for freedom is fought between the Axis powers (Germany, Italy, and Japan) and the Allies (France, Great Britain, the United States, the Soviet Union, Mexico, and to a lesser extent, China); it ends with the defeat of the Axis powers
1941	Attack on Pearl Harbor
1942–1946	Executive Order 9066: Internment of 110,000 Japanese Americans within the United States during World War II by President Franklin Roosevelt

1943	Zoot Suit Riots: Mexican American youth are attacked by United States servicemen in Los Angeles, California
1945	The United Nations is created
1946–1950	Chinese Communist Revolution
1946–1954	United States Senator McCarthy persecutes his enemies and falsely labels them as communists; more than 2,000 employees lose their jobs
1947	Indian Independence Act: India becomes independent from Britain
1948–1990	The Cold War: A period of ideological conflict between the communist East and Western democracies
1949	The North Atlantic Treaty Organization: A military alliance between 29 European and North American countries
1950–1953	Korean War: United States intervention against the communist revolutionary movement in Korea
1953	Cuban Revolution, led by Fidel Castro and Ernesto "Che" Guevara against the dictator Batista
1954–1968	Civil Rights movement: Mass protest movement against racial segregation and discrimination in the United States
1954	*Hernandez v. Texas* Supreme Court decision: Court rules that Mexican Americans and all other nationality groups have equal protection under the 14th Amendment of the United States Constitution
1954	*Brown v. Board of Education* Supreme Court decision: Court rules that American state laws establishing racial segregation in public schools are unconstitutional, even if the segregated schools are otherwise equal in quality
1955	Murder of 14-year-old Emmett Till, an African American boy falsely accused of assaulting a white woman
1955–1975	Vietnam War: United States intervention in Asia against their communist revolutionary movement. The war ended when United States forces withdrew in 1973 and Vietnam unified under communist control 2 years later
1955	Rosa Parks is arrested for refusing to give up her seat on a Montgomery bus
1955–1956	Montgomery Bus Boycott against racial segregation
1961	The United Nations passes a prohibition against marijuana, advocated by the United States
1961	Freedom Riders: White and black students travel across state lines to protest segregation

1962	Cesar Chavez and Dolores Huerta found the National Farmworkers Association
1962	Cuban Missile Crisis between the United States and the Soviet Union
1963	President John F. Kennedy is assassinated in Dallas, Texas
1964	Civil Rights Act is signed by President Lyndon B. Johnson
1965	Los Angeles Watts Riots erupt due to police brutality
1965	Voting Rights Act is signed by President Lyndon B. Johnson
1965	Malcolm X is assassinated
1965	Delano grape strike, led by Cesar Chavez and Dolores Huerta
1968	Martin Luther King, Jr., is assassinated, followed by rioting in 168 cities

Editor's Introduction

Part II presents the early theories of causation. At the onset of this section, we see the mass migration of 28 million Europeans to the United States over four decades beginning in 1880. Many of the immigrants come from eastern and southern Europe (Beck et al., 2014). By 1890, Native Americans have been dispossessed of their lands and culture and put in reservations. Meanwhile, in Mexico, the Indigenous peoples and Mestizos continue to face discrimination and exploitation under the dictatorship of Porfirio Diaz, who was eventually removed by the Mexican Revolution of 1910 (Library of Congress, n.d.-a). Under his rule, European investment grew, and class warfare increased.

In 1914, World War I began. It was described as the war to end all wars, as it utilized chemical warfare and strategic bombing. The war initially was between the Central Powers (Germany, Austria-Hungary, and Turkey) and the Allies (France, Great Britain, Russia, Italy, Japan, and the United States). The United States joined the war as a result of Germany sinking merchant ships near the British Isles. The war ended with the defeat of the Central Powers in 1918. The war was virtually unparalleled in the massacre, bloodshed, and annihilation it caused (Beck et al., 2014). There were over four million deaths on the side of the Central Powers and over five million of the Allies. Civilian casualties were 7.7 million in total. The war resulted in the formation of new countries in Europe and the Middle East. World War I was a significant turning point in the political, cultural, economic, and social climate of the world (Beck et al., 2014; Facing History and Ourselves, n.d.).

Also, as World War I was near its end, the Spanish Flu pandemic of 1918 was ravaging the world. The first wave occurred in the springtime and was mild, with symptoms of chills, fever, and fatigue. Social distancing measures were utilized at delayed rates. Businesses, schools, and restaurants were shut down. However, the second wave appeared in the fall of 1918, following the end-of-war festivities. Victims would die within hours and days of developing symptoms. Over 50 million people died, and 500 million people became infected, developing immunity after having near-death experiences

(Canales, 2020; Centers for Disease Control and Prevention, n.d.). The war and its aftermath of illness sparked revolutions and uprisings in the world. The Big Four (Britain, France, United States, and Italy) imposed their terms on the defeated powers in a series of treaties agreed on at the 1919 Paris Peace Conference, the most well-known being the German peace treaty, the Treaty of Versailles of 1918 (Beck et al., 2014; The National Archives, n.d.).

Inequality and racism continued in the United States against European immigrants and citizens of color. The Ku Klux Klan had a resurgence in 1915 in Protestant communities, advocating white supremacy and adding cross burnings to their tactics of intimidation. Actions of hate continued, with law enforcement perpetuating violence toward minorities (WGBH Education Foundation, 2020). In south Texas, Texas Rangers persecuted and lynched Mexican Americans. This was known as The Bandit Wars, in which the assassination squads conducted a campaign of annihilation of Mexicans. According to reports, over 300 men were wrongfully murdered (Proctor, 2010).

Furthermore, in 1919, there were the Chicago Race Riots, one of the most severe of 25 race riots in the United States during the Red (Bloody) Summer following World War I. The riot was triggered by the murder of a black young man by a white man. By the time the violence ended, 23 blacks and 15 whites were dead, along with more than 500 injured. The violence experienced highlighted the injustice and oppression faced by people of color (Fitzgerald, 2019; White, 1919). In 1921, Tulsa, Oklahoma, also experienced race riots between blacks and whites (Tulsa Historical Society & Museum, n.d.).

Additionally, according to the Library of Congress (n.d.-b), in the 1920s, the Prohibition movement passed the 18th Amendment, prohibiting the sale and consumption of alcohol, in an effort to decrease family violence. Following the ban, gangs, particularly the Italian American Mafia (La Costra Nostra), gained control of the beer and liquor supplies by engaging in bootlegging, leading to an increase of organized crime and violence. Prohibition ended as a result of the ratification of the 21st Amendment, which repealed the 18th Amendment. Even long after Prohibition, the mafia's presence would continue to rise.

By 1929, the world and the United States began to experience the Great Depression. It was a period of economic global downturn, and unemployment and poverty were experienced around the world until 1939 (Elliott, 2017; World Digital Library, n.d.-b). This led to the rise of political extremism, particularly of the Nazi Party in Germany (Beck et al., 2014). In the United States, Smith (2017) notes that Mexicans and Mexican Americans were used as scapegoats, and citizens were deported unjustly from their homes to Mexico, a foreign country to many of them. Injustice in the South continued, with nine black teenagers falsely accused of rape by two white women in Scottsboro, Alabama. Pardons by the state would not begin until 1947 and ended in 2013 (The National Archives, 2014).

Beck et al. (2014) explain that the US presidency was taken in 1933 by Franklin D. Roosevelt, who went on to serve four terms. To help the country recover from the Great Depression, he established the social welfare programs known as the New Deal (World Digital Library, n.d.-b). These programs were created to help stabilize the economy and to provide relief in the form of projects and programs for the government. During this time, Adolf Hitler became the Chancellor of Germany. Hitler attempted to conquer the world, expand Germany's territory, and engage in racial purification through the annihilation of those he deemed unworthy: the Jewish people, the Gypsy people, the disabled, and homosexuals. This would set the stage for World War II in 1939. The war for freedom was fought between the Axis powers (Germany, Italy, and Japan) against the Allies (France, Great Britain, the United States, the Soviet Union, Mexico, and to a lesser extent, China). In their racial purification efforts, the Nazis placed many people in concentration camps to face atrocities and death. The war ended with the defeat of the Axis powers in 1945. During that time frame, more than 50 million people lost their lives, as well as more than six million Jews (Beck et al., 2014; Geyer and Tooze, 2015; World Digital Library, n.d.-a).

Moreover, as the United States had fought for freedom abroad, following the bombing of Pearl Harbor, President Roosevelt enacted Executive Order 9066, which called for the internment of 110,000 Japanese Americans within the United States during World War II (Nagata et al., 2019). Discrimination was also being faced by Mexican Americans, who became the target of servicemen, resulting in the Zoot Suit Riots. These attacks on the Mexican American communities led to the rise of gangs in Los Angeles, created by minorities in order to protect themselves from state violence (Dundon, 2018).

Subsequently, after the defeat of the Axis powers in 1945, the Nuremberg Trials were set up by the Allies to enact justice for crimes against humanity by the Germans and Japanese. The United Nations (UN) was established to foster international cooperation and prevent future conflicts (Beck et al., 2014). Furthermore, the UN Commission on Human Rights was established a year later, in 1946. The Universal Declaration of Human Rights Drafting Committee, chaired by Eleanor Roosevelt, created the Universal Declaration of Human Rights, which was adopted by the UN General Assembly and became the International Bill of Human Rights (United Nations, n.d.).

References

Beck, R. B., Black, L., Krieger, L., Naylor, P. C., & Shabaka, D. I. (2014). *World history: Patterns of interaction.* Holt McDougal/Houghton Mifflin Harcourt.

Canales, K. (2020, April 13). Photos show the precautions US cities took to "flatten the curve" during the 1918 Spanish Flu pandemic. *Business Insider.* https://www.businessinsider.com/spanish-flu-pandemic-1918-precautions-us-cities-2020-4

Centers for Disease Control and Prevention. (n.d.). 1918 pandemic (H1N1 virus). https://www.cdc.gov/flu/pandemic-resources/1918-pandemic-h1n1.html

Dundon, R. (2018). The L.A. Zoot Suit Riots of 1943 were a targeted attack on Mexican and nonwhite youths. *Timeline.* https://timeline.com/zoot-suit-riots-of-1943-were-a-targeted-attack-on-mexican-youths-8e5b34775cff

Elliot, L. (2017). Crash course: What the Great Depression reveals about our future. *The Guardian.* https://www.theguardian.com/society/2017/mar/04/crash-1929-wall-street-what-the-great-depression-reveals-about-our-future

Facing History and Ourselves. (n.d.). Casualties of World War I. https://www.facinghistory.org/weimar-republic-fragility-democracy/politics/casualties-world-war-i-country-politics-world-war-i

Fitzgerald, M. (2019, July 27). Ensuring the Chicago Race Riot is not forgotten, with inspiration from Germany's Holocaust memorials. *Time Magazine*. https://time.com/5636039/chicago-race-riots-art-project/

Geyer, M., & Tooze, A. (2015). Part II- The social practice of people's war. In J. Ferris & E. Mawdsley (Eds.), *The Cambridge History of the Second World War* (Vol. 3, pp. 245–415). Cambridge University Press.

Library of Congress. (n.d.-a). Mexican Revolution: Topics in chronicling America. *Research Guides*. https://guides.loc.gov/chronicling-america-mexican-revolution

Library of Congress. (n.d.-b). Progressive Era to New Era, (1900–1929): Prohibition: A case study of progressive reform. *Classroom Materials*. http://www.loc.gov/teachers/classroommaterials/presentationsandactivities/presentations/timeline/progress/prohib/

Nagata, D. K., Kim, J. H. J., & Wu, K. (2019). The Japanese American wartime incarceration: Examining the scope of racial trauma. *American Psychologist, 74*(1), 36–48. https://doi.org/10.1037/amp0000303

Proctor, B. (2010). Texas Rangers. *Texas State Historical Association*. https://tshaonline.org/handbook/online/articles/met04

Smith, L. (2017). In the 1930s, we illegally deported 600,000 U.S. citizens because they had Mexican heritage. *Timeline*. https://timeline.com/in-the-1930s-we-illegally-deported-600-000-u-s-citizens-because-they-had-mexican-heritage-f0c5d589a5c3

The National Archives. (2014). The Scottsboro Boys: Injustice in Alabama. https://www.archives.gov/files/publications/prologue/2014/spring/scottsboro.pdf

The National Archives. (n.d.). The Great War. https://www.nationalarchives.gov.uk/education/greatwar/g5/cs1/background.htm

Tulsa Historical Society & Museum. (n.d.). Exhibit: Tulsa Race Massacre. https://www.tulsahistory.org/exhibit/1921-tulsa-race-massacre/

United Nations. (n.d.). Universal Declaration of Human Rights-History of the document. https://www.un.org/en/sections/universal-declaration/history-document/index.html

WGBH Educational Foundation. (n.d.). The Ku Klux Klan in the 1920s. Public Broadcasting Service. https://www.pbs.org/wgbh/americanexperience/features/flood-klan/

White, W. (1919, October). The causes of the Chicago Race Riot. *The Crises*, XVIII: 25.

World Digital Library. (n.d.-a). World history timelines. Library of Congress with support from United Nations Educational Scientific and Cultural Organization. https://www.wdl.org/en/sets/world-history/timeline/

World Digital Library. (n.d.-b). United States history timelines. Library of Congress with support from United Nations Educational Scientific and Cultural Organization. https://www.wdl.org/en/sets/us-history/timeline/n/sets/us-history/timeline/

READING 7

Anomie-Strain Theory
Timothy Brezina

The anomie tradition in criminology (also referred to as strain theory) can be traced to the early pioneering work of the French sociologist Emile Durkheim. Similar to Freud's notion of the "id," Durkheim assumed that individuals possessed a primal self that, in the absence of society, expressed itself through selfish wants and desires. Furthermore, Durkheim argued that the wants and desires of the primal self are more or less insatiable; in other words, the primal self is characterized by a relentless appetite "for more." In the context of modern society, this condition—when not adequately restrained—tends to express itself in an unquenchable thirst for pleasure or success, "overweening ambition," a "longing for infinity," and "perpetual dissatisfaction."

Given this view of human nature, Durkheim stressed the critical role played by society's moral institutions (such as family and religion) in placing limits on ambition, keeping egoistic or selfish desires "in check," and directing the energy of individuals into collective tasks and pursuits that provide meaning and fulfillment. In the absence of such restraint, society is at risk of degenerating into a state of *anomie*, in which the insatiable and potentially destructive desires of individuals are no longer regulated. In this condition, institutionalized norms lose their force and no longer guide behavior, individuals are freed to pursue egoistic goals, and rates of various deviant behaviors tend to increase, including crime and suicide.

In the 1930s, a young sociologist by the name of Robert K. Merton reformulated the anomie framework and applied it directly to deviant behavior in the United States. This seminal work, titled "Social Structure and Anomie" (Merton 1938), would become one of the most influential contributions to the study of crime and deviance, helping to shape all subsequent developments in the anomie-strain theory tradition.

Merton's reformulation retained the notion of insatiable desires, but instead of rooting such desires in human nature, they were now seen as products of culture and socialization. In particular, Merton observed that the cultural ethos known as the "American Dream" serves to promote the very type of overweening ambition and "longing for affinity" that Durkheim viewed as a threat to social order. Regardless of their current position in the stratification system, Americans are encouraged "never to stop trying," and to aspire to success, with an overwhelming emphasis on the accumulation of monetary wealth.

At the same time, Merton recognized that the opportunities required for monetary success are unevenly distributed in society, with large segments of society lacking prosocial means to achieve the ends they have been encouraged to pursue. Thus, for disadvantaged segments of the population, there exists a mismatch or *disjunction* between culturally prescribed success goals and the legitimate means available to achieve these goals. This disjunction between means and ends generates *strain* in the social structure and, especially among disadvantaged groups, contributes to a state of anomie. When large segments of the population have internalized a strong desire for material success, yet lack the legitimate means to attain this goal, the norms governing the legitimate ways to achieve success lose their relevance and force. When people no longer believe they can get ahead through "hard work" or "playing by the rules," their commitment to conformity weakens. This fact frees individuals to cheat, or to "innovate," by pursuing alternative and illegitimate avenues to success.

Merton recognized that innovation was not the only possible response to strain or anomie. Other adaptations to strain are possible, including *conformity* (in which individuals remain committed to legitimate means and goals, despite the odds), *ritualism* (in which individuals accept failure but remain committed to legitimate means, perhaps because they have simply become resigned to their fate), *retreatism* (in which individuals give up on society's prescribed goals *and* means, as exhibited by such escapist behaviors as alcoholism, drug abuse, and suicide), and *rebellion* (in which individuals or groups struggle to redefine the culturally approved goals and means). Nevertheless, while alternative adaptations are possible, strain is said to increase the rate of innovative behavior, including crime.

Thus, a defining feature of Merton's anomie-strain theory is that it locates the origins of deviant behavior in a contradictory configuration of cultural and structural arrangements. In fact, the theory was developed in reaction to biological and psychological theories that were popular at the time and located the roots of crime in individual pathology. Rejecting a pathological approach, Merton argued that crime more often represented "the normal reaction, by normal persons, to abnormal conditions" (Merton 1938: 672, note 2).

The alternative image of the offender suggested by strain theory, then, is that of a more or less rational, goal-seeking individual who has opted for non-conventional means to attain conventional goals. Offenders, therefore, are not distinct from conformists in terms of their biological or psychological makeup, or even in terms of the nature of their desires or goals. Indeed, a unique feature of Merton's anomie-strain theory is the implication that *both* conformist and deviant behaviors are motivated by a strong commitment to conventional success goals.

Contemporary research on drug dealers provides a useful illustration. This research indicates that successful participants in the illicit drug trade tend to share a number of traits in common. Not only do they share a particularly strong desire for monetary success but, in comparison to less successful dealers, individuals who reap high monetary returns from the illicit drug trade also tend to be relatively intelligent, willing to take risks, and willing to network with other dealers in order to secure advantages in the drug market (McCarthy and Hagan 2001). In short, the desires and traits exhibited by these dealers do not appear to differ substantially from the characteristics normally attributed to successful and legitimate business entrepreneurs. From a strain theory perspective, the key difference is that the former have rejected legitimate means of goal attainment in favor of illegitimate means.

Revised Strain Theories of Crime and Delinquency

Merton's strain theory was followed by a number of attempts to revise and expand the theory, and to make it more applicable to specific types of deviant group, especially juvenile gangs. In general agreement with Merton, Albert Cohen (1955) observed that much delinquency stems from the blockage of success goals experienced disproportionately by lower-class juveniles, especially in relation to the goal of middle-class status. Specifically, lower-class juveniles often arrive at school without the knowledge, values, and skills necessary to achieve success through legitimate means. As a result, they fall behind their middle-class peers and fail to meet the expectations of their middle-class teachers. In short, these juveniles are unable to live up to the middle-class "measuring rod." They are defined as problems by school officials and are effectively denied a legitimate pathway to middle-class status.

At the same time, however, Cohen observed that much juvenile delinquency is non-utilitarian in nature and is not specifically concerned with the goal of monetary success or conventional status. Vandalism, fights, and other "expressive" delinquencies can hardly be construed as innovative means to acquire middle-class status, for example. To explain such behavior, Cohen interpreted the delinquency of lower-class juveniles as an indirect response to strain. When strained juveniles come together, they cope with their collective frustration by setting up an alternative status system, which expresses hostility to the middle class and emphasizes goals they *can* achieve, such as toughness and fighting ability. Thus, according to Cohen's account, strain contributes to the formation of delinquent peer groups, which in turn encourage delinquent adaptations.

Cloward and Ohlin (1960) also explained the formation of juvenile gangs in terms of strain. Many lower-class juveniles desire monetary success but realize they will be unable to achieve this goal through legal channels. When these strained juveniles interact regularly and blame their goal blockage on the larger society, they may form gangs that facilitate and justify criminal activity. In contrast to Cohen, however, Cloward and Ohlin argue that delinquent gangs tend to specialize. Some gangs, for example, focus primarily on fighting, while others focus on theft or drug use. This specialization is believed to be a function, in part, of the "illegitimate opportunities" available to strained youth. In some communities, youth receive instruction and support from older individuals and are directed into theft and other money-oriented crimes. In other communities, strained youth receive little direction and may cope by forming gangs that are oriented toward violence. Thus, according to Cloward and Ohlin, strain provides the motivation for juvenile crime, but the illegitimate opportunity structure plays a crucial role in the type of delinquent adaptations that ultimately arise.

Recent Developments in the Anomie-Strain Theory Tradition

The "classic" strain theories of Merton, Cohen, and Cloward and Ohlin were highly influential during much of the 20th century, but were sharply criticized during the 1970s. Prominent criminologists criticized classic strain theories for their failure to explain the delinquency of middle-class individuals, their failure to explain why only *some* strained individuals turn to crime or delinquency, and their neglect of goals other than monetary success or middle-class status. Classic strain theories were also seen as lacking in empirical support. If such theories were correct, one would expect to find high levels of crime and delinquency among "strained" individuals; namely, among individuals who experience a disjunction between their aspirations and expectations. Yet, contrary to expectations, researchers observed that the highest levels of offending were to be found among individuals who lack aspirations for conventional success (e.g., among individuals who do *not* aspire to a college education or high-status occupation).

To address these criticisms, contemporary theorists have reformulated and reinvigorated the anomie-strain framework. The most influential of these reformulations include Agnew's (1992) general strain theory and Messner and Rosenfeld's (2001) institutional-anomie theory.

Agnew's General Strain Theory

To address some of the criticisms associated with classic strain theories, Agnew broadened the conception of strain to include a wider array of potential stressors, including stressors that are not limited to lower-class individuals but can also be experienced by individuals from middle-class backgrounds. According to Agnew's general strain theory (GST), the goals and outcomes that are important to individuals are not limited to income or middle-class status. Additional goals and outcomes that are recognized by the theory, and appear to be especially important to young males, include respect and masculine status (e.g., the expectation that one be treated "like a man"), autonomy (e.g., the goal or desire to enjoy a certain amount of personal independence), and the desire for thrills or excitement. GST, then, recognizes that individuals pursue a variety of goals beyond economic success and it expands the notion of goal-blockage accordingly. In particular, GST defines goal-blockage more broadly to include *the failure to achieve positively valued goals* (Agnew 1992, 2006).

In addition, Agnew highlights two other categories of strain, including *the loss of positively valued stimuli* and *the presentation of noxious or negatively valued stimuli*. The loss of positively valued stimuli includes a potentially wide range of negative events or experiences, including the theft of valued property, the loss of a romantic relationship, or the withdrawal of parental love. The presentation of noxious stimuli also includes a wide range of negative experiences, such as harassment and bullying from peers, negative relations with parents and teachers, and criminal victimization (Agnew 1992, 2006).

According to GST, strain increases the likelihood that individuals will experience negative emotions. Anger is one possible response and is of special interest to general strain theorists. Anger occurs when strain is blamed on others and it is believed to be especially conducive to crime and delinquency. Among other things, anger reduces one's tolerance for injury or insult, lowers inhibitions, energizes the individual to action, and creates desires for retaliation and revenge.

Of course, many people experience strains and stressors of various types, yet most do not resort to crime. In fact, GST recognizes that strain does not *automatically* lead to crime or delinquency. Rather, the theory specifies a number of conditions that are said to make a criminal/delinquent response to strain more or less likely. These conditions involve the nature of the strain in question, the coping abilities and resources available to the strained individual, and the extent to which the strained individual is predisposed to crime. Individuals may instead cope in legal or conventional ways. According to GST, for example, a criminal or delinquent response to strain is most likely to occur when conventional coping strategies are unavailable, when they prove ineffective, or when the coping resources of the individual become taxed (as may occur when the individual is subjected to chronic or repeated strain).

Like other strain theories, GST interprets offending behavior as an adaptation to strain—one that may allow individuals to cope with strain in the short run. However, the theory does *not* contend that crime is an effective solution (Agnew 2006). Crime is only one possible response to strain and, in the long run, may prove to be maladaptive, especially if it leads to other problems for the individual. Moreover, the intent of GST is not to excuse or justify criminal behavior. As Agnew is careful to note, the main purpose of the theory is to identify the processes that foster criminal conduct in the hopes that such knowledge may lead to improved strategies for the prevention and control of crime. The major crime control strategies that follow from GST include efforts that are designed to reduce or alleviate the strains that are conducive to crime or delinquency, equip individuals with the tools and skills that will allow them to avoid such strains, and reduce the likelihood that individuals will cope with strain in a criminal or delinquent manner (Agnew 1995).

A number of studies have attempted to assess the validity of GST. Although a comprehensive test of GST has yet to be conducted, researchers have managed to assess some of the core propositions of the theory. While the results of these research efforts have not always been consistent (Agnew 2006), the findings appear to indicate that, overall, GST has some potential for explaining crime, delinquency, and drug use.

Messner and Rosenfeld's Institutional Anomie Theory

Although Agnew (1999) contends that GST can be extended and applied to community-level crime rates, the primary focus of GST is on individual-level, social psychological processes. Messner and Rosenfeld's (2001) institutional anomie theory (IAT) concentrates on macro-level forces. In particular, IAT represents a contemporary elaboration and extension of Merton's earlier anomie-strain framework, with a special focus on the specific institutional arrangements that serve to magnify (or weaken) criminogenic aspects of the American Dream.

Like Merton, Messner and Rosenfeld highlight the criminogenic consequences of the American value system, with its exaggerated emphasis on achievement and competition. Although the American Dream fosters high levels of motivation and innovation, this cultural ethos defines success in excessively narrow and materialistic terms. Individual achievement and monetary success are glorified, while alternative measures of success (e.g., social or educational contributions to one's community) are implicitly devalued. In addition, the ethos of the American Dream tends to place greater emphasis on goal outcomes rather than the means used to attain success goals. In short, the American Dream generates strong pressures to succeed at any cost, and it does not discourage individuals from pursuing monetary success by the "technically most efficient means, that is, by any means necessary" (Messner and Rosenfeld 2001: 8).

According to Messner and Rosenfeld, at least two factors serve to magnify the criminogenic effects of the American Dream. The first factor involves the extent to which the economy dominates the institutional landscape. When, in a market society, "the pursuit of private gain becomes the organizing principle of all areas of social life" (Elliott Currie quoted in Messner and Rosenfeld 2001: 70), and when non-economic roles associated with family, school, and the larger community are consistently devalued, the norms surrounding prosocial means of goal attainment lose their perceived importance and become difficult to enforce. When, in turn, the normative order is weakened and individuals are not sufficiently restrained in terms of the means they select to pursue success, the result is a condition of anomie. At the individual level, this anomic condition is reflected in extreme competition, individualism, and an "anything goes" mentality (see also Konty 2005).

A second factor involves high levels of economic inequality. In light of extreme economic differences, the perceived consequences of winning or losing in the competitive struggle for society's rewards become all the more significant. Given extensive inequality, large segments of the population are positioned at the bottom rungs of the economic ladder and, by the standards of the American Dream, are relegated to the role of "failure." The desire to avoid this fate intensifies the pressure to succeed at any cost. As a result, normative means of goal attainment lose their restraining force and anomie prevails.

As IAT locates the major causes of crime in the dominant culture, the implications of the theory for crime control are fairly radical and go beyond traditional policy prescriptions. The crime control recommendations that follow from IAT involve nothing short of a cultural transformation, including alternative definitions of success and increased commitment to community, responsibility, and public altruism. Policies that strengthen non-economic institutions such as the family and school would facilitate this transformation, as these institutions help to restrain antisocial behavior (by enforcing norms that govern socially acceptable means of goal attainment). These institutions also provide a buffer against the corrosive forces of the market.

In an important test of IAT, Baumer and Gustafson (2007) examined the relationship between monetary success goals, commitment to legitimate means of goal attainment, and instrumental crime rates (robberies, burglaries, larcenies, and auto thefts) across 77 geographic units in the United States, including metropolitan areas and non-metropolitan counties. Several findings of the study are noteworthy. First, the authors observe significant variation in relevant value orientations across the communities they examined. For example, the percentage of survey respondents from each area who expressed a strong commitment to monetary success (agreeing that, "next to health, money is the most important thing") ranged from a low of 15 percent to a high of 49 percent. Likewise, the percentage of respondents from each area who expressed weak commitment to the legitimate means of pursuing monetary success (agreeing that "there are no right or wrong ways to make money, only hard and easy ways") ranged from 5 percent to 41 percent. These findings highlight the fact that, despite a shared American culture, individuals differ in the extent to which they internalize the values associated with the "dark side" of the American Dream. Moreover, these values appear to be exaggerated only in select communities.

Second, the authors observe a relationship between instrumental crime rates and commitment to monetary success, but only under certain conditions. As predicted by both classic and contemporary anomie-strain theories, strong commitment to monetary success is associated with relatively high crime rates only in those areas where commitment to legitimate means is weak. (In areas where people's commitment to legitimate means remains strong, the importance of monetary success has no bearing on the crime rate.) Furthermore, this particular value configuration tends to have the strongest impact on instrumental crime in those areas that suffer from extensive economic inequality and where many residents occupy positions of low economic standing.

Third, consistent with IAT, the authors find some evidence that non-economic institutions can lessen the pressures that contribute to instrumental crime. Specifically, they observe that values related to monetary success and legitimate means have no impact on the crime rate in those areas where family ties are strong and where the poor receive above-average levels of welfare assistance. According to the authors of the study, these results lend support to the policy recommendations that follow from IAT. In particular, policies that strengthen families and buffer people from the effects of poverty and unemployment "would contribute significantly to a comprehensive crime control policy" in the United States (Baumer and Gustafson 2007: 655).

Conclusion

Although additional research will be required before a complete assessment of anomie-strain theories can be made, the results of existing studies indicate that such theories have some potential to explain crime and deviance at both the micro- and macro-levels of analyses. Anomie-strain theories, then, may help to supplement the leading crime theories, including alternative theories that are rooted in the concepts of social learning or informal social control (Akers and Sellers 2008). Contemporary anomie-strain theories are intuitively compelling, have received considerable attention from criminologists, have helped to revitalize the anomie-strain theory tradition, and are certain to stimulate criminological research for years to come.

References

Agnew, Robert. 1992. "Foundation for a General Strain Theory of Crime and Delinquency." *Criminology* 30:47–87.

Agnew, Robert. 1995. "Controlling Delinquency: Recommendations from General Strain Theory." In H. Barlow (Ed.), *Crime and Public Policy* (pp. 43–70). Boulder, CO: Westview.

Agnew, Robert. 1999. "A General Strain Theory of Community Differences in Crime Rates." *Journal of Research in Crime and Delinquency* 36:123–155.

Agnew, Robert. 2006. *Pressured into Crime: An Overview of General Strain Theory.* Los Angeles, CA: Roxbury.

Agnew, Robert, Francis T. Cullen, Velmer S. Burton Jr., T. David Evans, and R. Gregory Dunaway. 1996. "A New Test of Classic Strain Theory." *Justice Quarterly* 13:681–704.

Akers, Ronald L. and Christine S. Sellers. 2008. *Criminological Theories.* 5th edition. New York: Oxford University Press.

Baumer, Eric P. and Regan Gustafson. 2007. "Social Organization and Instrumental Crime: Assessing the Empirical Validity of Classic and Contemporary Anomie Theories." *Criminology* 45:617–663.

Brezina, Timothy. 1996. "Adapting to Strain: An Examination of Delinquent Coping Responses." *Criminology* 34:39–60.

Cloward, Richard A. and Lloyd E. Ohlin. 1960. *Delinquency and Opportunity.* New York: Free Press.

Cohen, Albert. 1955. *Delinquent Boys.* New York: Free Press.

Durkheim, Emile. (1951 [1897]). *Suicide: A Study in Sociology.* Translated by J. A. Spaulding and G. Simpson. New York: Free Press.

Konty, Mark. 2005. "Microanomie: The Cognitive Foundations of the Relationship between Anomie and Deviance." *Criminology* 43:107–132.

McCarthy, Bill and John Hagan. 2001. "Capital, Competence, and Criminal Success." *Social Forces* 79:1035–1059.

Merton, Robert K. 1938. "Social Structure and Anomie." *American Sociological Review* 3:672–682.

Messner, Steven F. and Richard Rosenfeld. 2001. *Crime and the American Dream.* 3rd edition. Belmont, CA: Wadsworth.

READING 8

Learning Criminal Behavior

Social Process Theories

Mark M. Lanier, Stuart Henry, and Desiré Anastasia

"Criminals are made not born."

—Andrew Kehoe (mass murderer, 1927)

Military unit leaders, vampire cultures, and investment bankers appear to be at opposite ends of the moral and behavioral spectrum. The military represents discipline, uniformity, respect for authority, high ethical standards, hierarchical status, and the promotion and protection of American values. Goth and vampire (or "vampyre") cults represent anarchy, individualism, disregard for authority, and little in the way of ethics; they challenge the most deeply held religious and social values. Investment bankers are supposed to embody the society's trust and certainly embody its capitalist values and business ethics. They each, however, share some similarities that can socialize their members into ways of thinking that can result in crime. Consider the cases of William Calley, Charity Keesee, and Bernie Madoff.

On March 16, 1968, in Vietnam, as many as five hundred men, women, and children were killed by US Army platoons in what was to become known as the My Lai massacre. A squad sergeant from one of the platoons testified, "We complied with the orders, sir" (Calley 1974, 342). Lt. William Calley, who gave the order for his squad to "get rid of 'em," reasoned: "Well everything is to be killed. ... I figured 'They're already wounded, I might as well go and kill them. This is our mission'" (ibid., 347, 342). Calley, brought up as a "run of the mill average guy," did not learn this on the street in a criminal gang but in US schools. As he explained:

Mark M. Lanier, Stuart Henry, and Desiré Anastasia, Selections from "Learning Criminal Behavior: Social Process Theories," *Essential Criminology*, pp. 124-125, 128-145, 148-149, 341-396. Copyright © 2014 by Taylor & Francis Group. Reprinted with permission.

I went to school in the 1950s remember, and it was drilled into us from grammar school on, "Ain't is bad, aren't is good, communism's bad, democracy's good. One and one's two," etcetera: until we were at Edison High, we just didn't think about it. The people in Washington are smarter than me. If intelligent people told me, "Communism's bad. It's going to engulf us. To take us in," I believed them. I had to. Personally, I didn't kill any Vietnamese that day: I mean personally. I represented the United States of America. My country. (ibid., 342–344)

In May 1995, Charity Lynn Keesee was fifteen years old and a runaway from rural Kentucky. She weighed ninety-five pounds and was pregnant. She was a lonely, shy girl, intelligent but rebellious. She was also a member of a group of kids who belonged to a vampire cult that was responsible for the notorious "Vampire Clan Killings," which have been the topic of several books, movies, and television documentaries. Although not typically resulting in violence and death, more than four thousand people are estimated to practice this black art. Unlike most, Keesee's cult committed one of the most publicized crimes of the twentieth century. The leader of her cult, her boyfriend, Roderick (Rod) Ferrell, sixteen, and Scott Anderson, seventeen, broke into the home of cult member Heather Wendorf, fifteen, and beat her parents to death using a crowbar. Cigarette burns in the shape of a "V" were found on the victims. Keesee, Wendorf, and Dana Cooper, nineteen, were across town visiting with friends during the attack. After the brutal satanic murder Ferrell and Anderson stole the family SUV and picked up the girls. After successfully eluding the police for days, Keesee phoned her mother from a hotel in Louisiana. According to Keesee, she had her mother notify the authorities as to their whereabouts (personal correspondence, November 2002). Others dispute this claim, stating that she was simply trying to get money. In either case, this phone call resulted in the arrest of the group in Baton Rouge. On June 15, 1996, Charity Lynn Keesee was convicted of being an accessory to first-degree murder and sentenced to fifteen years in Florida correctional institutions. After meeting with her numerous times my [Lanier's] impression was that she was still in many ways a lost sixteen-year-old. She was shy, sweet, and very open about her life and activities. She was very willing to please, anxious to improve her life, and looking forward to an education. There was also an undercurrent of strength, anger, and defiance. Now released, she is a working single mother, who still bears the scars of her youth and lengthy incarceration.

Now consider the corporate "Ponzi scheme" perpetrated by Bernie L. Madoff.

Let's consider these three cases in more detail. Calley grew up in the 1950s as a privileged white male in a segregated patriarchal society. Calley represented America, discipline, success, and honor. Charity Keesee belonged to "Gen X" and was an abused, powerless, rural girl—individualistic, outside the mainstream, and a rebel. Madoff was brought up in a working-class ethnic Jewish family whose capitalist values were driven predominantly by profit making based on building trusted relationships. Yet all three participated in some of the most publicized crimes of our times. Is there a common set of characteristics that could explain these very different types of crimes and types of people? What do Lt. William Calley, Charity Keesee, and Bernie Madoff have in common?

Each case represents a segment of a learning matrix. The individual has either a "normal" or a "traumatic" upbringing and/or is subject to a "normal" or systemically problematic organizational learning environment. In the first case, Calley had a normal family socialization and a normal, if highly disciplined, organizational socialization. He learned through these processes that following orders for an ideal was the right thing to do, regardless of whether the outcome was harmful to others; Calley learned to follow orders, and not to question authority, and, therefore, did not see his slaughter of these Vietnamese citizens—old men, women, and children—as his responsibility.

Charity Keesee was subject to the opposite childhood extreme. Having been brought up in an abusive family, she first found relief through self-mutilation. Keesee became an active participant in role-playing games such as Dungeons & Dragons and Vampire: the Masquerade. Over time, she increasingly sought refuge with what she calls "kindred spirits"—similarly abused youth who were into the Goth scene; her particular band, however, went further than most. Like William Calley, Keesee belonged to an organized, hierarchically structured group. Cults and clans, though less formal than the military, still follow specific rituals, demand allegiance, and promote "values." Like William Calley, Keesee complied with whatever her "commander" demanded. Goths and vampire cults, like the military, also dress in a uniform of sorts. Despite their professed desire to be unique, they all wear black, have pale skin, and follow Victorian clothing styles. Goths look alike. The fantasy role-playing games and obedience to authority practiced by many self-proclaimed vampires is not so different from small children who play soldier and carry toy guns (like Calley did as a child). Also like the military, Goths are law-abiding citizens the vast majority of the time. They work, eat, and pay bills like everyone else. Occasionally, they "drift" into crime. They also learn justifications for their deviant behavior. Keesee, then, was subject to the cultural norms of a deviant organization (the cult); the result was harm without conscience to others.

Finally, Bernie Madoff, a "self-made man," experienced a normal childhood socialization and was also socialized into the norms of capitalist greed; the result was that he harmed massive numbers of others through a classic Ponzi scheme. Madoff, like Calley, came from a stable family, was not abused, but nonetheless was accused of the world's most costly fraud. At age twenty-two, in 1950, he invested $5,000 that he'd earned from his summer job as a Long Island lifeguard and from installing refrigeration systems to start his own investment firm. Madoff attended, but did not graduate from, Hofstra Law School. His brother was a part of his investment company, but it was his sons, who were partners in his firm, who turned him in.

These three different examples illustrate the central theme of this chapter: ordinary human beings can become criminal offenders as a result of social processes through which they learn harmful behaviors and attitudes, and rationalizations that excuse or justify harm to others. Whether they are conforming to the military objectives of the government, the code and conventions of a vampire cult, or the rules and practices of capitalist culture, what they learn can result in criminal harm.

In this chapter, we examine several perspectives on social learning, called social process theories, which explain how this comes about: "Social process theories hold that criminality is a function of individual socialization. These theories draw attention to the interactions people have with the various organizations, institutions and processes of society" (Siegel 2004, 214).

This chapter marks a transition from the individually oriented rational choice, biological, and psychological principles outlined in the previous chapters toward theories that explain criminal behavior based on social and group interactive factors. We thus move our understanding of crime and criminality toward the cultural, sociological, and structural principles that follow in the rest of the book. The two social process theories considered in this chapter—"differential association" and "neutralization and drift"—each in different ways addresses the important contribution of social interaction in the process of becoming criminal. But they each also make different assumptions about humans and the role of socialization in learning. As we shall see, "differential association" theory views crime and delinquency as the outcome of normal learning processes whereby youth learn the "wrong" behavior. "Neutralization and drift" theory views delinquency and crime as a result of juveniles learning to excuse, justify, or otherwise rationalize potential deviant and even criminal behavior (which allows them to be released from the constraints of convention and drift into delinquency). Let us look at these social process theories in more detail.

Common Themes and Different Assumptions

In the previous chapter, we reviewed various psychological explanations about how human minds "turn criminal" as well as how individuals develop "criminal personalities." We also examined other psychological theories that explained how both criminal thinking and behavior could be learned. Similar to these theories, several sociological theorists, notably Edwin Sutherland and his colleague Donald Cressey (1966), with their theory of differential association, rejected the psychological criminal personality analysis that criminals are different; instead, they argued that delinquents or criminals are no different from noncriminals. Criminals do not have different personalities and do not think or learn differently from noncriminals. In fact, criminals, and *all* humans for that matter, learn to commit crimes just as they learn any other behavior. Learning comprises "habits and knowledge that develop as a result of the experiences of the individual in entering and adjusting to the environment" (Vold and Bernard 1986, 205). Psychological learning theories provided a basis for social learning theory: "There are two basic modes of learning. People learn by experiencing the effects of their actions and through the power of social modeling" (Bandura 2001b, 170). In other words, people also learn vicariously through observation of others' behavior and consequences. Indeed, "much human learning either occurs designedly or unintentionally from the models in one's immediate environment" (ibid.).

The primary learning mechanism occurs in association with others. Those we are in close association and interaction with, usually through informal small groups, such as parents, family, friends, and peers, are most responsible for what we learn. In addition, "a vast amount of knowledge about people, places, and styles of thinking and behaving is gained from the extensive modeling in the symbolic environment of the electronic mass media [where] a single model can transmit new ways of thinking and behaving simultaneously to many people in vastly dispersed locales. Video and computer delivery systems feeding off telecommunication satellites are now rapidly diffusing new ideas, values and styles of conduct worldwide" (ibid., 170–171).

What is crucially different between lawbreakers and law abiders is not the learning process but the content of what is learned. Both law abiders and lawbreakers are socialized to conform to social norms. The norms that law abiders learn are those of conventional mainstream society, whereas the norms learned by delinquents and criminals are those of a delinquent subculture with values opposed to the larger society.

Early on, in their theory of neutralization and drift, some sociologists, such as David Matza (1964) and Gresham Sykes (Sykes and Matza 1957; Matza and Sykes 1961), argued that early social learning theory in criminology presented a too-simplistic and overly deterministic picture. First, the theory assumed that humans are passive social actors, or blank slates, to be provided with good or bad knowledge about how to behave. Second, it drew too stark a contrast between conventional mainstream values and delinquent subcultural values. Instead of being separate, these values are interrelated; delinquency forms a subterranean part of mainstream culture. Instead of being immersed in and committed either to convention or to delinquency, individuals are socialized to behave conventionally but can occasionally be released from the moral bind of law to drift between these extremes. Part of the contribution of social learning theory in criminology is to consider how these processes of learning occur and how their conflicting and often contradictory content is cognitively negotiated by humans to allow them to believe that what they are doing is, at least at the time of the acts, justifiable under the circumstances.

We begin our analysis of these two social process perspectives by considering the work of Edwin Sutherland, who has been described as "the leading criminologist of his generation" and "the most prominent of American criminologists" (Martin, Mutchnick, and Austin 1990, 139).

Sutherland's Differential Association Theory

Edwin Hardin Sutherland (1883–1950) earned a doctorate from the University of Chicago, with a double major in sociology and political economy, and eventually went on to chair the Sociology Department at Indiana University. He first presented his theory of differential association in the third edition of his textbook *Principles of Criminology* (1939). He subsequently revised and developed the theory and presented the final version in the next edition, published in 1947.

Sutherland discounted the moral, physiological, and psychological "inferiority" of offenders (Jacoby 1994, 78) and rejected "internal" psychological theories (Martin, Mutchnick, and Austin 1990). His perspective explained crime by learning in a social context through interaction and communication (influenced by the symbolic interactionist tradition discussed later). Differential association is an abbreviation for "differential association with criminal and anti-criminal behavior patterns" (ibid., 155; see also Cressey 1962). Its central concept parallels Gabriel Tarde's ideas ([1890] 1903) that behavior is imitated in proportion and intensity to the social closeness between people.

There are two basic elements to understanding Sutherland's social learning theory. First, the content of what is learned is key. This includes the specific techniques for committing the crime, motives, rationalizations, attitudes, and, especially, evaluations by others of the meaningful significance of each of these elements. Second, the process by which learning takes place is important, including the intimate informal groups and the collective and situational context where learning occurs (Vold, Bernard, and Snipes [1998] 2001). Reflecting aspects of culture conflict theory, Sutherland also saw crime as politically defined. In other words, people who are in positions of power have the ability to determine which behaviors are considered criminal. He also argued that criminal behavior itself is learned through assigning meaning to behavior, experiences, and events during interaction with others.

The systematic elegance of Sutherland's theory is seen in its nine clearly stated, testable propositions:

1. Criminal behavior is learned.
2. Criminal behavior is learned in interaction with other persons in a process of communication.
3. The principal part of the learning of criminal behavior occurs within intimate personal groups.
4. When criminal behavior is learned, the learning includes (a) techniques of committing the crime ... [and] (b) the specific direction of motives, drives, rationalizations, and attitudes.
5. The specific direction of motives and drives is learned from definitions of legal codes as favorable and unfavorable.
6. A person becomes delinquent because of an excess of definitions favorable to violation of law over definitions unfavorable to violation of law.
7. Differential associations may vary in frequency, duration, priority, and intensity.
8. The process of learning criminal behavior by association with criminal and anti-criminal patterns involves all of the mechanisms that are involved in any other learning.
9. Though criminal behavior is an expression of general needs and values, it is not explained by those general needs and values since non-criminal behavior is an expression of the same needs and values. (Sutherland [1939] 1947, 6–8)

The foundation of differential association is found in the sixth proposition; that a "person becomes a criminal when he or she perceives more favorable than unfavorable consequences to violating the law ... [and] individuals become law violators when they are in contact with people, groups, or events that produce an excess of definitions favorable toward criminality and are isolated from counteracting forces" (Siegel 2013, 238).

Both criminal and anticriminal associations can be affected by: (1) priority of learning: how early this is learned in life; (2) frequency: how often one interacts with groups encouraging the behavior in question; (3) duration: the length of exposure to particular behavioral patterns; and (4) intensity: the prestige or status of those manifesting the observed behavior. If each of these four aspects is more favorable toward law violation, there is a higher probability of the person choosing criminal behavior. In other words, associating with groups that value law violation can lead to learning criminal behavior.

A final aspect of Sutherland's theory is the shift from the concept of social disorganization to differential social organization. Social disorganization theory states that those who become criminals are isolated from the mainstream culture and are immersed in their own impoverished and dilapidated neighborhoods, which have different norms and values. Differential social organization suggests that a complex society comprises numerous conflicting groups, each with its own different norms and values; associations with some of these can result in learning to favor law violation over law-abiding behavior.

Empirical Support and Limitations of Differential Association Theory

The major difficulty with the original version of differential association theory is that some of its central concepts were not clearly defined and depended on a simple, passive definition of social learning. We saw that cognitive psychologists showed that learning is a creative and active process. Indeed, by focusing on learning in small groups, Sutherland ignored what social learning theorist Albert Bandura (1977, 1986, 2001b) later found to be significant modeling of images glorified in the media. As Bandura acknowledged, this is not surprising because most of these theories were crafted "long before the advent of revolutionary advances in the technology of communications" (2001b, 171).

Furthermore, Laub (2006) found that Sutherland failed to consider vital features of crime that opposed his theory. Early on, Sheldon Glueck (1956) raised another concern, asking if all criminal behavior is learned from others or if some people invent their own criminal behavior. If not, then how does criminal behavior begin? Differential association may explain why some people in high-crime areas commit crime, which several research studies have illustrated. But it does not explain how criminal behaviors originate or who starts them, nor does it explain how some individual crimes are committed without associates. It also does not explain what counts as an excess of definitions, nor does it explain irrational acts of violence or destruction. It *does* show how patterns of criminal behavior can persist over time, however, and how social and organizational groups of both the powerful and the powerless can sustain these.

Methodologically, research on differential association has been criticized on several counts. Glueck (1956) questioned the ability to test differential association, although others argued that it is testable (DeFleur and Quinney 1966), and considerable empirical research on the theory would seem to support this belief. A further criticism is that most studies rely on asking subjects about their relationships with significant others. This method does not determine causality, and thus researchers are unsure if differential associations cause deviant behavior or result from deviant behavior. In addition, most of the studies rely on cross-sectional rather than longitudinal samples, which make it impossible to know whether learning came before, after, or during criminal behavior.

Research on differential association has generally not been able to empirically validate the claims made, although it has received some support. Armstrong and Matusitz (2013) found that differential association theory explains how Hezbollah (a Shi'a Islamic militant group and political party based in Lebanon) has effectively managed to recruit new members and persuade them to commit terrorist attacks. The essence of any terrorist endeavor is communication among group members, therefore, by interacting with one another, Hezbollah terrorists develop their combat skills and learn new tactics. Hawdon (2012) found that learning hate online through information and communication technologies can be through imitation; conversely, it can also occur by "reading information, engaging in debate and dialogue, critically reflecting on arguments, and through all the learning mechanisms that all learning can occur" (2012, 41). Church II et al. (2008) examined Delbert Elliott's longitudinal National Youth Study (NYS) and found that being male was the strongest predictor of delinquency and carried a strong connection to having associations with delinquent peers (page 12). Fox et al (2011) found that, regarding stalking perpetration and victimization, "there may be responses, attitudes, and behaviors that are learned, modified, or reinforced primarily through interaction with peers" (2011, 39).

Conversely, in an examination of NYS data, Rebellon's (2012) analysis failed to support the notion that differential association at one point in time causes substance use at a later point. Rader and Haynes (2011) argue that "individuals differentially associate with others, both directly and indirectly, who expose them to differential gender associations, differential fear of crime associations, and differential gendered fear of crime associations" and, therefore, men and women have differing levels of fear of crime (2011, 298). Baier and Wright (2001) conducted a meta-analysis that examined the effects of religion on criminal behavior. Their reanalysis of sixty prior studies found that religious practices and belief do show a significant, moderate inhibiting effect on crime commission. Similarly, Cocoran et al. (2012) found that religious belief is associated with lower acceptance of white-collar crime. In summary, the empirical research provides mixed support for differential association.

Modifying Differential Association: Differential Reinforcement Theory and Differential Identification Theory

In an attempt to overcome some of the early limitations of Sutherland's original theory, C. Ray Jeffery (1965) along with Robert Burgess and Ronald Akers (1966; Akers [1977] 1985, 1998; Akers and Sellers 2008) developed versions of a differential reinforcement theory of crime based on a combination of Skinner's ideas of operant conditioning and Sutherland's ideas of differential association. Jeffery's version of differential reinforcement argues that individuals have differences in their reinforcement history with respect to being rewarded and punished: for some, being rewarded for minor rule breaking can lead to more serious law violation; for others, being punished may be interpreted as "attention receiving," and rather than reducing the tendency toward crime, punishment can actually increase it. Moreover, Jeffery claims that once a criminal behavior is learned, it can become self-reinforcing.

Rather than seeing a simple mechanical relationship between stimulus and response, Burgess and Akers (1966; Akers [1977] 1985, 2008), like Bandura, see a more complex relationship that depends on the feedback a person receives from the environment. Akers explains how people learn criminal behavior through operant conditioning and argues that people evaluate their own behavior through interaction with significant other people and groups. Burgess and Akers (1966) present a revised version of the propositional statement of Sutherland:

1. Criminal behavior is learned according to the principles of operant conditioning.

2. Criminal behavior is learned both in nonsocial situations that are reinforcing or discriminative and through that social interaction in which the behavior of other persons is reinforcing or discriminative for criminal behavior.

3. The principal part of the learning of criminal behavior occurs in those groups that make up the individual's major source of reinforcement.

4. The learning of criminal behavior (including specific techniques, attitudes, and avoidance procedures) is a function of the effective and available rein-forcers and the existing reinforcement contingencies.

5. The specific class of behaviors that is learned and their frequency of occurrence are a function of the reinforcers that are effective and available and the rules or norms by which these reinforcers are applied.

6. Criminal behavior is a function of norms that are discriminative for criminal behavior, the learning of which takes place when such behavior is more highly reinforced than noncriminal behavior.

7. The strength of criminal behavior is a direct function of the amount, frequency, and probability of its reinforcement. These interactions rely on norms, attitudes, and orientations.

Burgess and Akers are particularly interested in the role of punishment and who provides it. They see punishment as "positive" when it follows a behavior and causes it to decrease and as "negative" when it takes the form of a reduction or loss of reward or privilege. Burgess and Akers argue that differential reinforcement occurs when the rewards are given to two behaviors but one is more highly rewarded than the other.

Moreover, this differential rewarding is particularly influential when it comes from others with whom one is significantly identified, such as parents, teachers, peers, and so on. Furthermore, in his version of social learning theory, Akers, like Bandura, acknowledges that modeling can arise based on the rewards one sees others getting. Daniel Glaser (1956) called this identification with others, particularly the generalized characteristics of favored social groups or reference groups, differential identification theory.

Policy Implications of Differential Association and Social Learning Theory

The policy implications associated with differential association theory are relatively straightforward. If socialization in small groups provides an excess of definitions favorable to law violation, the implication for prevention is to keep young and impressionable individuals away from such groups as well as educate and train them to resist the messages of such groups. For those already influenced, "treatment" intervention involving resocialization is consistent with the theory's general principles. Specific prevention programs that follow from this theory include peer-led interventions, resistance-skills training, and personal and social skills training. In a review of research on such programs, however, Gorman and White noted that these "were shown to be of minimal effectiveness and conceptually limited in that they fail to address the complexity of the relationship between group associations and delinquency" (1995, 149). Gorman and White argued that because the relationship is reciprocal, it is insufficient to intervene at the adolescent peer-group level since doing so ignores the parent-child interaction in earlier years that led to involvement with antisocial peers in the first place. They suggested that family-based and community programs seem to be more conceptually consistent with differential association theory than the school-based skills programs, but the effectiveness of such programs has not yet been adequately demonstrated.

Also overlooked in the policy arena is the role of the law and public policy in influencing definitions favorable or unfavorable to law violation. For example, clearer and simplified laws provided by the dominant mainstream culture are indicated. A related policy would be to publicly proclaim the law and reasons for following it; the media may provide an effective format for delivering this message.

Limitations of Differential Reinforcement Theory

Empirical research has extensively tested differential reinforcement theory. Several large-scale studies (Akers et al. 1979; Krohn et al. 1985) have found it to be supported. Sellers et al., however, criticize narrative studies, stating that "the theory appears to have attracted a great deal of consensus on its predictive accuracy. This conclusion, however, has been based primarily on narrative reviews of numerous, widely disparate empirical tests of the theory," which can be compromised by subjective factors (2000, 1). Nevertheless, their own meta-analysis summarizing one hundred and forty other studies confirmed this support.

In spite of this empirical efficacy, this theory does not explain how people rewarded for conventional behavior (e.g., economically affluent youths) still commit crimes. Also, like Sutherland, Akers does not explain where the values transmitted through differential reinforcement come from in the first place. He does point out, however, that the social environment one is exposed to contains different content, some more conducive to illegal behavior than others. Indeed, in more recent work he has developed the macrolevel social structural side of this argument, proposing that environments impact individuals through learning (1998, 302).

Social learning theory's greatest merit is that not only does it draw together the psychological process components examined in the previous chapter of learning by role modeling and reinforcement of that learning, but "most significant, Akers contended that definitions and imitation are most instrumental in determining initial forays into crime" and that "continued involvement in crime, therefore, depends on exposure to social reinforcements that reward this activity. The stronger and more persistent the reinforcements ... the greater the likelihood that the criminal behavior will persist" (Lilly, Cullen, and Ball 2002, 46), and the more conducive the social environment to providing this reinforcement, the more likely are such structures to contribute to such criminogenesis (Akers 1998).

Going beyond Sutherland, Cressey, and Akers, we need to take into account Albert Bandura's significant contribution to social learning theory in its application to explain crime and deviance (1986, 1997, 2001a).

Neutralization Theory: Learning Rationalizations as Motives

One very important element of the behavior learned in intimate social groups and considered by Sutherland was the rationalizations that accompany behavior. These rationalizations are related to Sutherland's idea ([1939] 1947) about how law violations can be defined as favorable or unfavorable. Donald Cressey (1953, 1970), in a study of the "respectable" crime of embezzlement, found that three key elements were necessary for a violation of financial trust to occur: (1) a nonsharable financial problem (meaning a problem the offender feels embarrassed to tell others about, such as gambling debts); (2) the perception of their legitimate occupation as a solution to the problem, typically through using funds to which they have access; and (3) verbalizations, or words and phrases that make the behavior acceptable (such as "borrowing" the money and "intending" to pay it back). It is this third element, and the possibility that such words and phrases may be found in the common culture, that make the crime possible. As Cressey said: "I am convinced that the words and phrases that the potential embezzler uses in conversations with himself are actually the most important elements in the process that gets him into trouble" (1970, 111).

For Cressey, verbalizations were not simply rationalizations occurring after the fact of crime to relieve an offender of culpability. Instead, they were words and phrases that could, as C. Wright Mills (1940) had earlier argued, be "vocabularies of motive." They could inhibit someone from engaging in a criminal act by showing the potential offender that using such excuses or justifications after a criminal act might not be honored as acceptable. Alternatively, the excuses and justifications could be honored by future questioners, allowing the potential offender a sense of "freedom" that it might be acceptable to violate the law under the particular situation or circumstances described. The most sophisticated development of these ideas came from Matza (1964) and Sykes (Sykes and Matza 1957; Matza and Sykes 1961) in their studies of juvenile delinquency. Indeed, they stated that techniques of neutralization "make up a crucial component of Sutherland's 'definitions favorable to violation of law'. … It is by learning these techniques that the juvenile becomes delinquent" (Sykes and Matza 1957, 667).

Drifting In and Out of Delinquency: Matza and Sykes's Neutralization Theory

The central idea behind neutralization theory is that "the excuses and justifications that deviants use to rationalize their behaviors might themselves be implicated in the etiology of deviant behavior" (Maruna and Copes 2004, 2). In Matza and Sykes's terms, neutralizations "precede deviant behavior and make deviant behavior possible" (1957, 666), though not inevitable, as Matza was later at pains to point out through his concept of "drift," discussed below.

In 1957, while at Princeton University, Gresham Sykes teamed up with his former student David Matza to develop a new theory of crime that extended Sutherland's learning theory (Sykes and Matza 1957). The analysis originated in Sykes's studies of prison inmates and guards learning to rationalize rule breaking (Martin, Mutchnick, and Austin 1990). Matza argued that existing theories, whether biological, psychological, or sociological, were too deterministic. He argued that existing theories predict too much crime. Most juvenile delinquents do not continue their criminal behavior into adulthood; in other words, most desist from crime. If a biological or psychological factor "caused" crime, why would its influence diminish after adolescence? If delinquent subcultures were so compelling at socializing youths to define crime as acceptable, then what accounts for their maturational reform—the tendency for juvenile delinquents to relinquish their delinquency as they age into their twenties and thirties? Matza sought to combine these observations to explain most delinquency, arguing, "The image of the delinquent I wish to convey is one of drift; an actor neither compelled nor committed to deeds nor freely choosing them; neither different in any simple or fundamental sense from the law abiding, nor the same; conforming to certain traditions in American life while partially unreceptive to other more conventional traditions; and finally, an actor whose motivational system may be explored along lines explicitly commended by classical criminology—his peculiar relation to legal institutions" (1964, 28).

How Matza sought to combine these many orientations was, in part, by making a case for soft determinism. According to Matza, positivistic criminology (the scientific study of crime that had prevailed since the late nineteenth century) "fashioned an image of man to suit a study of criminal behavior based on scientific determinism. It rejected the view that man exercised freedom, was possessed of reason, and was thus capable of choice" (ibid., 5). Conversely, soft determinism argues that "human actions are not deprived of freedom because they are causally determined" (ibid., 9). The amount of freedom each person has varies. Some are more free than others and have a greater range of choices available. Moreover, this freedom varies according to circumstances, situations, and context.

Most important to understanding Matza and Sykes's argument is the concept of the "subculture of delinquency." As traditionally conceived, delinquent subcultures are considered separate and oppositional; their norms and values are different from those in the mainstream culture. The gang is the best example. For Matza and Sykes (1961), however, this was a false distinction. Most delinquents, they argued, are not full-fledged gang members but "mundane delinquents" who express remorse over their actions. Many admire law-abiding citizens. Furthermore, most differentiate between whom they will victimize and whom they will not. Finally, delinquents are not exclusively criminal; they also engage in many noncriminal acts. These factors suggest that delinquents are aware of the difference between right and wrong and are subject to the influence of both conventional and delinquent values.

Matza and Sykes argue that rather than delinquency and mainstream culture being separate, mainstream culture has an underbelly of "subterranean values" that exist side by side with conventional values. The subterranean subculture of delinquency makes it unnecessary for adolescent youths to join gangs or other subcultural groups to learn delinquent values. Instead, simply by learning and being socialized into conventional values and norms, adolescents are simultaneously socialized into the negation of those values. Nowhere is this more evident than in legal codes.

Legal codes are inconsistent and thus vulnerable. As Matza wrote, "The law contains the seeds of its own neutralization. Criminal law is especially susceptible [to] neutralization because the conditions of applicability, and thus inapplicability, are explicitly stated" (1964, 60). This means people can claim various kinds of exemptions in the belief that they are, under certain mitigating circumstances, not bound by the law. The classic example is "self-defense." Another example is the idea that criminal intent (*mens rea*) must be present for an act to be criminal. Such legal contradictions, and the implicit claims for exemption that follow from them, allow the possibility for choice and freedom because they render individuals intermittently free to choose to commit delinquent acts. Whether youths break the law depends not so much on their being in a delinquent subculture but, first, on whether they are freed into a state of drift and released from the larger culture's moral bind, and, second, on whether they then exercise free choice: "Drift stands midway between freedom and control. Its basis is an area in the social structure in which control has been loosened. The delinquent transiently exists in a limbo between convention and crime, responding in turn to the demands of each, flirting now with one, now with the other, but postponing commitment, evading decision. Thus he [or she] drifts between criminal and conventional action" (ibid., 28).

This "loosening" of control, or release from moral convention into a state of drift, occurs through neutralization. For Matza, neutralization comprises words and phrases that excuse or justify lawbreaking behavior, such as claiming an action was "self-defense." Unlike rationalizations, which come after an act to avoid culpability and consequences, and verbalizations that come after contemplating an act to allow oneself to commit it, neutralizations come before an act is even contemplated. Thus, for Matza, they are "unwitting," something that occurs to an actor that results from the unintended duplication, distortion, and extension of customary beliefs relating to when and under what circumstances exceptions are allowed: "Neutralization of legal precepts depends partly on equivocation—the unwitting use of concepts in markedly different ways" (ibid., 74; see also L. Taylor 1972). Neutralization frees the delinquent from the moral bind of law so that he or she may now choose to commit the crime. Crucially, whether or not a crime occurs no longer requires some special motivation.

Sykes and Matza (1957) classified excuses and justifications that provide a moral release into five types, which they called "techniques of neutralization":

1. *Denial of responsibility* (e.g., "It's not my fault—I was drunk at the time"): In this technique offenders claim their questioned behavior was not in their control, or that it was accidental. Offenders may list reasons such as alcohol, peer pressure, bad neighborhood, and so on that caused them to commit the act.

2. *Denial of injury* (e.g., "No one got hurt"): Here the extent of harm caused is minimized or negated. Offenders may deny that anyone or anything was harmed by their action. For example, shoplifters might claim that stores have so much money and insurance that "they can afford it," or employee thieves may claim their company wastes so much that "it'll never miss it." Embezzlers are also simply "borrowing the money," and joyriders are "borrowing" the car.

3. *Denial of victim* (e.g., "They had it coming to them"): Some offenders may claim that although someone got hurt, he or she deserved it. For example, corporations may treat their employees badly, paying them too little or instituting a stringent dress code. Employees may pilfer goods out of resentment "to get back at the company," saying they are the real victims of the corporation's abuse. Women who harm physically or psychologically abusive spouses may claim that the "victim" was actually an offender who had therefore forfeited his rights to victimhood and was finally getting what he deserved. Absent or abstract victims are also easy to deny victim status, which is another reason it is morally less challenging to steal from large diffuse organizations than the clearly identifiable "mom and pop" store owner.

4. *Condemnation of the condemners* (e.g., "Law enforcement is corrupt"): This technique involves negating the right of others to pass judgment. Offenders may reject the people who have authority

over them, such as judges, parents, and police officers, who are viewed as being just as corrupt and thus not worthy of respect.

5. *Appeal to higher loyalties* (e.g., "I didn't do it for myself"): Many offenders argue that their loyalties lie with their peers (fellow gang members, employees, police officers, and so on), and that the group has needs that take precedence over societal moral demands. Female embezzlers have claimed to have stolen for their families, and mothers have committed arson to provide work for their unemployed firefighter sons. Indeed, included are "corporate offenders who argue that their actions were conducted for 'higher' goals including profit for their stockholders and financial stability for their families." (Maruna and Copes 2004, 13)

Since Matza and Sykes's original studies on delinquency, researchers have applied neutralization theory to a variety of other crimes, including adult crime, especially to offenders who maintain a dual lifestyle and are both part of the mainstream yet also engage in crime, as in employee theft (Ditton 1977; Hollinger and Clark 1983; Hollinger 1991) and buying and selling stolen goods (Klockars 1974; Henry [1978] 1988). More recently a question has also been raised: is neutralization theory also pertinent to positive behaviors? A group of high-achieving students was interviewed and it was found that each of the five (main) techniques of neutralization was in fact advanced as a way of coping with the stigma, or the rate-busting portion, of their status. In a study of corporate crime, Nicole Leeper Piquero, S. G. Tibbetts, and M. B. Blankenship (2005) found that respondents used neutralizations in making decisions for a drug company about producing a drug that was harmful to consumers. As a consequence of this extended research, at least five additional types of neutralization have been identified (Henry 1990; Pfuhl and Henry 1993; Maruna and Copes 2004, 14):

1. *Metaphor of the ledger* (e.g., "I've done more good than bad in my life"): This was used by Klockars (1974) to show how the professional fence believed himself to be, on the balance of his life, more moral than immoral ("Look at all the money I've given to charity and how I've helped children. If you add it all up, I've got to come out on the good side").

2. *Claim of normality* (e.g., "Everyone is doing it"): This suggests that the law is not reflecting the popular will, and since everyone engages in, say, tax evasion, pilfering from the office, extramarital sex, and so on, then such acts are not really deviant and therefore are not wrong.

3. *Denial of negative intent* (e.g., "It was just a joke"): Henry (1990; Henry and Eaton 1999) found this was used by college students to justify their use of explosives on campus, among other things ("We were only having some fun"). The neutralization is partial denial, accepting responsibility for the act but denying that the negative consequences were intended.

4. *Claim of relative acceptability* (e.g., "There are others worse than me"), also called justification by comparison (Cromwell and Thurman 2003): unlike condemning the condemners, this appeals to the audience to compare the offender's crime to more serious ones and can go so far

as claiming to be moral. For example, Los Angeles police officers claimed that the beating of Rodney King, after being stopped for a traffic violation, helped prevent him from being killed by nervous fellow officers (Pfuhl and Henry 1993, 70).

5. *Claim of entitlement* (e.g., "For the sacrifices that I've made I deserve some special reward"): This was used by deployed naval officers to justify cheating on their wives back home (Shea 2007).

The important point about these techniques of neutralization is their timing in the cognitive process. All could be used as techniques or devices (1) *after* an illegal act to seek to reduce blame or culpability or (2) *before* committing the act while contemplating it in order to seek self-conscious approval that it is acceptable to go ahead. But for Matza and others (Taylor 1972; Henry 1976), the critical point is that they can also occur (3) *before contemplating the act*, releasing the actor to be morally free to choose the act. In the latter case, the context, situation, and circumstances provide a neutralizing discourse that removes the moral inhibition, releasing a person to commit criminal acts, as they would any other act.

Maruna and Copes argue that not only are the original five techniques of neutralization not necessarily the most important techniques, and are somewhat overlapping (e.g., denial of injury and denial of victim), but also that "researchers have identified dozens to even hundreds of techniques that seem to serve the same function as neutralization techniques. In fact, they maintain that "the individual use of specific neutralizations should be understood within the wider context of sense making that is the self-narrative process" (2004, 64). It is toward understanding this process that we now turn.

Bandura's Moral Disengagement Theory

In the context of his discussion of self-regulation Bandura comes close to Matza's concept of neutralization of morality. He describes the process of moral disengagement as one that uses psychological maneuvers or mechanisms for disengaging moral control, and he identifies two types. The first type is justificatory: "Investing harmful conduct with high moral purpose not only eliminates self-censure, but it engages self-approval in the service of destructive exploits as well. What was once morally condemnable, becomes a source of self-pride" (2001b, 178). Within the first type, three justificatory moral disengagement mechanisms are identified:

1. *Moral justification*, whereby harmful, inhumane, or otherwise detrimental conduct is made "personally and socially acceptable by portraying it as serving socially worthy or moral purposes" (ibid., 177).

2. *Sanitizing euphemistic language* is used to make harmful conduct personally respectable and more acceptable.

3. *Exonerating comparison* compares the questioned behavior to more harmful behavior such that "the more flagrant the inhumanities against which one's destructive conduct is contrasted, the more likely it will lose its repugnancy or even appear benevolent" (ibid., 178).

The second type of moral disengagement mechanism is that which diminishes a person's active human agency both to himself and others. This is a form of excuse, which Bandura calls "*displacement and diffusion of responsibility.*" Here someone or something is held responsible for the harm committed or when an individual sees him- or herself as a fragment of a much larger framework. He says that in this form of moral disengagement, "personal agency is obscured by diffusing responsibility for detrimental behavior by group decision making, subdividing injurious activities into seemingly harmless parts, and exploiting the anonymity of collective action" (ibid., 178), a form prevalent among corporate and government offenders.

Weakened moral control also comes about by:

1. *Disregarding or distorting harm*, which has similarities to Matza's denial of injury by ignoring, minimizing, distorting, or disbelieving in the harm caused.
2. *Blaming others* for harm "becomes a justifiable defensive reaction to perceived provocations," which is similar to Matza's denial of the victim (Bandura 2001b, 179).

Bandura also argues, "Self-censure for cruel conduct can be disengaged by de-humanization that strips people of human qualities. Once dehumanized, they are no longer viewed as persons with feelings, hopes and concerns but as subhuman objects" (ibid.). As others have noted, there are clearly close parallels between the major tenets of neutralization theory and Bandura's moral disengagement theory, even though Bandura does not acknowledge Matza's work in his own development of these ideas.

References

———. [1977] 1985. *Deviant Behavior: A Social Learning Approach*. Belmont, CA: Wadsworth.

———. 1998. *Social Learning and Social Structure: A General Theory of Crime and Deviance*. Boston: Northeastern University Press.

Akers, Ronald L., Marvin D. Krohn, Lonn Lanza-Kaduce, and Marcia Radosevich. 1979. "Social Learning and Deviant Behavior: A Specific Test of a General Theory." *American Sociological Review* 44: 635–655.

Akers, Ronald L., and Christine S. Sellers. 2008. *Criminological Theories: Introduction, Evaluation, and Application*. 5th ed. Oxford: Oxford University Press.

Armstrong, Taylor, and Jonathan Matusitz. 2013. "Hezbollah as a Group Phenomenon: Differential Association Theory." *Journal of Human Behavior in the Social Environment* 23, no. 4: 475–484.

Baier, Colin J., and Bradley R. E. Wright. 2001. "If You Love Me, Keep My Commandments: A Meta-Analysis of the Effect of Religion on Crime." *Journal of Research in Crime and Delinquency* 38: 3–21.

———. 1977. *Social Learning Theory*. Englewood Cliffs, NJ: Prentice Hall.

———. 1986. *Social Foundation of Thought and Acquisition: A Social Cognitive Theory.* Englewood Cliffs, NJ: Prentice Hall.

———. 1997. *Self-Efficacy: The Exercise of Control.* New York: Freeman.

———. 2001a. "Social Cognitive Theory: An Agentic Perspective." *Annual Review of Psychology* 52: 1–26.

———. 2001b. "Social Cognitive Theory of Personality." In *Handbook of Personality: Theory and Research,* edited by Lawrence A. Pervin and Oliver P. John, 154–196. 2d ed. New York: Guilford Press.

Burgess, Robert L., and Ronald L. Akers. 1966. "A Differential Association: Reinforcement Theory of Criminal Behavior." *Social Problems* 14: 128–147.

Calley, William L. 1974. "So This Is What War Is." In *In Their Own Behalf: Voices from the Margin,* edited by Charles H. McCaghy, James K. Skipper, Jr., and Mark Lefton. Englewood Cliffs, NJ: Prentice Hall.

Church II, Wesley T., Tracy Wharton, and Julie K. Taylor. 2008. "An Examination of Differential Association and Social Control Theory: Family Systems and Delinquency." *Youth Violence and Juvenile Justice* 7, no. 1: 3–15.

Corcoran, Katie E., David Pettinicchio and Blaine Robbins. 2012. "Religion and the Acceptability of White-Collar Crime: A Cross-National Analysis." *Journal for the Scientific Study of Religion* 51, no. 3: 542–567.

Cressey, Donald R. 1953. *Other People's Money.* Glencoe, IL: Free Press.

———. 1962. "The Development of a Theory: Differential Association." In *The Sociology of Crime and Delinquency,* edited by M. E. Wolfgang, L. Savitz, and N. Johnston. New York: John Wiley.

———. 1970. "The Respectable Criminal." In *Modern Criminals,* edited by James Short. New York: Transaction-Aldine.

Cromwell, Paul, and Quint Thurman. 2003. "The Devil Made Me Do It: Use of Neutralizations by Shoplifters." *Deviant Behavior* 24: 535–550.

DeFleur, Melvin, and Richard Quinney. 1966. "A Reformulation of Sutherland's Differential Association Theory and a Strategy for Empirical Verification." *Journal of Research in Crime and Delinquency* 2: 1–22.

Ditton, Jason. 1977. *Part-Time Crime: An Ethnography of Fiddling and Pilferage.* London: Macmillan.

Fox, Kathleen A., Matt R. Nobles, and Ronald L. Akers. 2011. "Is Stalking a Learned Phenomenon? An Empirical Test of Social Learning Theory." *Journal of Criminal Justice* 39, no. 1: 39–47.

Glaser, Daniel. 1956. "Criminality Theories and Behavioral Images." *American Journal of Sociology* 61: 433–444.

Glueck, Sheldon. 1956. "Theory and Fact in Criminology: A Criticism of Differential Association." *British Journal of Delinquency* 7: 92–109.

Gorman, D. M., and Helene Raskin White. 1995. "You Can Choose Your Friends, but Do They Choose Your Crime? Implications of Differential Association Theories for Crime Prevention Policy." In *Crime and Public Policy: Putting Theory to Work,* edited by Hugh D. Barlow. Boulder, CO: Westview Press.

Hawdon, James. 2012. "Applying Differential Association Theory to Online Hate Groups: a Theoretical Statement." *Research on Finnish Society* 5: 39–47.

Henry, Stuart. 1976. "Fencing with Accounts: The Language of Moral Bridging." *British Journal of Law and Society* 3: 91–100.

———. [1978] 1988. *The Hidden Economy: The Context and Control of Borderline Crime.* Oxford: Martin Robertson; Port Townsend, WA: Loompanics.

———, ed. 1990. *Degrees of Deviance: Student Accounts of Their Deviant Behavior.* Aldershot, UK: Avebury; Salem, WI: Sheffield.

Henry, Stuart, and Roger Eaton, eds. 1999. *Degrees of Deviance: Student Accounts of Their Deviant Behavior.* 2nd ed. Salem, WI: Sheffield Publishing.

Hollinger, Richard C. 1991. "Neutralizing in the Workplace: An Empirical Analysis of Property Theft and Production Deviance." *Deviant Behavior* 12: 169–202.

Hollinger, Richard C., and John P. Clark. 1983. *Theft by Employees.* Lexington, MA: D. C. Heath.

Jacoby, Joseph E. 1994. *Classics of Criminology.* 2d ed. Prospect Heights, IL: Waveland.

Jeffery, C. Ray. 1965. "Criminal Behavior and Learning Theory." *Journal of Criminal Law, Criminology, and Police Science* 56: 294–300.

Klockars, Carl. 1974. *The Professional Fence.* New York: Free Press.

Krohn, Marvin D., William Skinner, James Massey, and Ronald Akers. 1985. "Social Learning Theory and Adolescent Cigarette Smoking: A Longitudinal Study." *Social Problems* 32: 455–471.

Laub, John H. 2006. "Edwin H. Sutherland and the Michael-Adler Report: Searching for the Soul of Criminology Seventy Years Later." *Criminology* 44, no. 2: 235–257.

———. 2002. *Criminological Theory: Context and Consequences.* 3d ed. Thousand Oaks, CA: Sage.

Martin, Randy, Robert J. Mutchnick, and Timothy W. Austin. 1990. *Criminological Thought: Pioneers Past and Present.* New York: Macmillan.

———. 2004. "Excuses, Excuses: What Have We Learned from Five Decades of Neutralization Research?" In *Crime and Justice,* 1–100. Chicago: University of Chicago Press.

Matza, David. 1964. *Delinquency and Drift.* New York: John Wiley.

Matza, David, and Gresham Sykes. 1961. "Juvenile Delinquency and Subterranean Values." *American Sociological Review* 26: 712–719.

Mills, C. Wright. 1940. "Situated Actions and Vocabularies of Motive." *American Sociological Review* 5: 904–913.

Pfuhl, Erdwin H., and Stuart Henry. 1993. *The Deviance Process.* 3d ed. Hawthorn, NY: Aldine De Gruyter.

Rader, Nicole E. and Stacy H. Haynes. 2011. "Gendered Fear of Crime Socialization: An Extension of Akers's Social Learning Theory." *Feminist Criminology* 6, no. 4: 291–307.

Rebellon, Cesar J. 2012. "Differential Association and Substance Use: Assessing the Roles of Discriminant Validity, Socialization, and Selection in Traditional Empirical Tests." *European Journal of Criminology* 9, no. 1: 73–96.

Sellers, Christine, S., Travis C. Pratt, Thomas L. Winfree, and Frank T. Cullen. 2000. "The Empirical Status of Social Learning Theory: A Meta-Analysis." Paper presented at American Society of Criminology Conference, San Francisco: American Society of Criminology.

Shea, Jennifer Susan. 2007. "Naval Deployments and Adultery: The Neutralization of Moral Commitment." Master's thesis, San Diego State University.

———. 2004. *Criminology: Theories, Patterns, and Typologies.* 8th ed. Belmont, CA: Wadsworth.

———. 2012. *Criminology: Theories, Patterns and Typologies.* 11th ed. Belmont, CA: Wadsworth.

———. [1939] 1947. *Principles of Criminology.* Philadelphia: J. B. Lippincott.

Sutherland, Edwin H., and Donald R. Cressey. 1966. *Principles of Criminology.* Philadelphia: J. B. Lippincott.

Sykes, Gresham, and David Matza. 1957. "Techniques of Neutralization: A Theory of Delinquency." *American Sociological Review* 22: 664–670.

Tarde, Gabriel. [1890] 1903. *Gabriel Tarde's Laws of Imitation.* Translated by E. Parsons. New York: Henry Holt.

Taylor, Laurie. 1972. "The Significance and Interpretation of Motivational Questions: The Case of Sex Offenders." *Sociology* 6: 23–29.

Vold, George B., and Thomas J. Bernard. 1986. *Theoretical Criminology.* 3d ed. New York: Oxford University Press.

Vold, George B., Thomas J. Bernard, and J. B. Snipes. 1998 [2001]. *Theoretical Criminology.* 5th ed. New York: Oxford University Press.

READING 9

Labelling Theories

Roger Hopkins Burke

Labelling theories have their foundations in the various concepts and insights provided by interactionism, phenomenology and ethnomethodology—we encountered above—and focus on three central concerns. First, there is a consideration of why and how it is that some acts come to be defined as deviant or criminal while others do not. Thus, to this end there is an examination of legal codes and practices, and the social and professional interest groups that shape the criminal law. Second, it is recognised that certain people and groups are more likely to attract deviant, criminal and stigmatising labels than others. There is thus an examination of the differential applications of laws and labels by the various social control agencies and the relationship of this to organisational context. Unfortunately, these early, well-known and highly influential labelling theorists—with the limited exception of Becker (1963), Kitsuse (1962), Piliavin and Briar (1964) and Cicourel (1968)—did not address these concerns as thoroughly as they might have done, although they contributed significantly to the development of the radical criminology discussed in the following chapter, while the later far less well-known and significantly less influential labelling theorists such as Hartjen (1974), Ditton (1979) and Arvanites (1992) focus very much on the issue of state power. Most of the energy of the most active phase of the highly influential earlier labelling theory was nevertheless directed towards the third concern that assesses the experience of being labelled for the recipients of the label. We will consider each of these concerns in turn.

The Social Construction of Crime

Before labelling theories achieved prominence, most criminologists had a non-problematic conception of crime. Criminal behaviour was simply a form of activity that violates the criminal law. Once crime was thus defined, theorists—working in the predestined actor model tradition—could concentrate on their main concern of identifying and analysing its causes. This whole approach was nevertheless far too simplistic for proponents of the labelling perspective who argued that what is defined as 'criminal' is not fixed but varies across time, culture and even from one situation to the next. From this perspective, the conventional morality of rules and criminal laws in any given society should be studied and questioned and not merely accepted as self-evident.

Roger Hopkins Burke, "Labelling Theories," *An Introduction to Criminological Theory*, pp. 167-179, 351-393. Copyright © 2009 by Taylor & Francis Group. Reprinted with permission.

Labelling theorists fundamentally argue that no behaviour is *inherently* deviant or criminal, but only comes to be considered so when others confer this label upon the act. Thus, it is not the intrinsic nature of an act, but the nature of the societal reaction that determines whether a 'crime' has taken place. Even the most commonly recognised and serious crime of murder is not universally defined in the sense that anyone who kills another is everywhere and always guilty of murder. The essence of this position is neatly summarised in a well-known passage by Becker (1963: 4) whom, unlike most other labelling theorists, was concerned with the creators and enforcers of criminal labels and categories:

> Social groups create deviance by making the rules whose infraction constitutes deviance, and by applying those rules to particular people and labelling them as outsiders. From this point of view ... the deviant is one to whom the label has been successfully applied; deviant behaviour is behaviour that people so label.

Becker argued that rules—including criminal laws—are made by people with power and enforced upon people without power. Thus, even on an everyday level, rules are made by the old for the young, by men for women, by whites for blacks, by the middle class for the working class and we might add here, by schools for their students and parents for their children, an observation to which we return later in this chapter. These rules are often imposed upon the recipients against their will and their own best interests and are legitimised by an ideology that is transmitted to the less powerful in the course of primary and secondary socialisation. As a result of this process, most people internalise and obey the rules without realising—or questioning—the extent to which their behaviour is being decided for them.

Becker also argues that some rules may be cynically designed to keep the less powerful in their place while others may have simply been introduced as the outcome of a sincere—albeit irrational and mistaken—belief on the part of high-status individuals that the creation of a new rule will be beneficial for its intended subjects. Becker termed the people who create new rules for the 'benefit' of the less fortunate 'moral entrepreneurs'.

Becker noted two closely interrelated outcomes of a successful 'moral crusade': first, there is the creation of a new group of 'outsiders', those who infringe the new rule; second, a social control agency emerges charged with enforcing the rule and with the power to impose labels on transgressors, although more often this simply means an extension of police work and power. Eventually the new rule, control agency and 'deviant' social role come to permeate the collective consciousness and are taken for granted with the outcome being the creation of negative stereotypes of those labelled 'deviant'.

Becker (1963) cites the campaign by the US Federal Bureau of Narcotics (FBN) to outlaw marijuana use through the Marijuana Tax Act of 1937 which was justified on the grounds of protecting society—particularly young people—from the ill effects of this drug and relied heavily on propaganda of one sort or another to get its message across. In Becker's view the campaign was undertaken primarily as a means of advancing the organisational interests enjoyed by the state to be extended beyond mere breaches of the criminal law to cover 'status offences' such as truancy and promiscuity.

Tierney's (1982) analysis of domestic violence also provides evidence of the process of criminalisation. She argues that 'wife battering' only emerged as an important social issue worthy of criminal justice intervention after the mid-1970s, mainly because of the increasing strength of the women's movement and the determination to secure the provision of refuges, legislation and other measures aimed at protecting women.

In short, what these and similar studies show, is not the inherent harm of behaviour or its pervasiveness that prompts changes in the law, but rather the concerted efforts of sufficiently motivated and powerful social groups to redefine the boundaries of what is considered acceptable and legal.

Others have adopted a macro perspective in order to explain these processes. Thus, Erikson (1962) draws upon Durkheim in arguing that all social systems place certain boundaries on culturally permissible behaviour and deviancy is simply that which is defined as crossing these parameters. Indeed, deviant behaviour may be the only way of *marking* these boundaries. Thus, transactions between deviants and social control agents are 'boundary maintenance mechanisms' which attract a good deal of publicity and by acting outside of these system boundaries deviants demonstrate to society where the perimeters lie while, at the same time, giving those inside a sense of identity or 'belongingness'. These processes in turn help to preserve social stability. Thus, in viewing deviance as essentially 'boundary maintenance activity', the work of Erikson marks a point of convergence between the labelling perspective and the functionalism of Durkheim.

Quinney (1970) also employed a macro sociological perspective but one that combined labelling theory with conflict theory, differential association and deviant subculture theories. He was also influenced by Durkheim's notion of mechanical and organic solidarity in proposing two ideal types of society (or social organisation): *singular* and *segmental.* According to Quinney, in a singular or homogeneous society all crime must necessarily occur outside any value system since by definition all members of the society adhere to this value system. In a segmental or heterogeneous society some segments will share common values with others, but because there is unlikely to be a complete consensus, value systems will be in conflict to a certain extent. Thus, the criminal laws and their enforcement are a product of this conflict and the associated unequal distribution of political power.

Quinney argues that society is segmentally organised or pluralistic and, therefore, the criminal law tends to represent the values of politically powerful sections of society. Moreover, he suggests a direct relation between the possibility of someone being labelled as criminal and their relative position in the social structure.

The Recipients of Deviant Labels

It is conventional wisdom that those who break the law will be labelled as criminal. Becker (1963) nevertheless exposed the inadequacy of this perception, noting that the innocent are sometimes falsely accused, and more importantly, only some of those who violate the criminal law are eventually arrested and processed through the system. Kitsuse (1962) found—in a study of homosexuality that has much wider criminological ramifications—that it is not the behaviour *per se* that is the central issue. It is the interactional process through which behaviour is both defined as deviant and through which sanctions are initiated. Thus distinguishing deviants from non-deviants is not primarily a matter of behaviour but is contingent upon 'circumstance or situation, social and personal biography, and the bureaucratically organised activities of social control' (Kitsuse, 1962: 256).

A number of important studies conducted in the USA confirmed that the actual behaviour is not the only factor in determining whether a deviant or criminal label is conferred. Official responses are shaped by a range of extralegal variables, such as appearance, demeanour, ethnic group and age, for example, Piliavin and Briar (1964) looked at police encounters with juveniles and found that arrest decisions were based largely on physical cues—manner, dress and general appearance—from which the officer inferred the character of the youth. *Structural* factors, such as gender, social class, ethnic group, and time of day were also significant, thus a young, working-class, black male in a 'high delinquency area' at night was seen to have a very high chance of being at least stopped and questioned, if not arrested. The young man is quite simply *assumed* to be delinquent unless he can prove otherwise (Piliavin and Briar, 1964: 206). More recent studies undertaken in the UK have also shown that some police officers show class and/or race bias in the performance of their duties (see for example Smith and Gray, 1986; Institute of Race Relations, 1987).

Cicourel (1968) found that in the course of their interactions with juveniles, the 'background expectations' of the police—that is, their commonsensical theories as to the typical delinquent—led them to concentrate on certain 'types' of individuals. A further factor in determining how that encounter developed was found to be dependent on how the individual officer defined his or her own role. Those who defined their role in terms of a 'due process' model that emphasises the rights of the defendant attempted to follow the *letter* of the law and, therefore, tended to react only to specific, concrete evidence of the commission of a crime. In contrast, when officers perceived their role primarily in terms of a 'crime control' model that considers a theory of delinquency causation that focused on factors such as 'broken homes', 'permissive parenting' or 'poverty'. Thus, juveniles with this sort of background were seen as the likeliest candidates for a delinquent career and were often, albeit unwittingly, launched upon one. These findings had serious implications for the validity of crime statistics.

Many criminologists from quite different perspectives had previously acknowledged that official statistics were not a wholly accurate reflection of the reality of crime, for example, there was much concern over the hidden figure of unrecorded crime. Official statistics had been widely viewed as reasonably objective and thus providing a reliable basis for discerning patterns in crime and suggesting associations. From a labelling perspective official statistics were seen to be just another interpretation of the world and their only utility lay in the light they inadvertently shed on the agencies of social control that 'constructed' them. Quinney (1970) suggested four societal structures—age, gender, class and ethnic group—that would enhance the likelihood of someone receiving a criminal label and thus, there is a high probability that a young black working-class male will be defined as deviant. Moreover, the reality that this group is over-represented in the official crime statistics is not surprising since these figures are produced by agencies whose personnel, operating criteria and rationale are drawn from the more politically powerful segments of society. What Quinney was essentially arguing is that some people have the facilities for applying stigmatising labels to other people, ostensibly because these other people violate norms the labellers wish to uphold. This is only possible because these others are identified as members of society with little or no political power.

The Consequences of Labelling for the Recipients

It was noted earlier that labelling theories have for the most part concentrated on their third area of concern which is assessing the consequences of the labelling process for the future conduct of the recipient and this aspect is certainly the most widely discussed and best documented.

Frank Tannenbaum (1938)—who is usually regarded as founder of the labelling perspective—noted that of the many young males who break the law only some are apprehended. His 'dramatisation of evil' hypothesis described the process whereby a community first defines the *actions* of an individual as evil, but eventually goes on to define the *individual himself* as evil, thus casting suspicion on all his future actions. The evil is further 'dramatised' by separating the individual from his usual group and administering specialised treatment to 'punish' or 'cure' the evil. This leads to further isolation and the confirmation and internalisation of his new 'tag'. Eventually he will redefine his self-image in line with the opinions and expectations of others in the community and thereby come to perceive himself as criminal. This idea that in reacting to people as 'criminal', society actually encourages them to become so, and that criminal justice intervention can deepen criminality is the central contention of the labelling approach.

Edwin Lemert (1951) made a crucial distinction between *primary* and *secondary* deviance. The former—with affiliations to the predestined actor model—could arise out of a variety of sociocultural, psychological or even physiological factors. However, because these initial acts are often extremely tentative and certainly not part of an organised way of life, offenders can easily rationalise them as a temporary aberration or see it as part of a socially acceptable role, for example, a worker may observe that everyone pilfers a little from work. Thus such behaviour will be of only marginal significance in terms of the status and self-concept of the individual concerned. In short, primary deviants do not view their deviance as central to themselves and do not consider themselves to be deviant.

If, however, these initial activities are subject to societal reaction—and with each act of primary deviance the offender becomes progressively more stigmatised through 'name calling, labelling or stereotyping'—then a crisis may occur. One way of resolving this crisis is for the individual to accept their deviant status and organise their life and identity around the facts of deviance and it is at this stage that the person becomes a 'secondary deviant'. In short, it is proposed that a youth who steals something and is not caught may be less likely to persist in this behaviour than one that is apprehended and officially sanctioned. Deviance is simply the end result of a process of human interaction. Primary deviance may or may not develop into secondary deviance. It is the number of criminal transgressions and the intensity and hostility of societal reaction that determines the outcome.

It was with the influential work of Becker (1963), Erikson (1966) and Kitsuse (1962)—and their use of Merton's concept of the 'self-fulfilling prophecy': a false definition of a situation, evoking a new behaviour that makes the original false assumption come true—that the labelling perspective was to gain widespread popularity. These writers argued that most offenders are falsely defined as criminal. That is not to say that they are innocent in the sense of having not committed offences, but rather that the system, and thus society, not only judges their actions as criminal and 'bad', but extends this judgement to them as people. The consequences are that once someone has been deemed by society to be 'bad', there is an expectation that this 'badness' must again find expression in some way or another, leading to the commission of further offences. Armed with these stereotypes of offenders as wholly criminal and incapable of law-abiding behaviour, the general population reacts to them on this basis and treats them accordingly. Consequently, offenders may face general, labelling theorists view the processes outlined above as in any way deterministic or unavoidable. It is quite possible that some offenders may react to being labelled and stigmatised by refraining from the type of conduct that elicited such a reaction but as Downes and Rock (1998: 183) pertinently observe:

> Interactionism casts deviance as a process which may continue over a lifetime, which has no necessary end, which is anything but inexorable, and which may be built around false starts, diversions and returns. The trajectory of a deviant career cannot always be predicted. However constrained they may seem to be, people can choose not to err further.

The key point from a labelling perspective is that *many* offenders *do* internalise their criminal labels and thus stable or career criminality arises out of the reaction of society to them.

Moral Panics and Deviance Amplification

The labelling perspective has also been applied at the group level and a useful analytical tool in this context is that of the *deviancy amplification* feedback or spiral (Wilkins, 1964) where it is argued that the less tolerance there is to an initial act of deviance, the more similar acts that will be defined as deviant. This process will give rise to more reactions against offenders resulting in more social *alienation* or *marginalisation* of deviants. This state of affairs will generate more crime by deviant groups, leading to decreasing tolerance of deviants by conforming groups.

Deviancy amplification feedback is central to the phenomenon known as the 'moral panic' which Jock Young (1971) first used in his study of recreational drug users in north London and which was later developed by Stanley Cohen (1973) in his study of the societal reaction to the 'mods and rockers' disturbances of 1964. These studies marked a significant break with those approaches to delinquency—favoured by proponents of the predestined actor model—that were primarily concerned with finding the causes of delinquent behaviour. By contrast, definitional and structural questions relating to why certain groups define certain acts as deviant, and the consequences of this process, were asked.

Cohen (1973) found the press to be guilty of exaggeration and distortion in their reporting of the events in Clacton over the Easter bank holiday weekend in 1964. The sense of outrage communicated by such misrepresentation had set in motion a series of interrelated responses. First, there was increased public concern about the issue, to which the police responded by increasing their surveillance of the groups in question—mods and rockers. This resulted in more frequent arrests, which in turn appeared to confirm the validity of the original media reaction. Second, by emphasising the stylistic differences and antagonisms between the groups, the press reaction encouraged polarisation and further clashes between the groups.

Various moral entrepreneurs call for action to be taken against the groups involved in the outbreaks of lawlessness and usually pronounce that current controls are inadequate. Cohen (1973) shows that these entrepreneurs exaggerate the problem in order to make local events seem ones of pressing national concern and an index of the decline of morality and social standards. The extension of control leads to further marginalisation and stigmatisation of deviants which in turn leads to more demands for police action and so on into a deviancy amplification spiral. Cohen located the nature and extent of reaction to the mods and rockers in the social context of Britain during the 1960s. In particular, ambivalence about social change in the post-war period, the new affluence and freedom of young people and their apparent rejection of traditional social norms such as employment and the family are used as a context for the panic.

The concept of moral panic is also central to Hall *et al.*'s (1978) study of 'mugging' although the concept is used within a very different theoretical framework. While conceding that there can be no deviance without an agency of condemnation and control, it is argued that the notion of moral panic is limited if employed without reference to the social and political structures that empower a dominant minority to construct and implement the process of labelling. Within labelling theories moral panic is thus expressed in terms of a 'society' that creates rules and within the Marxism that informs Hall *et al.*'s approach, it is expressed in terms of a 'state' that has the power to criminalise

(Cohen, 1985: 272). Given its theoretical basis, this analysis falls more within the scope of the radical theories.

Goode and Ben-Yehuda (1994) have more recently challenged the assumption of earlier theorists that moral panics are in some way engineered at the behest—and in the interests—of dominant élites and distinguish three different models. First, there is the grass roots model where a panic has its origins within the general public and which expresses a genuinely felt—albeit objectively mistaken—concern about a perceived threat. Second, the elite-engineered model is where dominant groups deliberately and consciously generate concerns and fears that resonate with their wider political interests. Third, the interest-group model is where rule-creators and moral entrepreneurs launch crusades that coincide neatly with their own professional concerns and interests. Goode and Ben-Yehuda (1994) identify the following five characteristics of a moral panic: (i) a disproportionate reaction; (ii) concern about the threat; (iii) hostility to the objects of the panic; (iv) widespread use of the concept of moral panic to capture reaction to diverse themes or issues. For example, Watney (1987) has questioned the use of the concept to characterise media and policy reactions to HIV/Aids. McRobbie and Thornton (1995) argue that the whole idea of a moral panic needs to be reconsidered in an environment where there may be an institutionalised need for the media to generate 'good stories' and that these can easily become part of a promotional culture that 'ironically' uses sensationalism for commercial purposes.

Criticisms of Labelling Theories

As the labelling approach became more influential during the 1960s and early 1970s it attracted criticism from a variety of sources. Plummer (1979) noted that because the perspective is so loosely defined, it could harbour several diverse theoretical positions and therefore leave itself open to internal contradiction and criticism from all theoretical sides. Such ambiguity and eclecticism thus led some critics to claim that labelling is at best a vague perspective that does not contain consistent and interrelated concepts and which fails to make precise distinctions between mere description and causal statements (Taylor, Walton and Young, 1973). On the other hand, proponents of labelling theory such as Schur (1971) contend that the strength of the approach lies in its ability to analyse aspects of social reality that have been neglected, offer directions for research and thus complement other theoretical approaches.

Others argue that labelling theories fail to clearly define deviance. According to Gibbs (1966), labelling theorists claim that an act is deviant only if a certain reaction follows, yet at the same time refer to 'secret deviants' and 'primary deviants', and suggest that certain groups of people are licensed to engage in deviant behaviour without negative reactions. This implies, it is argued, that deviance can be identified not merely in terms of societal reactions to it but in terms of *existing social norms.* There may be ambiguity about certain kinds of 'soft' deviance—where criminal definitions are relative to time and place—but there can be no such ambiguity regarding 'hard' deviance, such as violent assault, robbery and burglary, which have always been universally condemned. 'Hard' deviants at least are fully aware that what they are doing is deviant or criminal but freely choose this course of action because it is profitable or exciting. Labelling is therefore an irrelevance.

Taylor, Walton and Young (1973) accept the notion that deviance is not simply an inherent property of an act but they do not agree that it is as arbitrary as labelling theorists imply. They take the view that the deviant is not a passive actor but a decision-maker whose rule breaking reflects initial motives and choices, and thus has meaning. This approach overlaps with a further criticism that observes the emphasis to be on the negative repercussions of labelling which implies an individual totally at the mercy of official labellers. A consequence of this overemphasis on societal reaction at the expense of individual choice has been the tendency to elevate the offender to the status of victim. Labelling theories have 'the paradoxical consequence of inviting us to view the deviant as a passive nonentity who is responsible neither for his suffering nor its alleviation—who is more 'sinned' against than sinning' (Gouldner, 1968: 38). Yet, as previously noted, labelling theories do not on the whole argue that the effects of labelling are determinant, but rather that negative societal reaction can, and in many cases will, deepen criminality. Thus as Downes and Rock (1998: 190) quite correctly observe, 'criticisms of the species offered by Gouldner really reflect a response to only the most narrow versions of interactionism'. As for the charge that labelling theorists take the side of the deviant and overlook the 'real' victims of crime some, most notably Becker (1967), make no apologies for this and argue that they are merely balancing out traditional approaches within criminology that are severely biased *against* the deviant.

Many of the criticisms of labelling theories would seem more justified had the approach been promoted as a developed theory rather than as a perspective comprising loosely connected themes. In the light of this, perhaps the most telling criticism of the perspective is that, though it focused on societal reaction, it stopped short of offering a systematic analysis of social structure and power relations. While acknowledging that political interest and social disadvantage influenced societal reaction, labelling theorists failed to make explicit the connection of the criminal justice system to the underlying capitalist economic order and the inequalities of wealth and power rooted therein. Some of these issues are addressed by later more recent labelling theorists and by the radical theorists we will encounter in the following chapter.

Labelling Theories Revisited

In more recent years the notions and concepts of labelling theories have been modified and developed. First, more recent attention has been devoted to informal labelling such as that carried out by parents, peers, and teachers which it has been argued has a greater effect on subsequent criminal behaviour than official labelling. Ross Matsueda (1992) and Heimer and Matsueda (1994) discuss the reasons why individuals may be informally labelled as delinquents and note that such labels are not simply an outcome of interaction with the criminal justice system—for example, arrest—but are crucially influenced by the individual's offending behaviour *and* their position in society. Powerless individuals such as urban, ethnic-minority, lower-class adolescents are far more likely to be negatively labelled by parents and peers than more affluent crime by passing legislation and, therefore, the substantive nature of the law is a legitimate object of study. These are sometimes referred to as criminalisation theories (Hartjen, 1974) and while they have some resemblance to societal reaction—or labelling perspectives—they are more closely linked to a field of study that some call the sociology of law perspective or the study of law as a mechanism of social control. Labelling theories that focus on state power can be considered as branches of controlology (Ditton, 1979) which refers to a group of theories with some interest in crime waves and moral panics but mostly take the view that criminal justice agencies are part of broader social control mechanisms, like welfare, mental health, education, the military, and the mass media, all of which are used by the state to control 'problem' populations (Arvanites, 1992). Controlology has its theoretical foundations in the work of Foucault (1971, 1977) who argued that various instruments of social control—more humane, enlightened, reasonable responses to deviance—are packaged and sold by the state to cover up the inherent coercion and power in the system. The state is thus always trying to portray a 'velvet glove' where its ultimate goal is to exercise its 'iron fist' to control troublesome populations, in other words, the pervasive 'hard' and 'soft' 'policing' strategies of the 'disciplinary-control-matrix' (Hopkins Burke, 2004b; 2008).

Link (1987), Link *et al.* (1987), and Link *et al.* (1989) have used labelling theory to understand how we view and respond to the mentally ill and observe that in the USA public attitudes have been conditioned so that such people are perceived in negative and devalued ways with the outcome being that many who need psychiatric help—and those who care for them—will either try to hide this reality from family friends, colleagues and their employers, or will withdraw from groups or people who they think might reject them.

Some have suggested that the criminal justice system and the public are increasing the stigmatisation of—particularly young—offenders and thus heightening the most negative effects of labelling. De Haan (2000) observes that levels of violence in society appear to be rising—even in the Netherlands where previously there had been reasonable tolerance of such behaviour—and explains this occurrence as a process of relabelling previously non-problematic actions as more serious. Indeed, it seems that there is an increasingly universal intolerance of violence and such behaviour is being dealt with much more harshly. Triplett (2000) claims that an increase in violent offences in the USA during the 1980s and 1990s had been accompanied by changes in the criminal justice system moving less serious offences—particularly status offences such as truancy—up the sentencing tariff, and by a change in the way in which (especially young) violent offenders come to be seen as evil. She observes that these judgements have been subsequently attached to all young offenders who have subsequently become isolated and excluded from mainstream society. Meossi (2000) argues that this demonising of offenders—observed both in Italy and the USA—tends to correlate closely with periodic economic downturns and Halpern (2001) asserts that the subsequent rise in crime levels leads to harsher treatment of offenders thus devaluing people through labelling which can itself lead to further acceleration in offending behaviour.

While many studies have been conducted to apply labelling theory to various types of deviance, Kenney (2002) considers it in relationship to the victims of crime and found that sympathy offered to a victim may be received as condescension and may result in a feeling of a loss of power. The victim may lose self-esteem as a result of this loss of power and if he or she seeks help from friends and loved ones, they may fear feeling or being viewed as incompetent. Once the individual has been labelled as a 'victim' they may well find that work colleagues, friends, and even family begin to avoid them due to feelings of guilt or not knowing how to react which can lead to further isolation of the victim. Many victims do not receive the support they seek from loved ones and may wonder if their feelings are normal. Similarly, Li and Dennis Moore (2001) concluded from their study of the relationship between disability and illicit drug use that discrimination against persons with disabilities leads to higher rates of illegal drug use by these people.

Others have utilised the concept of labelling in a more positive mode. Braithwaite (1989) thus introduces the concept of 'reintegrative shaming' where it is proposed that offenders should be shamed not in order to stigmatise them but to make them realise the negative impact of their actions on both individual victims and the wider community and then encourage others to forgive them and accept them back into society. Reintegrative shaming is an influential concept that underpins reparation and restorative justice programmes and has been widely introduced—in particular with young offenders—in New Zealand (see Morris, Maxwell and Robertson, 1993), Australia (see Strang, 1993; Forsythe, 1994; Hudson *et al.*, 1996), parts of the USA (see Alford, 1997) and Britain (see Dignan, 1999, Young and Goold, 1999; Maxwell and Morris, 2001). Some have suggested that such a policy would only work in rural communities with strong community bonds but Braithwaite (1993) considers that it could be even more effective in cities which are invariably constituted of many closely-knit micro-mechanical solidarities or communities (see Hopkins Burke and Pollock, 2004). Moreover, Braithwaite (1993) and Simpson, Lyn Exum and Smith (2000) consider reintegrative shaming to be an appropriate response to some white-collar and corporate violations of the law and propose that its application would be a considerable advance on a long established tradition of ignoring such cases.

References

Alford, S. (1997). 'Professionals Need Not Apply', *Corrections Today*, 59: 98–111.
Arvanites, T. (1992). 'The Mental Health and Criminal Justice System: Complementary Forms of Coercive Control', in A. Liska (ed.) *Social Threat and Social Control*. Albany, NY: SUNY Press.

Becker, H. (1963). *Outsiders: Studies in the Sociology of Deviance*. New York: Free Press.

Becker, H. (1967). 'Whose Side Are We On?', *Social Problems*, 14(3): 239–47.

Braithwaite, J. (1989). *Crime, Shame and Reintegration*. Cambridge: Cambridge University Press.

Braithwaite, J. (1993). 'Shame and Modernity', *British Journal of Criminology*, 33: 1–18.

Cicourel, A. (1968). *The Social Organisation of Juvenile Justice*. New York: Wiley.

Cohen, S. (1973). *Folk Devils and Moral Panics: The Creation of the Mods and Rockers*. London: Paladin.

Cohen, S. (1985). *Visions of Social Control*. Cambridge: Polity Press.

De Haan, W. (2000). 'Explaining the Absence of Violence: A Comparative Approach', in S. Karstedt and K.-D. Bussman (eds) *Social Dynamics of Crime and Control*. Oxford: Hart.

Dignan, J. (1999). 'The Criminal Justice Act and the Prospect for Restorative Justice', *Criminal Law Review*, 44–56.

Ditton, J. (1979). *Controlology: Beyond the New Criminology*. London: Macmillan.

Downes, D. and Rock, P. (1998). *Understanding Deviance, 3rd edition*. Oxford: Oxford University Press.

Erikson, K. (1962). 'Notes on the Sociology of Deviance', *Social Problems*, 9: 309–14.

Erikson, K. (1966). *Wayward Puritans: A Study in the Sociology of Deviance*. New York: Wiley.

Forsythe, L. (1994). 'Evaluation of Family Group Conference Cautioning Program in Wagga, NSW', Conference Paper Presented to the Australian and New Zealand Society of Criminology, 10th Annual Conference.

Foucault, M. (1971). *Madness and Civilisation: A History of Insanity in the Age of Reason*. London: Tavistock.

Foucault, M. (1977). *Discipline and Punish—the Birth of the Prison*. London: Allen Lane.

Gibbs, J. (1966). 'Conceptions of Deviant Behaviour', *Pacific Sociological Review*, 9: 9–14.

Goode, E. and Ben-Yehuda, N. (1994). *Moral Panics: The Social Construction of Deviance*. Oxford: Blackwell.

Gouldner, A. (1968). 'The Sociologist as Partisan: Sociology and the Welfare State', *The American Sociologist*, May: 103–16.

Hall, S., Critcher, C., Jefferson, T., Clarke, J. and Roberts, B. (1978). *Policing the Crisis*. London: Macmillan.

Halpern, D. (2001). 'Moral Values, Social Thrust and Inequality', *British Journal of Criminology*, 41: 230–44.

Hartjen, C. (1974). *Crime and Criminalization*. New York: Praeger.

Heimer, K., and Matsueda, R.L. (1994). 'Role-taking, Role Commitment, and Delinquency: A Theory of Differential Social Control', *American Sociological Review*, 59: 365–90.

Hopkins Burke, R.D. (2004b). 'Policing Contemporary Society' in R.D. Hopkins Burke, *'Hard Cop/Soft Cop': Dilemmas and Debates in Contemporary Policing*. Cullompton: Willan Publishing.

Hopkins Burke, R.D. (2008). *Young People, Crime and Justice*. Cullompton: Willan Publishing.

Hopkins Burke, R.D. and Pollock, E. (2004). 'A Tale of Two Anomies: Some Observations on the Contribution of (Sociological) Criminological Theory to Explaining Hate Crime Motivation', *Internet Journal of Criminology*.

Hudson, J., Morris, A., Maxwell, G. and Galway, B. (1996). *Family Group Conferences*. Annandale, NSW: Federation Press.

Institute of Race Relations (1987). *Policing Against Black People*. London: Institute of Race Relations.

Kenney, J.S. (2002). 'Victims of Crime and Labelling Theory: A Parallel Process?', *Deviant Behavior: An Interdisciplinary Journal*, 23: 235–65.

Kitsuse, J.I. (1962). 'Societal Reaction to Deviant Behaviour: Problems of Theory and Method', *Social Problems*, 9: 247–56.

Lemert, E. (1951). *Social Pathology: A Systematic Approach to the Theory of Sociopathic Behavior*. New York: McGraw-Hill.

Li, L., and Moore, D. (2001). 'Disability and Illicit Drug Use: An Application of Labeling Theory', *Deviant Behavior: An Interdisciplinary Journal*, 22: 1–21.

Link, B. (1987). 'Understanding Labelling Effects of Mental Disorders: An Assessment of the Effects of Expectations of Rejection', *American Sociological Review*, 54: 395–410.

Link, B., Cullen, F., Frank, J. and Wozniak, J. (1987). 'The Social Reaction of Former Mental Patients: Understanding Why Labels Work', *American Journal of Sociology*, 92: 145–67.

Link, B., Cullen, F., Struening, E., Shrout, P. and Dohrenwend, B. (1989). 'A Modified Labelling Theory Approach to Mental Disorders: An Empirical Assessment', *American Sociological Review*, 54: 400.

McRobbie, A. and Thornton, S. (1995). 'Rethinking "Moral Panic" for Multi-mediated Social Worlds', *British Journal of Sociology*, 46(4): 559–74.

Matsueda, R.L. (1992). 'Reflected Appraisals, Parental Labeling, and Delinquency: Specifying a Symbolic Interactionist Theory', *The American Journal of Sociology*, 97(6): 1577–611.

Maxwell, G. and Morris, A. (2001). 'Putting Restorative Justice Into Practice for Adult Offenders', *Howard Journal of Criminal Justice*, 40: 46–58.

Meossi, D. (2000). 'Changing Representations of the Criminal', *British Journal of Criminology*, 40: 290–305.

Morris, A., Maxwell, G.M. and Robertson, J.P. (1993) 'Giving Victims a Voice: A New Zealand Experiment', *Howard Journal of Criminal Justice*, 32: 304.

Piliavin, I. and Briar, B. (1964). 'Police Encounters with Juveniles', *American Journal of Sociology*, 69: 153–62.

Plummer, K. (1979). 'Misunderstanding Labelling Perspectives', in D. Downes and P. Rock (eds) *Deviant Interpretations*. London: Martin Robertson.

Quinney, R. (1970). *The Social Reality of Crime*. Boston, MA: Little, Brown.

Schur, E. (1971). *Labelling Deviant Behaviour: Its Sociological Implications*. New York: Harper and Row.

Simpson, S.S., Lyn Exum, M. and Smith, N.C. (2000). 'The Social Control of Corporate Criminals: Shame and Informal Sanction Threats', in S.S. Simpson (ed.) *Of Crime and Criminality: The Use of Theory in Everyday Life*. Thousand Oaks, CA: Pine Forge Press.

Smith, D. and Gray, J. (1986). *Police and People in London*. London: Policy Studies Institute.

Strang, H. (1993). 'Conferencing: A New Paradigm in Community Policing', Paper delivered to the Annual Conference of the Association of Chief Police Officers.

Tannenbaum, F. (1938). *Crime and the Community*. New York: Columbia University Press.

Taylor, I., Walton, P. and Young, J. (1973). *The New Criminology: For a Social Theory of Deviance*. London: Routledge & Kegan Paul.

Tierney, K. (1982). 'The Battered Women Movement and the Creation of the Wife Beating Problem', *Social Problems,* 29 (February): 207–20.

Triplett, R. (2000). 'The Dramatisation of Evil: Reacting to Juvenile Delinquency During the 1990s', in S.S. Simpson (ed.) *Of Crime and Criminality: The Use of Theory in Everyday Life*. Thousand Oaks, CA: Pine Forge Press.

Watney, S. (1987). *Policing Desire: Pornography, Aids and the Media*. London: Methuen.

Wilkins, L. (1964). *Social Deviance*. London: Tavistock.

Young, J. (1971). *The Drug Takers: The Social Meaning of Drugtaking*. London: Paladin.

Young, R. and Goold, B. (1999). 'Restorative Police Cautioning in Aylesbury—From Degrading to Shaming Ceremonies', *Criminal Law Review*, 123–34.

READING 10

Social Control Theories
Roger Hopkins Burke

Social control theories of crime and criminal behaviour have a long and distinguished pedigree with strong foundations in both the rational actor and predestined actor models of crime and criminal behaviour. Later variants have entailed explicit attempts to integrate notions from both models while even more recently elements from the victimised actor model have been incorporated.

The Origins of Social Control Theories

The origins of—or at least the underlying assumptions on—which social control theories are founded can be traced back to the work of Hobbes (1968 originally 1651) in the rational actor tradition, Freud (1927) and Durkheim (1951 originally 1897) from respectively the psychological and sociological variants of the predestined actor model.

Hobbes had been concerned with the apparent incompatibility between human nature and the notion of legal restraint. The answer to his question, 'why do men obey the rules of society?' was however simple enough. 'Fear ... it is the only thing, when there is appearance of profit or pleasure by breaking the laws that makes men keep them' (Hobbes, 1968: 247).

One of the central ideas of Freud that deviant impulses arise naturally when the id is not sufficiently constrained by the other components of the personality, the ego and superego, is also apparent in much of the work on control theory. This is particularly true of those earlier models that draw more explicitly on psychological rather than sociological factors (Reiss, 1951; Nye, 1958; Reckless, 1961).

The roots of the more sociologically oriented control theories can be found partly in the work of Durkheim (1951) who had argued that needs, desires or aspirations arise naturally within the individual; are unlimited and restrained only by the socialised moral norms of a given society. At the same time, it is society itself that creates needs and ambitions that are incapable of realisation in the particular social framework of the time. Merton (1938) later developed this idea in his analysis of *anomie* as a cause of crime.

Social control theory is fundamentally derived from a conception of human nature that proposes that there are no natural limits on elementary human needs and desires. People will always want and seek further economic reward and it is thus not necessary to look for special motives for engaging

---

Roger Hopkins Burke, "Social Control Theories," *An Introduction to Criminological Theory,* pp. 245-261, 351-393. Copyright © 2009 by Taylor & Francis Group. Reprinted with permission.

in criminal activity. Human beings are born free to break the law and will only refrain from doing so under particular circumstances. It is these fundamental assumptions that provide the foundations of later social control theories.

Most of the explanations of crime and criminal behaviour that we have encountered previously in this book view conformity as the normal or natural state of humanity. Criminal behaviour is simply abnormal. It is this orthodox way of thinking about crime that social control theory seeks to challenge. Therefore, in taking deviance for granted and treating conformity as problematic, social control theory offers not so much a theory of *deviance* but one of *conformity*. The central question asked is not the usual, 'why do some people commit crimes?' but rather, 'why do most of us conform?'

The unifying factor in the different versions of control theory is thus the assumption that crime and deviance is only to be expected when social and personal controls are in some way inadequate. Primacy is given to relationships, commitments, values, norms and beliefs that, it is proposed, explain why people do not break laws, in contrast to those theories we have seen in this book that accord primacy to motivating forces thought to explain why people do break laws. From this perspective it is thus recognised that lawbreaking is often the most immediate source of gratification or conflict resolution, and that no special motivation is required to explain such behaviour. Human beings are active, flexible organisms who will engage in a wide selection of activities, unless the range is limited by processes of socialisation and social learning.

Some writers in the rational actor tradition, for example Hobbes (1588–1678) and Bentham (1748–1832) had viewed human nature in general as essentially amoral and self-serving but later social control theories do not, on the whole, depict people in this way. They merely reject the underlying assumption contained in many of the theories discussed earlier in this book—for example, anomie and subcultural theories—that people are basically moral as a result of having internalised pro-social norms and values during socialisation.

Because they remove the assumption of morality and the positively socialised individual, control theories are not dependent on explanations such as 'relative deprivation', 'blocked opportunities', 'alienation' or 'status-frustration' to account for the motivated deviant. Crime is seen as a product of the weaknesses of the forces restraining the individual rather than of the strength of the impulse to deviate. It is the *absence* of control and the fact that delinquent or criminal behaviour 'usually results in quicker achievement of goals than normative behaviour' that leaves the individual free to calculate the costs of crime (Hirschi, 1969). Again, the influence of the rational actor model is apparent in this core idea of the 'rational' individual choosing crime only after a careful appraisal of the costs and benefits of such activity.

Early Social Control Theories

It was observed above that social control theories draw on both social and psychological factors in order to explain conformity and deviance. Probably the earliest sociological control theory was

Durkheim's theory of anomie where it is proposed that inadequate forms of social control are more likely that social disorganisation causes a weakening of social control, making crime and deviance more *possible* (a rational actor model argument).

The early control theories reviewed in the remainder of this section attach much more importance to psychological factors in their analysis of deviance and conformity. Albert Reiss (1951) thus distinguished between the effects of 'personal' control and 'social' control proposing that the former comes about when individuals internalise the norms and rules of non-deviant primary groups to such an extent that they become their own. The latter are founded in the ability of social groups or institutions to make rules or norms effective. Thus, conformity derived from social control tends to involve mere submission to the norms in question and does not necessarily require the internalisation of these within the value system of the individual. Reiss tested his theory on 1,110 children between the ages of eleven and seventeen who were subject to probation orders and found that personal controls were much more important in preventing deviance than social controls. He did not specify the specific control mechanisms which lead to conformity but did identify the failure of such primary groups as the family to provide reinforcement for non-delinquent roles and values as being crucial to the explanation of delinquency. His perspective was nevertheless true to control theory logic in that no specific motivational sources leading to delinquency were identified.

Jackson Toby (1957) argued that the adolescent without commitment to conventional society is a candidate for 'gang socialisation' which he acknowledged to be part of the causal, motivational, dynamic leading to delinquency, but introduced the concept of 'stakes in conformity' to explain 'candidacy' for such learning experiences. Thus, young people who had few stakes or investments in conformity were more likely to be drawn into gang activity than those who had more to lose. A variety of conventional social relationships and commitments could be jeopardised by involvement in delinquency and thus young people without such stakes were free to be recruited into gangs. This notion of 'stakes in conformity' was to be similar to concepts developed in later versions of social control theory.

Ivan Nye (1958) developed a much more systematic version of control theory and in attempting to locate and identify the factors that encourage conformity in adolescents, he focused on the family, which, because of the affectional bonds established between members, were considered to be the most important mechanism of social control. He identified four modes of social control generated by the family. First, *direct control* is imposed through external forces such as parents, teachers and the police using direct restraint and punishment. Second, individuals themselves in the absence of external regulation exercise *internalised control*. Third, *indirect control* is dependent upon the degree of affection that an individual has for conventional significant others. Fourth, *control through alternative means of needs satisfaction* works by reducing the temptation for individuals to resort to illegitimate means of needs satisfaction. Though independent of each other, these four modes of control were considered mutually reinforcing and to work more effectively in tandem. The focus on the family as a source of control was in marked contrast to the emphasis on economic circumstances as a source of criminogenic motivation at the time. Although he acknowledged motivational forces by stating that '*some* delinquent behaviour results from a *combination* of positive learning and weak and ineffective social control', he nevertheless adopts a control-theory position when he proposes that 'most delinquent behaviour is the result of insufficient social control' (Nye, 1958: 4). Hirschi (1969) was critical of Nye's use of concepts such as internal control, but (together with Gottfredson [Gottfredson and Hirschi, 1990]) was to propose 'self-control' as a key explanatory variable over 30 years later. Nye's work was the first major presentation of research from a social control perspective and most of his findings were to be found consistent with subsequent research using survey data.

Walter Reckless's (1967) containment theory sought to explain why—despite the various 'push' and 'pull' factors that may tempt individuals into criminal behaviour—for example, psychological factors such as restlessness or aggression, or adverse social conditions such as poverty and unemployment—most people resist these pressures and remain law-abiding citizens. Reckless argued that a combination of control factors, both internal and external to the individual, serve as insulators or 'containments' against these 'push' and 'pull' factors. The factors involved in outer containment were identified as being a) reasonable limits and expectations, b) meaningful roles and activities, and c) several complementary variables, such as, a sense of belonging and identity, supportive relationships especially in the family and adequate discipline.

Reckless nevertheless attached much more importance to factors in inner containment as he argued that these would tend to control the individual irrespective of the extent to which the external environment changed. Four key components of inner containment were identified. First, individuals with a strong and favourable *self-concept* are better insulated against those 'push' and 'pull' factors that encourage involvement in criminal activity. Second, *goal orientation* is the extent to which the individual has a clear direction in life oriented towards the achievement of legitimate goals such as educational and occupational success. Third, *frustration tolerance* is where contemporary society—with its emphasis on individualism and immediate gratification—might generate considerable frustration and, moreover, individuals were observed to have different capacities for coping with this factor. Fourth, *norm retention* is the extent to which individuals accept, internalise and are committed to become a significant challenge to other theories in the 1960s which emphasised status frustration and the adoption of oppositional values by delinquent youth. Matza proposed in contrast to the previous orthodox determinism that the delinquent merely 'flirts' with criminal and conventional behaviour while drifting among different social worlds. No specific constraints or controls were identified that keep young people from drifting, but those that did do were those who have few stakes in conformity and are free to drift into delinquency.

Scott Briar and Irving Piliavin (1965) presented one of the clearest statements of control theory rationale and they specifically challenged other theoretical perspectives of the 1960s by emphasising transitory, situational inducements as the motivating forces for involvement in delinquency in contrast to deviant subcultural or contracultural value systems and socially structured status problems. They found that motivation did not differentiate delinquent and non-delinquent young people as much as variable commitments to conformity and argued that the 'central process of social control' was 'commitments to conformity' and they included fear of material deprivations if apprehended, self-image, valued relationships, current and future statuses and activities. In his version of social control theory to which we now turn our attention, Hirschi (1969) was to limit the concept of commitment to the rational and emotional investments that people make in the pursuit of shared cultural goals.

Later Control Theories

Travis Hirschi (1969) made the most influential contribution to the development of later social control theory and asserts that at their simplest level all share the assumption that 'delinquent acts result when an individual's bond to society is weak or broken (Hirschi, 1969: 16). He identified four elements of the social bond: *attachment, commitment, involvement* and *belief* but unlike other control theorists who had emphasised the internal psychological dimension of control, these terms were employed in a much more sociological sense. The idea that norms and attitudes can be so deeply internalised as to constitute part of the personality is simply rejected and an individual's bonds to conventional society are much more superficial and precarious.

First, *attachment* refers to the capacity of individuals to form effective relationships with other people and institutions, in the case of adolescents, with their parents, peers and school. When these attachments are sufficiently strong, individuals are more likely to be concerned with the opinions and expectations of others and thus more likely to behave in accordance with them. Since this bond of attachment is considered by Hirschi to lie not in some psychological 'inner state', but in ongoing social relationships with significant others, the strength of these attachments can and may vary over time.

Second, *commitment* refers to the social investments made by the individual to conventional lines of action that could be put at risk by engaging in deviant behaviour. This is essentially a rational actor model cost–benefit type of argument where it is proposed that those investing most in conventional social life have a greater stake in conformity, and thus most to lose by breaking the rules. Third, *involvement* again refers not to some psychological or emotional state but to the more mundane reality that a person may be too busy doing conventional things to find time to engage in deviant activities. Fourth, *beliefs* are not—as we might expect—a set of deeply held convictions but rather a set of impressions and convictions in need of constant reinforcement. In this context, beliefs are closely bound up with—and dependent upon—the pattern and strength of attachments an individual has with other people and institutions. These four variables, though independent, are also highly interrelated and are theoretically given equal weight: each helps to prevent law-breaking activities in most people.

For many the main strength of Hirschi's work is empirical rather than theoretical (see Box, 1981; Downes and Rock, 1998). This view tends to be based on the results of a large-scale study conducted by Hirschi of over 4,000 adolescents from mixed social and ethnic backgrounds where a variety of propositions derived from control, strain and cultural diversity theories were tested and for the most part it was the control variables that appeared to correlate most closely and consistently with offending behaviour. Hirschi's data indicates that the closer a relationship a child enjoyed with its parents, the more it is attached to and identifies with them, the lesser the likelihood of involvement in delinquent behaviour. Moreover, it is those who do not like school and do not care what teachers think of them who are more likely to commit delinquent acts. Not that attachment to delinquent peers is, in itself, found to undermine conventional bonds and lead to offending behaviour. It is rather, weak social bonds and a low stake in conformity that leads to the acquisition of delinquent friends. The data showed that high aspirations give a stake in conformity that ties an individual to the conventional social order, and not the reverse suggested by the anomie theory tradition. Moreover, social class and ethnic background were found to be 'very weakly' related to offending behaviour.

Numerous other attempts have been made to test the theoretical and empirical adequacy of Hirschi's original theory and the models derived from it. One notable example is Thomas and Hyman's (1978) study, which is particularly illuminating as it employed a much more sophisticated methodology than strong attachments to their family are less likely to engage in delinquency. The evidence on the association between attachment and commitment to the school, particularly poor school performance, not liking school and low educational and occupational aspirations and delinquency, is even stronger.

Despite its impressive empirical support, Hirschi's original formulation of control theory has not escaped criticism. He himself conceded that it overestimated the significance of involvement in conventional activities and underestimated the importance of delinquent friends. Moreover, both of these problems appeared to have stemmed from the same conceptual source, the taken-for-granted assumption of a natural motivation towards offending behaviour (Box, 1981; Downes and Rock, 1998). There have been other criticisms. First, the theory cannot account for the specific form or content of deviant behaviour, or 'why some uncontrolled individuals become heroin users, some become hit men, and others price fixing conspirators' (Braithwaite, 1989: 13). Second, there is a failure to consider the underlying structural and historical context in which criminal behaviour takes place (Elliot, Ageton and Canter, 1979; Box, 1981, 1987). Third, while it plainly considers primary deviance among adolescents, habitual 'secondary deviance' appears to be outside its conceptual boundaries (Box, 1981). Subsequently, other researchers have sought a remedy for these various identified defects by integrating control theory with other theoretical perspectives.

Integrated Theoretical Perspectives

Elliot, Ageton and Canter (1979) developed a model that sought to expand and synthesise anomie theories, social learning and social control perspectives into a simple explanatory paradigm. They begin with the assumption that individuals have different early socialisation experiences, leading to variable degrees of commitment to, and integration into, the conventional social order, in other words, strong and weak social bonds. These initial bonds can be further reinforced or attenuated by such factors as positive experiences at school and in the wider community, positive labelling in these new settings and continuing stability in the home.

The structural dimension of Elliot *et al.*'s model is most explicit in their analysis of the factors that serve to loosen social bonds. Limited or blocked opportunities, negative labelling experiences at school, for example streaming, social disorganisation at home and in the wider community—high rates of geographic mobility, economic recession and unemployment—are all identified as experiences that may weaken or break initially strong ties to the conventional order.

Such structural impediments to achieving conventional success goals will constitute a source of strain and can of themselves—where commitment to conventional goals is strong enough—provide *the* motivational stimulus to delinquency. In most cases, however, and specifically for those whose ties and commitments to conventional groups and goals are weak in the first place, then some further motivation is necessary for sustained involvement in delinquent behaviour. For Elliot, Ageton and Canter (1979: 15), it is 'access to and involvement in delinquent learning structures that provides this positive motivation and largely shapes the form and content of delinquent behaviour'.

Elliot *et al.* propose two primary explanatory routes to delinquency. The first and probably most frequent represents an integration of control theory and social learning theory and involves weak bonds to conventional society and exposure and commitment to groups involved in delinquent activity. The second path represents an integration of traditional strain and social learning perspectives and this involves strong bonds to conventional society, conditions and experiences that accentuate those bonds and in most cases exposure and commitment to groups involved in delinquency.

Stephen Box (1981, 1987) sought to explain the discrepancy between the findings of self-report studies—such as those conducted by Hirschi—and which suggest only a weak relationship between social class and delinquency, and official statistics that show strong links. By integrating control theory with a labelling/conflict perspective—incorporated from the victimised actor model of crime and criminal behaviour—Box showed how the 'primary' deviants of the self-report studies become the largely economically disadvantaged and minority group 'secondary' deviants of the official statistics. He argues that differential policing practices and institutional biases at different stages of the criminal justice system all operate in favour of the most advantaged sections of society and to the detriment of its less favoured citizens. However, this is not merely a product of discriminating decision-making criteria made on the basis of the individual characteristics of the suspect. Employing a more macro and historical view of the criminalisation process, Box (1981: 20) suggested that it may be plausible to view such outcomes as a response to social problems of which the individual is merely a symbol:

> Thus, the economically marginalised and the oppressed ethnic minorities—because they will also be economically marginalised—will be treated more harshly

> by the judicial system not simply because of who they are, but also because of what they symbolise, namely the perceived threat to social order posed by the growth of the permanently unemployed.

an attachment to other human beings, who might introduce a controlling influence in his or her life, is substantially reduced.

John Braithwaite's (1989) theory of 'predatory' crime—that is, crimes involving the victimisation of one party by another—builds upon and integrates elements of control, labelling, strain and subcultural theory and argues that the key to crime control is a cultural commitment to shaming in ways that are described as 'reintegrative'; thus, 'societies with low crime rates are those that shame potently and judiciously' (1989: 1). Braithwaite makes a crucial distinction between shaming that leads to stigmatising 'to outcasting, to confirmation of a deviant master status' and shaming that is: 'reintegrative, that shames while maintaining bonds of respect or love, that sharply terminates disapproval with forgiveness. The latter controls crime while the former pushes offenders toward criminal sub-cultures' (1989: 12–13).

Braithwaite argues that criminal subcultures become attractive to those who have been stigmatised by their shaming because they can provide emotional and social support. Participation in these groups can also supply criminal role models, knowledge on how to offend and techniques of 'neutralisation' (see Matza, 1964) that taken together can make the choice to engage in crime more attractive and likely. Therefore, a high level of stigmatisation in a society is a key factor in stimulating the formation of criminal subcultures. The other major societal variable that encourages this configuration is the 'systematic blockage of legitimate opportunities for critical fractions of the population' (1989: 103).

Braithwaite claims that individuals are more susceptible to shaming when they are enmeshed in multiple relationships of *interdependency* and, furthermore, societies shame more effectively when they are *communitarian*. It is such societies or cultures—constituted of dense networks of individual interdependencies characterised by mutual help and trust—rather than individualistic societies that are more capable of delivering the required more potent shaming and more shaming that is reintegrative. This is a crucial observation.

Both Box and Braithwaite have significantly sought to rescue the social control theory perspective from its emphasis on the individual—or more accurately family—culpability that had made it so popular with conservative governments both in the UK and the USA during the 1980s. Box (1981, 1987) located his radical reformulation of social control theory within the victimised actor model but it is the notion of 'reintegrative shaming' developed by Braithwaite that has been central to the populist socialist perspective. Significantly, neither Box nor Braithwaite—like Hirschi whom they sought to improve upon—manage to offer a satisfactory explanation of all crime and criminal behaviour. Hirschi sought subsequently—in collaboration with Michael Gottfredson—to do just that.

A General Theory of Crime

In their *General Theory of Crime*, Gottfredson and Hirschi (1990) manage to combine rational actor model notions of crime with a predestined actor model theory of criminality. In line with the hedonistic calculus of rational actor model thinking, crime is defined as acts of force or fraud undertaken in the pursuit of self-interest. The authors propose that the vast bulk of criminal acts are trivial and mundane affairs that result in little gain and require little in the way of effort, planning, preparation or skill, and their 'versatility construct' points to how crime is essentially interchangeable. The characteristics of ordinary criminal events are simply inconsistent with notions of specialisation or the 'criminal career'. Since the likelihood of criminal behaviour is also closely linked to the availability of opportunity, the characteristics of situations and the personal properties of individuals will also affect the use of force or fraud in the pursuit of self-interest. This concept of criminality—low self-control—is not confined to criminal acts but is also causally implicated in many 'analogous' acts, such as promiscuity, alcohol use and smoking where such behaviour is portrayed as the impulsive actions of disorganised individuals seeking quick gratification.

Gottfredson and Hirschi turn to the predestined actor model in order to account for the variation in self-control among individuals, arguing that the main cause is 'ineffective parenting' and this failure to instil self-control early in life cannot easily be remedied later, any more than effective control, once established, can be later undone. According to this 'stability postulate', levels of self-control will remain stable throughout the life course and 'differences between people in the likelihood that they will commit criminal acts persist over time' (1990: 107).

The *General Theory of Crime* is essentially a radical restatement of the control theory set out by Hirschi in his earlier work successfully addressing many of the key criticisms aimed at the original. It is more explicitly grounded in a rational actor model conception of crime and thus offers a more consistent notion of criminal motivation than has been the case with previous control theories. By asserting that crime is essentially interchangeable while the propensity to commit crime remains stable throughout the life course, the theory has no need to provide separate explanations for different *types* of crime, nor for *primary* or persistent *secondary* deviation.

Evidence that high-ranking governmental and corporate officials, acting independently or on behalf of the organisations they serve, use fraud and force in carefully planned ways to enrich themselves and maintain their positions. Barlow (1991: 238) observes that, 'compared to low-end crime, high-end crime is much more likely to involve planning, special expertise, organisation, delayed gratification, and persistence—as well as considerably larger potential gains'.

The existence of high-level crime also seems to cast considerable doubt on Gottfredson and Hirschi's 'stability postulate', that is, the notion that levels of self-control remain constant throughout the life course. Since low self-control is also incompatible with the discipline and effort normally required to attain high office, it is difficult to see how corporate offenders managed to climb the corporate ladder in the first place!

Even if the proposition that low self-control is a causal factor in some—or even most types of crime—is accepted, can we also accept the straightforward association Gottfredson and Hirschi propose between low self-control and ineffective parenting? Although the literature discussed elsewhere in this book does suggest a relationship between parenting and delinquency, this is compromised and complicated when structural factors are considered; for example, while her study of socially deprived families in Birmingham did find that parental supervision was an important factor in determining adolescent offending behaviour, Harriet Wilson (1980: 233–4) warned against the misinterpretation of her findings:

> The essential point of our findings is the very close association of lax parenting methods with severe social handicap. Lax parenting methods are often the result of chronic stress ... frequent or prolonged spells of unemployment, physical or mental disabilities amongst members of the family, and an often-permanent condition of poverty. It is the position of the most disadvantaged groups in society, and not the individual, which needs improvement in the first place.

These findings show quite clearly that even by relocating the source of control from the nature of an individual's bond to society back to within the individual him- or herself, Gottfredson and Hirschi cannot escape the need to incorporate some sense of underlying structural context into their analysis. Their work has however been influential and Hirschi has himself subsequently outlined the policy implications of the general theory. Hirschi (1995) argues that policies designed to deter (the rational actor model) or rehabilitate (the predestined actor model) will continue to have little success in reducing criminal behaviour. Effective state policies are those that support and enhance socialisation within the family by improving the quality of child-rearing practices with the focus on the form, size, and stability of the family unit. Thus, there should always be two parents for every child, no more than three children in a family and the relationships between parents and children strong and durable. Furthermore, it is not young teenage mothers who are a problem that causes delinquency in children. It is having a mother without a father. Therefore, effective policies are those that focus not on preventing teenage pregnancies, but on maintaining the involvement of the father in the life of the child. It is proposed that these policy reforms would strengthen family bonds, increase socialisation and create greater self-control in the child that will make it unlikely that they will become involved in offending behaviour (1995: 138–9).

Developments in Social Control Theories

Various developments in and modifications to social control theories have occurred in the USA in the later decades of the twentieth and the first decade of the twenty-first centuries. We will here consider three of the most significant: power control theory, control balance theories and differential coercion theory.

Power control theory developed by John Hagan (Hagan, Gillis and Simpson, 1985, 1987, 1990; Hagan, 1989) combines social class and control theories of criminal behaviour in order to explain the effects of familial control on gender differences in crime. Hagan, Gillis and Simpson (1987) argue that parental position in the workforce affects patriarchal attitudes in the household and these, in turn, result in different levels of control placed on boys and girls in the home. Moreover, differing levels of control affect the likelihood of the children taking risks and ultimately becoming involved in deviant behaviour. In other words, because of the greater levels of control placed on girls in patriarchal households, boys are more delinquent than girls.

Power control theory begins with the assumption that mothers constitute the primary agents of socialisation in the family. In households in which the mother and father have relatively similar levels of power at work—'balanced households'—the former will be less likely to differentially exert control over their daughters, and both sons and daughters will experience similar levels of control thus leading them to develop similar attitudes regarding the risks and benefits of engaging in deviant behaviour. It is thus assumed that balanced households will experience fewer gender differences in deviant behaviour. In contrast, households in which mothers and fathers have dissimilar levels of behaviour probably decrease because *both* male and female delinquents are affected. Moreover, in less patriarchal households, sons are shown to have more controls placed on them thus decreasing their levels of delinquency.

Charles Tittle (1995, 1997, 1999, 2000) proposes a general theory of deviant behaviour—control balance theory—which provides a definition of deviancy that goes well beyond that of criminality and into the realm of social harms that preoccupies zemiologists. From this perspective, deviancy is simply any activity which the majority find unacceptable and/or disapprove of and occurs when a person has either a surplus or deficit of control in relation to others. Those, whose position in society allows them to exert more control over others and their environment than is exerted over them, enjoy a control surplus. A control deficit arises where people are controlled more by others than they are able to control. Tittle proposes that any control imbalance—surplus or deficit—is likely to lead to deviancy. A deficit of control could well lead to resentment, envy and the loss of any stake in society thus removing any incentive to conform; a surplus can lead to corruption, a desire to extend the surplus, enhance autonomy and increase domination. The link with criminal behaviour is founded on the supposition that the subservience of others largely removes the risk of being caught. A more specific claim is that any breakdown of subservience provokes angry outbursts and this has been used to explain some incidents of domestic violence (see Hopkins and McGregor, 1991). The dual aspect of the theory seems to provide explanations of street crime (most likely to be associated with a control deficit) and corporate crime (most likely to be associated with a control surplus).

Tittle does not assume that an imbalance alone will inevitably lead to criminality but emphasises the drive for autonomy. Criminal motivation arises for those with a control surplus because they want to extend it (greed) and for those with a deficit (need) because they want to alleviate it. For criminal behaviour to occur, motivation has to be triggered by provocation and facilitated by both opportunity and an absence of constraint.

Linking crime with power is not new. Violent crime invariably involves an element of control or power over the victim and sex crimes have often been explained in this way (see Lansky, 1987; Scheff and Retzinger, 1991). Property offences can also be explained in this manner, thus burglars have power over their victims, the power to decide what to take and leave, how much mess and trauma to cause, and for some this is part of the attraction of burglary (Katz, 1988). Control balance theory is nevertheless helpful in explaining gender differentials in offending rates for there is still a tendency for women to be controlled to a greater extent than men and in more spheres of their lives. Women experience control deficits more frequently than men and become easily enmeshed in the full range of submissive deviancy without access to predatory criminal opportunity. In contrast, fewer women are presumed to have a control surplus so that they would be under-represented in the areas of exploitation, plunder and decadence, the converse being true for a considerably higher proportion of males.

Braithwaite (1997) proposes a policy strategy of redistributing control imbalances and argues that a more egalitarian society will reduce both control surplus and deficit with the outcome that deviance in general and offending behaviour in particular will be reduced. He acknowledges that some form of control will be inevitable to maintain order in even the most equal of societies but proposes that this should be exercised in ways which respect those who are subjected to the control.

Differential coercion theory developed by Mark Colvin (2000) seeks to extend our existing understanding of the coercion-crime relationship. Other recent criminological theories have also highlighted the theme of coercion. Athens (1997) thus describes coercive interpersonal relations as primary forces in the creation of dangerous violent criminals. Regoli and Hewitt (1994) argue that coercive acts by adults in their quest for order play a major role in creating an oppressive environment for young people that produces delinquency. Tittle (1995) contends that repression—a concept similar to coercion—creates control deficits that, depending on the strength and consistency of the repression produce predatory, defiant, or submissive forms of deviance. Hagan and McCarthy (1998) focus on the coercive forces in both the background and foreground in their explanation of delinquency among homeless, street youth.

Colvin (2000) observes that coercion has multiple sources—including families, schools, peer relations and neighbourhoods—and then specifies how each of these coercive experiences foster criminal involvement. He uses the term differential because individuals vary in the extent to which they are exposed to coercion and it is a central premise of his perspective that criminal involvement will be positively related to the degree of duress experienced by individuals.

There are two proposed dimensions of differential coercion: the *degree* of the coercive force—on a continuum from none to very strong coercion—and the *consistency* with which it is applied or experienced. In most ordinary circumstances—in families, schools, peer groups and a neighbourhood, for example—coercion is most likely to be experienced on an inconsistent basis, in which case, the extent, or degree, of the coercion is the most significant element in producing delinquency.

Coercion, it is argued, produces a set of 'social-psychological' deficits that are conducive to greater involvement in delinquency. Thus, to the degree that threatened use of physical force and/or the actual or threatened removal of social supports. Impersonal coercion is experienced as pressure arising from larger circumstances beyond the control of the individual and these macro-level sources of coercion can include economic and social pressures created by structural unemployment, poverty, or violent competition among groups.

An example of impersonal coercion discussed by Colvin (2000: 124) is the violent environment within neighbourhoods created by gang rivalries. Such neighbourhoods—perceived as dangerous and violent by the young people who live in them—are a strong, impersonal force that creates an environment of threat (Decker and Van Winkle, 1996) which enhances 'coercive ideation' and other social-psychological deficits that Colvin (2000) argues are conducive to delinquency. Moreover, the school setting can be perceived as coercive if school administrators fail to curtail a threatening school environment created by bullying and other forms of aggression at school.

In summary, for Colvin (2000), the accumulated coercion that juveniles experience in their families, schools, peer relations, and neighbourhoods creates social-psychological deficits that makes involvement in delinquent activities more likely. The logic of differential coercion theory is that the effects of coercion are general and thus are implicated in most, if not all, forms of criminality, including white-collar and corporate crime.

Unnever, Colvin and Cullen (2004) sought to test the core propositions of differential coercion theory and collected data from 2,472 middle school students at six different public schools in a metropolitan area of Virginia. Variables included demographic information including gender, measures of economic status, race, and grade level, as well as various measures of coercion, such as parental coercion, peer coercion, school coercion, and neighbourhood coercion. Other variables included four measures of social-psychological factors: anger, parental social bonds, school social bonds, and coercive ideation. Their results largely supported the general proposition that different types of coercion would be positively associated with delinquent involvement. Parental coercion, including verbal abuse, threats, and physical punishment, were significantly related to delinquency. School and neighbourhood coercion were also significantly related to delinquency, although the associations were less strong than parental coercion. Peer coercion was found to have no relationship to delinquency. Unnever, Colvin and Cullen (2004) conclude from their data that students exposed to coercive environments develop social-psychological deficits which may lead them to engage in delinquent activities.

References

Athens, L. (1997). *Violent Acts and Actors Revisited*. Urbana, IL: University of Illinois Press.

Barlow, H. (1991). 'Review Essay of "A General Theory of Crime"', *Journal of Criminal Law and Criminology*, 1: 82–96.

Box, S. (1981). *Deviance, Reality and Society, 2nd edition.* London: Rinehart and Winston.

Box, S. (1987). *Recession, Crime and Punishment.* London: Macmillan.

Braithwaite, J. (1989). *Crime, Shame and Reintegration.* Cambridge: Cambridge University Press.

Braithwaite, J. (1997). 'Charles Tittle's Control Balance and Criminal Theory', *Theoretical Criminology*, 1: 68–79.

Briar, S. and Piliavin, I. (1965). 'Delinquency, Situational Inducements and Commitments to Conformity', *Social Problems*, 13(1): 35–45.

Colvin, M. (2000). *Crime and Coercion: An Integrated Theory of Chronic Criminality.* New York: St Martin's Press.

Decker, S.H. and Van Winkle, B. (1996). *Life in the Gang.* New York: Cambridge University Press.

Downes, D. and Rock, P. (1998). *Understanding Deviance, 3rd edition.* Oxford: Oxford University Press.

Durkheim, E. (1951, originally published in 1897) *Suicide.* New York: Free Press.

Elliot, D., Ageton, S. and Canter, J. (1979). 'An Integrated Theoretical Perspective on Delinquent Behaviour', *Journal of Research in Crime and Delinquency,* 16: 126–49.

Freud, S. (1927). *The Ego and the Id.* London: Hogarth.

Gottfredson, M.R. and Hirschi, T. (1990). *A General Theory of Crime.* Stanford, CA: Stanford University Press.

Hagan, J. (1989). *Structural Criminology.* New Brunswick, NJ: Rutgers University Press.

Hagan, J. Gillis, A.R. and Simpson, J. (1985). 'The Class Structure of Gender and Delinquency: Toward a Power-Control Theory of Common Delinquent Behavior', *American Journal of Sociology*, 90(2): 1151–78.

Hagan, J. Gillis, A.R. and Simpson, J. (1987). 'Class in the Household: A Power-Control Theory of Gender and Delinquency', *American Journal of Sociology*, 92(4): 788–816.

Hagan, J., Gillis, A.R. and Simpson, J. (1990). 'Clarifying and Extending Power-Control Theory', *American Journal of Sociology*, 95(4): 1024–37.

Hagan, J. and McCarthy, B. (1998). *Mean Streets: Youth Crime and Homelessness.* Cambridge: Cambridge University Press.

Hirschi, T. (1969). *Causes of Delinquency.* Berkeley, CA: University of California Press.

Hirschi, T. (1995). 'The Family', in J.Q. Wilson and J. Petersilia (eds) *Crime.* San Francisco, CA: ICS Press.

Hobbes, T. (1968 originally 1651) *Leviathan,* edited by C.B. Macpherson. Harmondsworth: Penguin.

Hopkins, A. and McGregor, H. (1991). *Working for Change: The Movement Against Domestic Violence.* Sydney: Allen & Unwin.

Katz, J. (1988). *Seductions of Crime: Moral and Sensual Attractions in Doing Evil.* New York: Basic Books.

Lansky, M. (1987). 'Shame and Domestic Violence', in D. Nathanson (ed.) *The Many Faces of Shame.* New York: Guilford.

Matza, D.M. (1964). *Delinquency and Drift.* New York: Wiley.

Merton, R.K. (1938). 'Social Structure and Anomie', *American Sociological Review,* 3: 672–82.

Nye, F.I. (1958). *Family Relationships and Delinquent Behaviour.* New York: Wiley.

Reckless, W. (1961). *The Crime Problem, 3rd edition.* New York: Appleton Century Crofts.

Reckless, W. (1967). *The Crime Problem, 4th edition.* New York: Appleton Century Crofts.

Regoli, R. and Hewitt, J. (1994). *Delinquency in Society, 2nd edition.* Boston, MA: McGraw Hill.

Reiss, A.J. (1951). 'Delinquency as the Failure of Personal and Social Controls', *American Sociological Review,* 16: 213–39.

Scheff, T. and Retzinger, S. (1991). *Emotions and Violence: Shame and Rage in Destructive Conflicts.* Lexington, VA: Lexington Books.

Thomas, D.W. and Hyman, J.M. (1978). 'Compliance, Theory, Control Theory and Juvenile Delinquency', in M. Krohn and R.L. Acker (eds) *Crime, Law and Sanctions.* London: Sage.

Tittle, C.R. (1995). *Control Balance: Towards a General Theory of Deviance.* Boulder, CO: Westview Press.

Tittle, C.R. (1997). 'Thoughts Stimulated by Braithwaite's Analysis of Control Balance', *Theoretical Criminology,* 1: 87–107.

Tittle, C.R. (1999). 'Continuing the Discussion of Control Balance', *Theoretical Criminology,* 3: 326–43.

Tittle, C.R. (2000). 'Control Balance', in R. Paternoster and R. Bachman (eds) *Explaining Criminals and Crime: Essays in Contemporary Theory.* Los Angeles, CA: Roxbury.

Toby, J. (1957). 'Social Disorganization and Stake in Conformity: Complementary Factors in the Behavior of Hoodlums', *American Sociological Review,* 22(5): 505–12.

Unnever, J.D., Colvin, M., Cullen, F.T. (2004). 'Crime and Coercion: A Test of Core Theoretical Propositions', *Journal of Research in Crime and Delinquency,* 41(3): 244–68.

Wilson, H. (1980). 'Parental Supervision: A Neglected Aspect of Delinquency', *British Journal of Criminology,* 20: 315–27.

PART III

New Directions in Criminology

In the Pursuit of Equality, Freedom, and Justice

....

Part III Timeline

1945	The United Nations is created
1947	The Universal Declaration of Human Rights Drafting Committee is convened, chaired by Eleanor Roosevelt
1948	The Universal Declaration of Human Rights is adopted by the UN General Assembly
1954–1968	Civil Rights movement: Mass protest movement against racial segregation and discrimination in the United States
1954	*Hernandez v. Texas* Supreme Court decision: Court rules that Mexican Americans and all other nationality groups have equal protection under the 14th Amendment of the United States Constitution
1954	*Brown v. Board of Education* Supreme Court decision: Court rules that American state laws establishing racial segregation in public schools are unconstitutional, even if the segregated schools are otherwise equal in quality

1955	Murder of 14-year-old Emmett Till, an African American boy falsely accused of assaulting a white woman
1955–1975	Vietnam War: United States intervention in Asia against their communist revolutionary movement; the war ends when United States forces withdraw in 1973, and Vietnam unifies under communist control two years later
1955	Rosa Parks is arrested for refusing to give up her seat on a Montgomery bus
1955–1956	Montgomery Bus Boycott against racial segregation
1961	The United Nations passes a prohibition against marijuana, advocated by the United States
1961	Freedom Riders: White and black students travel across state lines to protest segregation
1962	Cesar Chavez and Dolores Huerta found the United Farm Workers
1962	Cuban Missile Crisis between the United States and the Soviet Union
1963	President John F. Kennedy is assassinated in Dallas, Texas
1964	Civil Rights Act is signed by President Lyndon B. Johnson
1965	Los Angeles Watts Riots erupt due to police brutality
1965	Voting Rights Act is signed by President Lyndon B. Johnson
1965	Malcolm X is assassinated
1965	Delano grape strike led by Cesar Chavez and Dolores Huerta
1968	Martin Luther King, Jr., is assassinated, followed by rioting in 168 cities
1973	*Roe v. Wade* Supreme Court decision: Court rules that the Due Process Clause of the 14th Amendment to the United States Constitution provides a fundamental "right to privacy" that protects a pregnant woman's liberty to choose whether to have an abortion or not; abortion is made widely available
1974	US President Richard Nixon resigns due to the Watergate scandal
1975	The Voting Rights Act is extended to include Mexican Americans
1979–1981	Iran hostage crisis
1980s	Rise of the Mexican and Colombian cartels
1985-1987	Iran-Contra Affair: The United States sells arms to Iran and funds the Contras in Nicaragua to fight the new socialist democratic government
1986	Chernobyl nuclear disaster
1989	Fall of the Berlin Wall
1990–1991	Gulf War: Iraq invades Kuwait and the United States intervenes in expelling Iraq

1991	The Union of Soviet Socialist Republics is dismantled, and the Cold War against communism ends
1992	LA riots: Officers are videotaped beating up an African American and are acquitted; this leads to outrage and rioting in Los Angeles
1993	European Community is established
1993	Waco Siege of the Branch Davidians Compound
1994	The North American Free Trade Agreement is signed by Canada, Mexico, and the United States
1995	Oklahoma City bombing
1999	Columbine school shooting
2001	Terrorist attacks of 9/11

Editor's Introduction

Part III establishes new directions in criminology, embracing the ideals set by the liberal philosophers: equality, freedom, and justice. After World War II, the United Nations (UN) was established in 1945 to foster international cooperation and to prevent future global conflicts (Beck et al., 2014). The UN Commission on Human Rights was established a year later and was responsible for the drafting of the Universal Declaration of Human Rights, which was adopted by the UN General Assembly (United Nations, n.d.). After World War II, the Allies set up the North Atlantic Treaty Organization to oversee the defeated Axis countries, as well as the division of the Eastern and Western Blocs. This was the beginning of the Cold War (1948–1990), 45 years of nuclear arms tension between the superpowers the Soviet Union and the United States, along with their respective allies (Beck et al., 2014; Miami Valley Teaching American History Project, 2009).

In 1948, President Harry Truman issued Executive Order 9981 to end segregation in the Armed Services, but the Civil Rights movement reached momentum from 1954 to 1968 (Beck et al., 2014). In the 1954 Supreme Court case of *Brown v. Board of Education*, racial segregation was found unconstitutional. The transition was difficult and violent. The fight for desegregation continued with Rosa Parks, who refused to give up her bus seat to a white man. She garnered attention, as she was the secretary of the NAACP chapter in Montgomery, Alabama. Her bold stance prompted a yearlong Montgomery bus boycott. Across the South, Martin Luther King, Jr., led the Civil Rights movement with nonviolent protests (Beck et al., 2014; History, Art, & Archives, n.d.). While civil rights were being fought for, unrest and violence arose due to the U.S. intervention in Asia against the communist movement. This created the conditions for the Vietnam War. The war was a manifestation of the conflict of the Cold War between the Soviet Union and the United States. It ended when United States forces withdrew from Vietnam in 1973, and the country unified under communist control several years later (Beck et al., 2014; U.S. History, n.d.).

Moreover, as African Americans were fighting for their rights, Mexican American farm workers were fighting for a living wage and civil rights. According to United Farm Workers (n.d.), these farm workers had long been exploited, though they were essential to the industry of agriculture. Under the leadership of Cesar Chavez and Dolores Huerta, they organized United Farm Workers in 1962 to secure better working conditions. In 1963, over 250,000 people participated in The March on Washington for Jobs and Freedom (World Digital Library, n.d.). Dr. King gave his "I Have A Dream" speech as the closing address, right in front of the Lincoln Memorial, stating, "I have a dream that one day this nation will rise and live out the true meaning of its creed: 'We hold these truths to be self-evident: that all men are created equal,'" (The Martin Luther King, Jr. Research and Education Institute, n.d.-b). That same year, President John F. Kennedy was assassinated in Dallas, Texas. President Kennedy was a staunch advocate for civil rights, and upon his death, many of his proposals were pushed forward by Congress. President Lyndon B. Johnson signed the Civil Rights Act of 1964 and the Voting Rights Act of 1965, prohibiting discrimination due to race, color, sex, religion, or national origin (Beck et al., 2014; Bomboy, 2019).

As the federal government signed legislation against racial discrimination, police brutality against people of color continued. In 1965, the Watts Riots erupted as a result of police brutality (Civil Rights Digital Library, 2013). That same year, Malcolm X was assassinated; he was another strong advocate for civil rights, who inspired the Black Panther Party, a civil rights organization targeted by the FBI. In 1968, Martin Luther King, Jr., was assassinated on the balcony of his hotel room in Memphis, Tennessee. His assassination led to rioting in 168 cities. Dr. King's murder, like the killing of Malcolm X, radicalized many moderate African American activists, fueling the growth of the Black Power movement and the Black Panther Party into the 1970s (Beck et al., 2014; Hall, 2007).

Additionally, women's rights gained momentum in the 1970s, with feminists demanding agency over their bodies. In 1973, the Supreme Court decision on *Roe v. Wade* found that the Due Process Clause of the 14th Amendment provides a fundamental "right to privacy," protecting a pregnant woman's liberty to choose whether to have an abortion or not (Legal Information Institute, n.d.). In 1974, President Nixon resigned before facing impeachment for his crimes against the Democratic National Committee. During his presidency, his stance as a crime fighter led to his war on drugs. And although it had been recommended by his Presidential Commission that marijuana be decriminalized, he refused to listen and instead created the Drug Enforcement Agency (Phillips, 2010).

Subsequently, following Nixon's resignation, Gerald Ford took the reins of the presidency. In 1975, President Ford expanded the Voting Rights Act to include Mexican Americans, although they had been conquered citizens since 1848 and were still considered second class citizens (Gamboa, 2015). According to Haberman (2018), in the 1980s, Ronald Reagan, an actor and ex-governor of California, became president of the United States under a conservative right-wing, Christian platform. Furthermore, Campbell (1990) explains that Reagan's domestic and international policies resulted in the decimation of the middle class, as well as an increase of homelessness, while the United States was fighting and supporting guerrilla warfare against countries fighting for justice and democratic socialism. His presidency was disgraced as a result of the Iran-Contra Affair (1985–1987), in which the United States sold weapons to Iran to fund warfare in Nicaragua. After Ronald Reagan's presidency, his vice president, George H. W. Bush, would become president. His experience beyond the vice presidency included tenure as the director of the CIA. Under President Bush, the United States engaged in the Gulf War (1990–1991), protecting its oil interests in Kuwait from Iraq. By 1991, the USSR collapsed and became a free-market capitalist economy, leading to an increase in organized crime and human trafficking (Beck et al., 2014; Combs, 2018). In 1994, the North American Free Trade Agreement was signed by Canada, Mexico, and the United States. The passage of NAFTA resulted in the elimination or reduction of barriers to trade and investment, which increased the exploitation and impoverishment of developing countries (U.S. Customs & Border Protection, n.d.).

Also, Wallace (2017) notes how on the domestic front, police brutality led to the L.A. Riots in 1992, and in 1993, the U.S. Bureau of Alcohol, Tobacco, Firearms, and Explosives and FBI confronted David Koresh and his white cult followers in Waco, Texas. The federal government went under fire for mishandling the situation and putting children in harm's way (Combs, 2018; Kettler, 2019). Indignation against the federal government was seen in the bombing of the Murrah Federal Building in Oklahoma City in 1995 by Timothy McVeigh and Terry Nichols. They murdered 68 people and injured over 600, including children. McVeigh timed his attack to coincide with the second anniversary of the deadly fire that ended the Waco siege at the Branch Davidian compound (Combs, 2018; Federal Bureau of Investigation, n.d.).

In 1999, the family of Dr. King filed a civil lawsuit against Loyd Jowers. Mr. Jowers had publicly confessed on television to being part of the conspiracy to assassinate Dr. Martin Luther King, Jr., and frame James Earl Ray for the murder. The jury found that James Earl Ray was not responsible for the murder but that Loyd Jowers had been aided by other governmental entities to conspire to assassinate King. The family was awarded damages of one hundred dollars (The Martin Luther King, Jr. Research and Education Institute, n.d.-a). Combs (2018) notes that in the same year, 1999, domestic terrorism in the form of mass shootings by white young males began with Columbine. Twelfth-grade students Eric Harris and Dylan Klebold, who had a history of being bullied, went on to shoot their classmates and then turned the weapons on themselves. In 2001, the nation was attacked on 9/11 by the Islamic terrorist group Al-Qaeda in retaliation for the continued presence of the United States in the Middle East (Beck et al, 2014; Combs, 2018).

References

Beck, R. B., Black, L., Krieger, L., Naylor, P. C., & Shabaka, D. I. (2014). *World history: Patterns of interaction.* Holt McDougal/Houghton Mifflin Harcourt.

Bomboy, S. (2019). How JFK's assassination led to a constitutional amendment. *Constitution Daily*. National Constitutional Center. https://constitutioncenter.org/blog/how-jfks-assassination-led-to-a-constitutional-amendment

Campbell, J. (Rev.). (1990). Consistency Of U.S. foreign policy: The Gulf War and the Iran-contra affair. *Foreign Affairs*. https://www.foreignaffairs.com/reviews/capsule-review/1990-03-01/consistency-us-foreign-policy-gulf-war-and-iran-contra-affair

Combs, C. (2018). *Terrorism in the twenty-first century* (8th ed.). Pearson.

Civil Rights Digital Library. (2013). Watts Riot. *Digital Library of Georgia*. http://crdl.usg.edu/events/watts_riots/?Welcome

Federal Bureau of Investigation. (n.d.). Oklahoma City bombing. *History*. https://www.fbi.gov/history/famous-cases/oklahoma-city-bombing

Gamboa, S. (2015, August 6). For Latinos, 1965 Voting Rights Act impact came a decade later. *NBC News*. https://www.nbcnews.com/news/latino/latinos-1965-voting-rights-act-impact-came-decade-later-n404936

Haberman, C. (2018, October 28). Religion and right-wing politics: How Evangelicals reshaped elections. *The New York Times*. https://www.nytimes.com/2018/10/28/us/religion-politics-evangelicals.html

Hall, S. (2007). The NAACP, Black Power, and the African American freedom struggle, 1966–1969. *The Historian, 69*(1), 49–82. https://doi.org/10.1111/j.1540-6563.2007.00174.x

History, Art, and Archives. (n.d.). The Civil Rights movement and the Second Reconstruction, 1945–1968. United States House of Representatives. https://history.house.gov/Exhibitions-and-Publications/BAIC/Historical-Essays/Keeping-the-Faith/Civil-Rights-Movement/

Kettler, S. (2019). David Koresh and the Waco siege. *Biography*. https://www.biography.com/news/david-koresh-waco-ae-documentary

Legal Information Institute. (n.d.). Roe v. Wade. Cornell Law School. https://www.law.cornell.edu/supremecourt/text/410/113

Miami Valley Teaching American History Project. (2009). The history success kit. High school history resources for the Ohio Graduation Test. Section 5: 1939–1953 World War II and the rise of the Cold War. Wright State University. https://corescholar.libraries.wright.edu/mvtah/3

Phillips, P. (2010). Drug War Madness: A call for consistency amidst the conflict. *Chapman Law Review, 13*, 645–680.

The Martin Luther King, Jr. Research and Education Institute. (n.d.-a). Assassination of Martin Luther King, Jr. *Martin Luther King, Jr. Threats/Attacks Against Collection*. Stanford University. https://kinginstitute.stanford.edu/encyclopedia/assassination-martin-luther-king-jr

The Martin Luther King, Jr. Research and Education Institute. (n.d.-b) (2020). "I have a dream," address delivered at the March on Washington for Jobs and Freedom. *The Martin Luther King, Jr. Estate Collection*. Stanford University. https://kinginstitute.stanford.edu/king-papers/documents/i-have-dream-address-delivered-march-washington-jobs-and-freedom

United Farm Workers. (n.d.). The Rise of the UFW. UFW History. https://ufw.org/research/history/ufw-history/

United Nations. (n.d.). Universal Declaration of Human Rights: History of document. https://www.un.org/en/sections/universal-declaration/history-document/index.html

U.S. Customs and Border Protection. (n.d.). North American Free Trade Agreement. https://www.cbp.gov/trade/nafta

U.S. History. (n.d.). The Vietnam War. https://www.ushistory.org/us/55.asp

Wallace, C. (2017, April 28). The unrest that led to the L.A. Riots, twenty-five year on. *The New Yorker*. https://www.newyorker.com/culture/culture-desk/the-unrest-that-led-to-the-l-a-riots-twenty-five-years-on

World Digital Library. (n.d.). United States history timelines. Library of Congress with support from United Nations Educational Scientific and Cultural Organization. https://www.wdl.org/en/sets/us-history/timeline/n/sets/us-history/timeline/

SECTION A

Feminist Criminology

READING 11

Feminist Criminology
Tim Newburn

Introduction

This chapter considers the emergence, nature, and impact of feminist criminology. Like all the other perspectives we have considered it is very much a product of a particular time. Straightforwardly, the scholarship covered in the main sections of this chapter was a product of the re-emergence of feminism from the late 1960s onwards. In part, feminist criminology was a reaction to pre-existing ways of 'doing' criminology:

> [T]he reaction was against an old, established male chauvinism in the academic discipline. Women were either invisible to conventional criminologists or present only as prostitutes or marginal or contingent figures. Further, when women were discussed it was in crude sexist stereotypes which were widely and thoughtlessly disseminated. Feminist criminology has been quite successful in developing and establishing this critique, although it has been much more difficult to get it taken into mainstream criminology. (Heidensohn, 1996: 161–2)

The focus here is on criminological theory and, in particular, how it has been influenced by feminist scholarship. Arguably the most important development in critical criminological theory in the past 30–40 years, feminist theory has transformed thinking in this area. There are continuing debates about what constitutes feminist criminology, but what seems undeniable is that feminist scholarship has had a substantial impact on criminology in recent decades.

Developing in the United States in the late 1960s and in the UK in the 1970s, feminist scholarship has been heavily critical of much mainstream criminological theorising. Heidensohn (1996: 111) put it starkly when she observed: 'criminology, mainstream and tributary, has almost nothing to say of interest or importance about women'.

Tim Newburn, "Feminist Criminology," *Criminology*, pp. 308-324, 1009-1064. Copyright © 2013 by Taylor & Francis Group. Reprinted with permission.

Early Criminology and the Female Offender

Early criminology, often characterised as 'biological positivism' or something similar, is in some ways unusual. It is unusual less for its emphasis on matters such as biology and physiognomy than for the fact that it did actually pay some attention to women. In this it may be distinguished from much that followed which was, as we will see, almost wilfully blind to female offending and female victimisation. There are two key aspects to work on female offending from within this tradition: it is seen as particularly influenced by biology—more so than male offending—and it is highly sexualised.

Lombroso and Ferrero

For Lombroso, women were especially influenced by their biology. Lombroso and Ferrero's work on the female criminal concluded that there were far fewer 'born female criminals' than males. The reason that women commit less crime, they argued, is that they are less highly developed than the male. They are more primitive, the consequence of which was that they have less scope for degeneration. The most common form of regression for the woman, Lombroso and Ferrero argued, was prostitution.

Rock has argued that the primary reason that Lombroso's work continues to be referred to in contemporary criminology is as a result of his role as the primary *bête-noir* of feminist criminology—as 'the man they loved to hate' (Rock, 2007: 125). According to many feminist critics, it was not just in the early twentieth century that views of women as

Left Gabriella Bompard. Source: Lombroso, *La donna delinquente*, 1893. *Editor's note:* Lombroso considered Bompard, a French prostitute convicted of premeditated murder, to be an example of the full born criminal type.

Above Berland (2 views). Source: Lombroso, *La donna delinquente*, 1893. *Editor's note:* Lombroso describes this criminal as lascivious, homicidal, and virile in appearance.

Below Thomas (2 views). Source: Lombroso, *La donna delinquente*, 1893. *Editor's note:* In this photo, Lombroso detected the wrinkles, protruding ears, twisted nose, and overall virility that he considered typical of female born criminals.

Illustrations from Lombroso and Ferrero's *La Donna Delinquente* (1893), now republished in a new translation (Lombroso and Ferrero: 1893/2004).

Lombroso and Ferrero on the 'Female Born Criminal'

While the majority of female criminals are merely led into crime by someone else or by irresistible temptation, there is a small subgroup whose criminal propensities are more intense and perverse than even those of their male counterparts. These are the female born criminals, whose evil is inversely proportionate to their numbers. … The extreme perversity of female born criminals manifests itself in two characteristics: the variety of their crimes and their cruelty.

Variety of Crimes

Many female born criminals specialize in not just one but several types of crime and often in two types that in males are mutually exclusive, such as poisoning and murder. … In history we find Agrippina, an adulterer, incest offender, and party to homicide, and Messalina, a prostitute, adulterer, accomplice in homicide and thief.

Cruelty

Second, the female born criminal surpasses her male counterpart in the refined, diabolical cruelty in which she commits her crimes. Merely killing her enemy does not satisfy her; she needs to watch him suffer and experience the full taste of death. … In short, while female born criminals are fewer in number than male born criminals, they are often much more savage. What is the explanation?

We have seen that the normal woman is by nature less sensitive to pain than a man. Because compassion is an effect of sensitivity, if one is lacking, the other will be too. We have also seen how women have many traits in common with children; that they are deficient in the moral sense; and that they are vengeful, jealous, and inclined to refined cruelty when they take revenge …

In addition, the female born criminal is, so to speak doubly exceptional, first, as a woman and then as a criminal. This is because criminals are exceptions among civilized people, and women are exceptions among criminals, women's natural form of regression being prostitution, not crime. Primitive woman was a prostitute rather than a criminal. As a double exception, then, the criminal woman is a true monster. Honest women are kept in line by factors such as maternity, piety, and weakness; when a woman commits a crime despite these restraints, this is a sign that her power of evil is immense.

Source: Lombroso and Ferrero (1893/2004: 182–185).

outmoded as Lombroso's were expressed, but that they could be found within contemporary criminology too. Heidensohn (2002) argues that Lombroso and Ferrero's work had a significant influence on women's penal treatment. Similarly, Carol Smart (1976) suggested the work of Lombroso, though considered by many to be archaic and desperately outdated, remained typical in its attitude toward and portrayal of women. Ironically, it appears that whereas much of what Lombroso had argued was largely discredited and abandoned, the relative invisibility of female crime meant that many of the assumptions that underpinned Lombroso's work continued to exert influence long afterward.

By and large, the idea that it is biological differences that are the primary cause of the distinctive patterns of male and female offending has disappeared from criminology, though Gelsthorpe (2002) points to the work of Maccoby and Jacklin (1975) as an exception to this, as is the work of Dalton (1977) on the link between menstruation and crime.

W.I. Thomas and Otto Pollak

W.I. Thomas was another who propounded a view of female deviance that emphasised sexuality, with promiscuity being regularly equated with delinquency. Much of Thomas's focus was on prostitution and soliciting, and these activities were seen as typical of female deviance. The female criminal, according to Thomas (1923), was cold, calculating and amoral. They had failed, in essence, to learn appropriate female roles and required greater control and oversight. In an echo of Durkheim he argued that the rapid social transformations taking place resulted in the undermining of previously existing social constraints and the development of greater awareness of the deprivations that people, and women in particular, were forced to suffer. This frustration led to the disorganisation of women's lives and potentially to delinquency (often defined as sexual delinquency).

A similar, sex-based theory was that developed by Otto Pollak (1961). He sought to explore the phenomenon of hidden female crime—being convinced that the relatively low official rates of female offending disguised the real situation. In part, this is a reflection of the lenient way in which women are treated by the criminal justice system, he argued. It also reflects the fact that women are in many ways manipulative and deceitful, this being a reflection of the nature of their sexuality and biology. In particular, women's passive role in sex, he argued (1961: 10), forms the basis for women's skill in deceit:

> Not enough attention has been paid to the physiological fact that man must achieve an erection in order to perform the sex act and will not be able to hide his failure. His lack of positive emotion in the sexual sphere must become overt to the partner and pretense of sexual response is impossible for him, if it is lacking. Woman's body, however, permits such pretense to a certain degree and lack of orgasm does not prevent her ability to participate in the sex act.

Women therefore have a different relationship with the truth. In particular, through sexual intercourse, women are able to develop both the ability and the confidence to deceive men. As Smart (1976) argues, rather than ask what might lie behind women's experience of sex, Pollak assumes that such behaviour is illustrative of fundamental characteristics—characteristics that are played out in relation to crime also. Much male offending, he argued, is actually stimulated or instigated by women.

Crimes committed by women tend to reflect their nature and may often be hidden (poisoning, infanticide), or reflect the psychological make-up of women (kleptomania, for example) or their sexuality (prostitution, sexual blackmail).

Heidensohn (1987: 17) says that 'what is striking about [Lombroso's, Pollak's and Thomas's] theories is not merely their sexism, or even their misogyny, but their resilience and persistence'. Indeed, she points out that a second generation of writers (Cowie *et al.*, 1968; Richardson, 1969; Gibbens, 1971) continued to advance very similar ideas and such views had a practical impact on women's treatment in prison in particular (Dobash *et al.*, 1986). Nevertheless, though the work of the likes of Lombroso, W.I. Thomas and Pollak is much discredited now, there are at least two important reasons for studying them (Heidensohn 1996):

- Such theories have been used to lend 'intellectual respectability' to long-standing folk ideas about women and women's behaviour.
- Until relatively recently such work was rarely questioned or criticised.

Sociological Criminology and the Continued Invisibility of Women

By contrast with the earlier work of the likes of Lombroso, W.I. Thomas and Pollak, the female offender hardly appears at all in much of the classic criminological theory of the mid-twentieth century, such as the work of the Chicago School, in strain, subcultural or control theory or, indeed, in much later 'radical' work. In a path-breaking article in 1968 in the *British Journal of Sociology* Frances Heidensohn drew attention to the notable failure to examine and research female deviance. This, she said, was remarkable for at least three reasons:

- Deviance in general (male and female) has long aroused much sociological and other academic interest (from at least the time of Durkheim). It is surprising therefore that the actual or potential deviance of approximately half the members of any society elicits such little concern.
- Interest in other aspects of women's experiences and social position has been very substantial, and has included almost every 'type' of sociologist.
- The differences between male and female offending have also long been noted, and these differences appear to occur with the kind of regularity and uniformity that normally attracts the interest of the social scientist.

This is not to say that mid-century sociological criminology made no reference to gender. It is merely to observe that, as a number of feminist scholars have argued, such work often relied on a set of assumptions about gender and took as its core concern the behaviour of men. Heidensohn (1996: 127) quotes the eminent mid-century criminologist Herman Mannheim making just such a point:

> Hitherto female crime has, for all practical purposes, been dealt with almost exclusively by men in their various capacities as legislators, judges, policemen; and ... the same was true of the theoretical treatment of the subject. ... This could

not fail to create a one-sided picture ... this centuries-old male predominance in theory.

One of the big differences between early criminological thought and the more sociologically informed theorising that succeeded it was the abandonment of the idea that crime is abnormal or pathological, and its replacement with a more understanding and appreciative set of approaches which sought to make sense of the circumstances in which offending took place and of the view of the world as it was seen through the eyes of the offender

It is precisely this appreciative sociology, Heidensohn argues, that led male researchers to ignore or exclude women from their studies: 'treating delinquency as normal made female delinquency problematic because it was both statistically unusual and also deemed role-inappropriate' (1996: 129). Delinquency is viewed as unfeminine, precisely because it is *male* behaviour. Moreover, Heidensohn argues it was not just that male sociologists were concerned to study male delinquency that was important, it was that their appreciative stance led them to *celebrate* it that reinforced the short-sightedness so far as women were concerned.

Heidensohn provides a number of examples, including the following from Albert Cohen's *Delinquent Boys* (1955: 140):

> The delinquent is the rogue male. His conduct may be viewed not only negatively ... [but also] ... positively ... as the exploitation of modes of behaviour which are traditionally symbolic of untrammelled masculinity, which are renounced by middle-class culture because incompatible with its ends, but which are not without a certain aura of glamour and romance.

Neither labelling theory nor British subcultural theory had much to say about female crime. The dominant focus of British subcultural theory in the 1970s was on white, working-class, male culture (Dorn and South, 1982). There were, at least in the earliest years of such writing, few attempts to understand either female delinquency or the styles associated with female subcultures, though the work of Angela McRobbie was both an early and a consistent exception to this (McRobbie and Garber, 1976; McRobbie, 1980, 1991).

According to McRobbie and Garber (1976), because of their position within public and private worlds, girls tend to be pushed to the periphery of social activities, and much 'girl culture' becomes a culture of the bedroom rather than the street (see also Frith, 1983). It is this, McRobbie (1980: 40) argues, that most subcultural theorists ignore:

> in documenting the temporary flights of the Teds, Mods or Rockers, they fail to show that it is monstrously more difficult for women to escape (even

temporarily) and that these symbolic flights have often been at the expense of women (especially mothers) and girls. The lads' ... peer group consciousness and pleasure frequently seem to hinge on a collective disregard for women and sexual exploitation of girls.

The 'lonely, uncharted seas of human behaviour', as Heidensohn (1968) described female deviance, were consequently long overdue serious academic consideration. Where is the equivalent of Shaw's *The Jackroller* or Sutherland's *The Professional Thief* she asked? What is needed, she suggested, 'is a crash programme of research which telescopes decades of comparable studies of males.' Such work when it begins must avoid treating its subject matter either as if it must be understood simply as a question of sex, or simply in comparison with men. A start would be to develop a 'natural history' of female deviance, in which knowledge of the parameters, types and nature of such activities would be a central focus.

Why such silence in criminological theory in relation to female offending—or, indeed, female conformity? Heidensohn (1996) suggests that there at least four important reasons:

1. What she terms the 'delinquent machismo tradition' in criminology treated male deviance as heroic and romantic—'the "college boys" became fascinated by the "corner boys"' (1996: 141).
2. This was reinforced by male dominance in academic life (the emphasis on 'founding fathers'; the preponderance of men in senior positions; and the 'ideology of gender' which constructs reality in sexually stereotyped ways).
3. The relative infrequency and relatively mundane nature of female offending made its public profile much lower.
4. The primary theoretical concerns in mainstream criminology are easier to sustain if one ignores the issue of sex differences in offending.

The Development of Modern Feminist Criminology

Feminist criminology proceeds from the assertion, therefore, that women at best have been marginal in criminology, are all too often entirely invisible, and, even when they are the focus of attention this is rarely directed in a sympathetic or rounded fashion. At the heart of feminist criminology lies a critique of extant criminology for a number of highly significant oversights. These include:

- The failure to theorise or to engage in the empirical study of female offending.
- The neglect of female victimisation and, particularly, male violence against women.
- The over-concentration on the impact of the criminal justice system on male offenders.

The period since the early 1970s has seen the emergence of new feminist and/or feminist-influenced criminologies. In fact, as we will see, there has been a considerable debate as to whether a 'feminist criminology' is desirable or even possible. Nevertheless, what is undeniable is the huge expansion of work in this area during this period. Writing in 1990, Carol Smart observed, 'some ten years ago it was *de rigueur* to start any paper on this topic [feminism and crime] with a reference to a dearth of material in the field. Now it is difficult to keep up with the production of papers and books' (1990: 71).

Female Emancipation and Crime

Two books published in America in 1975 set the tone for much that was to follow. In *Sisters in Crime* Freda Adler argued that changes to women's roles were leading to greater aggressiveness, competitiveness and criminality. In short, as women were leaving traditional housebound roles they were becoming more involved in violence and other forms of offending. The differences between the sexes in this regard were declining. Similarly, Rita Simon in *Women and Crime* also considered some of the changes in female criminality, but argued that it was the new opportunities that came with women's new roles, rather than some fundamental change in women themselves, that was crucial in understanding what was occurring. However, as Gelsthorpe (2002: 22) observes:

> A major assumption underlying the suggestion that increased opportunities lead to increases in women's crime is that women's roles have changed, that women now play an equal part in social, economic and political life. Moreover, women's earnings continue to be lower than those of men, and women remain a minority in high-ranking positions in society. Women also continue to bear the brunt of domestic and childcare responsibilities even when they are in full-time employment. Thus, women may be more involved in crime than hitherto, but this may be due to reasons of poverty, economic marginalisation and so on, and not due to women's emancipation.

Nevertheless, Gelsthorpe suggests that there are at least two reasons to think that the 'emancipation thesis' had value (2002: 24):

1. It focused attention on female crime.
2. The feminist critique of existing theories made an immense contribution in stimulating a proper evaluation of theories and their importance and relevance in explaining women's crime.

Moreover, it is far from the case that arguments that link alleged or actual changes in women's social position and social roles to female offending have disappeared. Heidensohn (2006) suggests that media preoccupation with female (mis)conduct seems even more disproportionate than it was previously and Alder and Worrall (2004) detail the apparent rise of public concern about violence by young women and the suggestion in the media and elsewhere that alleged increases in such behaviour are evidence of the emergence of a new breed of violent young women. Worrall (2004a: 47) describes the build-up of a moral panic in the late 1990s focusing on 'younger and younger girls becoming increasingly aggressive, mushrooming girl gangs, increased use of drugs and, especially, alcohol, and the wilful abandonment of gender role expectations'.

Although the early focus of much feminist work was on the changing social position of women and the impact, often assumed, that this was having on female criminality, it was fairly quickly superseded by theories that were more concerned with patriarchy and male domination. Carol Smart (1976: xiii), for example, argued that criminology tended to adopt 'an entirely uncritical attitude towards sexual stereotypes of women and girls'. In this context, 'patriarchy' has been defined as 'a sex/gender system in which men dominate women and what is considered masculine is more highly valued than what is considered feminine. Patriarchy is a system of social stratification, which means that it uses a wide array of social control policies and practices to ratify male power and to keep girls and women subordinate to men' (Chesney-Lind, 2006: 9).

Feminist scholarship in criminology has a number of characteristics that distinguish it from traditional male-dominated work. Daly and Chesney-Lind (1988: 504) suggest that there are five key elements underpinning feminist work:

- Gender is not a natural fact, but rather a complex social, historical and cultural product; it is related to, but not simply derived from, biological sex differences and reproductive capacities.
- Gender and gender relations order social life and social institutions in fundamental ways.
- Gender relations and constructs of masculinity and femininity are not symmetrical, but rather are based on an organising principle of men's superiority and social and political-economic dominance over women.
- Systems of knowledge reflect men's views of the natural and social world; the production of knowledge is gendered.
- Women should be at the centre of intellectual inquiry, not peripheral, invisible or appendages of men.

A number of questions are raised by this. Most obviously, is whether theories derived from the study of, and designed to aid understanding of, male offending can be used or applied to female offending. This approach to theorising has been referred to as the 'generalisability approach', or the 'add women and stir approach' (Heidensohn, 2006; Chesney-Lind, 2006). Miller (2000) suggests there have been two main lines of criticism of the generalisability approach.

The first suggests that it overlooks ethnic and economic inequality, failing to focus on the very different structural circumstances occupied by men and women and ignoring the racial and class inequalities that are important in explaining patterns of offending. Thus, for example, Lisa Maher's (1997) study of a Brooklyn drug market illustrates the highly gendered and racialised division of labour in the local drug economy—a division of labour that in important respects replicates and reinforces women's typically disadvantaged position in relation to men.

The second line of criticism is that whatever the benefits in using traditional criminological theory in attempting to explain female offending, what it is clearly unable to do is address the pivotal issue of the differential rates of male and female offending.

Carol Smart and Feminist Criminology

The book that has perhaps had greatest impact on this debate, both in stimulating much of it, and in setting the parameters for many successive arguments, is Carol Smart's (1976) *Women, Crime and Criminology*. In the preface to the book she raised two crucial concerns: first, that there was a particular danger that studying women separately from men would lead to continued marginalisation and to the perpetuation of a male-dominated criminology; and second, that increasing academic attention on female crime could have the unintended, and arguably undesirable, consequence of increasing public and criminal justice attention on such activities.

In the text, Smart argued that women offenders were treated as being *doubly deviant* because they were perceived as having not only broken the law, but also as having transgressed their gender roles. Early research by Eaton (1986) found that female defendants in court were simultaneously located and understood as dependants within the family setting and also as being responsible for their own behaviour and for that of other family members. As Edwards (1984: 213) put it: 'Female defendants are processed within the criminal justice system in accordance with the crimes which they committed and the extent to which the commission of the act and its nature deviate from appropriate female behaviour.'

Though making an enormously important contribution to the development of feminist scholarship in this area, Smart has been generally sceptical about elements of the project, particularly more recent attempts to develop a policy-oriented and pragmatic 'feminist criminology':

> The problem which faces criminology is not insignificant, however, and, arguably, its dilemma is even more fundamental than that facing sociology. The whole *raison d'être* of criminology is that it addresses crime. It categorises a vast range of activities and treats them as if they were all subject to the same laws—whether laws of human behaviour, genetic inheritance, economic rationality, development or the like. The argument within criminology has always been between those who give primacy to one form of explanation rather than another. The thing that criminology cannot do is deconstruct crime. It cannot locate rape or child sexual abuse in the domain of sexuality, nor theft in the domain of economic activity, nor drug use in the domain of health, to do so would be to abandon criminology to sociology, but more important it would involve abandoning an idea of a unified problem which requires a unified response—at least at the theoretical level.
>
> (Smart, 1990: 77)

Women, Crime and Criminology

Carol Smart's 1976 book is one of the most important contributions to feminist scholarship in this area. The book began life as a Master's dissertation and it was at this time that Smart says she 'became aware of the overwhelming lack of interest in female criminality displayed by established criminologists and deviancy theorists' (1976: xiii).

In the book Smart discusses the nature of female offending and examines classical and modern criminological work. Existing work, where it considers women at all, is generally inadequate and may be divided into two main categories: those that make an explicit reference to female criminality and those in which it remains implicit. Women generally remain invisible within criminology, she suggests, and, more particularly, their victimisation is especially ignored.

The silence around women's victimisation raises the question, she suggests, 'whether the victims of these offences being women has influenced the criminologist's or sociologist's interest, especially where the majority are male' (1976: 180). Not only is it vital for there to be more research on female criminality, Smart argued, but that such research should be situated in the broader moral, political, economic and sexual spheres which influence women's position in society.

If criminology and the sociology of deviance are truly to play a significant role in the development of our understanding of crime, Smart concludes, then they must 'become more than the study of men and crime' (1976: 185).

Smart's questioning of the criminological enterprise stimulated a considerable debate within feminism (Edwards, 1981; Heidensohn, 1985; Rafter and Stanko, 1980; Young, 1996). Pat Carlen (1992: 53) described the idea of feminist criminology as neither 'desirable nor possible' but, as we will see, still considered it possible for feminists to study 'women and crime'. Gelsthorpe and Morris (1990: 2) suggested that criminology 'has for many feminist writers and researchers been a constraining rather than a constructive and creative influence'. Maureen Cain (1989: 3), another long-standing critic of the limitations of the traditional criminological project, argued that:

> Crimes, criminals, victims, courts, police officers, lawyers, social workers may be objects of investigation, but our explanations must reach beyond and encompass all of them, as life histories and the victim studies, the continuity studies and the ideology studies already strain to do. I am arguing that, in a sense, feminist criminology is impossible; that feminist *criminology* disrupts the categories of criminology itself.

Cain's argument was that work in this arena should question the assumptions of traditional criminology and, in particular, should seek to examine how gender is constructed by official bodies and also more broadly within social life. Despite the scepticism voiced in the quote above, Cain (1989) was by no means entirely dismissive of a feminist criminology. Carlen (1992), though similarly sceptical, nonetheless defended the potential within feminist scholarship to transcend the existing limitations of the discipline of criminology as it was currently constituted.

The left realist response to Smart's critique of the criminological enterprise is to suggest that it leads to 'infinite regress'. If deconstruction is the key, when does one stop? Everything eventually disappears because it is argued to have no essence. More particularly, they suggest that the critique is inconsistent, on the one hand criticising criminology for its *essentialism* in treating crime as if it were a meaningful category, and on the other using terms like *rape* and *child sexual abuse* as they too could not be subject to the same criticism (Matthews and Young, 1992). The deconstructionist impulse, and the antipathy toward grand theory displayed in the radical feminist critique 'too easily lead towards nihilism, cynicism and conservatism', they argue (1992: 13).

Nevertheless, feminist criminology had an important impact on left realism and the perspectives are in many ways much more compatible than the 'debate' between Smart and Matthews and Young might imply. In part, the existence of disagreement is more a reflection of the fact that there is no single feminist criminology (Gelsthorpe, 1988). Rather, there are a number of different forms of feminist scholarship that can be identified within recent criminology, and although there have been a number of attempts to categorise these (see, for example, Harding, 1987), such is the wealth of scholarship available now that it is debatable whether such distinctions are especially helpful.

Contemporary Feminist Criminology

Rather than reworking existing criminological theories in ways that incorporate consideration of female offending, a substantial strand of feminist scholarship has focused on the development of new theoretical tools and on the utilisation of particular methodological approaches. Leonard (1982: xi–xii; quoted in Valier, 2002: 132) describes it as follows:

> Initially I thought it might be possible simply to add what had been overlooked, and to elaborate an analysis of women in terms of existing theory. I quickly discovered that this is impossible. Theoretical criminology was constructed by men, about men. It is simply not up to the analytical task of explaining female patterns of crime. Although some theories work better than others, they all illustrate what social scientists are slowly recognizing within criminology and outside the field: that our theories are not the general explanations of human behaviour they claim to be, but rather particular understandings of male behaviour. A single theoretical canopy has been assumed for men and women, although their social realities are extremely diverse.

A range of feminist responses has begun to fill this void. Daly (1997) identifies three modes of conceptualising sex/gender in feminist theory, and the implications of each for criminology. The three she identifies as: 'class–race–gender', 'doing gender' and 'sexed bodies'.

Class–race–gender has also been referred to as 'multiple inequalities'. This perspective, Daly says, conceptualises inequalities as intersecting, interlocking and contingent matters, rather than as being discrete or separate. Despite the terminology, such approaches are not restricted to the main inequalities of class, race and gender, but also incorporate age, sexuality and physical ability/disability. Attempting to show how multiple inequalities work has resulted in the utilisation of particular methods, such as literary and story-telling forms. The relevance and contribution of this perspective to criminology 'is an insistence that everyone is located in a matrix of multiple social relations', i.e. that race and gender are just as relevant to an analysis of white men as they are to black women. With an emphasis on contingency, one can explore the varied positions of 'black women'—as offenders, victims and mothers and wives of offenders and victims—to 'white justice' (1997: 35; and see Johnson, 2003).

The second mode is what she refers to as 'doing gender', a phrase taken from West and Zimmerman (quoted in Daly, 1997: 36) in which gender is conceived not as the property of individuals, but as:

> An emergent feature of social situations ... an outcome of and a rationale for ... social arrangements ... a means of legitimating [a] fundamental division ... of society. [Gender is] a routine, methodical, and recurring accomplishment ... not a set of traits, nor a variable, nor a role [but] itself constituted through interaction.

Such a view has been an important influence on feminist writing and, more recently, has particularly informed the growing body of work on 'masculinity' (Newburn and Stanko, 1994). As the quote suggests, in this view gender is viewed as a social accomplishment—something constructed and attained in particular social settings. As such, crime, like other activities, may be viewed as a practice or set of practices through which particular articulations of gender—particular styles of masculinity or femininity—are 'done'. One of the difficulties that authors such as Messerschmidt (1993) who work in this tradition encounter 'is how to conceptualize crime as a gendered line of action without once again establishing boys and men as the norm, differentiating themselves from all that is "feminine"' (Daly, 1997: 37).

The third mode Daly identifies is what she refers to as 'sexed bodies'. This is work which builds on Foucault's analysis of the body as a site of 'disciplinary practices' together with feminist work which seeks to acknowledge sex differences whilst avoiding biological essentialism (that these sex differences *determine* gendered differences in behaviour, status and similar). What is the relevance of this position to criminology? Building on work by Katz (1988), Daly (1997: 40) argues that it enables us, among other things, to:

> explore how the 'sensual attractions' of crime are differently available and 'experienced' by male/female bodies and masculine/feminine subjectivities. We could analyse the variable production of sexed (and racialized, etc.) bodies across many types of harms (not just rape) or for other sites of legal regulation such as family law. We could take Howe's (1994) theoretical lead by investigating women's bodies as the object of penality.

Crucially, she says, such a perspective allows that the allegedly gender-neutral penal policies and practices are tied to specific male bodies. The danger of such a perspective lies in the prominence given to sex differences, and the possibility that these may come to dominate other aspects of social life and practice.

Understanding Women's Involvement in Crime

Given the failures of traditional criminology in this area, it can be of little surprise that a substantial element in feminist criminology has involved attempts to understand the nature of female offending and, linked with this, the treatment of women within the criminal justice process. In particular, feminist work has been concerned to examine what has variously come to be called 'the gender gap' or the 'sex–crime ratio': the generally higher levels of offending among men. Here we look more briefly at some of the key theoretical developments of recent decades. By the late 1980s, Frances Heidensohn (1987) was able to examine the growing body of research and identify four characteristics of many of the female offenders that had been the subject of recent research. These were:

- *Economic rationality*—In contrast to earlier portrayals, such as those of Lombroso, Pollak and others, which took female criminality to be illustrative of irrationality and the influence of biology, feminist research had produced considerable evidence that women offenders were predominantly involved in property crimes and were motivated by economic concerns.
- *Heterogeneity of their offences*—'Women commit fewer crimes than men, are less likely to be recidivists or professional criminals and contribute very little to the tariff of serious violent crime' (Heidensohn, 1987: 19). Moreover, the differences between male and female offending derive not from the innate characteristics of men and women, but from social circumstances, differing opportunities, the socialisation process and the differential impact of informal and formal social control.
- *Fear and impact of deviant stigma*—The process of criminalisation has a differential impact on men and women, producing a greater sense of what Goffman (1968) called 'spoiled identity' among female offenders. The fact that female offending is considerably less extensive than male offending, together with the generally more sensational treatment it receives by public authorities and especially the media, produces a greater sense of stigmatisation.
- *The experience of double deviance and double jeopardy*—The experience, highlighted earlier, of being damned for being criminal, and doubly damned for behaving 'unlike a woman'. Such double deviance produces the potential for double jeopardy—excessive intervention by the criminal justice system which not only punishes the crime but, often justified in paternalistic terms, seeks also to impose particular controls over women's behaviour, together with the potential for additional informal sanctions from family and community (Heidensohn, 2006).

Frances Heidensohn (here with Roger Hood), a pioneer in feminist perspectives in criminology. In 2004, she won the Sellin Glueck Award of the American Society of Criminology for contributions to international criminology.

So, where are we left in attempting to understand female offending? As we have seen, much critical feminist scholarship has emphasised the role of patriarchy (Edwards, 1984) in explaining the role of criminal justice in women's oppression, and the importance of women's economic marginalisation (Carlen, 1985) in making sense of why some women make the decisions that they do (and see work by Hansen, 2006).

More recently it is perhaps control theory that has proved to have the greatest resonance for some feminist scholars. With its emphasis on conformity rather than deviance, control theory offers possibilities for understanding the lower levels of female offending compared with male offending, together with the specific nature of female offending. Heidensohn (1996: 199) argues that 'If we start from the broader issues of conformity and control and observe and analyse how these affect *all* women to some degree and *some* groups of women more than others, we can then learn rather more about those who become involved in crime as compared with other kinds of activities which might be available to them.'

In essence, her position rests on the argument that it is crucial to understand the varied and multiple ways in which women's lives are ordered and controlled. From this point of view it becomes important to acknowledge the varied and often subtle ways in which women's lives are subjected to high levels of informal social control (Feeley and Little, 1991). Female roles and behaviour are fundamentally shaped, she argues, at four levels:

- *The home*—There is a considerable sociological literature (e.g. Gavron, 1966) detailing the multiple ways in which women's lives are constrained in the private, domestic world of the home.
- *In public*—Here Heidensohn suggests that there are three separate, but linked, aspects to the control of women's behaviour:
  - the male quasi-monopoly of force and violence—note the very high (relative) levels of fear reported by women in relation to physical attack and sexual violence in particular;
  - the notion of reputation and 'name'—the ways traditionally girls and women have been 'kept in their place' through male control over reputation;
  - the ideology of separate spheres—the notion that men and women operate in different ways in the public and private realms and are subject to different rules.
- *At work*—Again Heidensohn notes three ways in which the normative constraints on women are either greater or different from those on men:
  - most women have to cope with both home and work;
  - the bulk of supervisors of women's work are male;
  - women have to deal with sexual harassment at work.
- *In social policies*—A range of social policies—not least welfare benefits—have traditionally been organised in ways that reinforce women's roles.

The essence of Heidensohn's argument, therefore, is that in these many ways we can begin to understand the highly constrained and controlled environments that women have generally inhabited in modern society, and that this should be helpful to us in understanding their (more limited) offending behaviour. Moreover, they 'face distinctively different opportunity situations and ... an additional series of controls' (1996: 198). Thus, the predominance of property offending in female crime is likely related, she argues, to women's general powerlessness and economic marginality.

One further question raised by such an analysis concerns how such controls are to be understood normatively: i.e. whether they should be perceived as benign or malign. In this regard, Carlen (1995) is clear that there is much here that is far from benign, and argues consequently that a more appropriate term to capture such processes might be 'anti-social control':

a variety of malign institutionalized practices that may either set limits to individual action by favouring one set of citizens at the expense of another so as to subvert equal opportunities ideologies in relation to gender, race and class (or other social groupings); or (in societies without equal opportunities ideologies) set limits to individual action in ways that are anti-social because they atrophy an individual's social contribution and do so on the grounds of either biological attributes or exploitative social relations.

(Carlen and Worrall, 2004: 122)

Women, Prison and Punishment

The body (or soul) upon which punishment is inflicted is gendered and, yet, as Carlen (2002) has noted, it is relatively rare within criminology that the words 'women' and 'punishment' are brought together. The reason for this, she suggests, is in part a product of a more general need to deny or repress knowledge about the social inequalities between those who impose punishment and those upon whom it is imposed. In addition, however, there are a number of more specific reasons:

- Women commit fewer crimes than men and commit fewer serious crimes than men. Consequently, 'the nightmarish and murderous felon in the shadows has not traditionally lurked in female form' (2002: 4).
- One result of this is that, traditionally, women have tended to be controlled through informal rather than formal means.
- When women are prosecuted there has been a tendency not to view them, simply, as criminal and rather to see them as mad or as subject to forces beyond their control (Zedner, 1991).
- Finally, Carlen (2002) argues that connecting women with punishment has potential sexual or pornographic connotations and that this has served to inhibit discourse in this area.

From the outset therefore feminist penology was grappling with a set of difficult problems. As a consequence, there is a number of questions that have become central to this area. They begin with the core question of whether women are treated differently from men in the penal sphere and, if so, in what ways? Relatedly, feminist scholarship also asks whether women *should* be treated differently. In relation to imprisonment, feminist writers inquire as to its purpose, why it takes the forms it does and whether, in most cases, it is an appropriate setting for female offenders.

The Nature of Women's Imprisonment

Carlen and Worrall (2004) identify four themes which, they argue, are central to answering the question, 'why do women's prisons take the forms they do?'

- *Prisonisation*—An idea with a long history in the study of imprisonment, which suggests that inmates take on a set of behaviours and values that reflect the culture of the institution (Sykes, 1958). Feminist work has identified a number of problems particular to women's imprisonment, notably that prisons and prison systems are usually organised in relation to men's needs and are often very poorly equipped to deal with the often very different needs of female prisoners. Moreover, feminist work suggests that female prisoners are more adversely affected by the separation brought about by imprisonment. In relation to 'prisonisation', studies have tended to focus on how women adapt to the experience of imprisonment and to what extent their behaviour 'inside' is a product of the nature of the regime and the culture of the prison itself.
- *Discrimination*—Focusing on the way in which female prisoners are treated differently from male prisoners, 'though not usually in ways which have been to their advantage' (Carlen and Worrall, 2004: 82; see also Zedner, 1991). In this connection they quote a historical study by Rafter looking at women's imprisonment in nineteenth- and early twentieth-century America, in which she noted that:

  > The custodial model was a masculine model: derived from men's prisons, it adopted their characteristics—retributive purpose, high-security architecture, a male-dominated authority structure, programmes that stressed earnings and harsh discipline ... women's custodial institutions treated women like men.

  > (Rafter, 1985: 21)

- As Carlen (1983) and others have noted elsewhere, although women may be treated somewhat as if they are men, their experience of imprisonment is generally different from men's:
  – They tend to be imprisoned at greater distances from home than male prisoners (because of the smaller number of women's prisons).
  – The nature and range of regimes tends to be more restricted (for the same reason).
  – Women prisoners tend to suffer greater social stigma than men—largely as a result of being perceived as being doubly deviant.
- *Resistance*—In contrast to the idea of prisonisation, one theme in feminist work on women's imprisonment has explored and stressed ways in which women can and do resist aspects of the experience of imprisonment, including using femininity as a tool (Bosworth, 1999) and in developing vibrant, highly organised inmate cultures (Barton, 2005; Denton, 2001).
- *Carceral clawback*—A term coined by Pat Carlen (2002, 2004) to capture the ideological project engaged in within prison systems to promote the idea that prisoners *need* to be kept inside. Without this, prisons lose one, if not the, central reason for their continued existence. The consequence of this ideological project is that reform programmes which challenge prison security and traditional prison functioning tend to be modified, reformed or even suppressed. This is one of the key barriers to the development of regimes that are better suited to women's needs (Hannah-Moffat, 2002; Hayman, 2006).

The Criminalisation of Women

As we have seen, feminist scholars have been concerned with why women are criminalised less than men. Beyond the straightforward empirical observation that women commit less crime than men, one consistent line of argument has focused around how women are 'constructed' and 'presented' within criminal justice. In particular, a number of authors have argued that one element of the criminal justice process involves rendering female offenders harmless by (re)locating them within traditional gendered roles:

> The female lawbreaker is routinely offered the opportunity to neutralise the effects of her lawbreaking activity by implicitly entering into a contract whereby she permits her life to be represented primarily in terms of its domestic, sexual and pathological dimensions. The effect of this 'gender contract' is to strip her lawbreaking of its social, economic and ideological dimensions in order to minimise its punitive consequences.
>
> (Worrall, 1990: 31)

One consistent theme running through many of the chapters in this book concerns the growing punitiveness visible at the end of the twentieth century and the beginning of the twenty-first. Arguably, this has affected women at least as much, if not more than, men. Worrall (2002) argues that the politicisation of crime control, and the emergence of new forms of actuarial justice (the new penology, have seen what she refers to as a 'search for equivalence' in relation to female offending. Such equivalence blurs or ignores the differences between men and women (and male and female offenders) and serves to make women punishable, and requiring of punishment. 'The political and moral justification for such punishment is that either more women are committing punishable acts or more women are being *discovered* committing punishable acts' (Worrall, 2002: 48). One consequence of this, Worrall argues, has been a retreat from the medicalisation, welfarisation, sexualisation and domestication that has traditionally characterised responses to much women's offending.

A Feminist Methodology?

Much feminist scholarship, especially from the 1980s onward, was particularly critical of aspects of traditional, mainstream criminology's approach to inquiry (Stanley and Wise, 1979; Cain, 1986). By contrast, feminist work promoted appreciative, generally qualitative methodologies (Gelsthorpe, 1990) and was highly critical of claims to objectivity and neutrality (Kelly, 1978). In large part, this reflected the fact that much feminist writing was located—indeed, often deeply embedded in—practical, political campaigning activity (Stanko, 1990). Chesney-Lind (1997) has written of the importance of seeing female offenders as 'people with life histories' (Gelsthorpe, 2002). A more recent edited collection on gender and justice (Heidensohn, 2006) illustrates that contemporary scholarship in this area is still predominantly characterised by qualitative research methods, though by no means exclusively so (also see Oakley, 2000).

Gelsthorpe (1990) identifies four major themes in debate around the nature of feminist methodology:

- *Choice of topic*—This, Gelsthope suggests, has generally meant selecting objects of study that are linked to women's oppression and, in particular, seeking to identify topics of political and practical importance that have the potential to contribute to ending that oppression. Within this context one area of debate has concerned the extent to which it is appropriate for men to be involved in the enterprise (Stanley and Wise, 1983; Cain, 1986).
- *Process*—Also, in particular, the strengths and weaknesses of quantitative and qualitative approaches to research has been debated. As suggested above, there has been a consistent view put forward that qualitative methods are in many respects best suited to feminist research studies. It is not quantitative methods *per se* that Gelsthorpe (1990: 91) says are the problem, but 'insensitive quantification'.
- *Power and control*—Here the focus is on the nature of the relationship between the researcher and those they are researching. Gelsthorpe quotes Stanley and Wise's (1983: 170) observation that the traditional relationship 'is obscene because it treats people as mere objects, there for the researcher to do research "on". Treating people as objects—sex objects or research objects—is morally unjustifiable'. One consequence of this has been to attempt to engage the subjects of research more fully in the project itself (Ramazanoglu and Holland, 2002).
- *The subjective experiences of doing research*—Feminist researchers have been concerned to attempt to record elements of the research experience, to be open about what is involved, and emphasising the personal aspects of research. Again, as with the three other themes, this arises from the importance of personal experience to all aspects of research, captured in McRobbie's (1982: 52) observation that 'Feminism forces us to locate our own autobiographies and our experience inside the questions we might ask'.

Although work in this area has given rise to a number of potentially contentious debates—in particular around how feminist criminology should be conducted, and who should do it—Heidensohn and Gelsthorpe (2007: 385) in their review of the area conclude that a close reading reveals 'no fixed "absolutes" beyond the need for sensitivity in the research task, for personal reflexivity—to reflect on the subjectivities of all involved—and commitment to make the research relevant to women'.

Feminist Victimology

One very important strand of feminist scholarship has been what might be called feminist victimology. The focus of this work is on uncovering, assessing and responding to the victimisation of women and, in particular, men's violence against women. Historically, relatively little attention was paid to rape, sexual assault and to domestic violence. The private world of the family, and the behaviour of men within it, was subject to little critical scrutiny. Moreover, there was tacit acceptance of much male violence against women and a range of justifications or rationalisations for such behaviour.

From the 1970s onwards there was a substantial growth in work—both practical and intellectual—in these areas. Campaigning around, and research on, domestic violence (Dobash and Dobash, 1979), and violence against women more generally (Hanmer *et al.*, 1989) began significantly to challenge many mainstream (sometimes referred to as 'malestream') ideas in criminology. Feminist work in this area had a number of themes and objectives:

- Making visible forms of victimisation that hitherto had been largely ignored.
- Illustrating the extent to which violence against women was primarily an issue of men's violence against women.
- Illustrating that whilst popular representations highlight the idea of 'stranger danger', in practice women have been most at risk 'within the home'. As Stanko (1990: 6–7) put it:

    > While other criminological works concern themselves only with the potential threat posed by strangers outside the home, I do not assume that the home is safe. The place where people are supposed to find solace from the perils of the outside world should not be presumed to provide a respite from interpersonal violence. For far too many, menace lurks there as well. The prevalence of battering among women's experiences of intimate relationships with men, the growing awareness amongst adult women of potential and actual sexual danger from male intimates, acquaintances and friends, and the memories of adults of physical and sexual abuse during their childhoods shatter the illusion of the safe home.

- Arguing that sexual violence by men against women was not primarily an issue of sex, but one of power (Daly and Chesney-Lind, 1988).
- Illustrating the ways in which the criminal justice system failed to respond appropriately to women's victimisation and how this was frequently the result of the male-dominated and oriented nature of the system, and the stereotyped views of women that structured the working of the major agencies such as the police and the courts.
- Identifying aspects of secondary victimisation—the negative consequences of the criminal justice process for women complainants, often experienced as further victimisation (Stanko, 1985).

Assessing Feminist Criminology

Though there is much debate about what constitutes 'feminist' criminology, one can probably agree with Gelsthorpe's (2002: 135) identification of its key elements:

- a focus on *sex/gender* as a central organising principle in social life;
- recognition of the importance of *power* in shaping social relations;

- sensitivity to the influence of social *context* on behaviour;
- recognition that social reality is a *process* and that research methods need to reflect this;
- a political commitment to *social change*;
- personal and theoretical reflexivity on epistemological, methodological, and ethical choices and commitments; and
- openness and creativity in thinking about producing and evaluating knowledge.

It is impossible to deny that feminist scholarship has had anything but an important impact on criminological thought in recent decades. As a consequence of its impact it is no longer the case that criminology is gender-blind—though some critics might quite reasonably claim that it continues to be dominated by discussion of male offending and by theories that are more concerned with men than women. Carlen and Worrall (1987: 9) have argued that a focus on gender has had three crucial consequences for criminology:

1. It has called into question previous theories of lawbreaking and/or criminalisation.
2. It has suggested new lines of investigation for empirical research programmes.
3. It has either provoked new uses for old concepts, or has displaced old theories with new ones.

Feminist scholarship had an important impact in refocusing elements of criminological attention on the impact of the criminal justice system (Heidensohn, 1968). Examining the ways in which the police, the courts and the prisons dealt with women, such work argued that there were numerous structural disadvantages faced by women—in contrast to the oft-held assumption that, in fact, the criminal justice system tended to treat women more leniently (an assumption that one can still hear repeated regularly—for assessments of the arguments see Hedderman and Hough, 1994; Hedderman, 2004).

In terms of its more particular impact, Downes and Rock argue that the 'study of victimization constitutes the sole area in which gender has transformed research' (Downes and Rock, 2007: 265). They go on to argue, nevertheless, that there are four substantive areas where feminist scholarship has led to significant work:

1. Mounting a significant challenge to the 'female emancipation leads to crime' debate.
2. Challenging and undermining the hypothesis that women are treated more leniently than men by the criminal justice system.
3. The development of a gender-based theory of both male and female delinquency focusing on differential or segregative social control systems.
4. The raising to greater prominence of the female victim and, indeed, of the plight of victims generally—male or female. As Chesney-Lind (2006: 7) remarks: 'the naming of the types and dimensions of female victimization had a significant impact on public policy, and it is arguably the most tangible accomplishment of both feminist criminology and grassroots feminists concerned about gender, crime, and justice.'

Intriguingly, one of the more recent areas that has developed from the insights derived from feminist scholarship is that which has led a number of criminologists to focus on ideas of 'maleness'. This is a relatively recent development and traditional criminology has tended to ignore the issue of masculinity, leading Heidensohn (1987: 23) to refer to this as the 'lean-to' approach to gender and deviance in which:

> Gender is no longer ignored ... but it is consigned to an outhouse, beyond the main structure of the work and is almost invariably conflated with *women*; males are not seen as having gender; or if their masculinity does become an issue, it is taken-for-granted and not treated as problematic.

In fact, as Renzetti (1993: 232) has observed, 'the goal of feminism is not to push men out so as to bring women in, but rather to gender the study of crime'. Underpinning much work on masculinity is the idea that much extant criminology has tended to treat men in a somewhat stereotypical and uni-dimensional form—as if there were only one way of *being* male. Borrowing from Connell (1987), Messerschmidt (1993) focuses on the way in which men are socialised into a form of 'hegemonic masculinity'. This term, utilising Gramsci's notion of 'hegemony' has proved something of a mixed blessing in relation to understanding maleness and crime. At heart, it picks up the idea that there are certain core attributes—toughness and other forms of physical prowess, authority, heterosexuality, competitiveness—which are associated with a dominant model of how to be a man. Such hegemonic masculinity is contrasted with 'subordinated masculinities' (associated with other ways of being male such as being bi-sexual or gay) and with femininity.

Certainly, early usage of the idea of hegemonic masculinity added little to the existing literature on male offenders, doing little other than identifying characteristics that had long been associated with young, particularly working-class males (Willis, 1977). Moreover, in some of the literature the links between 'doing masculinity' and crime were far from clear. One attempt at clarification, by Messerschmidt (1993), argued that deviance is a core method which men who experience goal blockages use to communicate their masculinity. There is no single method of achieving this but many, mediated by race and class, that have differing effects on offending behaviour. At one extreme, therefore, domestic violence is a 'resource for affirming "maleness"' (1993: 173). In an echo of strain theory, he argues that such offending will be more common among lower-class males because of the problems they face in securing the necessary resources for constructing their masculinity.

The concept of 'hegemonic masculinity' was criticised on a number of accounts:

- *Essentialism*—Under-emphasising the fluid, contested and changing nature of masculinity (Hearn, 1996).
- *Inconsistency*—What does hegemonic masculinity actually mean? Is it an ideal-type, not found in reality, or is it an attempt to identify the attributes of particular types of men, or men in certain

situations or positions—'Is it John Wayne or Leonardo DiCaprio; Mike Tyson or Pelé?' (Connell and Messerschmidt, 2005: 838).
- *Emphasising the negative*—Treatments of hegemonic masculinity, especially within criminology, have tended to focus on negative male attributes rather than positive ones (Collier, 1998).

Connell and Messerschmidt (2005) have responded to these and other criticisms. They argue for the retention and reformulation of the concept. They defend the idea that there exists both a plurality and a hierarchy of masculinities, and they suggest it is important to emphasise that the 'hegemonic' form of masculinity need not be the commonest pattern of masculinity, its characteristics being established through exemplars such as sports and pop stars. Despite some far-reaching criticisms of both the theory and its application (see also Hood-Williams, 2001), the sense persists that the study of masculinities has potential explanatory power within the field of criminology even if, as yet, this potential remains some distance from realisation.

Feminist writing has had an impact, therefore, on our understanding of women's offending, their victimisation—particularly at the hands of men—and their treatment by the criminal justice system. Feminist emphasis on the idea of 'doing gender' has also given rise to a growing concern with masculinities and how such a notion might be linked to the ways in which we understand and research male offending. Although feminist scholarship has undoubtedly fallen far short of the impact on criminology than many of its most important advocates would wish (Smart, 1990; Heidensohn, 1996), and criminology remains male-dominated and male-oriented, it is important not to underestimate the ways in which feminism resonates through criminological work. It can be seen in criminological theory, in the nature and style of criminological methods, and in all the major policy debates of the moment. Nevertheless, in attempting to wield *influence* (changing the nature of the enterprise), there is the constant danger of *incorporation* (simply becoming absorbed into the mainstream—or 'malestream'). No doubt this is the balancing act that feminist criminologists will continue to confront for the foreseeable future.

References

Adler, F. (1975). *Sisters in Crime*, New York: McGraw-Hill.

Alder, C. and Worrall, A. (eds) (2004). *Girl's Violence: Myths and realities,* Albany, NY: State University of New York Press.

Barton, A. (2005). *Fragile Moralities and Dangerous Sexualities,* Aldershot: Ashgate.

Bosworth, M. (1999). *Engendering Resistance: Agency and power in women's prisons,* Aldershot: Ashgate.

Cain, M. (1986). 'Realism, feminism, methodology and law', *International Journal of the Sociology of Law,* 14, 3/4, 255–67.

Cain, M. (1989). *Growing Up Good: Policing the behaviour of girls in Europe,* London: Sage.

Carlen, P. (1983). *Women's Imprisonment,* London: Routledge and Kegan Paul.

Carlen, P. (1985). *Criminal Women,* Oxford: Polity Press.
Carlen, P. (1992). 'Criminal women and criminal justice: the limits to, and potential of, feminist and left realist perspectives', in Matthews, R. and Young, J. (eds) *Issues in Realist Criminology,* London: Sage.
Carlen, P. (1995). 'Virginia, criminology and the anti-social control of women', in Blumberg, T. and Cohen, S. (eds) *Punishment and Social Control,* New York: Aldine de Gruyter.
Carlen, P. (ed.) (2002). *Women and Punishment: The struggle for justice,* Cullompton: Willan.
Carlen, P. and Worrall, A. (eds) (1987). *Gender, Crime and Justice,* Milton Keynes: Open University Press.
Carlen, P. and Worrall, A. (2004). *Analysing Women's Imprisonment,* Cullompton: Willan.
Chesney-Lind, M. (1997). *The Female Offender: Girls, women and crime,* Thousand Oaks, CA: Sage.
Chesney-Lind, M. (2006). 'Patriarchy, crime and justice: Feminist criminology in an era of backlash', *Feminist Criminology,* 1, 1, 6–26.
Cohen, A.K. (1955). *Delinquent Boys: The culture of the gang,* New York: The Free Press.
Collier, R. (1998). *Masculinities, Crime and Criminology: Men, heterosexuality and the criminal(ised)other,* London: Sage.
Connell, R. (1987). *Gender and Power: Society, the person and sexual politics,* Cambridge: Polity Press.
Connell, R. and Messerschmidt, J. (2005). 'Hegemonic masculinity: Rethinking the concept', *Gender and Society,* 19, 6, 829–59.
Cowie, J., Cowie, V. and Slater, E. (1968). *Delinquency in Girls,* London: Heinemann.
Dalton, K. (1977). *The Premenstrual Syndrome and Progresterone Therapy,* London: Heinemann.
Daly, K. (1997). 'Different ways of conceptualizing sex/gender in feminist theory and their implications for criminology', *Theoretical Criminology,* 1, 1, 25–51.
Daly, K. and Chesney-Lind, M. (1988). 'Feminism and criminology', *Justice Quarterly,* 5, 497–538.
Denton, B. (2001). *Dealing: Women in the drug economy,* Sydney: University of New South Wales Press.
Dobash, R.E. and Dobash, R.P. (1979). *Violence Against Wives,* Basingstoke: Macmillan.
Dobash, R., Dobash, R., and Gutteridge, S. (1986). *The Imprisonment of Women,* Oxford: Blackwell Publishing.
Dorn, N. and South, N. (1982). 'Of males and markets: A critical review of youth culture theory', *Research Paper 1, Centre for Occupational and Community Research,* London: Middlesex Polytechnic.
Downes, D. and Rock, P. (2007). *Understanding Deviance,* 5th edn, Oxford: Oxford University Press.
Eaton, M. (1986). *Justice for Women?,* Milton Keynes: Open University Press.
Edwards, S. (1984). *Women on Trial,* Manchester: Manchester University Press.
Edwards, S.M. (1981). *Female Sexuality and the Law,* London: Martin Robertson.
Feeley, M. and Little, D. (1991). 'The vanishing female: The decline of women in the criminal process, 1687–1912', *Law and Society Review,* 25, 4, 719–57.
Frith, S. (1983). *Sound Effects: Youth, leisure and the politics of rock and roll,* London: Constable.
Gavron, H. (1966). *The Captive Wife: Conflicts of housebound mothers,* London, New York: Routledge and Kegan Paul.
Gelsthorpe, L. (1988). 'Feminism and criminology in Britain', *British Journal of Criminology,* 28, 2, 93–110.

Gelsthorpe, L. (1990). 'Feminist methodologies in criminology: A new approach or old wine in new bottles?', in Gelsthorpe, L. and Morris, A. (eds). *Feminist Perspectives in Criminology,* Milton Keynes: Open University Press.

Gelsthorpe, L. (2002). 'Feminism and criminology', in Maguire, M., Morgan, R., and Reiner, R. (eds) *The Oxford Handbook of Criminology,* 3rd edn, Oxford: Oxford University Press.

Gelsthorpe, L. and Morris, A. (eds) (1990). *Feminist Perspectives in Criminology,* Milton Keynes: Open University Press.

Gibbens, T. (1971). 'Female offenders', *British Journal of Hospital Medicine,* 6, 279–286.

Goffman, E. (1968). *Asylums: Essays on the social situation of mental patients and other inmates,* Harmondsworth: Penguin.

Hannah-Moffat, K. (2002). 'Creating choices? Reflecting on the choices', in Carlen, P. (ed.) *Women and the Struggle for Justice,* Cullompton: Willan.

Hanmer, J., Radford, J. and Stanko, E.A. (1989). *Women, Policing and Male Violence,* London: Routledge.

Hansen, K. (2006). 'Gender differences in self-reported offending', in Heidensohn, F. (ed.) *Gender and Justice: New concepts and approaches,* Cullompton: Willan.

Harding, S. (1987). *Feminism and Methodology,* Milton Keynes: Open University Press.

Hayman, S. (2006). 'The reforming prison: A Canadian tale', in Heidensohn, F. (ed.) *Gender and Justice: New perspectives,* Cullompton: Willan.

Hearn, J. (1996). 'Is masculinity dead? A critique of the concept of masculinity/ masculinities', in Mac an Ghail, M. (ed.), *Understanding Masculinities: Social relations and cultural arenas,* Buckingham: Open University Press.

Hedderman, C. (2004). 'Why are more women being sentenced to custody?', in McIvor, G. (ed.) *Women Who Offend,* London: Jessica Kingsley.

Hedderman, C. and Hough, M. (1994). *Does the criminal justice system treat men and women differently?* Home Office Research Findings 10, London: Home Office.

Heidensohn, F. (1968). 'The deviance of women: a critique and an inquiry', *British Journal of Sociology,* 19, 2, 160–73.

Heidensohn, F. (1985). *Women and Crime,* London: Macmillan.

Heidensohn, F. (1987). 'Women and crime: Questions for criminology', in Carlen, P. and Worrall, A. (eds) *Gender, Crime and Justice,* Milton Keynes: Open University Press.

Heidensohn, F. (1996). *Women and Crime,* 2nd edn, Basingstoke: Macmillan.

Heidensohn, F. (2002). 'Gender and crime', in Maguire, M., Morgan, R. and Reiner, R. (eds) *The Oxford Handbook of Criminology,* 3rd edn, Oxford: Oxford University Press.

Heidensohn, F. (ed.) (2006a). *Gender and Justice: New concepts and approaches,* Cullompton: Willan.

Heidensohn, F. (2006b). 'New perspectives and established views', in Heidensohn, F. (ed.) *Gender and Justice: New concepts and approaches,* Cullompton: Willan.

Heidensohn, F. and Gelsthorpe, L. (2007). 'Gender and crime', in Maguire, M., Morgan, R. and Reiner, R. (eds) *The Oxford Handbook of Criminology,* 4th edn, Oxford: Oxford University Press.

Hood-Williams, J. (2001). 'Gender, masculinities and crime: From structures to psyches', *Theoretical Criminology,* 5, 1, 37–60.

Howe, A. (1994). *Punish and Critique: Towards a feminist analysis of penality*, New York: Routledge.

Johnson, P. (2003). *Inner lives: Voices of African American women in prison.* New York: New York University Press.

Katz, J. (1988). *Seductions of Crime: Moral and sensual attractions in doing evil,* New York: Basic Books.

Kelly, A. (1978). 'Feminism and research', *Women's Studies International Quarterly,* 1, 225–232.

Leonard, E. (1982). *Women, Crime and Society: A critique of criminology theory,* New York: Longman.

Lombroso, C. and Ferrero, G. (1893/2004). *Criminal Woman, the Prostitute and the Normal Woman,* translated, and with a new introduction, by Rafter, N.H. and Gibson, M., Durham: Duke University Press.

McRobbie, A. (1980). 'Settling accounts with subcultures: A feminist critique', *Screen Education,* 39.

McRobbie, A. (1982). 'The politics of feminist research: Between talk, text and action', *Feminist Review,* 12, 46–57.

McRobbie, A. (1991). *Feminism and Youth Culture: From Jackie to Just Seventeen,* London: Macmillan.

McRobbie, A. and Garber, J. (1976). 'Girls and subcultures: An exploration', in Hall, S. and Jefferson, T. (eds) *Resistance through Rituals,* London: Hutchison.

Maccoby, E.E. and Jacklin, C.N. (1975). *The Psychology of Sex Differences*, Stanford: Stanford University Press; London: Oxford University Press.

Maher, L. (1997). *Sexed Work,* Oxford: Oxford University Press.

Matthews, R. and Young, J. (eds) (1992). *Rethinking Criminology: The realist debate,* London: Sage.

Messerschmidt, J. (1993). *Masculinities and Crime: Critique and reconceptualisation of theory,* Lanham, MD: Rowman and Littlefield.

Miller, J. (2000). 'Feminist theories of women's crime: Robbery as a case study', in Simpson, S. (ed.) *Of Crime and Criminality,* Thousand Oaks, CA: Pine Forge Press.

Newburn, T. and Stanko, E.A. (1994). *Just Boys Doing Business: Men, masculinities and crime,* London: Routledge.

Oakley, A. (2000). *Experiments in Knowing: Gender and method in the social sciences,* Cambridge: Polity Press.

Pollak, O. (1961). *The Criminality of Women,* New York: A.S. Barnes.

Rafter, N. (1985). 'Chastizing the unchaste: Social control functions of a women's reformatory', in Cohen, S. and Scull, A. (eds) *Social Control and the State,* Oxford: Blackwell Publishing.

Rafter, N.H. and Stanko, E. (1982). *Judge, Lawyer, Victim, Thief: Women, gender roles and criminal justice*, Boston: Northeastern University Press.

Ramazanoglu, C. and Holland, J. (2002). *Feminist Methodology: Challenges and choices,* London: Sage.

Renzetti, C.M. (1993). 'On the margins of the malestream (or, they *still* don't get it, do they?): Feminist analyses in criminal justice education', *Journal of Criminal Justice Education,* 4, 2, 219–234.

Richardson, H. (1969). *Adolescent Girls in Approved Schools*, London: Routledge and Kegan Paul.

Rock, P. (2007). 'Cesare Lombroso as a signal criminologist', *Criminology and Criminal Justice*, 7, 2, 117–134.

Simon, I. (1975). *The Contemporary Woman and Crime*, Washington, DC: National Institute of Mental Health.

Smart, C. (1976). *Women, Crime and Criminology: A feminist critique*, London: Routledge and Kegan Paul.

Smart, C. (1990). 'Feminist approaches to criminology or postmodern woman meets atavistic man', in Gelsthorpe, L. and Morris, A. (eds) *Feminist Perspectives in Criminology*, Milton Keynes: Open University Press.

Stanko, E. (1985). *Intimate Intrusions: Women's experiences of male violence*, London: Virago.

Stanko, E. (1990). *Everyday Violence: How women and men experience sexual and physical danger*, London: Pandora.

Stanley, L. and Wise, S. (1979). 'Feminist research, feminist consciousness and experiences of sexism', *Women's Studies International Quarterly*, 2, 259–279.

Stanley, L. and Wise, S. (1983). *Breaking Out: Feminist consciousness and feminist research*, London: Routledge and Kegan Paul.

Sykes, G. (1958). *The Society of Captives*, Princeton, NJ: Princeton University Press.

Thomas, W.I. (1923). *The Unadjusted Girl*, Boston, MA: Little, Brown.

Valier, C. (2002). *Theories of Crime and Punishment*, Harlow: Longman.

Willis, P. (1977). *Learning to Labour: How working class kids get working class jobs*, Farnborough: Saxon House.

Worrall, A. (1990). *Offending Women*, London: Routledge.

Worrall, A. (2002). 'Rendering them punishable', in Carlen, P. (ed) *Women and Punishment: The struggle for justice*, Cullompton: Willan.

Worrall, A. (2004). 'Twisted sisters, ladettes and the new penology: The social construction of violent girls', in Alder, C. and Worrall, A. (eds) *Girl's Violence: Myths and realities*, Albany, NY: State University of New York Press.

Young, A. (1996). *Imagining Crime: Textual outlaws and criminal conversations*, London: Sage.

Zedner, L. (1991). *Women, Crime and Custody in Victorian England*, Oxford: Oxford University Press

READING 12

At the Intersections

Race, Gender and Violence

Nikki Jones and Jerry Flores

Over the last several decades, scholars have paid increased attention to gender and trends in violent offending and victimization (DeHart and Lynch, 2013; Goodkind, 2009; Males, 2010). Most recently, interest in this area was piqued by changes in arrest statistics for women and girls beginning in the late 1980s and continuing into the early 2000s. During this time, girls' arrests for violent offenses increased more rapidly and decreased more slowly than arrests of boys for similar offenses (Chesney-Lind and Shelden, 2004). Over this time period, more girls entered secure detention for crimes against persons like simple assault and aggravated assault. The number of women incarcerated for violent offenses also increased over the first decade of the twenty-first century from 109,340 in 1999 to 183,986 in 2009 (Bureau of Justice Statistics, 2011). During this time, women also continued to experience high rates of victimization. Women were 45 percent of simple assault victims in 2008 (Bureau of Justice Statistics, 2011). Women remain the most common victims of rape and sexual assault (80 percent). Data from 2009 find that women who reported rapes were raped by men 78 percent of the time and most often by a friend, relative or intimate partner.

These data reveal a complicated trend: women and girls remain common targets of violent victimization, especially at the hands of men and intimate partners, but are also more likely than ever to be arrested and incarcerated for violent offending. This is especially true for poor women of color who are disproportionately represented in the juvenile and criminal justice systems (Renzetti and Maier, 2002). How do researchers account for these recent trends? How are these recent trends in gender, violent offending and victimization patterned by intersections of race, gender and class? How do these explanations challenge or extend previous studies of gender and violence, especially studies of women's experience with violence and victimization? Finally, how do these explanations help us to understand the hype surrounding the so-called "new violent girl" and the punitive institutional responses that have emerged as a result of socially constructing girls as "wild" or "bad"?

In this chapter we review key contributions to the literature on gender, violence and victimization. Instead of providing an exhaustive review of the literature, we highlight key theoretical and empirical

Nikki Jones and Jerry Flores, Selection from "At the Intersections: Race, Gender and Violence," *Routledge International Handbook of Crime and Gender Studies*, ed. Claire M. Renzetti, Susan L. Miller, and Angela R. Gover, pp. 73-85. Copyright © 2013 by Taylor & Francis Group. Reprinted with permission.

contributions that illustrate *how intersections of race, gender and class shape the criminological literature on gender, violence and victimization,* and *the implications of "intersectionality" for helping us to better understand trends in violence and victimization among women and girls.* We begin with a discussion of Dorie Klein's (1973) "The Etiology of Female Crime: A Review of the Literature," which is one of the earliest and most significant reviews of the traditional criminological canon. Klein's critique was among the first to challenge the representation of women in the traditional criminological literature. Subsequent critiques of the literature encouraged the development of gender and crime and feminist criminology as valid areas of study in the criminological literature. These critiques also paved the way for the development of Black feminist criminology (Potter, 2006), which encourages the use of an intersectional analysis to understand trends in violent offending, victimization and institutional responses to each. In contrast to the early criminological works surveyed in the first section of this chapter, recent work on gender, violence and victimization draws on an intersectional framework to explain how categorical variables like race, gender or class, pattern violence and victimization. In addition to explaining differences in patterns across and within groups, these explanations also help us to better understand how race, gender and class inform institutional responses to violence and victimization.

On Etiology: Gender and Criminology

It is almost impossible to disentangle the earliest explanations for women's and girls' experiences with violence—either as victims or offenders—from researchers' essentialist understandings of the inherent biological or psychological qualities of women and girls. Early theorists concerned with delinquent, deviant, or criminal behavior argued that women and girls were "naturally" constrained from engaging in all forms of crime, including violence. These pseudoscientific arguments of the late nineteenth and early twentieth centuries were also racialized. For example, in *The Female Offender*, Lombroso and Ferrero (1895) argued that only "savage" women are capable of violent crimes. Among the so-called savage women cited by Lombroso: the Hottentot, a Negro woman and a Red Indian woman. In contrast, Lombroso argued, "civilized" white women did not use violence because it was inconsistent with their essential female nature.

Dorie Klein's analysis of the representation of women in early criminological theory exposed the taken-for-granted assumptions embedded in essentialist arguments that continued to influence theories about women's offending well into the 1970s. In "The Etiology of Female Crime: A Review of the Literature," Klein (1973) explains how these narrow theories of women's crime, developed from the turn of the twentieth century until the mid-1950s, relied on the fundamental assumption that women's criminal behavior was a result of their deficient biology or individual psychological deficiencies. Among the traditional theorists critiqued by Klein were Lombroso, who once wrote that "the born female criminal is, so to speak, doubly exceptional, as a woman and as a criminal"

(Lombroso and Ferrero, 1895, p. 184). In each of these texts, Klein writes, assumptions of inherent biological differences between the sexes manifest themselves into physiological and psychological differences which, while tangentially influenced by social structure, ultimately explain women's offending (Klein, 1973). An example of this type of essentialist theorizing is perhaps best reflected in Otto Pollak's suggestion, published in *The Criminality of Women* (1950), that the majority of women's crime is hidden *and* that women are favorably situated to hide their criminality because of an inherent biological quality particular to women: their need to hide their menstruation from others.

Klein (1973) offers that when read side-by-side these theorists represent "a tradition" of explaining women's criminality that relies on "implicit or explicit assumptions about the *inherent nature of women*" (p. 31). Such theories suggest that women's criminality is inherently physiological or psychological in nature and only partially related to their position within the larger social structure. These theorists, Klein argues, along with their contemporaries, "create two distinct social classes of women: good women who are 'normal' non-criminals, and bad women who are criminals" (p. 31). This type of theorizing reflects, Klein argues, "a moral position that often masquerades as scientific distinction" (p. 31).

In her review of the literature, Klein also reveals how the taken-for-granted sexism of early theorists was joined with racist characterizations of non-white women. A critical review of the literature reveals that the work of many positivist theorists reflected a belief in a racial hierarchy that situated white, upper class men located at the top and Black, lower class women at the bottom. Regarding Lombroso and Ferrero's (1895) classic biological atavistic approach Klein (1973) writes that Lombroso "theorizes that individuals develop differentially within sexual and racial limitations which differ hierarchically from the most highly developed, the white men, to the most primitive, the nonwhite women" (p. 186). Klein (1973) argues that Thomas' socio-psychological explanation for women's criminal offending is also rooted not only in flawed assumptions about biology, sex and gender, but also race. According to Klein (1973), Thomas argues that in civilized nations the sexes are more physically different as are the "races." The implication of the intersection of the two is obvious: "[t]he most highly developed races would therefore have the most feminized women, that is, the most 'good' women and in turn the most 'noncriminal' women" (p. 36). Klein argues that these forms of sexism and racism influenced theories of women's criminal offending into the 1970s.

Klein's critical review was an early feminist critique of the criminological canon; it was also a critique of many of her contemporaries who, Klein argued, were "guilty of the same undocumented and poorly researched work as earlier criminologists" (p. 33). In response to the return of biological theories to explain girls' offending and the persistent emphasis on the role of women's sexuality in contemporary theories of women's offending Klein (1973) concludes, "[t]he road from Lombroso to the present is surprisingly straight" (p. 33). These narrowly focused explanations for women's offending led to narrowly focused strategies to respond to women's offending: strategies developed to solve the problem of women's criminal behavior were largely focused on the individual adjustment of women to "gender appropriate" behavior (Goodkind, 2009; Klein, 1973).

In the years following Klein's (1973) "Etiology," feminist criminologists would rely heavily on her initial critical review of the criminological literature in the development of their own research agendas (Chesney-Lind and Shelden, 2004; Miller, 2001; Naffine, 1987, 1996). In this line of research, scholars deliberately sought to challenge some of the commonsense assumptions about gender and patterns of women's violence and victimization. Ngaire Naffine (1987) extended Klein's critical review of the traditional criminological literature in *Female Crime: The Construction of Women in Criminology*. Naffine (1987) provides a critical review of the construction of women in mainstream criminology and the implications of this construction for criminological theory. Naffine (1987) suggests that, "[i]f one were to typify the average female offender, she would be a once-only shoplifter who tends to steal items of little value" (p. 12). Here, Naffine highlights how women's use of violence and, in turn, women's victimization were routinely ignored and instead replaced with a romanticized version of the delinquent as "the rogue male" while his female counterpart remains, predictably, primarily concerned with the "narrow set of relations with the opposite sex" (p. 11). Naffine expands her critique in *Feminism and Criminology* (1996) where she extends her theoretical critique of criminological theory to a large-scale disciplinary critique of contemporary criminological literature (cf. Leonard, 1982). In a call that is consistent with the intellectual shifts of the time, Naffine argues for greater reflexivity on the part of researchers: not only should researchers rethink how they see women, but they should also think critically about how their own positions or "standpoints" inform their research (Collins 1990; DeHart and Lynch, 2013; Harding, 2004). In contrast to an unreflective embrace of empirical research, Naffine (1996) argues for a feminist criminology that is willing to "put itself about, to engage with its detractors, and to subject itself to precisely the sort of critical scrutiny it has applied to others" (p. 4). It is the role of the feminist criminologist, Naffine (1996) suggests, to critique this tendency within the discipline and to then move beyond this critique and into the "work of criminology."

The shift to reflexivity that Naffine describes led to a number of theoretical and conceptual breakthroughs that have influenced the development of gender and crime over the last quarter of a century. As Daly (1998) writes, a significant "source of field expansion [in the area of gender and crime] comes from feminist scholars" (p. 100) who are concerned with theories of gender and studies of women's lives as well as the application of this research to crime. Daly (1998) explains, "this group is less interested in devising a grand theory of gender and crime, and more inclined to identify the ways in which gender structures men's and women's life worlds, identities, and thinkable courses of action" (p. 100). Scholars writing in this tradition often emphasize the influence of inequality, oppression and marginalization on girls and women's pathways to crime. Early examples of works produced within this tradition include Eleanor Miller's (1986) study of female street hustlers in Milwaukee and Meda Chesney-Lind's (2010) study of the criminalization of girls and women's survival strategies, among others. In the next section, we describe how the theoretical contributions of intersectionality, "race-gender-class" (Daly, 1998) and black feminist criminology (Potter, 2006) have shaped contemporary understandings of gender, violence and victimization.

At the Intersections: Understanding Gender, Violence and Victimization

In the decades following the publication of Klein's "Etiology," feminist criminologists continued to challenge simplistic assertions about gender that characterized the discipline. Feminist criminologists also encouraged a new generation of scholars to account for how *intersections* of gender, race and class patterned violence and victimization among women, especially women of color who were disproportionately represented in arrest and incarceration statistics as the twentieth century neared its end (Britton, 2000; Collins, 2004; Daly, 1997; DeHart and Lynch, 2013; Renzetti and Maier, 2002; Shelden, 2010). Sally Simpson's (1991) direction to fellow criminologists was one of several calls to expand the criminological literature in this way:

> Criminologists have been mistaken to ignore important variations in criminal behavior among females. The simplistic assertion that males are violent and females are not contains a grain of truth, but it misses the complexity and texture of women's lives. A review of the empirical literature on violence reveals the confounding effects of gender, race, and class. Although their combined influences are difficult to tease out, a firm understanding of how they interact is fundamental for a more inclusive and elegant criminological theory.
>
> *(p. 129)*

In an early examination of the variation in causal factors for Black women and white women's offending Hill and Crawford (1990) also argue for a more careful examination of the intersections of race, gender and class within studies of gender and crime. In the introduction to their analysis the authors write that theories about female criminality "are theories about white females" (Hill and Crawford, 1990, p. 603). The authors later conclude that Black women "fit less" into current theoretical models and that "the empirical neglect of the Black female offender has had important consequences for the development of theory" (Hill and Crawford, 1990, p. 621). In "Different Ways of Conceptualizing Sex/Gender in Feminist Theory and the Implications for Criminology" Daly (1997) suggests that these types of empirical and theoretical challenges to the literature, "were part of a general mood to unsettle social theory and to re-engage a critique of positivist social science" (Daly, 1997, p. 33). One of the most influential concepts to arise out of these challenges to both mainstream social science and feminist theory was what Daly (1997) terms "class-race-gender." On the conceptualization of multiple inequalities Daly (1997) writes, "[c]lass-race-gender conceptualizes inequalities, not as additive and discrete, but as intersecting, interlocking and contingent" (p. 33). This concept has been particularly influential on Daly's (1997) work: "My work has been most influenced by class-race-gender or what I have come to term multiple inequalities" (p. 33). Daly (1997) continues, "In the 1980s, it was ... Black women whose critique of feminist thought had the greater influence on my thinking" (p. 33).

Over the last two decades, researchers have adopted an intersectionality framework to explain variations in violence and victimization across and within groups. In "Caste, Class and Violent Crime: Explaining Difference in Female Offending" Simpson (1991) explores differences in violent offending both within and between gender and racial groups. Regarding the peculiar position of black women, Simpson (1991) writes, "Black females appear to respond differently to conditions of poverty, racism, and patriarchy than their class, gender, and racial counterparts. Race and gender merge into a theoretically interesting and important case, one that deserves more systematic inquiry" (p. 116). Simpson's (1991) examination of trends in the literature that address variations in violent offending by gender and race suggests that:

> Black women, especially those in the "underclass" engage in what might be considered anomalous behavior for their gender (i.e., violent crimes) but not their race. ... On the other hand, given the high level of violence among black males, black female rates of violent crime are relatively low.
>
> (p. 116)

Like Daly, Simpson (1991) offers that "[c]lass, gender and race are best understood as intersecting systems of dominance and control" (p. 125). This type of theorizing, Simpson (1991) suggests, can better explain variations in black women's and white women's willingness to "buy into" the dominant "patriarchal power system" which may exert some control over women's use of interpersonal violence (p. 127). Regarding culture and violent offending in particular, Simpson (1991) suggests that, "As structural conditions increasingly preclude mobility for the bottom of the surplus population, cultural redefinitions and adjustments may influence perceptions of, and beliefs about, the emergence and appropriateness of violence" (p. 128). Here, Simpson (1991) suggests that it is the varying structural positions of white women and Black women, and their dynamic interaction with culture, that explain, at least in part, why white women and Black women apparently use and experience violence differently: "Class is an oppressive structure for both black and white females, but black women's experiences of their material circumstances and their perceptions of self and choice vary qualitatively from those of whites" (p. 128). Simpson (1991) concludes:

> The observed gender differences in how violence is interpreted and incorporated into one's behavioral repertoire emerge from the contradictory cultural tendencies of caste (i.e., female = nonviolent, black = violent; Lewis 1981). Black females ... are more apt than black males to delegitimate violence. However, given their

racial oppression and differential experience of patriarchy, in the family, black females are perhaps less apt to delegitimate violence than their white counterparts.

(p. 129)

Over the last two decades, feminist criminologists and gender and crime scholars have examined women's and girls' experiences with aggression and violence with increasing complexity.[1]

Meda Chesney-Lind's studies of delinquent girls reveal how gender specific violence shapes girls' pathways to delinquency (DeHart and Lynch, 2013; Bosworth and Fili, 2012; Chesney-Lind and Shelden, 2004; Daly, 1997, 1998); and feminist criminologists using Collins' concept of "intersectionality" (Collins, 2004) have contributed new insights into the study of women's experiences with violence by challenging the "universality" implied by popular theories on the relationship between gender, violence and victimization (Daly, 1997). Scholars have shown how intersections of race, gender and class expose women to unique life experiences, which, in turn, may influence and shape their social relationship to violence (Renzetti, 2004; Simpson 1991; Simpson and Elis, 1995).[2]

An understanding of how material circumstances influence women's and girls' relationships to violence is illustrated in Beth Richie's (1996) study of black battered female offenders. Richie's analysis examines the impact of what she describes as "multiple marginality." Richie's analysis of the life histories of African American battered women incarcerated at Riker's Island Correctional Facility in New York City also blurs the boundaries between victim and offender—a common experience for incarcerated African American women. Richie argues that African American women were "compelled to crime" by a range of structural and personal circumstances that included pressures to adhere to socially appropriate gender roles. Richie describes how the ability of women to adequately respond to the violence they experienced at the hands of their partners was made more difficult by simultaneous experiences of racism. Black gender ideologies (Collins, 2004) also placed pressure on women to demonstrate loyalty to their black male partners. These experiences were compounded by poverty, which limited the options available to women to respond to the violence in their lives. Under these conditions, women often chose survival strategies, like using violence against their male partners, which increased their social isolation and made them more vulnerable to criminal sanctions, including long periods of incarceration.

Recent contributions from Jody Miller, Gail Garfield, Hillary Potter and Nikki Jones echo Richie's argument and further demonstrate how intersections of race, gender and class shape violence and victimization in the lives of African American girls who come of age in distressed urban neighborhoods. In *Getting Played: African American Girls, Urban Inequality, and Gendered Violence* (2008), Miller draws on an analysis of surveys and interviews conducted with at-risk and delinquent African American youth to explain how structural circumstances foster troubling cultural adaptations that result in the prevalent threat of gender-specific violence for girls and the normalization of participation in this violence for boys. Miller's analysis reveals how violent victimization in urban settings is shaped by extreme poverty. Girls' and boys' accounts of violence reveal both their vulnerability and marginality in these settings. The violence reported by girls includes verbal harassment, unwanted touching, and sexual assault. Miller reports that over half of the 75 girls interviewed experienced some form of sexual coercion or assault; nearly a third of interview respondents reported multiple experiences of victimization. Generally, girls were hesitant to report gender-specific harassment or violence to institutional authorities.[3]

Miller's work highlights how intersections of gender and class shape experiences of violence and victimization among poor urban youth of color. Recent work from Hillary Potter and Gail Garfield extends her analysis by emphasizing how intersections of race, gender and class shape violent victimization and the use of violence among African American women and girls. In her research on black women and intimate partner abuse, *Battle Cries: Black Women and Intimate Partner Abuse* (2008), Hillary Potter reports on how intersecting identities shape women's experience with violence and victimization. Among the contributions of Potter's work is her explanation of how images and expectations of the "Strong Black Woman" shape how women make sense of the abuse in their lives. Potter writes that the women in her study confronted numerous forms of domination and discrimination "because of their abusive circumstances and their interwoven identities due to race, gender and other social, cultural, and individual circumstances" (pp. 9–10). Potter introduces the concept of "dynamic resistance" to explain how these intersections shape women's responses to the abuse in their lives, including ways that challenge typical notions of mainstream femininity, like fighting back against their abuser. She explains:

> The women's self-perception as Strong Black Women, and not as victims, is considered to account for their efforts to resist abuse and other life distress. Included in this resistance is the propensity for the women to verbally and physically retaliate against their abusers.
>
> *(Potter, 2008, p. 10)*

Potter's use of Black Feminist Criminology (Potter, 2008) also helps to uncover how intersecting oppressions (Collins, 2004) pattern black women's experiences with violence and victimization over the life course. Potter explains that Black feminist criminology "extends beyond traditional feminist criminology to view African American women (and conceivably, other women of color) from the multiple marginalized and dominated positions in society, culture, community and families" (2006, p. 107). Potter (2006) argues that much of contemporary criminology fails to address how multiple forms of oppression influence the experiences of women. These experiences shape the meanings of violence among Black women and the set of responses available to women who want to end the violence in their lives. Potter encourages other scholars to draw on Black feminist criminology when examining how black women experience and respond to crime and victimization (Potter, 2006).

Gail Garfield takes an approach that is consistent with Black feminist criminology in her examination of African American women's experiences with violent victimization. In *Knowing What We Know: African American Women's Experiences of Violence and Violation* (2005), Garfield draws on an intersectionality framework introduced by legal scholar Kimberlé Crenshaw and other feminist scholars: "Kimberlé Crenshaw suggests that the social, personal, and physical dimensions of uneven power relations intersect rather than stand as isolated or discrete relations. And through this intersection, differences are created that give texture and shape to women's day-to-day experiences" (Garfield, 2005, p. 3). Garfield also draws on an intersectionality framework in her study of violence in the lives of African American men in *Through Our Eyes: African American Men's Experiences of Race, Gender and Violence*. Garfield extends her analysis of the "relational context of violence and violation" and uses the life histories of African American men to complicate common images of Black manhood and masculinity. Her work reveals the "tensions, dilemmas, and contradictions" that characterize African Americans' experiences with violence. Her work provides a unique perspective on men who are actively involved in creating a more progressive manhood that is less harmful to others and to their own sense of self. These studies reveal the benefit of interrogating experiences of violence and victimization at the intersections of race, gender, class and other categorical identities. As we describe in the following section, an intersectional analysis is especially useful in understanding the underlying dynamics that have contributed to recent increases in arrests for violent offenses among women and girls.

Race, Gender and the New Violent Girl

Over the last decade, researchers have focused more attention on girls' participation in violent acts, and the subsequent victimization that results from these physical encounters (Jones, 2010; Schaffner, 2006). Some popular and scholarly explanations for recent trends in girls' violence and victimization reflect the same sort of essentialist understandings of gender and race that informed the earliest explanations of women's and girls' offending. For example, popular explanations of girls' changing nature suggest that girls today are "moody," "insecure" and "meaner" than ever before, making them more likely to participate in crime and violence (Wiseman, 2002). Psychologists Dellasega and Nixon (2003) claim that this generation of girls is "rotten" and has simply gone "wrong" because of the increased "bullying" that happens among teenage girls. They attribute this behavior to "superstar singers acting like sexy schoolgirls and movie stars firing machine guns or using martial arts on opponents while wearing skintight jumpsuits," paying little attention to poverty, discrimination and inequality (Dellasega and Nixon, 2003, p. 3). Some explanations are reminiscent of the "liberation hypothesis" (Adler, 1975), which offered that the women's movement "freed" women to participate in crime, especially crimes dominated by men. For example, Prothrow-Stith and Spivak (2005) have argued that encouraging girls to participate in sports and excel in academics has also made them more competitive and aggressive, which in turn encourages girls' violent behavior.

These explanations ignore recent self-report data that do not reveal a dramatic change in girls' behavior (Males, 2010, p. 27). These explanations also fail to uncover the social meaning of violence for girls in distressed urban neighborhoods, and neglect recent changes in institutional responses to girls' violent or aggressive behavior. Recent research has filled this gap in the literature. In Between Good and Ghetto: African American Girls and Inner-city Violence (2010) Jones draws on an intersectional framework to examine the social meaning of violence and victimization among African American adolescent girls. Her ethnographic study reveals how gender patterns girls' use of violence in ways that are similar and distinct to boys' use of violence in the same settings (cf. Jones, 2008). Her analysis also reveals variation in the use of violence among similarly situated African American girls. The study reveals how growing up in neighborhoods characterized by concentrated poverty and a visible and unpredictably violent drug trade pushes both adolescent boys and girls into a preoccupation with survival. Girls' accounts reveal the array of interpersonal and situational strategies they draw on to manage the violence they confront in neighborhood and school settings where interpersonal violence is governed largely by a hyper-masculine, eye-for-an-eye ethic that Elijah Anderson has described as the "code of the street." A form of street justice, the code emerges where the presence of civil law is weak and thrives in settings where social institutions like schools or the police have abdicated responsibility for ensuring the well-being of inner city residents (Anderson, 1999, p. 10). While adolescent girls in these settings have no manhood to defend, girls' accounts reveal that they do have many reasons to be preoccupied with protecting themselves from threats of violence. The need to avoid or overcome dangers throughout their adolescence presents a gendered challenge for inner-city girls whose experience is complicated by intersections of gender, race and class.

Jones explains that African American inner-city girls who live in distressed urban neighborhoods must learn how to effectively manage potential threats of interpersonal violence—that is, they must work the code of the street—at the risk of violating mainstream and local expectations regarding appropriate feminine behavior.[4] The gendered expectations surrounding girls' and women's use or control of violence are perhaps the most constraining. Girls are expected to use relational aggression—as popular media suggests—and fight with words and tears, not fists, knives or box cutters. Inner-city girls, like most American girls, feel this pressure to be "good," "decent" and "respectable." Yet, like some inner-city boys, they may also feel pressure to establish a "tough front" in order to deter potential challengers on the street or in the school setting. Girls who are deeply invested in crafting a public persona as a tough girl or a "fighter," as some in Jones's study did, are especially open to being evaluated by peers, adults, and outsiders as "street" or "ghetto." Such distinctions are powerful, Jones argues, because community members and institutional actors—teachers, judges, police officers—use them as a basis for understanding, interpreting, and predicting their own and others' actions, attitudes, and behaviors, especially when it comes to interpersonal violence (Anderson, 1999). These understandings help to pattern institutional responses to girls' violence as well, including expulsion, arrest and entry into secure detention.

Recent research, including chapters in this volume, also reveals how responses to girls' violent behavior are patterned by intersections of race, gender and class (Chesney-Lind and Jones, 2010). These studies find that girls' arrests for violent offenses like simple assault or aggravated assault are influenced by policy shifts implemented over the last several decades, including a shift in responses to domestic violence incidents (Chesney-Lind, 2010) and "zero-tolerance" policies toward fighting in schools (Losen and Skiba, 2010). In one of the most definitive studies in this area, Darrell Steffensmeier and colleagues (2005) dismissed claims that the twenty-first century girl is committing more crimes than girls in previous periods. Instead, girls' arrests for violent offenses like simple assault or aggravated assault are artifacts of "recent changes in public sentiment and enforcement policies for dealing with youth crime and violence that has elevated the visibility and reporting of girls' violence" (Steffensmeier, Schwartz, Zhong and Ackerman, 2005, p. 356). Steffensmeier and colleagues describe the increased arrests of girls for violent offenses as a consequence of a "net-widening effect": girls today are much more likely to receive an official criminal sanction for behavior that would not have been addressed by law enforcement in years past. Policy shifts in responding to student behavior in school is an example of this net-widening effect. Steffensmeier and colleagues (2005) explain:

> Many schools, especially in the large urban centers, have adopted zero tolerance policies toward violence ... Both male and female youth are being arrested in substantial numbers for behavior that, before these preventive measures, would have likely been handled as a school disciplinary matter.
>
> (p. 366)

These changes in policies and practices have "disproportionately escalated girls' arrests for violent crimes," the researchers continue, "particularly for assaults involving minor physical confrontations or verbal threats—most frequently with another girl—that in the past would have been ignored or responded to less formally" (Steffensmeier et al., 2005, p. 367). The authors conclude that the rise in girls' violence is "more a social construction than an empirical reality."

Girls today are no more violent than in years past. However, girls' violent or aggressive behavior is more likely to trigger an official sanction from the juvenile or criminal justice system than in years past. This is especially true for girls of color. For example, in a recent study Tia Stevens, Merry Morash and Meda Chesney-Lind used data from the National Longitudinal Youth Survey to examine the probability of conviction and institutionalization for violent behavior among youth in 1980 and 2000 (Stevens, Morash and Chesney-Lind, 2011). The researchers found that while self-reports of attacks on other people did not increase over this time period, "an increased proportion of youth penetrated into the juvenile justice system in 2000." In 2000, girls were "nearly twice as likely as girls in 1980 to report they had been charged with a crime." These changes were particularly dramatic for black girls: "Black girls in 2000 were nearly seven times more likely as their 1980 counterparts to have been charged with a crime" (Stevens et al., 2011, p. 19). Stevens et al. (2011) conclude that "the justice system is getting tougher on girls but girls do not appear to be getting tougher" (p. 22).

It might also be said that the justice system is getting especially tough on girls of color. Changes in policies and institutional practices have led to increases in the involvement of African American, Latina and Native American girls in the justice system (Bosworth and Fili, 2013). Girls who enter institutions of confinement are increasingly being arrested for behavior that previously did not warrant criminal sanctions: "once these girls enter the system, they tend to stay in the system, despite fairly clear evidence that in previous decades their behavior would not have warranted a criminal justice response, much less an arrest" (Chesney-Lind and Jones, 2010, p. 4). In turn, entry into secure detention often increases girls' vulnerability to a unique set of risks, including exposure to violence and victimization (Bosworth and Fili, 2013; Schaffner, 2006). Empirical research conducted in the US suggests that emotional, physical and sexual abuse of inmates is ubiquitous in institutions of confinement (Friedman, 2003). Schaffner (2006) found that girls regularly encountered violence and the threat of violence while incarcerated in California. In secure detention settings, girls must contend with threats of violence from other girls and, at times, from correctional staff. In a review of the literature in this area Burton-Rose (2003) found that girls and women across the US face the constant threat of sexual and physical assault inside of detention facilities by correctional staff. Girls and women in detention are more likely than males to experience verbal abuse by staff members for behavior that is deemed "unladylike" (Bosworth and Fili, 2013; Goodkind, 2009). Researchers have also documented the frequency of child abuse and neglect inside group homes in the US and Canada (Chesney-Lind and Shelden, 2004). In an ethnographic study of a Canadian group home Brown (2010) found that girls constantly worried about potential threats of violence. They continually shifted from using violence to being victims of violent acts perpetrated by staff members and other residents (Brown, 2010). Crosland et al. (2008) found that staff members in American group homes are often ill equipped and under-trained to deal with these types of situations, which tends to exacerbate already volatile situations.

These challenges are exacerbated for youth who are perceived by institutional actors to be "gender non-conforming." Recent studies of LGBT youth in detention have shown LGBT youth are likely to receive additional sanctions for behavior that is otherwise age-appropriate (Estrada and Marksamer, 2006). This secondary punishment—the punishment delivered to those who violate gender norms—is built into the earliest phases of the system. In a study of gender non-conforming youth in the juvenile justice system, Angela Irvine (2010) found that LGBT youth are twice as likely to be detained during pre-trial for nonviolent offenses like truancy, running away and prostitution. These youth are also much more likely to be subject to verbal and sexual harassment and to experience violence at the hands of other youth while in detention (Estrada and Marksamer, 2006). Lisa Pasko's recent research on the experiences of LBQ girls in custody also reveals how girls' lesbian identities are pathologized or minimized among correctional staff. Her work also documents how recent policy interventions like the Prison Rape Elimination Act have had the unintentional consequence of intensifying punitive responses to sexual activity among incarcerated girls (Pasko, 2011).

Conclusion

Dorie Klein's (1973) critique of the etiology of criminological theory reveals how taken-for-granted assumptions about women distorted explanations for women's offending, including women's experiences with violence and victimization. Since the publication of Klein's critical review, the field of gender and crime has expanded significantly. Feminist contributions have been especially important to the development of this area: "feminist researchers have made women offenders and victims visible" partly by demonstrating how "girls are penalized for behavior which is condoned or encouraged in boys" (Morris and Gelsthorpe, 1991, p. 4). Feminist scholars have also complicated the study of women's lives by integrating understandings of "intersecting oppressions" and "class-race-gender" into theory and methods. An early example of this approach includes Simpson's (1991) use of Black feminist thought in her examination of gender and race variation in violent offending. In recent years, this work has been extended and complicated by scholars like Jody Miller, Hillary Potter, Beth Richie, Nikki Jones and others who have drawn on an intersectionality framework to provide more nuanced accounts of how race, gender and class shape experiences of violence and victimization. Such approaches to understanding violence and victimization are necessary in order to adequately explain recent trends in the arrest and detention of women and girls for violent offenses. For example, in contrast to popular and scholarly claims about a new violent girl, the best available data reveal that girls' behavior has not changed in any substantial ways over the last several decades. However, it is clear that institutions and adults have changed the way we respond to violent or aggressive behavior among women and girls. This is especially true for girls of color who are overrepresented at every stage of the juvenile justice system. Future research should continue to explore the social meaning of violence among women and girls along with the consequences of punitive policies and practices for women and girls. Researchers should also continue to examine how intersections of race, gender, class and sexuality pattern trends in gender, violence and victimization.

Notes

1. See Dana Britton's "Feminism in criminology: Engendering the outlaw" (2000) for an analysis of how Black feminist thought and feminism, respectively, can influence criminological theory and research. For recent studies of gender, crime, violence and victimization see *Gender and crime: Patterns of victimization and offending* (Heimer and Kruttschnitt, 2005).

2. The introduction of the ethnomethodologically driven concepts of "doing gender" and "doing difference" also helped to complicate criminological theories on gender and violence (Fenstermaker and West, 2002; West and Zimmerman, 1987; for a comprehensive review and critical analysis of feminist criminologists' use of "doing gender" see Miller, 2002).

3. Miller's earlier work explored how gender patterns the use of violence among gang-involved and non-gang-involved girls. For more details see Miller, J. (2001) *One of the guys: Girls, gangs and gender*. New York: Oxford University Press.

4. For further discussion see Mullins, C. W., Wright, R., and Jacobs, B. A. (2004). Gender, streetlife and criminal retaliation, *Criminology*, 42(4), 911–40.

References

Adler, F. (1975). Sisters in crime. New York: McGraw-Hill Press.

Anderson, E. (1999). *Code of the street: Decency, violence, and the moral life of the inner city*. New York: W. W. Norton and Company.

Bosworth, M. and Fili, A. (2013). Corrections, gender-specific programming and offender re-entry. In C.M. Renzetti, S.L. Miller and A.R. Gover (eds), *Routledge international handbook of crime and gender studies* (pp. 231–242). New York: Routledge.

Brown, M. (2010). Negotiations of the living space: Life in the group home for girls who use violence. In M. Chesney-Lind and N. Jones (eds), *Fighting for girls: New perspectives on gender and violence* (pp. 175–99). Albany: State University of New York Press.

Britton, D. M. (2000). Feminism in criminology: Engendering the outlaw. *Annals of the American Academy of Political and Social Science*, 57(1), 571–92.

Bureau of Justice Statistics. (2011). *Criminal victimization in the United States 2008*. Washington, DC: US Department of Justice.

———. (2011, September 15). *Federal criminal case processing statistics*. Retrieved from http://bjs.ojp.usdoj.gov/fjsrc/var.cfm?ttype=trends&agency=USMS&db_type=ArrestsFed&saf=IN.

Burton-Rose, D. (2003). Our sisters' keepers. In T. Herivel and P. Wright (eds), *Prison nation: The warehousing of America's poor* (pp. 258–61). New York: Taylor and Francis.

Chesney-Lind, M. (2010). Jailing "bad" girls: Girls' violence and trends in female incarceration. In M. Chesney-Lind and N. Jones (eds), *Fighting for girls: New perspectives on gender and violence* (pp. 57–79). Albany: State University of New York Press.

Chesney-Lind, M. and Jones, N. (eds) (2010). *Fighting for girls: New perspectives on gender and violence*. Albany: State University of New York Press.

Chesney-Lind, M. and Shelden, R. G. (2004). *Girls, delinquency, and juvenile justice* (3rd edn). Belmont, CA: Wadsworth Cengage Learning.

Collins, P. H. (1990). *Black feminist thought: Knowledge, consiousness, and the politics of empowerment*. New York: Routledge.

———. (2004). *Black sexual politics: African Americans, gender and the new racism.* New York: Routledge.

Crosland, K. A., Dunlap, G., Sager, W., Neff, B., Wilcox, C., and Blanco, A. et al. (2008). The effects of staff training on the types of interactions observed at two group homes for foster care children. *Research on Social Work Practice*, 18(5), 410–20.

Daly, K. (1997). Different ways of conceptualizing sex/gender in feminist theory and their implications for criminology. *Theoretical Criminology, 1*, 25–51.

———. (1998). Gender, crime and criminology. In M.H. Tonry (ed.), *The handbook of crime and punishment* (pp. 85–110). New York: Oxford University Press.

DeHart, D. and Lynch, S. (2013). Gendered pathways to crime: The relationship between victimazition and offending. In C.M. Renzetti, S.L. Miller and A.R. Gover (eds), *Routledge international handbook of crime and gender studies* (pp. 120–133). New York: Routledge.

Dellasega, C. and Nixon, C. (2003). *Girl wars: 12 strategies that will end female bullying.* New York: Simon and Schuster.

Estrada, R. and Marksamer, J. (2006). The legal rights of LGBT youth in state custody: What child welfare and juvenile justice professionals need to know. *Child Welfare League of America, 85*(2), 171–94.

Friedman, A. (2003). Juveniles held hostage for profit by CSC in Florida. In T. Herivel and P. Wright (eds), *Prison nation: The warehousing of America's poor* (pp. 164–65). New York: Taylor and Francis.

Garfield, G. (2005). *Knowing what we know: African American women's experiences of violence and violation.* New Brunswick, NJ: Rutgers University Press.

Goodkind, S. (2009). "You may even be president of the United States one day"? Challenging commercialized feminism in programming for girls in juvenile justice. In L.M. Nybell, J.J. Shook, and J. L. Finn (eds), *Childhood, youth, and social work in transformation* (pp. 364–384). New York: Columbia University Press.

Harding, S. G. (ed.) (2004). *The feminist standpoint theory reader.* New York: Routledge.

Heimer, K. and Kruttschnitt, C. (eds) (2005). *Gender and crime: Patterns in victimization and offending.* New York: New York University Press.

Hill, G. and Crawford, E. (1990). Women, race and crime. *Criminology*, 28, 601–23.

Irvine, A. (2010). We've had three of them: Addressing the invisibility of lesbian, gay, bisexual and gender nonconforming youths in the juvenile justice system. *Columbia Journal of Gender and the Law*, 12(3), 675–700.

Jones, N. (2008). Working "the code": On girls, gender, and inner-city violence. *Australia and New Zealand Journal of Criminology*, 41(1), 63–83.

———. (2010). *Between good and ghetto: African American girls and inner-city violence.* New Brunswick, NJ: Rutgers University Press.

Klein, D. (1973). The etiology of female crime: A review of the literature. In B. R. Price and N. J. Sokoloff (eds), *The criminal justice system and women* (pp. 30–53). New York: McGraw-Hill.

Leonard, E. (1982). *Women, crime and society: A critque of theoretical criminology.* New York: Longman Inc.

Lombroso, C. and Ferrero, G. (1895). *The female offender.* New York: D. Appleton and Company.

Losen, D. J. and Skiba, R. (2010). *Suspended education: Urban middle schools in crisis.* Montgomery, AL: Southern Poverty Law Center.

Males, M. (2010). *Girls myths*. Retrieved September 1, 2010, from www.youthfacts.org/girlphob.

Miller, E. M. (1986). *Street woman*. Philadelphia, PA: Temple University Press.

Miller, J. (2001). *One of the guys: Girls, gangs, and gender*. New York: Oxford University Press.

———. (2002). The strengths and limits of "doing gender" for understanding street crime. *Theoretical Criminology, 6*, 433–60.

———. (2008). *Getting played: African American girls, urban inequality, and gendered violence*. New York: New York University Press.

Morris, A. and Gelsthorpe, L. (1991). Feminist perspectives in criminology: Transforming and transgressing. *Women and Criminal Justice*, 2, 3–26.

Mullins, C. W., Wright, R. and Jacobs, B. A. (2004). Gender, streetlife and criminal retaliation. *Criminology*, 42(4), 911–40.

Naffine, N. (1987). Female crime: The construction of women in criminology. Boston, MA: Allen & Unwin.

———.(1996). *Feminism and criminology*. Philadelphia, PA: Temple University Press.

Pasko, L. (2011). Setting the record "straight": Girls, sexuality and the juvenile correctional system. *Social Justice, 37*(1), 7–26.

Pollak, O. (1950). *The criminality of women*. Philadelphia, PA: University of Pennsylvania Press.

Potter, H. (2006). An argument for black feminist criminology. *Feminist Criminology, 1*(2), 106–24.

———. (2008). *Battle cries: Black women and intimate partner abuse*. New York: New York University Press.

Prothrow-Stith, D. and Spivak, H. R. (2005). *Sugar and spice and no longer nice: How can we stop girls' violence?* San Francisco, CA: Josey-Bass Press.

Renzetti, C. M. (2004) Feminist theories of violent behavior. In M. Zahn, H. Brownstein, and S. Jackson (eds), *Violence: From theory to research* (pp. 131–143). Cincinnati, OH: Anderson Publishing.

Renzetti, C.M. and Maier, S. (2002). "Private" crime in public housing: Violent victimization, fear of crime and social isolation among women public housing residents. *Women's Health and Urban Life, 1*, 46–65.

Richie, B. (1996). *Compelled to crime: The gender entrapment of battered black women*. New York: Routledge.

Schaffner, L. (2006). *Girls in trouble with the law*. New Brunswick, NJ: Rutgers University Press.

Simpson, S. (1991). Caste, class and violent crime: Explaining differences in female offending. *Criminology, 29*, 115–35.

Simpson, S. and Elis, L. (1995). Doing gender: Sorting out the castle and crime conundrum. *Criminology, 33*, 47–81.

Stevens, T., Morash, M. and Chesney-Lind, M. (2011). Are girls getting tougher, or are we tougher on girls? Probability of arrest and juvenile court oversight in 1980 and 2000. *Justice Quarterly, 28*(5), 719–44.

Steffensmeier, D., Schwartz, J., Zhong, H. and Ackerman, J. (2005). An assesment of recent trends in girls' violence using diverse longitudinal sources: Is the gender gap closing? *Criminology, 43*(2), 355–406.

West, C. and Fenstermaker, S. (1995). Doing difference. *Gender & Society, 9*(1), 8–37.

West, C. and Zimmerman, D. H. (1987). Doing gender. *Gender & Society, 1*(1), 125–51.

Wiseman, R. (2002). *Queen bees and wannabes: Helping your daughter survive cliques, gossip, boyfriends, and other realities of adolescence*. New York: Three Rivers Press.

READING 13

Identities and Intersectionalities

Structured Action Theory, Left Realism, Postmodern Feminism, and Black/Multiracial Feminist Criminology

Claire M. Renzetti

Let me begin with a confession: I struggled with the title for this chapter. For one thing, including all the theories to be discussed makes for an accurate, but not very eloquent title. It certainly does not roll easily off the tongue. More importantly, I do not want to give the impression that this is a "kitchen sink" chapter; that this is the chapter in which one throws in anything and everything that has not yet been covered but needs to be. Such would diminish the significance of each of the theories—an outcome that is opposite to what I intend and also somewhat ironic given that "othering" is a primary concern of these theories. It may also appear at first glance that, apart from the feminist tie, this is a theoretically disparate list. But as I will show, these theories are linked in several ways and together they have made a significant impact on criminology and criminal justice. To begin, then, let us examine the notion of gender as "situated accomplishment" and consider how it has been applied to the study of criminal offending.

Masculinities, Femininities, and Crime

Sex and *gender* are terms typically used interchangeably in everyday conversation, but sociologists distinguish *sex*, a biological category, from *gender*, a socially constructed category. Nevertheless, even in sociological analyses, both sex and gender were—and, unfortunately, often still are—presented as binaries: categories with two mutually exclusive components. An individual is *either* male *or* female (sex), masculine *or* feminine (gender), and their masculinity or femininity derives "naturally" from their biological sex. A radical departure from this framework was introduced in 1987 by Candace West and Don Zimmerman in what has since become "the most cited article ever published in *Gender & Society*," one of the most prestigious academic journals in the fields of sociology and women's studies (Jurik and Siemsen, 2009: 72). Not only did West and Zimmerman attempt to break with the gender binary, they also replaced the traditional conceptualization of gender as a role or

Claire M. Renzetti, "Identities and Intersectionalities: Structured Action Theory, Left Realism, Postmodern Feminism, and Black/Multiracial Feminist Criminology," *Feminist Criminology*, pp. 50-74, 107-111, 115-137. Copyright © 2013 by Taylor & Francis Group. Reprinted with permission.

attribute of individuals with a more fluid, dynamic conceptualization of gender as accomplishment. Less than ten years later, West and Fenstermaker (1995) expanded the "doing gender approach" to other social categories, such as race and class, in an examination of the interactional aspects of "doing difference."[1] The doing gender/difference approach is also often referred to as *social construction feminism* because it sees gender as being socially created through people's actions and interactions with one another on a daily basis. The build-up of these interactions in the course of everyday life produces not only gendered self-identities, but also gendered social structures that, as Lorber (2009: 245) put it, "congeal" inequality.

To understand this perspective better, let us begin with the observation that social behavior is governed by norms, including gender norms (i.e. rules about masculinity and femininity), and these norms vary by social context or situation, although one consistent outcome is differentiation. In learning these norms, we learn how to "correctly" categorize people—and ourselves (e.g. male *or* female). As we interact, we constantly engage in this categorization, and we also know that others are categorizing us, so we make choices about how we look and act in a given situation based on how we think others might interpret our appearance and behavior. Social constructionists call this process *accountability*. Thus, people "do gender" by appearing and acting in ways that will lead others to identify them in a given situation as "male" or "female." Likewise, one may "do race" to be identified "white" or "Latino" or another race; one may "do sexual orientation" to be identified "gay" or "straight"; and so on. But this is not a process of constructing separate but equal categories, because these categories and the normative traits and behaviors attached to them are also ascribed differential value; some categories are valued more highly than others, and this inequality is reflected and reproduced in social relations and social structures in which people interact everyday—in, for example, families, schools, workplaces. As individuals continuously do gender (or race, or class), then, their "performance" is both constrained by and reproduces these unequal social relations and structures (West and Fenstermaker, 1995).

Before discussing how feminist criminologists have applied social constructionism in their theorizing and research, let us take a closer look at some of the central elements of this perspective. Notice first the importance of agency in social constructionism. From this perspective, individuals do not passively internalize pre-scripted gender roles that subsequently determine their attitudes and behavior; rather, gender is something people must do, or accomplish, in their everyday interactions with others (Connell, 1995). Moreover, how people do gender and what they accomplish varies situationally and is influenced by structural conditions. This means, then, that gender is not static or fixed. Social constructionism allows for multiple varieties of gender, for masculini*ties* and feminini*ties*, that an individual will likely change—and may change dramatically, in fact—as their circumstances change (Miller, 2002). It also allows for the possibility that in some situations individuals may "improvise" their performance of gender, or innovate new ways of doing gender (Messerschmidt, 1997).

But while this element of agency is critical, keep in mind, too, that social constructionists recognize the importance of how structural constraints—for example, in the form of power differences within and across groups—impinge on how gender and other differences can be accomplished. One may be more powerful than others in one context (e.g. a husband exercising power over his wife and children at home), but less powerful than others in a different context (e.g. the same man being subject to the power of his boss at work). "Consequently," as Messerschmidt (1997: 7) argues, "rather than viewing gender, race, and class as discreet 'things' that somehow relate to each other, it is important to visualize them as mutually constituting one another …" Furthermore, as Lorber (2009: 245) points out:

> While the social construction perspective allows for changes in gendered practices, change does not come easily, because many of the foundational assumptions of the gendered social order and its ubiquitous processes are legitimated by religion, taught by education, upheld by the mass media, and enforced by systems of social control.

It is James Messerschmidt who has been credited with pioneering the application of social constructionism to criminological theorizing and research through the development of his *structured action theory*. Although Messerschmidt has studied young women's involvement in crime, particularly in the context of street gangs (see Messerschmidt, 1995, 1997, 2002), much of his work focuses on understanding the relationship between masculinities and crime for as he correctly notes, for most criminologists the study of gender and crime means the study of women and crime. But men and boys are gendered too, and although historically they have been viewed as the "normal subjects" of criminological research, "the gendered content of their legitimate and illegitimate behavior has been virtually ignored" (Messerschmidt, 1993: 1; see also Messerschmidt, 1997, 2000).

In examining masculinities in relation to crime, Messerschmidt (1993, 1997) argues that crime is a resource used by men and boys to do gender—more specifically, to accomplish masculinity in a particular setting. Through secondary analyses of others' research as well as his own in-depth interviews with young men, Messerschmidt (2000, 2002) has studied how boys and men ascribe meaning to their behavior and make conscious choices, albeit in the context of structural constraints, about how to behave in a particular situation. He reports, for example, that boys and men living in disadvantaged urban neighborhoods use street crime, such as robbery, not only as a way of getting money or other valuable items, but also as a means for constructing a particular type of masculinity that he calls "hardman" (Messerschmidt, 1993). In another example—an analysis of the 1986 space shuttle *Challenger* disaster—Messerschmidt (1997) explores the construction of corporate masculinities by the white, middle-class managers and engineers involved in the launch decision that resulted in the deaths of all seven *Challenger* astronauts.

Importantly, Messerschmidt (1995, 1997) also discusses how crime may be a resource for some young women to construct particular femininities. He maintains, for instance, that girls in street gangs engage in behaviors, such as fighting and other forms of violence, that some observers might interpret as their attempts to act like boys, but to the girls themselves the behavior has a different meaning. These girls describe themselves as "feminine," but as acting "bad" (see also Jones, 2009). Messerschmidt (1995: 183) labels this femininity "bad-girl femininity," stating that the girls "are doing femininity in terms of activities appropriate to their sex category and in a specific social situation [i.e. the urban street gang]." Elsewhere, Messerschmidt (2002) describes third-wave feminism,[2] including the hip hop and Riot Grrrl subcultures, as constructing a "tough-girl femininity." Messerschmidt (ibid.: 465) makes the significant point that when women and girls are violent they are not just acting like or mimicking men and boys, but rather are "engaging in violence authentically as [women and] girls and as a legitimate aspect of their femininity." Their accomplishment of gender, though, like that of men and boys, is simultaneously shaped by various structural inequalities, such as sexism, racism, social class inequality, and heterosexism.

Structured action theory, as we have noted, advances our understanding of gender and crime in several ways. One important contribution is that it broadens the criminological lens beyond women's victimization. Recall that the feminist theories we discussed in Chapter 3 have been critiqued for overemphasizing women's victimization, subverting their agency and, perhaps inadvertently but nonetheless effectively, reinforcing stereotypes of female passivity and weakness. It follows from such stereotyping that the woman or girl who is aggressive or who "fights back" is anomalous, or worse, pathological, whereas the structured action theorist sees her as doing what everyone must do: accomplishing gender. What is more, in addition to drawing attention to the gendered nature of male criminal offending, structured action theorists do not depict male or female offenders as simply acting out a predetermined "gender role," but rather as actively constructing gender (and race, class and other differences) within the parameters of structural constraints through criminal offending. As Miller (2002: 434) points out, structured action theory "provides a means of bridging the agency/structure divide ... but does so in a way thoroughly grounded in the contexts of structural inequalities such as those of gender, sexuality, race, class, and age." Criminologists who have conducted research informed by structured action theory have found that crime is not only a means for accomplishing gender in certain contexts, but also that efforts to do gender affect who is victimized. For instance, in their studies of the characteristics of hate crime (e.g. the group nature of the offending, perpetrators' language, their use of alcohol) as well as the characteristics of hate crime perpetrators and victims, Bufkin (1999) and Perry (2001) argue that hate crime is a resource used by some groups of young men to accomplish a particular type of masculinity, specifically, *hegemonic masculinity*: white, Christian, able-bodied, and heterosexual.[3]

Structured action theory, however, has been criticized on a number of grounds.[4] Some critics argue, for example, that the way structured action theory is often applied in criminological analyses is tautological. A tautology is circular reasoning. The concern here is with what critics characterize as structured action theorists' rather myopic view that "whatever groups of boys and girls, or men and women, do is a kind of gender" (Risman, 2009: 81). And as Miller (2002) notes, the tautology problem is related to a second criticism of structured action theory: the tendency to reinforce, rather than challenge, *gender dualism* or what we referred to earlier as the gender binary. For instance, when young straight men engage in gay bashing it is interpreted by structured action theorists as an effort to construct a specific masculine identity, and when young women in a street gang fight with rival gang members, it is interpreted as an effort to construct a specific feminine identity. But to paraphrase Risman (2009), why label behaviors adopted by groups of males or females as alternative masculinities or femininities just because the group itself is made up of biological males and females?[5] For one thing, constructing gender in some situations may not be a primary motivation. Second, as Miller's (2001) research shows, some girls and women strongly identify with boys and men and describe their behavior as masculine, not feminine; that is, they see themselves as "one of the guys." So despite the theoretical conception of multiple masculinities and femininities, these critics maintain that structured action theory often falls short in applying this notion to real-life males and females because of its "selective attention" to gender difference, thereby overlooking instances of "gender crossing," contradictory or contingent gender constructions, gender resistance, and efforts to "undo gender" (Butler, 1990; Jones, 2009; Miller, 2002, Risman, 2009). This concern is extended to studies of differences, such as race and social class, which intersect with gender. Such research shows tremendous variation both across *and within* social groups. For example, there is evidence that some African American gang girls take pride in masculine identities (Miller, 2001), while others embrace feminine identities (Messerschmidt, 2002), and still others are "aggressive for the streets, pretty for the pictures" as part of a strategy to stay safe and survive the very dangerous neighborhoods in which they live their everyday lives (Jones, 2009: 89; see also Miller, 2002, 2008).

It is interesting to note that this latter point actually supports structured action theory in terms of documenting a multitude of masculinities and femininities as well as the agency that social actors exercise in constructing these multiple identities—sometimes highly constrained in their efforts and at other times pushing back hard enough at these constraints to create alternatives and bring about change. But this diversity and both potential and realized social change are precisely what critics do not want structured action theorists to lose sight of. Certainly, it is not easy to think outside the gender binary/dualism box, but it is necessary if we are to understand and appreciate the rich complexity and diversity of people's lived experiences, which for some include criminal offending.

Taking the Gendered Nature of Crime Seriously: Left Realism

We mentioned the emergence of a "new criminology" in the late 1960s and 1970s that was critical of mainstream criminologists for focusing on crimes committed by the powerless (e.g. street crime committed by young men of color in impoverished urban neighborhoods) and ignoring the crimes of the powerful (e.g. white-collar and corporate crime committed by wealthy, white businessmen; human rights violations committed by police or military personnel acting on behalf of governments). In the mid-1980s, though, another form of critical criminology was developed that, while not unconcerned with crimes of the powerful, nevertheless called for more criminological attention to street crime as well as the harsh social control techniques being adopted to address it (e.g. stop and frisk practices, saturation policing, three-strikes-and-you're-out sentencing laws).[6] This perspective, which originated in Great Britain, is known as *left realism*; left realists urged fellow critical criminologists to take crime in the streets, and its effects, seriously (Carlen, 1995).

Left realists acknowledge that many people are seriously harmed by white-collar, corporate, and governmental crime, but at the same time, they argue that many radical and Marxist criminologists have neglected the fact that "ordinary people," especially people who live in impoverished and working-class, high-crime neighborhoods, must cope daily with the severe negative consequences of predatory street crime and thus, rightly, fear it (Currie, 1992; Lea and Young, 1984). Moreover, de-emphasizing the significance of this type of crime relinquishes responsibility for responding to "the crime problem" to right-wing conservatives whose solution is to "crack down on crime," resulting in more people enmeshed in an increasingly draconian criminal justice system (DeKeseredy, 2011b; DeKeseredy and Schwartz, 2010). Such responses, however, may just compound crime's painful effects, since both perpetrators and victims typically live in the same communities and, not infrequently, in the same households.

In developing their theory, left realists originally drew heavily on Marxism as well as on mainstream strain and subcultural theories of crime. For instance, British left realists Lea and Young (1984) maintained that when people who are poor perceive their situation as unfair, they grow discontented and, if they have no legitimate way to address the inequity they are experiencing, they become increasingly frustrated. When unhappy, frustrated people are segregated together in whole communities of disadvantage, they form subcultures that encourage and legitimate criminal behavior.

Left realism has been criticized by criminologists on the political left (e.g. Carlen, 1995; Henry, 1999; Smart, 1990) as well as mainstream criminologists (e.g. Gibbons, 1994). But some critical criminologists see value in the left realist perspective, particularly in accounting for the crimes committed "behind closed doors by patriarchal, abusive men" (DeKeseredy, 2011b: 38). DeKeseredy and Schwartz (2010) distinguish their brand of left realism from other iterations of the theory by foregrounding gender, noting that even recent revisions of left realism have been gender-blind, and by examining how gender intersects with race and social class to shape behavior, including criminal behavior.

DeKeseredy and Schwartz (2010) point out that laissez-faire economic policies in recent years have cost many men their jobs, as corporations move production overseas to countries where labor costs are lower and regulations are weak or nonexistent. Young, working-class men have been especially hard hit by deindustrialization and the restructuring of the economy in countries such as the U.S., Canada, and Great Britain. If they can find work, it is increasingly in low-paying and menial jobs. Yet, these men are steeped in their culture's gendered norms of hegemonic masculinity, including being self-reliant; taking responsibility as the family "breadwinner"; maintaining the "upper hand" over "their" women and children; being unemotional, tough, and aggressive; and steadfastly disdaining even the slightest appearance of femininity, so as not to be ridiculed as "gay" by male peers. If legitimate means (e.g. gainful employment) to live up to the principles of hegemonic masculinity are blocked, then other means, such as violence, may be used to accomplish this type of masculinity. According to DeKeseredy and Schwartz (ibid.: 163):

> Men at the bottom of the socioeconomic ladder flocking together with members of all-male sexist subcultures is not surprising, since they are more likely than their more affluent counterparts to adhere to an ideology of familial patriarchy ... Arguably, such subcultures are likely to flourish in the near future because areas with high levels of poverty and unemployment are fertile breeding grounds for male-to-male and male-to-female violence ...

In addition to theorizing how particular social constructions of masculinity combine with social class constraints to encourage criminal offending, DeKeseredy and Schwartz (2010) also examine the role of institutionalized racism, which exacerbates the impact of many social problems, including unemployment and underemployment, for men of color. Young black, Asian, Latino, and other minority men experience heightened negative effects of social and economic disadvantage, which block their ability to attain the masculine status they value. It is not surprising, then, that many of these young men support and reinforce one another's views regarding "respect," the use of drugs and alcohol, and the objectification and control of women, and engage in crime as a type of "compensatory masculinity" or as a means of "repairing 'damaged masculinity'" (ibid.: 164).

DeKeseredy and Schwartz's left realism may be considered a form of feminist left realism. Others (e.g. Carlen, 1995) have also identified compatibilities between left realism and feminism. Yet, one of the difficulties with left realism, even of the feminist variety, is that it does not pay much attention to female offending. Left realism focuses on how and why socially and economically marginalized men victimize one another as well as their female intimate partners and women in their communities. But these women share this disadvantaged status. Can women's lower rates of offending be explained simply in terms of their adherence to gendered norms of "emphasized femininity" (Messerschmidt, 1997)? That raises the tautology problem that we noted earlier with regard to structured action theory. More empirical research is needed to test the applicability of feminist left realism to women's offending as well as women's resistance to men's violence. At the same time, while DeKeseredy and Schwartz (2010: 164) acknowledge that there are "diverse subcultural ways of doing masculinity" such that there are many marginalized men who are nonviolent and who treat women with dignity just as there are many affluent men who abuse women, neither of these two groups is carefully studied by feminist left realists.[7] DeKeseredy and Schwartz (ibid.: 163) point out, for example, that "there is a large empirical and theoretical literature on the strong correlation between patriarchal male peer support and various types of woman abuse in university/college dating, which involves, for the most part, middle- and upper-class young adults ..." Is this literature grounded in feminist left realism, or is feminist left realism limited to explaining only the criminal offending of socially and economically disadvantaged men? It is likely that the middle- and upper-class young *female* adults on university campuses, who are disproportionately affected by the offending of their male peers, would argue that this crime, too, should be "taken seriously." This is not to indict DeKeseredy and Schwartz, both of whom are recognized internationally as pro-feminist men and pioneering violence-against-women scholars, but rather to point out that the broader applicability of feminist left realism remains to date largely untested.

Postmodern Feminist Criminology

Most of us, throughout our lives, are exhorted to "tell the truth." We accept unquestioningly that there is an objective truth to be told. Similarly, most scientists, including criminologists and other social scientists, undertake empirical research in the pursuit of truth. Indeed, one of the foundational principles of science is that truth is knowable. But there is a group of criminologists who reject this claim. They are *postmodern* criminologists. Truth to postmodernists is a social construction, or, as postmodern feminist Nancy Wonders (1999: 116) explains:

> what passes for objectivity and the "truth" is really just one possible story about reality.... Thus, truth is always *contingent* on historical understandings, particular circumstances, and individual judgments; truth, therefore, is always temporary and partial—it can always change. Truth is also always political, privileging some perspective over others.

Postmodern theory has its origins in Europe, primarily France and Germany, where in the 1970s and 1980s, philosophers, literary theorists, and sociologists such as Jacques Derrida, Jean-Francois Lyotard, and Jean Baudrillard developed it as a sweeping critique of science, philosophy, and modernity. The theory quickly gained a sizeable following among academics in a variety of disciplines, including criminology, in Great Britain, Australia, and the United States during the 1980s and 1990s. Within criminology, various strains of postmodern theory have emerged, including postmodern feminist theory, and these, like left realism, have been critiqued by both the right and the left. One common criticism is that postmodernists' use of "jargonistic and insider language" does more to obfuscate than to elucidate their theoretical tenets; in fact, postmodernist prose has not infrequently been described as convoluted, incomprehensible, and vacuous (see, for example, Akers and Sellers, 2008; Naffine, 1995). Others maintain that postmodern criminologists offer little in the way of useful suggestions for public policy changes or an agenda of social activism, adopting instead a politically neutral stance or, worse, appearing reactionary at times (see, for instance, Friedrichs, 2009). Postmodern criminologists themselves often strongly criticize the ideas of fellow postmodernists (see, for example, Howe, 2000). Consequently, I undertake this attempt to offer a simplified, general overview of postmodern feminist criminology fully aware that I am unlikely to please or satisfy many criminologists, especially postmodern criminologists of any stripe.[8]

As noted at the outset of this section, postmodernists conceptualize "truth" as *contingent* or relative, not absolute. What is accepted as truth changes over time, and across places, and from one individual to the next. In the late 1800s, for example, it was widely accepted as a scientifically established truth that criminals were evolutionary throwbacks who could easily be identified by certain anatomical characteristics or "stigmata" such as big ears, a sloping forehead, and facial asymmetry, but today we understand this perspective to be fiction. Postmodernists, then, examine how realities are constructed through social interaction. However, unlike the social constructionists whose work we discussed earlier in the chapter, postmodernists do not emphasize social structure; they focus instead on culture, especially language, or *texts*. A text may be what we conventionally mean by the word—i.e. books, newspapers, diaries, or other written artifacts—but postmodernists also expand the term to include anything that people "read" or give meaning to. Every text has a *discourse*, that is, "what it says, does not say, and hints at (sometimes called a *subtext*)" (Lorber, 2009: 268). Also included in a text's discourse are the historical and social contexts and material conditions under which it is produced, as well as its intended audience (even though people in the actual audience may end up "reading" it differently from what the creators intended) (Lorber, 2009).

A central task for the postmodernist is to *deconstruct* or *decode* a text to expose or "unpack" its covert messages; that is, all the taken-for-granted assumptions, arbitrary distinctions, group interests, and values that undergird any "truth claim." In Humphries' (1999) analysis of "crack mothers," for instance, she shows how media reports, frequently drawing on medical and social science research that has since been widely criticized, constructed images "linking race, addiction, poverty, sexuality, and motherhood [and] turned the country's least powerful group, poor women of color, into a potent symbol of all that was wrong with America" (Humphries, 2013: 37). And despite the childhood chant that "words can never hurt me," such cultural representations often have very real and harmful consequences in people's lives because they promote particular courses of action. In this case, instead of offering treatment to substance-abusing women, some women were prosecuted in high-profile trials on charges of child abuse or endangerment, or for "delivering drugs to a minor;" many lost custody of their children.

In this example we also see another major concern of postmodernists: That some individuals and groups are able to get their values and beliefs represented as "truth," while others "do not participate in the construction of 'truth' because they have been systematically excluded from access to the tools of science, the power of the state, and the writing of history" (Wonders, 1999: 116). This exclusion has been based on difference, which is typically constructed as a dichotomy—e.g. male or female, heterosexual or homosexual, white or non-white—with one category ascribed greater value and, therefore, greater privilege, than the other. Although the differences that are used to divide members of these respective categories are represented as "natural" or biologically based, which gives the false impression that they are stable and largely immutable, postmodern analyses demonstrate how these categories in fact vary and change over time and across place or location. The U.S. Census provides a vivid example. The Census Bureau asks people to self-identify their race, but gives them predetermined categories from which to choose their racial identification; these categories, however, have changed in some way almost every decade since the 1800s. In 1890, for instance, there were eight racial categories on the census form, four of which were used to distinguish black people: you were "black" if you had three-quarters or more black ancestry, "mulatto" if you had three-eighths to five-eighths black ancestry, "quadroon" if you had one-quarter black ancestry, and "octoroon" if you had one-eighth or "any trace" of black ancestry. By 1900, there were five categories because "mulatto," "quadroon," and "octoroon" had been eliminated. Just 30 years later, in 1930, though, there were ten racial categories on the census form: white, negro, Indian (American Indian), Chinese, Japanese, Korean, Filipino, Hindu, Mexican, and "other." The 1930 census was the first and only time "Mexican" was identified as a distinct race. By 1950, Korean and Hindu (which is a religion) were deleted from the census form. Obviously, these dramatic changes on the census do not reflect actual changes in "races"; rather, they are the results of the fluctuating social, economic, and political concerns of those with the power to make "truth claims" about "race": the dominant white population during each historical period (Lee, 1993; see also Muhammad, 2010). "Thus, race is produced and reproduced all the time; indeed, we are continually changing the meaning of race" (Wonders, 1999: 117).

But by revealing the non-neutral, value-laden, often unjust character of various texts, postmodernists' deconstructions present the possibility of alternatives: If truth is provisional, individuals may reject, subvert, or appropriate specific depictions of "reality" and essentially reconstruct "reality" from their own standpoints and experiences. And herein lies the potential for social change from a postmodern perspective. In fact, it has been argued that while postmodern criminology on its own appears politically neutral or, worse, "intellectually and politically bankrupt" (Howe, 2000: 221), postmodern criminology joined with feminist criminology offers strategies for constructing "justice." For instance, Wonders (1999: 122), drawing on Elam's (1994) concept of "ethical activism" argues that, "We have a responsibility—and obligation to ourselves and others—to understand our daily role in defining and creating reality and justice, and to do our best to make judgments that make the world a good place to be for all of us." Similarly, Grant (1993) urges the use of deconstruction to actively resist the negative, harmful, and hierarchical group identities that have been constructed by the powerful for the oppressed. Nevertheless, postmodern feminists continually caution against falling into the trap of advocating universal solutions to any social problem and warn criminologists not to assume we know what is "best" for oppressed groups. Justice, like all other "texts," is contingent: it changes over time, across location, and among individuals and groups. Thus, "local people everywhere need to develop their own definitions of their experiences and to work out their own methods of resistance to oppression" (DeKeseredy and Schwartz, 1996: 274).

There are, not surprisingly, many criminologists, including feminist criminologists, who find these postmodern and postmodern feminist strategies unsatisfying or insufficient. Some critics see such approaches as too individualistic, as little more than exhortations to "play nice" and make "good life choices," which do little to address or attack the inequalities embedded in major social institutions, such as the legal system (see, for example, Lorber, 2009). Others are critical of the strict relativism of postmodern feminism—for instance, the position that all knowledge is subjective, that "reality" is unknowable. Flavin and Artz (2013: 23), who have conducted extensive research on violence against women in post-apartheid South Africa, articulate this concern well:

> It is easy to argue that there is no essential experience with violence (and structural discrimination) for women in South Africa. However, it could also be argued that it is the very historical experience, and the horrific social impact of this experience, that may somehow be the binding agent of South African women. To no small extent, there are shared histories (apartheid rule), a common current reality (high risk of indiscriminate violence, including sexual violence) and a struggle (such as being free from violence, securing freedom of movement and a responsive criminal justice system) affecting all women. Are these issues not sufficiently common to South African women as women? Do they need to be entirely exposed and divided into individual segments so that each experience or struggle is so finely deconstructed and dissected that feminist advocacy is fractured? What is feminist theory if the core of it is not about women; some common thread of experience that differentiates us from men or masculinist law or justice? What makes it feminist? In this context, the weighty cautions and strict rationing of legitimate voices by feminism is counterintuitive.

While the uncompromising relativism of postmodern feminist theory has been viewed by some criminologists as actually undermining feminism, other feminist criminologists continue to challenge the discipline's tendency to ignore the significant impacts of multiple, simultaneous inequalities. An analysis of what has been called the "matrix of domination and resistance" (Collins, 2000) is the primary focus of black and multiracial feminist criminologists whose work we examine next.

Intersectionality: Black and Multiracial Feminist Criminology

Black feminist sociologist, Patricia Hill Collins (2012), in a recent reflection on her experiences teaching a course on "Contemporary Black Women" in a Black Studies department during the 1980s while she was writing her book, *Black Feminist Thought* (1990), reports that she avoided using the term "feminism" in class because her students strongly rejected it. "In their minds, feminism was for white women, not them" (Collins, 2012: 19). Indeed, Collins' students' complaints about feminism were widespread among women of color, particularly women of color in the academy, who, during the 1970s and 1980s, pointed to the fallacy of essentialist thinking in mainstream feminist scholarship and theorizing, which purported to speak on behalf of *all* women (Higgenbotham, 2012). Criminologist Amanda Burgess-Proctor (2006), citing Thompson (2002), points out, in fact, that second-wave feminism was often referred to by women of color and antiracist white women as "hegemonic feminism" because it regarded the experiences of white, middle-class, heterosexual women as the normative standard. Women academics of color, as "outsiders within the ivory tower" (Higgenbotham, 2012: 25), were well situated to see that one's standpoint or social locations shape one's construction of knowledge or "truth" and that knowledge production is never divorced from power relations (Baca Zinn, 2012; Collins, 2012; Yuval-Davis, 2012). This critique, and the alternative theorizing it generated, became the foundation on which black and multiracial feminist criminology was built.

Collins (1986, 1990) and others (e.g. Baca Zinn *et al.*, 1986; Baca Zinn and Thornton Dill, 1996; Crenshaw, 1994; Rice, 1990) argued that although hegemonic feminists acknowledge differences across groups of women, this acknowledgment rarely moves beyond a "tolerance" of pluralism, or as Baca Zinn and Thornton Dill (1996: 323) put it, "a long list of diversities which begin with gender, class, and race, and continue through a range of social structural as well as personal characteristics" (see also Laslett and Brenner, 2000). Overlooked, though, are differences of *power* among women that are attached to these "diversities." In addition, hegemonic feminism foregrounds gender inequality—specifically, dominance of men over women—while leaving unaddressed other subordinating statuses based on race, social class, sexual orientation, and other social locating factors that intersect with gender to produce different experiences of oppression and privilege. In other (and rather simplistic) words, women of color may experience sexism at the hands of men, including men of color, but they (and men of color) also experience racism in their interactions with white men *and* white women. Black and multiracial feminism, then, emphasizes both the *power relations* embedded in socially constructed differences and the *intersectionality* of these differences.

Black and multiracial feminism, therefore, is distinct from hegemonic and other feminisms in several significant ways. First, as we have already noted, black and multiracial feminists examine how various social locating factors—gender, race, ethnicity, social class, sexuality, age, national origin, physical ability—"*mutually construct one another* as unjust systems of power" (Collins, 2012: 19, emphasis added). Each of these social locations is structured hierarchically, with differential power and privilege attached to each rung of each hierarchy. But the hierarchies do not operate side by side; rather, they are overlapping hierarchies, forming what has been variously called the "matrix of domination" (Collins, 2000), "multiple marginality" (Richie, 1996), or "multiplicative identity" (Wing, 2003), because all women and men occupy rungs of all the hierarchies simultaneously (i.e. we are, at once, gendered, raced, classed, and so on, even though in any given situation one or two of these factors may have more salience than others). "[Y]ou cannot look at one of these social statuses alone, nor can you add them one after another. Their interaction is synergistic—together they construct social locations that are oppressive because they result in multiple systems of domination" (Lorber, 2009: 198).[9] These interlocking inequalities shape who we are as individuals and our interactions with one another within the groups to which we belong and across social groups, as well as our access to opportunities, rewards, privileges, and power. This means, then, that these interlocking hierarchies operate both at the institutional (macro) level and within the realm of everyday (micro) social interaction.

The omnipresence of these intersecting hierarchies or inequalities, however, does not mean that people are completely determined by them and lack agency. Nor does it mean that all members of the same group have the same experiences or that they "agree on the significance of [their] varying experiences" (Collins, 2000: 25). Thus, people's simultaneously held multiple identities will result in members of a specific group facing both common and divergent challenges, to which they may sometimes respond in unified, and at other times in diverse, ways. To paraphrase Potter (2006: 112), the experiences of women of color are collective, yet also individualized. This observation raises another fundamental principle of black and multiracial feminism: that all people are *both* privileged *and* oppressed; no one enjoys total privilege or suffers total oppression. Closely associated with this idea is the concept of *relationality*, which "assumes that groups of people are socially situated in relation to other groups of people based on their differences" (Burgess-Proctor, 2006: 37). Burgess-Proctor illustrates this point by noting that "some women benefit from the oppression of other women who occupy a lower social position, even when (or perhaps especially when) the former are not cognizant of the benefits that their privileged status provides" (p. 37). Baca Zinn and Thornton Dill (1996) underline the importance of this point by noting that while the intersectional framework was developed by black and multiracial feminists, it applies not only to women of color, but to all groups of women *and* men, because everyone experiences advantages and disadvantages resulting from intersecting inequalities.

Before turning to an assessment of the impact of black and multiracial feminism on feminist criminology, let us first discuss some of the concerns about this perspective that have been raised by feminist sociologists and criminologists. One issue has to do with the anti-essentialism of black and multiracial feminism and is similar to the objection voiced in regards to the relativism of postmodern feminism. Ngaire Naffine (2002), for instance, agrees that the perspectives and experiences of white, middle-class, heterosexual, and well-educated feminists long dominated feminist theorizing, scholarship, and activism, further marginalizing the voices of women from already marginalized groups. At the same time, however, she cautions against the counter-approach, which she sees as an overemphasis on what she calls "localized narratives": "The concerted effort to do justice to the world views of those differently situated, by declaring them the final authority on their own situation, contains the tacit proposition that their experience is somehow always beyond reach, always in some way incommensurable to one's own experience" (ibid.: 91; see also Rudy, 2000). Flavin and Artz

(2013: 23) echo this concern, drawing again on their research in South Africa, where they note that despite the existence of 11 official languages and many more cultural groups, as well as tremendous variations in income and education, shared experiences among women nevertheless exist.

> If we assert that the lived experiences of women are all, always, so radically different from each other, then the future is grim indeed for feminist legal and criminological scholarship and policymaking. The end result is an analysis of women and their relationship to law and criminal justice that is so fragmented and oppositional that feminist jurisprudence and feminist reforms are simply too obscure and idiosyncratic to be tenable.

Some critics have also expressed the related concern that black and multiracial feminism produces "identity politics," which is also divisive and exclusionary because it assumes that only those who share the same marginal or oppressed identity or social location can truly understand it. Collins (1990), though, and others (e.g. Yuval-Davis, 2012) explicitly reject this position, with Harding (1993: 59) labeling it "ethnocentric." Yuval-Davis (2012: 51) emphasizes that advocates do not necessarily have to be members of the group for whom they are advocating, since "it is the message, not the messenger, that counts." She further cautions advocates who are members of the groups for whom they are advocating not to assume they can speak for everyone in their group. She points out that one of the problems with identity politics is that outspoken activists and "community leaders" often become identified as the "authentic voice" of their communities, and this may be harmful to other members, such as women, who may be marginalized *within* these communities. In her admonition she highlights the significance of intersectionality: "even as advocates, it is important that the activists should be reflective and conscious of the multiplexity of their specific positionings" (Yuval-Davis, ibid.; see also Rudy, 2000).

Finally, some critics have argued that the focus on intersecting inequalities may produce an "oppression olympics" (Hancock, 2011), in which various groups vie for recognition as "most oppressed," again producing divisiveness, rather than solidarity, across marginalized groups and undermining efforts toward progressive social change. While examples of this problem certainly exist, especially during periods when marginalized groups are forced by economic recession and budget cuts to compete with one another for limited funding and other resources, this criticism also stems from a misunderstanding (and perhaps, misuse) of black and multiracial feminism generally, and of intersectionality in particular. Collins (1997), for example, sees no value in constructing hierarchies of oppression. For one thing, she maintains, there is no single "worst" position. In addition, she believes that in order to arrive at an approximation of "truth" it is crucial to engage in dialogue with people holding various social positionings—not only those on the margins, but also those in the "hegemonic center."

Regardless of these criticisms, the impact of black and multiracial feminism, particularly the intersectionality framework, on feminist criminology cannot be overstated.[10] Baca Zinn (2012: 30) asserts that, "In the past three decades, intersectionality has become a sociological specialty in its own right, with unique concepts, methodologies, and a distinctive process through which knowledge is shaped. Today, the distinguishing features of intersectionality are part of the gender studies canon." Her observation characterizes feminist criminology equally as well. Let us consider, then, some examples of this influence.

Intersectionality in Feminist Criminological Research

Feminist criminologists began calling for greater attention to intersecting inequalities—in particular, the intersections of gender, race, and class—in criminological research in the late 1980s and 1990s (see, for example, Daly, 1993, 1997; Daly and Stephens, 1995; Hill and Crawford, 1990; Simpson, 1991; see also Britton, 2000). In the ensuing years, a large number of studies have examined how intersecting inequalities based on gender, race, class, age, and sexuality construct and constrain the life experiences of various groups of women and men, including their experiences as criminal offenders and as crime victims. Much of this work has focused on violent crime and has shown how, especially for young women of color growing up in severely disadvantaged neighborhoods, violent victimization is intimately tied to violent offending. For instance, Nikki Jones' (2010) ethnographic research with African American inner-city girls reveals the various strategies these young women use to deal with the very real threats to their survival posed by living in impoverished communities plagued by an active and violent drug trade and a hyper-masculine "code of the street." Although their male peers confront the same environmental conditions, Jones shows how both the threats of violence and the adolescents' responses to them are gendered, with girls' use of violence being in some ways similar to, but in other ways distinct from, boys' use of violence, and how use of violence varies even among girls who share these circumstances (see also Miller, 2008). Jones examines how the young women feel pressure to conform to the idealized notion of the "good, respectable girl," but how some also feel the need to construct a public image as a "tough girl" or a "fighter" as a way to protect themselves at school or in their neighborhood. Such a public persona, though, may result in harsh responses to their violent behavior by teachers, the police, and judges, increasing their risk of being expelled from school, arrested, and placed in a juvenile detention facility, a point that we return to shortly.

We see in Jones' research not only how gender, race, class, and age intersect to shape vulnerability to violence, but also potential victims' efforts to prevent or resist such violence. Recent research on intimate partner violence reinforces the importance of analyzing intersectionality in order to develop a fuller understanding of victimization, resistance, and offending. For example, Hillary Potter (2006, 2008) considers, among other factors, how interactions within the black community based on distinctive aspects of black culture explain African American women's experiences of and responses to intimate partner violence. Potter (2006: 116) reports, for instance, that:

Black women remain in abusive relationships more so out of fear of being without companionship, being without a father or father figure for minor children, and being stigmatized as yet another single black mother than fear of further and more perilous battering incidents or of financial independence.

She sees these fears as direct outgrowths of African American women's unique experiences in U.S. society as well as within the African American community.[11] Moreover, she identifies the image or ideal of the "Strong Black Woman," which has developed out of African American women's need to confront various types of domination and discrimination in their everyday lives, as playing a critical role in influencing their responses to intimate partner violence. More specifically, as "Strong Black Women," African American women are more likely than other women to fight back against their abusive partners (Potter, 2008; see also Garfield, 2005; Gillum, 2002; Richie, 1996, 2012).[12]

It may be argued, however, that it is in research on criminal justice processing, particularly sentencing, that one can see the greatest influence of black and multiracial feminism. Consider, for instance, recent feminist criminological analyses of *sentencing disparity*, which occurs when offenders charged with the same or a similar crime are given different punishments. Looking at the data in Table 13.1, we see that racial and ethnic minorities, both male and female, are disproportionately represented among state and federal prison populations. While black men make up 13.2 percent of the U.S. male population, they are 38.8 percent of the U.S. male *prison* population. Similarly, Hispanic men are 16.5 percent of the U.S. male population, but 22.6 percent of the U.S. male prison population. The disparities are less dramatic for women, but are present nonetheless: Black women are 14.0 percent and Hispanic women 15.0 percent of the U.S. female population, respectively, but they are 25.4 percent and 17.9 percent of the U.S. female prison population, respectively (Guerino *et al.*, 2012). Women, though, regardless of race, make up a very small percentage of the prison population in the United States (less than 7 percent), although the number of women incarcerated in state and federal

Table 13.1 Estimated Number of Sentenced Prisoners Under State and Federal Jurisdiction, By Sex and Race, 2010

Race	Male	Female
White	451,600	48,000
Black	561,400	26,600
Hispanic	327,200	18,700
Total	1,446,000	104,600

Source: Guerino *et al.*, (2012: 26).

prisons has increased dramatically since 2000 and at a rate higher than that of men (ibid.). Are these differences across groups caused solely by legal factors (e.g. crime severity, previous record), or do extra-legal factors, such as the offenders' race and/or sex, influence sentencing decisions thereby producing sentencing disparities? Studies by feminist criminologists utilizing an intersectionalities framework have begun to answer such questions.

Traditionally, criminologists would approach the question of how extra-legal factors affect sentencing decisions by looking at a single variable at a time: sex *or* race. For example, data consistently show that, among adults, female defendants are significantly less likely than male defendants to be sentenced to prison, and even when women are sentenced to prison, their incarceration periods are shorter, on average, than those of men. These differences are found not only in the United States, but in the United Kingdom, Australia, and New Zealand, too (Spohn and Brennan, 2013). Spohn and Brennan (ibid.) review numerous studies of gender disparities in sentencing and report that even when accounting for crime seriousness, prior criminal record, and other legally relevant factors, women receive more lenient sentences than men, a finding that suggests judges and juries view female offenders differently—perhaps as less threatening, perhaps as less blameworthy—than male offenders. Thus, gender stereotypes may be influencing sentencing decisions, but, drawing attention to the question of intersectionality, Spohn and Brennan (ibid.: 218) point out that, "What is generally missing from the extant theoretical literature is a discussion of how racial/ethnic stereotypes may condition gender stereotypes." Given that hegemonic culture constructs "the criminal" as a young, black or Latino male and the media consistently reinforce this image, judges and juries may be influenced by intersecting racial and gender stereotypes that associate threat, dangerousness, and criminality with men of color, but not women of color. There are, of course, negative racialized and gendered stereotypes of women of color, too (see, for instance, Gillum, 2002; Landrine, 1985) and the media generally treat minority female offenders less sympathetically than white female offenders (Brennan and Vandenberg, 2009).[13] How might the intersecting inequalities of gender and race affect sentencing outcomes, then? Spohn and Brennan (2013) report that women receive more lenient sentences than men of the same race, such that women of color fare better than men of color in sentencing, thereby benefiting from their gender status. At the same time, however, white women are afforded preferential treatment relative to white men *and* men of color, whereas black and Hispanic men are punished more harshly than white women, women of color, *and* white men, indicating that they pay a "race penalty" when sentenced.[14]

The brevity of this book does not allow me to adequately cover all of the important contributions being made by feminist criminologists whose work is framed by black and multiracial feminism. I do hope, however, that the sampling I have offered gives readers an inkling of black and multiracial feminism's impact on feminist criminology, as well as a strong sense of how black and multiracial feminism pushes criminologists beyond the conceptualization of gender, race/ethnicity, and other social locators as mere "control variables" and allows us to more fully understand the complexity of people's lived experiences. More startling—and energizing—is the fact that black and multiracial feminism is still in its infancy as criminological theory, and those of us who apply it in our work recognize the need for much more research that explores the multiple and intricate ways that gender intersects with race and ethnicity, social class, age, sexuality, ability, and other status markers to shape differential outcomes for crime victims and offenders, for students, and for criminal justice professionals. We have truly only scratched the surface.

Notes

1. Although the doing gender/doing difference approach is widely used—and, according to its creators (West and Zimmerman, 2009), often misused—today, West and Zimmerman persevered for ten years (through multiple revisions) to get their paper accepted for publication, a fact of which up-and-coming theorists and authors in particular should take note.

2. The label "third-wave feminism" is often applied to the feminism of many young women today to set it apart from the feminism of the 1960s, 1970s, and 1980s, which has been referred to as the "second wave of feminism," distinguishing it from late eighteenth- and early nineteenth-century feminism (i.e. the "first wave") (Renzetti et al., 2012). Third wave feminism is commonly described as rebellious in terms of its celebration of female sexuality, and its emphasis on women's autonomy and agency (Lorber, 2005, 2009). An important element of third-wave feminism is inclusion. Many third-wave feminists have developed a multiracial/multicultural worldview focusing on the consequences of racism, social class inequality, and homophobia in addition to sexism (Baumgardner and Richards, 2000; Renzetti et al., 2012). We discuss this perspective in greater detail later in the chapter.

3. See also Goodey's (1997) analysis of masculinities and fear of crime and Miller's (1998) study of gender and the accomplishment of robbery in the U.S., as well as Brookman et al.'s (2007) study of gender and robbery in the UK. Stroud (2012) offers a fascinating analysis of how carrying concealed handguns helps "relatively privileged men" to accomplish hegemonic masculinity "through fantasies of violence and self-defense," especially against racial and ethnic minority men.

4. Here I will highlight only a few of what I consider the most salient criticisms of structured action theory. For a more thorough and nuanced discussion of these criticisms, see the exchange between Miller and Messerschmidt in the November, 2002 issue of *Theoretical Criminology*, which we repeatedly cite in this chapter. See also the symposium on doing gender in the February, 2009 issue of *Gender & Society*; several of the contributions to the symposium are cited in this chapter as well.

5. Once again, the challenge is to recognize that even sex is not a binary category. When we speak of an individual's sex, we may be referring to *chromosomal* sex, *hormonal* sex, *gonadal* sex, or *genital* sex. Although for many people all of these are consistent with the category male or the category female, for some people they are not. For instance, some individuals (approximately 1 in 5,000 to 1 in 15,000 births) are born with a pair of XX sex chromosomes, which makes them chromosomally female, but because of prenatal exposure to androgens (male sex hormones) their external genitals may look more like those of

boys than girls. This is a condition known as congenital adrenal hyperplasia. Similarly, some fetuses with male sex chromosomes (XY) are insensitive to androgens—a condition known as androgen insensitivity syndrome—and they are then born with the external genitalia of females. Typically, physicians advise parents of children with these conditions to have their genitals surgically reconstructed or "corrected." But this position has come under increasing criticism because such conditions usually are not threatening to the child's health; as one critic put it, they are only threatening to the child's culture (Kessler, 1996). For further discussion of *intersexuality*, genital ambiguity, and cross-cultural research on multiple genders, see Preves (2003) and Renzetti *et al.* (2012).

6. Stop and frisk refers to the ability of police to stop a person they deem "suspicious" to question them and pat them down (i.e. frisk them) in order to detect weapons. This controversial practice has been challenged as an unconstitutional search, but the U.S. Supreme Court has upheld it as a legitimate way to prevent crime, especially violent crime, and has given police considerable discretion in terms of what they deem "reasonably suspicious." Some people, however, are automatically labeled suspicious because of their membership in a particular group, such as people of color, so they are disproportionately—and unfairly—subjected to this practice. Saturation policing refers to the practice of concentrating large numbers of police officers in small, high-crime areas (known as "hot spots"). The rationale is to have a highly visible and overwhelming police presence in order to deter crime, which, on its face, makes sense. However, the police may be perceived as an "occupying army," particularly in racially segregated and economically disadvantaged neighborhoods. Ironically, some residents of such neighborhoods point out that despite saturation policing, the police are often quite slow to respond to their calls for help (see, for example, Websdale, 2001). Finally, the three strikes law, adopted in California, was originally intended to reduce the recidivism of violent felons by imposing a life sentence in prison on individuals convicted of a third offense. Most "strike crimes" (i.e. criminal convictions that count in the three-strike tally) are violent felonies, but other, less serious crimes are included as well as are juvenile convictions and out-of-state convictions. The law has resulted in many grossly unfair outcomes (e.g. an individual being sentenced to life in prison for a shoplifting conviction because it was his or her "third strike" while an individual convicted of manslaughter is sentenced to 15 years because it is his or her first conviction). The law has also contributed to the serious—and inhumane—prison overcrowding in California, where one in four inmates is a "striker" (Shouse Law Group, 2012). See also Alexander (2010) for further discussion of these and other, similar practices.

7. As the economic downturn that began in 2007 began to worsen, the media reported an upsurge in cases of domestic violence, both intimate partner violence and child abuse, and attributed the increase to growing depression among men who had recently lost their jobs or who were experiencing severe financial problems. This group included middle-class and wealthy men who had lost positions in high-paying, high-status professions. But while research indicates a strong association between economic hardship and domestic violence, the relationship is complex and, often, economic distress is only one factor that must be considered in conjunction with a host of other risk factors. See Renzetti (2011a) for a further discussion of these issues.

8. Wonders (1999: 112) points out that "some postmodern theorists argue that it is not possible to summarize the field at all, since postmodernism is a response against 'totalizing' theory or efforts to explain the world in a unified and unifying way." Wonders herself maintains that it is unproductive to try to force postmodernism and feminism into a single theory because in doing so one runs the risk of "losing something from each perspective" (ibid.). Rather, she advocates "bridging" the two theories by identifying their "points of convergence."

9. Other terms that have been applied to these intersecting inequalities are "trilogy of oppression" (Gordon, 1987), referring to the disadvantaged status of women of color in terms of gender, race, and class, and "multiple jeopardy" (King, 1988), which encompasses the multiple forms of oppression experienced simultaneously by women of color.

10. We wish to emphasize here that the impact has largely been limited to *feminist* criminology and not the discipline as a whole. The extent to which feminism generally, or any specific feminist theory, has influenced the discipline of criminology is debatable.

11. Wood (2012) notes that many abused black women experience additional pressure not to report their violent intimate partners to police in order to "protect" black men from the racist criminal justice system. Wood indicates that this pressure comes from several sources within the black community, such as black clergy who characterize the black male as an "endangered species," and others who send the message that "if you report and/or prosecute your abuser, you are contributing to the problem because black men are stigmatized and 'selectively' over-penalized. In this way, a woman of color may be discouraged from making the choice to protect herself from an abuser by a sense of cultural duty to keep a black man out of the hands of 'white authority figures'" (p. 50). But see also Beth Richie's (2012) excellent analysis of how, over the past two decades, the anti-violence movement, in an effort to win mainstream public support for its cause as well as funding from an increasingly conservative government, abandoned its more radical demands and practices, thereby abandoning women who fall outside hegemonic femininity and heteronormative sexuality—for example, black women in marginalized positions—while at the same time embracing policies, such as mandatory arrest laws, which support what she calls the "prison nation." Her research shows that under these conditions, "the more socially disadvantaged black women are, the more they will be stigmatized by or, worse, punished, for [sic] their victimization" (p. 159).

12. Ransby (2000) offers several excellent examples of black feminists' resistance to women's oppression within the black community. She notes black feminists' protests of Clarence Thomas' nomination to the U.S. Supreme Court in 1991. She also discusses black feminists' rallies against plans by "the predominantly male political establishment" in Harlem (New York City) and St. Louis, Missouri to celebrate boxer Mike Tyson's release from prison after serving his sentence on a rape conviction. And she relates how black feminist law professor Kimberle Creshaw organized a national meeting in 1995 for black feminists to develop responses to Louis Farrakhan's "Million Man March," one of the central purposes of which was to exhort black men to reclaim their rightful titles as heads of their families and communities. As Ransby (2000: 1217) explains, however, "The issue, for many, was not clear cut: for some, opposing Clarence Thomas's sexism had been easy because there were so many other reasons (having to do with

his conservative antiblack politics) to oppose him, but to challenge a charismatic religious icon like Farrakhan or a superstar athlete like Tyson was a different matter altogether. Nevertheless, black feminists once again mobilized on fairly short notice to do precisely that."

13. See Muhammad (2010) for a historical analysis of how the association of Blackness with crime has been socially constructed in the United States. In a commentary on Muhammad's book, Kay Harris (2012) observed that the cultural racialization of crime may be summed up in the sentence, "white people commit crimes; black people are criminals."

14. In an interesting analysis of juvenile court decision making, Guevara *et al.* (2006) found that the effect of race on both pre-adjudication detention and case disposition decisions varied by gender, but in different ways. For example, white girls were more likely than nonwhite girls to receive an out-of-home placement—a harsher disposition and the opposite of what occurred for the boys in the study—which they speculate may reflect the racialized gender stereotypes of juvenile court authorities who regard delinquency by white girls as a more serious violation of gender norms than delinquency by non-white girls. Spohn and Brennan's (2013) discussion of sentencing in capital cases also indicates that racialized gender stereotypes may affect sentencing in capital cases. The studies they review (Holcomb *et al.*, 2004; Williams *et al.*, 2007) showed that offenders convicted of capital crimes against females were two and a half times more likely to be sentenced to death than offenders convicted of capital crimes against males, but when the race of the victim was also examined, the data showed that offenders convicted of killing white females had the greatest likelihood of being sentenced to death, whereas those convicted of killing black males had the lowest likelihood of receiving a death sentence. An offender who killed a white female was 14 times more likely to be sentenced to death than an offender who killed a black male. Factors that further affected the imposition of the death sentence in cases involving white female homicide victims included whether the victim had been raped, whether the victim's body was unclothed when found, and whether there was evidence that the victim had been forced to disrobe.

References

Akers, R.L., and Sellers, C.S. (2008). *Criminological Theories*, New York: Oxford University Press.

Alexander, M. (2010). *The New Jim Crow: Mass Incarceration in the Era of Colorblindness*, New York: New Press.

Baca Zinn, M. (2012). "Patricia Hill Collins: Past and future innovations", *Gender & Society*, 26: 28–32.

Baca Zinn, M., Cannon, L.W., Higgenbotham, E., and Thornton Dill, B. (1986). "The cost of exclusionary practices in women's studies", *Signs*, 11: 290–303.

Baca Zinn, M., and Thornton Dill, B. (1996). "Theorizing difference from multiracial feminism", *Feminist Studies*, 22: 321–31.

Baumgardner, J., and Richards, A. (2000). *Manifesta: Young Women, Feminism, and the Future*, New York: Farrar, Straus, and Giroux.

Brennan, P.K., and Vandenberg, A.L. (2009). "Depictions of female offenders in front-page newspaper stories: The importance of race/ethnicity", *International Journal of Social Inquiry*, 2: 141–75.

———. (2000). "Feminism in criminology: Engendering the outlaw", *Annals of the American Academy of Social Sciences*, 571: 57–76.

Brookman, F., Mullins, C., Bennett, T., and Wright, R. (2007). "Gender, motivation, and the accomplishment of street robbery in the United Kingdom", *British Journal of Criminology*, 47: 861–84.

Bufkin, J. (1999). "Bias crime as gendered behavior", *Social Justice*, 26: 155–76.

Burgess-Proctor, A. (2006). "Intersections of race, class, gender, and crime: Future directions for feminist criminology", *Feminist Criminology*, 1: 27–47.

Butler, J. (1990). *Gender Trouble: Feminism and the Subversion of Identity*, New York: Routledge.

———. (1995). "Women, crime, feminism, and realism", in N. Naffine (ed.) *Gender, Crime and Feminism*, Aldershot, UK: Dartmouth Publishing Company.

Collins, P.H. (1986). "Learning from the outsider within: The sociological significance of black feminist thought", *Social Problems*, 33: 14–32.

———. (1990). *Black Feminist Thought*, New York: Routledge.

———. (1997). "Comment on Hekman's 'Truth and method: Feminist standpoint theory revisited': Where's the power?" *Signs*, 22: 375–81.

———. (2000). *Black Feminist Thought*, 2nd ed., New York: Routledge.

———. (2012). "Looking back, moving ahead: Scholarship in service to social justice", *Gender & Society*, 26: 14–22.

Connell, R.W. (1995). *Masculinities*, Berkeley: University of California Press.

Crenshaw, K. (1994). "Mapping the margins: Intersectionality, identity politics, and violence against women of color", in M.A. Fineman and R. Mykitiuk (eds.) *The Public Nature of Private Violence*, New York: Routledge.

Currie, E. (1992). "Retreatism, minimalism, realism: Three styles of reasoning on crime and drugs in the United States", in J. Lowman and B.D. MacLean (eds.) *Realist Criminology: Crime Control and Policing in the 1990s*, Toronto: University of Toronto Press.

———. (1993). "Class-race-gender: Sloganeering in search of meaning", *Social Justice*, 20: 56–71.

———. (1997). "Different ways of conceptualizing sex/gender in feminist theory and their implications for feminist criminology", *Theoretical Criminology*, 1: 25–51.

Daly, K., and Stephens, D. (1995). "The 'dark figure' of criminology: Towards a black and multi-ethnic feminist agenda for theory and research", in N.H. Rafter, and F. Heidensohn (eds.) *International Feminist Perspectives in Criminology: Engendering a Discipline*, Philadephia: Open University Press.

———. (2011b). *Contemporary Critical Criminology*, London: Routledge.

DeKeseredy, W.S., and Schwartz, M.D. (1996). *Contemporary Criminology*, Belmont, CA: Wadsworth.

———. (2010). "Friedman economic policies, social exclusion, and crime: Toward a gendered left realist subcultural theory", *Crime, Law and Social Change*, 54: 159–70.

Elam, D. (1994). *Feminism and Deconstruction: Ms. En Abyme*, New York: Routledge.

Flavin, J., and Artz, L. (2013). "Understanding women, gender, and crime: Some historical and international developments", in C.M. Renzetti, S.L. Miller, and R.A. Gover (eds.) *Routledge International Handbook of Crime and Gender Studies*, London: Routledge.

Friedrichs, D.O. (2009). "Critical criminology", in J.M. Miller (ed.) *21st Century Criminology: A Reference Handbook, Volume 1*, Thousand Oaks, CA: SAGE.

Garfield, G. (2005). *Knowing What We Know: African American Women's Experiences of Violence and Violation*, New Brunswick, NJ: Rutgers University Press.

Gibbons, D. (1994). *Talking about Crime and Criminals: Problems and Issues in Theory Development in Criminology*, Englewood Cliffs, NJ: Prentice Hall.

Gillum, T.L. (2002). "Exploring the link between stereotypic images and intimate partner violence in the African American community", *Violence Against Women*, 8: 64–86.

Goodey, J. (1997). "Boys don't cry: Masculinities, fear of crime, and fearlessness", *British Journal of Criminology*, 37: 401–18.

Gordon, V.V. (1987). *Black Women, Feminism, and Black Liberation: Which Way?* Chicago: Third World Press.

Grant, J. (1993). *Fundamental Feminism: Contesting the Core Concepts of Feminist Theory*, New York: Routledge.

Guerino, P., Harrison, P.M., and Sabol, W.J. (2012). *Prisoners in 2010*, Washington, DC: U.S. Department of Justice, Bureau of Justice Statistics. Retrieved from http://bjs.ojp.usdoj.gov/index.cfm?ty=pbdetail&iid=2230.

Guevara, L., Herz, D., and Spohn, C. (2006). "Gender and juvenile decision making: What role does race play?" *Feminist Criminology*, 1: 258–82.

Hancock, A. (2011). *Solidarity Politics for Millenials*, New York: Palgrave MacMillan.

Harding, S. (1993). "Rethinking standpoint epistemology: 'What is strong objectivity?'", in L. Alcoff and E. Potter (eds.) *Feminist Epistemologies*, New York: Routledge.

Harris, K. (2012, March) [Commentary on K. G. Muhammad's *The Condemnation of Blackness: Race, Crime, and the Making of Modern Urban America*], Author Meets Critics Session, Annual Meeting of the Academy of Criminal Justice Sciences, New York, NY.

Henry, S. (1999). "Is left realism a useful theory for addressing the problems of crime? No", in J.R. Fuller and E.W. Hickey (eds.) *Controversial Issues in Criminology*, Boston: Allyn and Bacon.

Higgenbotham, E. (2012). "Reflections on the early contributions of Patricia Hill Collins", *Gender & Society*, 26: 23–7.

Hill, G., and Crawford, E. (1990). "Women, race and crime", *Criminology*, 28: 601–23.

Holcomb, J.E., Williams, M.R., and Demuth, S. (2004). "White female victims and death penalty disparity research", *Justice Quarterly*, 21: 877–902.

Howe, A. (2000). "Postmodern criminology and its feminist discontents", *Australian and New Zealand Journal of Criminology*, 33: 221–36.

Humphries, D. (1999). *Crack Mothers: Pregnancy, Drugs and the Media*, Columbus: Ohio State University Press.

———. (2013). "Media, crime and gender", in C.M. Renzetti, S.L. Miller, and A.R. Gover (eds.) *Routledge International Handbook of Crime and Gender Studies*, London: Routledge.

Jones, N. (2009). " 'I was aggressive for the streets, pretty for the pictures': Gender, difference, and the inner-city girl", *Gender & Society*, 23: 89-93.

———. (2010). *Between Good and Ghetto: African American Girls and Inner-city Violence*, New Brunswick, NJ: Rutgers University Press.

Jurik, N.C., and Siemsen, C. (2009). " 'Doing gender' as canon or agenda: A symposium on West and Zimmerman", *Gender & Society*, 23: 72-5.

Kessler, S.J. (1996). "The medical construction of gender: Case management of intersexed infants", in B. Laslett, S.G. Kohlstedt, H. Longino, and E. Hammonds (eds.) *Gender and Scientific Authority*, Chicago: University of Chicago Press.

King, D.K. (1988). "Multiple jeopardy, multiple consciousness: The context of black feminist ideology", *Signs*, 14: 42-72.

Landrine, H. (1985). "Race x class stereotypes of women", *Sex Roles*, 13: 65-75.

Laslett, B., and Brenner, J. (2000). "Twenty-first century academic feminism in the United States: Utopian visions and practical actions", *Signs*, 25: 1231-36.

Lea, J., and Young, J. (1984). *What is to Be Done About Law and Order?* New York: Penguin.

Lee, S.M. (1993). "Racial classifications and the U.S. census, 1890-1990", *Ethnic and Racial Studies*, 16: 75-94.

Lorber, J. (2005). *Breaking the Bowls: Degendering and Feminist Change*, New York: W.W. Norton.

———. (2009). *Gender Inequality: Feminist Theory and Politics*, New York: Oxford University Press.

———. (1993). *Masculinities and Crime*, Lanham, MD: Rowman & Littlefield.

———. (1995). *From Patriarchy to Gender: Feminist Theory, Criminology, and the Challenge of Diversity*, Philadelphia: Open University Press.

———. (1997). *Crime as Structured Social Action: Gender, Race, Class, and Crime in the Making*, Thousand Oaks, CA: SAGE.

———. (2000). *Nine Lives: Adolescent Masculinity, The Body, and Violence*, Boulder, CO: Westview.

———. (2002). "On gang girls, gender, and a structured action theory: A reply to Miller", *Theoretical Criminology*, 6: 461-75.

Miller, J. (1998). "Up it up: Gender and the accomplishment of street robbery", *Criminology*, 36: 37-66.

———. (2001). *One of the Guys: Girls, Gangs and Gender*, New York: Oxford University Press.

———. (2002). "The strengths and limits of 'doing gender' for understanding street crime", *Theoretical Criminology*, 6: 433-60.

———. (2008). *Getting Played: African American Girls, Urban Inequality, and Gendered Violence*, New York: New York University Press.

Muhammad, K.G. (2010). *The Condemnation of Blackness: Race, Crime, and the Making of Modern Urban America*, Cambridge, MA: Harvard University Press.

Naffine, N. (1995). "Criminal conversation", *Law and Critique*, 6: 193-207.

———. (2002). "In praise of legal feminism", *Legal Studies*, 22: 77–101.

Perry, B. (2001). *In the Name of Hate: Understanding Hate Crime*, New York: Routledge.

Potter, H. (2006). "An argument for black feminist criminology: Understanding African American women's experiences with intimate partner violence using an integrated approach", *Feminist Criminology*, 1: 106–24.

———. (2008). *Battle Cries: Black Women and Intimate Partner Violence*, New York: New York University Press.

Preves, S.E. (2003). *Intersex and Identity: The Contested Self*, New Brunswick, NJ: Rutgers University Press.

Ransby, B. (2000). "Black feminism at twenty-one: Reflections on the evolution of a national community", *Signs*, 25: 1215–21.

———. (2011a). "Economic issues and intimate partner violence", in C.M.

Renzetti, C.M., Curran, D.J., and Meier, S.L. (2012). *Women, Men, and Society: The Sociology of Gender*, 6th ed., Boston: Allyn and Bacon.

Rice, M. (1990). "Challenging orthodoxies in feminist theory: A black feminist critique", in L. Gelsthorpe and A. Morris (eds.) *Feminist Perspectives in Criminology*, Philadelphia: Open University Press.

Richie, B. (1996). *Compelled to Crime*, New York: Routledge.

———. (2012). *Arrested Justice: Black Women, Violence, and America's Prison Nation,* New York: New York University Press.

———. (2009). "From doing to undoing: Gender as we know it", *Gender & Society*, 23: 81–4.

Rudy, K. (2000). "Difference and indifference: A U.S. feminist response to global politics", *Signs*, 25: 1051–54.

Shouse Law Group (2012). "California three strikes law explained by criminal defense attorneys". Retrieved from http://www.shouselaw.com/three-strikes.html.

———. (1991). "Caste, class and violent crime: Explaining differences in female offending", *Criminology*, 33: 47–81.

———. (1990). "Feminist approaches to criminology: Or postmodern woman meets atavistic man", in L. Gelsthorpe and A. Morris (eds.) *Feminist Perspectives in Criminology*, Milton Keynes, UK: Open University Press.

Spohn, C., and Brennan, P.K. (2013). "Sentencing and punishment", in C.M. Renzetti, S.L. Miller, and A.R. Gover (eds.) *Routledge International Handbook of Crime and Gender Studies*, London: Routledge.

Stroud, A. (2012). "Good guys with guns: Hegemonic masculinity and concealed handguns", *Gender & Society*, 26: 216–38.

Thompson, B. (2002). "Multiracial feminism: Recasting the chronology of second wave feminism", *Feminist Studies*, 28: 337–60.

Websdale, N. (2001). *Policing the Poor: From Slave Plantation to Public Housing*, Boston: Northeastern University Press.

West, C., and Fenstermaker, S. (1995). "Doing difference", *Gender & Society*, 9: 8–37.

West, C., and Zimmerman, D.H. (1987). "Doing gender", *Gender & Society*, 1: 125–51.

———. (2009). "Accounting for doing gender", *Gender & Society*, 23: 112–22.

Williams, M.R., Demuth, S., and Holcomb, J.E. (2007). "Understanding the influence of victim gender in death penalty cases: The importance of victim race, sex-related victimization, and jury decision making", *Criminology*, 45: 865–91.

Wing, A.K. (ed.) (2003). *Critical Race Feminism: A Reader* (2nd ed.), New York: New York University Press.

Wonders, N.A. (1999). "Postmodern feminist criminology and social justice", in B.A. Arrigo (ed.) *Social Justice, Criminal Justice*, Belmont, CA: Wadsworth.

Wood, K. (2012, April/May). "Women of color, the pressure not to report, and sisterhood", *Domestic Violence Report*, 17: 49–50, 57–9.

Yuval-Davis, N. (2012). "Dialogical epistemology—an intersectional resistance to the 'oppression olympics'", *Gender & Society*, 26: 46–54.

SECTION B
Critical Criminology

READING 14

The History of Critical Criminology in the United States

Raymond Michalowski

Introduction

In 1915 the literary historian Van Wyck Brooks (1915, p. 339) observed that history is the "search for a usable past." Brook's view that writing history is a selective assembling of the past so as to render it useful in building some desired future recognizes that history is always the product of authors who necessarily write from some standpoint.

In keeping with this vision of historiography, I acknowledge that the history of critical criminology in the United States that I offer here is the story as I tell it, shaped by the vantage points from which I experienced it. My vantage point begins as a young scholar drawn to radical criminology in the early 1970s, who a decade later participated in the routinization of U.S. critical criminology through the creation of a Division of Critical Criminology (DCC) within the American Society of Criminology (ASC). My perspective is also shaped by 40 years of writing, editing, and organizational activity in radical and critical criminology, my personal linkages to other critical criminologists, and my work with social movements and non-governmental organizations seeking social justice. Others with different vantage points would likely write a different history, slanting the attention this way or that, giving greater attention to some events or publications to which I give less, and less to some that I give more. This is to be expected. It is the way of historiography.

In seeking a usable past for critical criminology in the United States, I am particularly interested in learning what an intellectual movement born in an era that coupled social upheaval with optimism about a progressive future can tell us about our present age, a time when significant conflicts between classes, races, and sexes operate, less as sources for collective social action, and more as subterranean tensions beneath the hegemony of neo-liberal capitalism at a time when there is little political appetite for progressive solutions to crime and other social problems.

Raymond Michalowski, "The History of Critical Criminology in the United States," *Routledge Handbook of Critical Criminology*, ed. Walter S. DeKeseredy and Molly Dragiewicz, pp. 32-45. Copyright © 2012 by Taylor & Francis Group. Reprinted with permission.

Framing History

Historiography raises a number of questions. There is the matter of periodization. When did the particular "history" in question begin? Another is localization. Where did history happen? Yet another is characterization. Who made history happen?

Histories of intellectual movements often focus primarily on the evolution of some set of ideas. The individuals who circulated the ideas and the organizational arrangements that made this circulation possible are often treated mainly as conduits of intellectual development rather than integral to it. In contrast, the perspective I bring here presumes that context, people, and organizations play significant roles in the development of schools of thought. Thus, the story I tell gives particular attention to two cities, two time periods, and two groups of people. The cities are Berkeley and Chicago. The times are the early 1970s and the mid-1980s. The people are those who were part of the Union of Radical Criminology (URC) and those who participated in the creation of the DCC within the ASC. For sure, the entire history of U.S. critical criminology is not encompassed by these particular places, times, and people. However, as many more recent developments are discussed in other chapters in this volume, I focus here primarily on the first 20 years of critical criminology in the United States, roughly from 1968 to 1988. My central question is "How did the 'radical criminology' of the 1970s, characterized by historical-materialist methods and socialist politics, evolve by the turn of the century into a polyvocal critical criminology comprising three overlapping meta-theoretical frameworks: historical materialism, identity, and ideation (see Figure 14.1).

Historical materialism characterizes the early years of "radical criminology" with its focus on the role of social class, class conflict, and capitalist state formation in shaping the social construction of crime and the normative practices justice. Key foci within this perspective include instrumentalist, structuralist, and post-structuralist Marxian approaches to state and law, analyses of the political economy of crime and punishment, studies of crimes

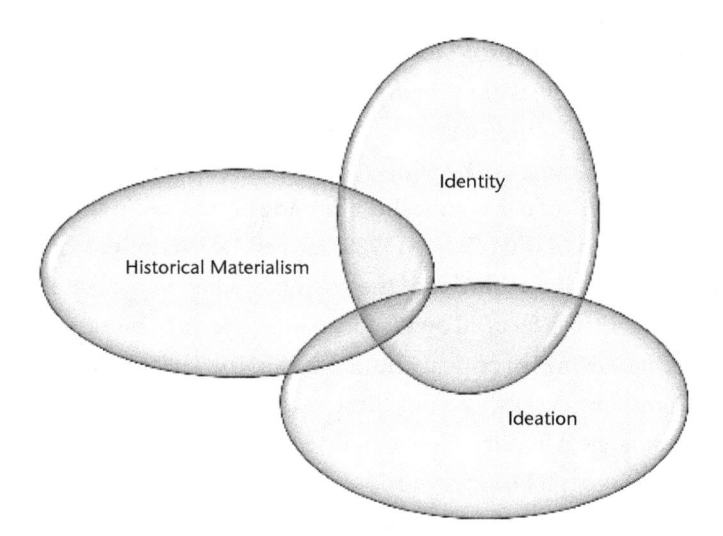

Figure 14.1 The meta-theoretical frameworks of critical criminology. Historical materialism: (a) instrumental and structural Marxism, (b) political economy of crime and punishment, (c) corporate, state and political crime, (d) state and ideology. Identity: (a) women and crime, (b) gender and justice, (c) critical race theory, (d) queer theory, (e) ethnicity, (f) youth and crime. Idealism: (a) moral panics, (b) media and crime, (c) subcultures, (d) cultural criminology, (e) constitutive criminology, (f) semiotics.

of power such as corporate crime, state crime, and state–corporate crime, and inquiries into the relationship between state and ideology.

The meta-framework of *identity* replaces social class as the central explanatory force shaping deviant behavior and justice policies with one or more key components of personhood, such as gender, race, ethnicity, age, or sexual orientation. Within this framework we find liberal, radical, Marxist, socialist, and post-modern feminism, critical race/ethnicity theory, queer theory, and critical studies of youth deviance.

Ideation refers to approaches that focus specifically on communicative structures, mass-mediated imagery, subcultures, social resistance, and style. Analyses of moral panics, studies of the intersections between mass media and fear of crime, critical inquiries into subcultures, cultural criminology, constitutive criminology, and the semiotics of law and justice figure prominently in this framework.

As indicated by the areas of overlap, the meta-frameworks in Figure 14.1 are not wholly discrete. For example, Marxist and socialist feminist criminologies are located somewhere in the overlap between historical materialism and identity, while studies of youth subculture styles blend the perspectives of ideation and identity.

Figure 14.1 is not meant to suggest the relative size or importance of the different meta-theoretical frameworks in terms of their respective influences on contemporary critical criminology insofar as the influence of each of these meta-frameworks has fluctuated over time. Rather, Figure 14.1 is best seen as a taxonomy for identifying the major frames of critical criminological inquiry and locating key research foci within them.

Figure 14.1 does suggest a rough timeline with respect to the emergence of the different meta-theoretical frameworks within U.S. critical criminology. Specifically, the historical materialism characteristic of early radical criminology emerged in the late 1960s as the first appearance in the United States of what Cohen (1988) termed "anti-criminology." Identity theories, particularly feminist criminology and critical race theory, followed on in the late 1970s and early 1980s. By the mid-1980s critical writings focused on the ideational aspects of moral panics, mass media, and subcultures were entering the mix of critical criminology in the United States.[1]

Contemporarily, each of these meta-theoretical frameworks is a vibrant location for critical criminological inquiry. However, three important changes have transpired since the early 1970s. One is that, although historical-materialist and political-economic analyses remain an active component of critical criminology, the predominant image of critical criminology since the mid-1990s has come to center around analyses focused on ideation and identity. The second is that the organizational framework for U.S. anti-criminology evolved from being concentrated primarily within the DCC to one in which many critical criminologists concerned with the intersections of identity, deviance, and justice are now more closely affiliated with the ASC's divisions on Women and Crime and People of Color and Crime. The third change is that academic subspecialization has rendered critical criminology subspecialties more self-contained than was the case within radical criminology during the 1968–88 period.

Early Developments: 1968–76

In contrast to the constellation of sometimes overlapping and sometimes discrete orientations we find today, critical criminology began as a somewhat more homogeneous radical intellectual movement in the United States and Great Britain in the 1960s.[2] In the United States, a small group of criminologists, animated by the social upheavals of the age, began questioning the then (and still) dominant practice of basing criminological research on state definitions of crime, and using these definitions to pursue research questions aligned with the interests of dominant classes, the state, and its subsidiary justice agencies. As an alternative, early radical criminologists created various blends of symbolic interactionism, labeling theory, Marxist political-economics, and critiques of sociological positivism (Gouldner, 1970) in their search for a foundation for criminological inquiry that was internal rather than external to the discipline. The resulting "radical criminology," to use the contemporaneous name for this movement in the United States, challenged the dominant sociology of crime and justice rooted in structural-functionalist theories that emphasized equilibrium as the normal social condition (Merton, 1949; Parsons, 1951).

Since the 1940s criminology had been a structural-functionalist and liberal enterprise that accepted state definitions of crime as non-problematic, approached the justice system as a reformist project designed to rehabilitate and reintegrate criminals into what was presumed to be an otherwise well-running society, and promoted value-free behaviorist research (Cardarelli & Hicks, 1993). For most criminologists, the primary question during the first two-thirds of the twentieth century was "why did *they* do it?"—the "they" being most often working-class white gang youth, low-income men of color charged with street crimes, and minority women prosecuted for "vice" crimes. The emergent radical criminology sought to reach beyond the dominant focus on the individual causes of working-class crime by building more macro-sociological frameworks that could explicate how large-scale social structures and their related state apparatus create and reproduce systems of law and justice that shape the distribution of "criminality" by subordinating those whose presence, pleasures, or predations are perceived as threats to the dominant order, while choosing to define most of the harms committed by political, economic, and cultural elites as acceptable, and sometimes even laudable behavior (Michalowski, 2009).

Early radical criminology differed from its putatively value-free, behaviorist predecessors in three very significant ways. First, it utilized expressly Marxist theories as a basis for its inquiries (Groves & Sampson, 1986). Insofar as class *conflict* is arguably the fundamental theoretical starting point of Marxian social analysis, incorporating Marxist models of society into criminology constituted a fundamental break with the dominant structural-functionalist presumption that societies were rooted in equilibrium. Second, early radical criminologists were explicit in their intention to use criminological inquiry as a vehicle to further the development of a more socialist society (Platt, 1974). Third, early radical criminologists frequently took partisan roles on behalf of those they saw as victims of the capitalist justice system. Radical criminologists actively participated in local struggles to advance the interests of the poor, African Americans, prisoners, and female victims of rape (Shank, 1999). This commitment, which James Inciardi (1980, p. 1), a leading mainstream critic of radical criminology, dismissed as "over identification with the underdog," violated the positivist mandate that criminologists eschew so-called "ideological" commitments in favor of putative "value-neutral" inquiry.

The Marxism of early radical criminology in the United States was not an intellectual outgrowth of some existing Marxist intellectual tradition in U.S. universities because there was no Marxist tradition in the U.S. universities. The repression of Marxist scholars, first during the Red Scare of the 1920s, and then the McCarthy era of the 1950s and early 1960s, negated any continuum of Marxist thought in the U.S. Academy comparable to that in British and European universities (Caute, 1978; Schrecker, 1985).[3]

In the absence of a ready Marxist tradition, early U.S. radical criminologists drew from other intellectual sources as well as from Marxist writings. One was a non-Marxist conflict criminology based in the conflict sociology of Coser (1956), Dahrendorf (1959), and Mills (1956). Before the emergence of a distinctly radical criminology in the United States, some criminologists had deployed social conflict perspectives to analyses of crime and justice (see, for example, Chambliss, 1964; Chambliss & Siedman, 1971; Hills, 1971; Quinney 1970; Sellin, 1938; Turk, 1969; Vold, 1958).

Like later radical criminologists, conflict criminologists recognized the significance of social class in determining who would be positioned to make law and who would most likely feel its weight. Unlike radical criminologists, their analysis was more Weberian than Marxist. That is, they approached social class as a set of complex, shifting interest groups aligned along a broad continuum of prestige, status, and wealth, rather than as more categorical social groupings defined by location with respect to the ownership and control of means of production (Domhoff, 1990; Wright, 1985). For conflict criminologists, conflict was a normal characteristic of modern societies resulting from their complex divisions of labor and uneven distributions of material wealth. For Marxist criminologists, these conflicts were not automatically occurring offshoots of modernity; they resulted from the efforts of a small class of powerful political-economic actors to ensure their class would retain its control over the life conditions of all other classes.

Despite these important differences, early radical criminology owes a significant and often unrecognized intellectual debt to the work of conflict theorists who first challenged the dominance of structural-functionalist thought in mid-twentieth-century U.S. criminology. Most importantly, these early conflict criminologists laid the foundations for a "definitional" paradigm in criminology. As Blum-West and Carter (1983) observe, the central project of the definitional paradigm is to understand how some harms become "crimes," that is, targets for state control, while others do not. This contrasts with the focus of the "behavioral" paradigm on why some people engage in behaviors that the state has defined as crimes. Although radical and critical criminologists significantly expanded the definitional paradigm, conflict criminologists were the first to challenge the ontology of crime, transforming it from a meta-theoretical foundation for criminological inquiry into a social construct in need of explanation.

The emergence of a distinctly Marxist radical criminology in the United States was also an artifact of the political ferment of the 1960s and early 1970s. Although some of the early founders of critical criminology were established scholars who migrated leftward from earlier standpoints within conflict criminology, the rank-and-file of the emergent radical criminology consisted of newer scholars whose relatively recent transition into adulthood had been marked by what many historians have termed the "Spirit of '68," a feeling of rebellion and a sense that widespread human liberation was just around the corner. Horn (2007, p. 2) characterizes this era as a time when "idealism was far more universal than cynicism and nihilism," when young activists believed they could "construct a different and more egalitarian social order, a world where company and university paternalism were to make way for workers' control, student power, and generalized self-management of all walks of life." Revolutionary moments such as these tend to be dominated by powerful emotions and attractive new styles of action (Kushner, 2008). Many young scholars in the late 1960s and early 1970s, like many others in their age cohort, were drawn to the fearful excitement and hope that they could play a pivotal role in making a better future for their nation and the world.

By the 1980s, the Spirit of '68, with its hopes for sweeping social change, was on its way to becoming a nostalgic memory, as it was gradually replaced by a more cynical, neo-liberal view of social life. Those who retained a commitment to alternative visions of the future began to focus their energies less on sweeping national reforms and more on localized struggles for change (Boyt, 1981).

The decline of the Spirit of '68 in the United States was due in part to its role in bringing down the presidency of Lyndon Johnson and to the eventual end of the Vietnam War (Gitlin, 1993). By the 1970s, anti-war struggles had come to dominate what began as a more broadly focused U.S. student movement aimed at combining students and workers into a political force to promote socialist policies (Hayden, 2005). With the war over, movement exhaustion set in. The broader socialist goals of pre-war student politics, largely lost from sight during the anti-war years, were never recaptured as a national political agenda.

Three other factors, however, figured equally, if not more importantly, in dampening the Spirit of '68. First, by the late 1970s, U.S. global economic dominance was in decline as the capitalist countries of Europe and Asia emerged as significant economic competitors once recovered from the material and social devastation of World War II. Declining rates of profit in the United States led to a fundamental restructuring of the U.S. political economy, including reducing the power of labor to a point where it could no longer protect the economic gains it had made during and after World

War II, let alone support egalitarian social and economic policies typical of the Spirit of '68 (Gordon, Edwards, & Reich, 1982).

Second, labor discontent was channeled to the political right by an orchestrated backlash against civil rights and environmental movements, creating a new anti-progressive political culture within a significant proportion of the U.S. working class. Conservative opinion-makers claimed that civil rights and anti-discrimination laws would cost white workers jobs and promotions because of the "special rights" being given to African Americans. Other conservatives argued that environmental regulations would destroy the industrial base that employed much of the white working class. The result was a significant shift of working-class voters away from the Democratic party and toward a Republican party increasingly characterized by a conservative economic and cultural agenda (Block, Cloward, & Ehrenreich, 1987). This conservative turn in U.S. politics ended the era of normative liberalism that began with the presidency of Franklin Roosevelt. In its place there emerged a conservative cultural and political climate that saw egalitarian social change as unaffordable, unnatural, and undesirable.

Third, the collapse of the Soviet Union and anything resembling a socialist bloc ushered in an era of capitalist triumphalism in which calls for social justice were increasingly dismissed by political leaders and opinion-makers as the irrelevant babblings of "leftists" who refused to accept that "socialism does not work." By portraying calls to expand social justice as a pathway to repeating the failed practices of the Soviet Union, neo-liberal, conservative, and right-wing politicians in the United States fashioned a powerful weapon to mobilize the working class against policies such as health-care reform and greater regulation over business that would actually benefit the working class. The ability of conservatives to successfully portray U.S. President Barack Obama as a "socialist" shortly after his election in 2008, even though most of his agenda was, at best, centrist by European standards, is a particularly sharp example of how far to the right the United States had moved from the Spirit of '68.

At the time of this writing in 2010, most of those who were directly involved in the progressive social movements of the 1960s and early 1970s are in their late fifties or older. Those now in their forties had barely reached their early teenage years by the time these movements had begun to fade. From the vantage point of the early twenty-first century in the United States, dominated by hyper-materialism, militarism, conservative ideology, and racism recoded as an anti-immigration sentiment, the hopes for a more egalitarian, less materialist, and more peaceful country that animated the Spirit of '68 can seem naïve or foolish to anyone who was not there—and that probably includes many reading these words. There was, however, a reason for the optimism of the young activists, including the early radical criminologists, who both experienced and created the progressive movements of the 1960s and 1970s. As young adults they had witnessed fundamental changes, and most of these seemed to point toward a new age of human liberation and social integration.

After the end of World War II, anti-colonial struggles in European colonies in Africa, India, and Southeast Asia wrested independence from once invincible overlords. In 1959, a small band of leftist fighters overthrew a U.S.-backed dictator in Cuba, and within five years began reorganizing the country in order to provide universal health care, education, employment, and social security. By the mid-1960s, the U.S. civil rights movement, with activist students playing important roles, was successfully challenging segregation in a number of venues, bringing social and legal changes that would alter the public and political face of the South. The student "Free Speech" emanating from Berkeley galvanized students around the country to challenge curricula, academic policies, and university ties to the military–industrial complex. By the late 1960s university students had also taken the lead in an increasingly broad anti-war movement.

The sexual revolution, ushered in by the availability of reliable birth control, had fractured the more rigid sexual mores of previous generations, inaugurating a new era of sexual exploration and openness. What was then know as "the women's movement" was challenging everyday patriarchies and changing how young men and women related to one another, while a fledgling gay rights movement had begun to confront that most absolute bastion of patriarchy, normative heterosexuality (Diski, 2009).

For young people who had been raised within a profoundly racist, sexist, militarist, sexually repressed, and authoritarian society, these were not small changes. In their short lifetimes, those caught up in the Spirit of '68 saw seemingly fixed components of U.S. society and culture radically altered. If established racial, sexual, educational, and geo-political dynamics could be changed, it seemed reasonable to many young people that creating a society organized around cooperative principles of socialism rather than competitive ones of capitalism was the future.

I suggest that it is not possible to understand the energy, socialist commitments, passion, and occasional excesses of early radical criminology—such as the moment at the 1974 ASC meeting when a prominent radical criminologist called a prominent mainstream criminologist "a racist pig," and stormed out of the room—without appreciating the climate of the age. Many early radical criminologists incorporated Marxist theory and Marxist politics into their work, not because they had been reared in radical traditions, but because Marxism seemed to offer the best set of explanations for the oppressions against which the Spirit of '68 struggled, and the best set of options for an alternative vision of society. Their crystal ball proved murky on a number of accounts. Nevertheless, these early attempts to link Marxism to criminology were to have a lasting effect on the field.

Berkeley, Backlash and *Social Justice*

In 1965, criminology graduate students at Berkeley, influenced by the Free Speech movement, established a student journal, *Issues in Criminology*, as a venue for articles challenging dominant criminological thinking. One of the foundational manifestos of radical criminology, "Defenders of Order or Guardians of Human Rights" (Schwendinger & Schwendinger, 1970) was first published in *Issues*.

By the early 1970s, progressive faculty and students at the Berkeley School of Criminology were deeply involved in local social movements such as the struggle for "People's Park," efforts to bring Berkeley police under community control, and the Bay Area Women Against Rape. In 1971, a group of criminology students and faculty at Berkeley founded the Union of Radical Criminologists (URC) with the goal of creating a national organization of criminologists that would promote radical ideas and solidarity with progressive community organizations (Shank, 1999).

The URC published several inquiries into policing: *Policing America* (Platt & Cooper, 1972) and *The Iron Fist and the Velvet Glove* (Platt et al., 1975). It also constituted the apex of radical criminology in the Berkeley School of Criminology. Troubled by the growing radicalism of faculty and students, particularly students associated with Tony Platt, Herman Schwendinger, Julia Schwendinger, and Paul Takagi, in 1976 the University of California administration closed the school. Tenured professors were relocated to other departments. Those without the protection of tenure such as Platt and the Schwendingers lost their appointments, and subsequently were never offered university positions that enabled them to educate doctoral students. This, however, did not end their influence on criminology.

Rather than being a crushing blow to the development of U.S. radical criminology, repression of the Berkeley School of Criminology became a rallying point for anti-criminologists. At the moment the School of Criminology teetered on the brink of closure, URC spread nationally through its publications and via the ASC. The ASC meeting in Chicago in 1974 proved to be a watershed moment for the development of U.S. radical criminology. In addition to heated debates between orthodox and radical criminologists, the meeting resulted in the creation of a mailing list of interested criminologists, most of whom were outside the Berkeley orbit. This list evolved into an informal newsletter linking emerging radical criminologists in the United States and United Kingdom.[4] What had been once been a localized collective was now a broader-based intellectual movement.

Within this same time frame, the journal *Crime and Social Justice* replaced the former *Issues in Criminology*. The new journal, independent of UC-Berkeley but under the editorial direction of many of the school's former faculty and students, began publishing radical theory and research in criminology and analyses of community struggles for social justice. As the first radical/critical journal in criminology, *Crime and Social Justice*[5] paved the way for others that would eventually follow, such as *Contemporary Crises* (now *Crime, Law and Social Change*), *Human Justice*, and *Critical Criminology*. It also provided an outlet for the academic writings of radical criminologists when more mainstream journals rejected their work as unsuitable for "serious" criminological discourse, making it possible for many to maintain academic careers.

It is possible that a critical criminology might have emerged in the United States without the influence of the Berkeley collective, URC, and *Crime and Social Justice*. This counter-factual, however, in no way minimizes the actual role these people and events played in bringing anti-criminology to the consciousness of U.S. criminologists.

From Radical to Critical Criminology

From the beginning, the adjectives "radical" and "critical" have always been problematic descriptors for anti-criminology. Even as the Union of Radical Criminology was expanding its influence, writers such as Gresham Sykes (1974) and Taylor, Walton, and Young (1975) were writing about the development of "critical" criminology. To further muddy the waters, most of the works that came to be understood as critical criminology had relatively little intellectual linkages to critical theory in sociology as developed by the Frankfurt School (Groves & Sampson, 1986). Nevertheless, by the late 1980s, the term "radical criminology" had been largely displaced by "critical criminology." This shift in naming anti-criminology in the United States, I suggest, was animated by two factors. One was strategic. The other reflected the emergence of new ideas and an attendant growth in criminological subspecialization.

Strategic Factors

At the 1988 ASC meeting in (once again) Chicago, a group of about 30 radical criminologists gathered to discuss requesting a separate division within the society. After considerable debate the group agreed on "critical criminology" as the name of the proposed division. This decision was motivated significantly by the belief of many participants that the ASC would not approve a division with "radical" as its descriptor. Like an earlier decision by the Union of Radical Sociology (Levine, 2004), those favoring "critical" argued that this term would help minimize opposition from the ASC leadership for two reasons. First, it was not as directly linked with a Marxist approach as was radical criminology. Second, "critical" implied an academic undertaking rather than one committed to direct activism and social change.

I think it is fair to say that most of those debating the new division's name were committed to using criminological inquiry to challenge and transform systems of domination in the wider social order, rather than being proponents of knowledge-for-its-own-sake forms of scholarly inquiry. Indeed, most in the room that day were veterans of political struggles in their communities, the Academy, and the national stage. Many, also accepted, however, that securing a separate ASC division would be difficult enough without the criticisms of being ideological and unscholarly that would attach to any proposal that contained the term "radical."

In addition to the strategic concern with avoiding backlash, there were also suggestions that "critical criminology" would imply a bigger theoretical tent. The reasoning was that, although "radical criminology" implied a primary focus on Marxist approaches, a number of newer anti-criminologists, particularly feminists, were challenging the dominant order from frameworks that were not expressly (or exclusively) Marxist or political-economic in nature. The idea of creating a welcoming organizational home for all anti-criminologists was appealing. When coupled with the concern with avoiding backlash, it sealed the adoption of "critical criminology" as the organizational name for the division.

Words matter. The ASC approved the creation of a Division of Critical Criminology. It is unlikely it would have accepted a Division of Radical Criminology. The shift of names also broadened the division's appeal beyond Marxist criminology. As a consequence, for a brief time the DCC became an important site for interaction between Marxist and feminist criminologists, so much so that its first chair, Susan Caringella, was a feminist criminologist. The term "critical" also implied a more esoteric and scholarly organization. Over time, engaging in political activism became less of a common marker among division members than engaging in critical scholarship. Although many division members continued to be social activists and public intellectuals, the forces of history and the pressures of contemporary academic life gradually rendered critical criminology a more scholastic enterprise than its radical predecessor.

The name "critical criminology" became a handy term of art embracing many varieties of anti-criminology. Because it is a sliding signifier—an "empty center of meaning" in Lacan's (1977, p. 27) terms—divergent anti-criminology subspecialists can all see themselves reflected in the term "critical criminology." If intellectual diversity, like biological diversity, is an important key to long-term survival, the selection of a vague name for U.S. anti-criminology may have been a wiser move than anyone thought that day in Chicago.

Substantive Factors

Although the selection of a name "critical criminology" may have been strategic, it also reflected the evolution of U.S. anti-criminology into a more polyvocal endeavor. The majority of early radical criminological analyses were typically informed by "plain Marxist" approaches that addressed issues of crime and justice as manifestations of political-economic structures designed to facilitate the reproduction of free-market and state-capitalist societies (Balbus, 1977; Chambliss, 1990; Pearce, 1976; Quinney, 1977; Spitzer, 1975). Rather quickly, radical criminology moved beyond these early Marxist models to encompass a plethora of theories focused on independent forces at play within the complex social dynamics of power, justice, and lived human experience (Morrison, 1995).

In less than a decade after the publication of the earliest writings in radical criminology, it was no longer accurate to speak of *a* radical or *a* critical criminology, for what had emerged was many anti-criminologies co-existing side by side, sometimes intersecting, and sometimes generating independent literatures with little substantive overlap. Just as the larger discipline of criminology—essentially a subspecialty of sociology—had fractured in its early years into many sub-subspecialties, critical criminology, as yet another subspecialty of criminology, subdivided inquiry even further.

Between 1985 and 1986 three books were published that, I suggest, are emblematic of the evolution that was under way in U.S. anti-criminology at that juncture. Each represented a comprehensive application of one of the frameworks shown in Figure 14.1. My work, *Order, Law and Crime* (Michalowski, 1985) was a core text in criminology grounded in an explicitly historical-materialist framework. Pfohl's (1985) *Images of Deviance and Social Control* was a similarly wide-ranging criminological text, but one that gave primary attention to ideational forces, particularly the social construction of cultural frameworks within which we imagine self and other, normalcy and deviance. Finally, Messerschmidt's

(1986) *Capitalism, Patriarchy and Crime* was grounded in a "socialist-feminist perspective." The near simultaneous appearance of these works with their distinct lenses for criminological inquiry underscores the importance of the mid-1980s as a turning point for anti-criminology in the United States. This was the point at which the more singular Marxist criminology of the 1970s was joined by anti-criminologies of ideation and identity.

The multiplicity of critical criminologies and special topics that constitute this present book are themselves testimony to the complex mitosis that has taken place in critical criminology. To some extent this reflects a process of disciplinary specialization, fueled in part by deepening understandings of the complexity of the subject matter: state, law, crime, consciousness, and identity.

It is also fueled by institutional mandates within the contemporary Academy. Without being directly aware of it, scholars, particularly newer ones, experience pressures to identify and colonize new academic niches. As Cardarelli and Hicks (1993, p. 548) noted, the rate of expansion in journals and articles is "so overwhelming in numbers that one is forced to define one's academic interests more narrowly than at any time in the past." This leads to changes in attention as new areas of inquiry emerge and eventually become older and less attractive, leading to other, newer foci. Indeed, many of us who teach graduate students direct them to identify new areas of inquiry on which to focus theses and dissertations as a way of helping them establish their own academic careers. I suggest this not as critique, but as description, and to remind us that, although critical criminology is certainly a powerful body of ideas, for very many it is also an occupation embedded within powerful institutional frameworks whose cultures and mandates play an important role in shaping action.

Conclusion

In many ways the history of critical criminology in the United States reflects the history of the United States. Early radical criminology was an artifact of the social turmoil of the 1960s and 1970s. During this time key pillars of the dominant political, economic, military, sexual, and racial order experienced radical challenges from a variety of social movements (Piven & Cloward, 1978). Out in the streets, dominant authorities used guns, tear gas, and barricades to contain these movements. It is predictable that in this climate an emergent anti-criminology would focus on state and class conflict as its most important explanatory variables.

By the 1980s not only had the national mood tempered politically, but also many of the gains of the Spirit of '68 were appearing more complicated than they first appeared. Women were entering the workforce in greater proportions than any time since World War II, but gender bias in the workplace remained, and when these women returned home they were still expected to do the laundry. The sexual revolution had loosened many of the strictures that had distorted sexuality for young men and women in the past, yet finding meaningful and comfortable relationships with a life partner remained both desirable and challenging for many. The civil rights movement had taken down the barriers of *de jure* segregation, but racial and ethnic injustice remained powerful forces limiting the full participation of non-white minorities in U.S. society, except for continually expanding opportunities to serve time in prison. It is in this climate that inquiries into how sexual and racial identities influenced the likelihood of criminality, victimhood, and becoming ensnared (or not) in the justice system sank deep roots in critical criminology.

By the 1980s, everyone, everywhere in the United States was the continual target of mass-mediated messages, particularly marketing messages. Commodities and style, key components of "the American way of life" since the rise of consumer culture in the later decades of the nineteenth century, had become core components of self-consciousness and identity (Lears, 1995). Between the end of the nineteenth century and the last third of the twentieth, the anxieties associated with conspicuous consumption moved from a concern of the *nouveau riche,* to one that troubled white, middle-class adults struggling to "keep up with the Joneses" in post-World War II suburbs, to one that was felt across all classes and ages. By the 1980s many children feared ridicule if they went to school without wearing the preferred desired designer labels of the moment, and young urban boys found high-status basketball shoes and team jackets a motivation for assault. In a world where mass-mediated images were central to everyday life, a growing number of critical criminologists saw consciousness, communication, and culture as key forces.

There were also other factors at play in the rise of attention to ideation. One was the somewhat belated exposure of U.S. scholars to the works of French post-modernists once translations became widely available to U.S. anglophone scholars (Foucault, 1980). I suggest, however, that the attractiveness of these works and the "postmodern turn" in U.S. scholarship they triggered, a turn that eventually made its way into criminology (Arrigo, Schehr, & Milovanovic, 2005), was itself a response to the external realities of a post-modern world where image and fact were becoming indistinguishable.

U.S. critical criminology has entered its late forties. Whether this portends a mature and productive middle age or a mid-life crisis is difficult to foresee. Certainly, it remains an energetic, expanding area of inquiry informed variously by the paradigmatic areas of historical materialism, identity, and ideation. Unlike orthodox criminology, which remains focused on finding new answers for the old question of "why did they do it," critical criminology continues to build on a history of asking new and challenging questions about how power, subordination, and resistance constitute practices of state, law, crime, and justice. Contemporarily critical criminology operates within an Academy subject to powerful external pressures to eliminate the protections against politically motivated firings that the concept of "academic freedom" and the practice tenure were created to prevent (Krebs, 2008; Leiser, 1994). This change could threaten the ability of critical criminologists working in universities to pursue inquiries that challenge the dominant social order. Even if this particular threat does not mature, the current political, economic, and social climate in the United States offers limited space for approaches to law and justice animated by the Spirit of '68 that lies at the heart of critical criminology. However, history is never over. Times and social forces change. The present era in which proto-fascist ideologies, calls for ever-harsher treatment of criminals and those accused of crimes, and anti-immigrant hysteria have become accepted political discourse is not eternal. Nor does it represent, at least in my view, the deepest aspirations of humanity. These aspirations, and the political history they have produced over the long sweep of modern society, favor restraining the powerful and empowering the powerless. For this reason, critical criminology will endure and grow because, at its core, it shares with the greater mass of humanity a fundamental desire: the desire for social justice.

Notes

1. It should be noted that ideational analysis emerged earlier in the United Kingdom, particularly within the Birmingham Centre for Contemporary Cultural Studies, and there had also been some earlier work on media and crime in the United States (e.g. Fishman, 1978).

2. Although this chapter is a history of critical criminology in the United States, as is clear from the opening chapter on critical criminology in Great Britain, the U.S. scene was considerably influenced by the writings of radical scholars in the United Kingdom.

3. As one example of this lack of a Marxist tradition, I obtained a Ph.D. in a department ranked among the top ten in sociology in the United States in 1974 without *any* professor ever suggesting that I read *any* work by Karl Marx or other Marxian analysts. This absence of Marxist thought in U.S. universities as late as the early 1970s differed from the European and British contexts, where Marxist thought had continued to be part of the intellectual environment in the decades following World War II, despite the Cold War.

4. In the interests of full disclosure I should note that I proposed this mailing list and newsletter, and for a time managed this particular line of communications among the emergent national network of radical criminologists.

5. The journal continues to publish under the name of *Social Justice*.

References

Arrigo, B., Schehr, R. & Milovanovic, D. (2005). *The French connection in criminology: Rediscovering crime, law, and social change*. Albany, NY: SUNY Press.

Balbus, I. D. (1977). Commodity form and legal form: An essay on the "relative autonomy" of the law. *Law & Society Review, 11*(3), 571–588.

Block, F., Cloward, R. A., & Ehrenreich, B. (1987). *Mean season*. New York: Pantheon.

Blum-West, S., & Carter, T. J. (1983). Bringing white collar crime back in: An examination of crimes and torts. *Social Problems, 30*(5), 545–554.

Boyt, H. C. (1981). *The backyard revolution: Understanding the new citizen movement.* Philadelphia: Temple University Press.

Brooks, V. W. (1918). On creating a usable past. *Dial, 64,* April 11.

Cardarelli, A. P., & Hicks. S. C. (1993). Racialism in law and criminology: A retrospective view of critical legal studies and radical criminology. *Journal of Criminal Law and Criminology, 84*(3), 502–553.

Caute, D. (1978). *The great fear: The anti-communist purge under Truman and Eisenhower.* New York: Simon and Schuster.

Chambliss. W. J. (1964). A sociological analysis of the law of vagrancy. *Social Problems,* Summer, 67–77.

Chambliss, W. J. (1990). Toward a radical criminology. In D. Kairys (Ed.), *The politics of law: A progressive critique* (pp. 242–297). New York: Basic Books.

Chambliss, W. J., & Siedman, R. (1971). *Law, order, and power.* Reading, MA: Addison-Wesley.

Cohen, S. (1988). *Against criminology.* New Brunswick, NJ: Transaction.

Coser, L. (1956). *The functions of social conflict.* New York: Free Press.

Dahrendorf, R. (1959). *Class and class conflict in industrial society.* Palo Alto, CA: Stanford University Press.

Diski, J. (2009). *The sixties.* New York: Picador.

Domhoff, G. W. (1990). *The power elite and the state: How policy is made in America.* Hawthorne, NY: Alidine de Gruyter.

Fishman, M. (1978). Crime waves as ideology. *Social Problems, 25*(5), 531–543.

Foucault, M. (1980). *Power/knowledge: Selected interviews and other writings, 1972–1977.* New York: Pantheon.

Gitlin, T. (1993). *The sixties: Years of hope, days of rage.* New York: Bantam.

Gordon, D., Edwards, D., & Reich, M. (1982). *Segmented work, divided workers: The historical transformation of labor in the United States.* London: Cambridge University Press.

Gouldner, A. (1970). *The coming crisis of Western sociology.* New York: Basic Books.

Groves, B. W., & Sampson, R. J. (1986). Critical theory and criminology. *Social Problems, 33*(6), 58–80.

Hayden, T. (2005). *The Port Huron statement: The vision call of the 1960s revolution.* New York: Public Affairs Press.

Hills, S. (1971). *Crime, power and morality.* Scranton, PA: Chandler.

Horn, G. R. (2007). *The Spirit of '68: Rebellion in Western Europe and North America, 1956–1976.* New York: Oxford University Press.

Indicardi, J. A. (1980). *Radical criminology: The coming crisis.* Thousand Oaks, CA: Sage.

Krebs, P. (2008) The future of tenure. AAUP Academe OnLine. Available at http://www.aaup.org/AAUP/pubsres/academe/2008/SO/col/fte.htm (accessed October 12, 2010).

Kushner, R. (2008). *Telex from Cuba.* New York: Scribner.

Lacan, J. (1977). The agency of the letter in the unconscious or reason since Freud, in *Écrits: A selection,* translated by A. Sheridan. New York: W. W. Norton.

Lears, J. (1995). *Fables of abundance.* New York: Basic Books.

Leiser, B. M. (1994) Threats to academic freedom and tenure. *Pace Law Review*. Available at http://www.aaup.org/AAUP/pubsres/academe/2008/SO/col/fte.htm (accessed October 11, 2010).

Levine, R. (2004). *Enriching the sociological imagination: How radical sociology changed the discipline*. Leiden, the Netherlands: Brill.

Merton, R. K. (1949). *Social theory and social structure*. New York: Free Press.

Messerschmidt, J. (1986). *Capitalism, patriarchy and crime*. Lanham, MD: Rowman & Littlefield.

Michalowski, R. J. (1985). *Order, law and crime*. New York: Random House.

Michalowski, R. J. (2009). Power, crime and criminology in the new imperial age. *Crime, Law and Social Change, 51*(3–4), 303–325.

Mills, C. W. (1956). *The power elite*. New York: Free Press.

Morrison, W. (1995). *Theoretical criminology: From modernity to post-modernism*. London: Routledge-Cavendish.

Parsons, T. (1951). *The social system*. New York: MacMillan.

Pearce, F. (1976). *Crimes of the powerful*. London: Pluto Press.

Pfohl, S. (1985). *Images of deviance and social control*. New York: McGraw-Hill.

Piven, F. F., & Cloward, R. (1978) *Poor people's movements: Why they succeed, how they fail*. New York: Vintage.

Platt, T. (1974). Prospects for a radical criminology in the United States. *Crime and Social Justice, 1*, 1.

Platt, T. (1975). *The iron fist and the velvet glove*. Berkeley, CA: Synthesis Publications.

Platt, T., & Cooper, L. (1972). *Policing America*. Englewood Cliffs, NJ: Prentice Hall.

Quinney, R. (1970). *Social reality of crime*. Boston: Little Brown.

Quinney, R. (1977). *Class, state and crime*. Providence, RI: Longman.

Schrecker, E. W. (1985). *No ivory tower: McCarthyism and the universities*. New York: Oxford.

Schwendinger, H., & Schwendinger, J. (1970). Defenders of order or guardians of human rights? *Issues in Criminology, 5*(2), 123–157.

Sellin, T. (1938). *Culture conflict and crime*. New York: Social Science Research Council.

Shank, G. (1999). Looking back: Radical criminology and social movements. *Social Justice*, Summer, 4–6.

Spitzer, S. (1975). Toward a Marxian theory of deviance. *Social Problems, 22*, 638–651.

Sykes, G. M. (1974). The rise of critical criminology. *Journal of Criminal Law and Criminology, 65*(2), 206–213.

Taylor, I., Walton, P., & Young, J. (1975). *Critical criminology*. London: Routledge and Kegan Paul.

Turk, A. (1969). *Criminality and the legal order*. New York: Rand McNally.

Vold, G. (1958). *Theoretical criminology*. New York: Oxford University Press.

Wright, E. O. (1985). *Classes*. London: Verso.

READING 15

Keynote Address

Critical Criminology for a Global Age[1]

Raymond Michalowski
Northern Arizona University

A Short Preface

I want to begin by thanking all those who worked to make possible what I hope will be looked upon as the first annual Critical Criminology and Justice Studies Conference. I also want to thank the organizers for the honor of being invited to deliver the keynote address for the conference.

Being in the room that day with so many like-minded criminologists seemed a long way from the early 1970s when small groups of U.S. and British "radical criminologists"—the *bête noir* of what Don Gibbons (1979) so aptly termed "the criminological enterprise"—were struggling for, while being ambivalent about, a place within academic criminology. Today, in 2009, there is a sufficient critical mass of critical criminologists within even the relatively limited geographical reach of the Western Society of Criminology to hold a separate conference.

Stanley Cohen (1988), to my mind one of the best sociologists of criminological knowledge, has questioned whether such gains are to be lauded or lamented. It is certainly the case that while radical, critical, and feminist criminologists were scaling the ramparts of academia with some success, the forces of repressive control were successfully capturing levers of state power, unleashing thirty years of mass incarceration fueled by wars on crime, drugs, and poor people (Austin and Irwin 2000; Patillo, Weiman and Western 2004). Despite this triumph of repressive control, it remains important, nevertheless, for those of us that Cohen termed "anti-criminologists" to continue reaffirming our commitment to critical analyses and honing our public policy alternatives to unequal justice. Doing so is not academic woolgathering, as conservative politicians and managerial criminologists might suggest. It is, instead, purposeful action.

Public policy inevitably articulates the interests and consciousness of those with the positional power to determine state law, rather than codifying some pure form of scholarly knowledge or

Raymond Michalowski, "Keynote Address: Critical Criminology for a Global Age," *Western Criminology Review*, vol. 11, no. 1, pp. 3-10. Copyright © 2010 by Western Criminology Review. Reprinted with permission. Provided by ProQuest LLC. All rights reserved.

reflecting positivist visions of "evidence based" practice. Politics is always political, and justice policy is politics *par excellence* because it always announces a particular worldview about human nature and social order.

One need not have read Foucault (2003) to know that power determines what is understood as truth and that this politically determined truth is the basis for state policy. The inability of critical criminology to substantially slow the tide of state repression against the dispossessed is not a failure of intellectual effort or political commitment. Nor is it some failure to "get the message out." Speaking truth to power comes with no guarantee that power will listen. In fact, it probably comes with exactly the opposite. Small groups of dissidents, by themselves, rarely make headway against the forces of history. They can, however, create, nurture, and grow an intellectual framework that offers alternatives to a moribund system of thought and action once that system's failings become too weighty to ignore. It seems to me that this has been largely what critical criminologists have been doing these last 30 years, British "left-realists" excepted.

With the collapse of the neo-liberal dream of global economic hegemony, the burgeoning costs of a wildly overgrown justice system, and the election of the first mixed-race president in U.S. history, I think that moment for broad, public reconsideration of our justice practices might not be too far ahead. Thus, this is a timely opportunity to reflect on the challenges and promises of growing a criminology that is capable of understanding crime and justice as an expression of social order rather than as just an annoying social problem to be managed in what is otherwise the best of all possible worlds.

Key Note

Once I had agreed to be the keynote speaker for the Critical Criminology and Justice Studies Conference, I began to ponder, as is often my inclination, the *meaning* of the task before me. Long ago, as an apprentice musician, I learned that a *key note* is the lowest note in a scale, the one that determines the subsequent notes and gives its name to the scale. And I had a colloquial understanding of the idea of a *keynote* address. However, I thought that perhaps it would be interesting to consider the linguistic foundation of these terms.

Delving into my favorite source, *The Oxford English Dictionary*, I found two distinct meanings of key note when applied to the spoken word. In one, the two-word phrase "key note" is internal to the presentation, and in the other, the meaning of the single word "keynote" is external to it. When referring to the internal character of a presentation, a key note is "the leading idea of a discourse ... the prevailing tone of thought or feeling." Thus, according to a 1783 rhetoric text, "Much of the Orator's art and ability is shown, in striking properly at the commencement, the key note ... of the rest of his Oration" (OED, 2009).

When speaking of its external focus, a keynote is "an opening address, designed to state the main concerns or to set the prevailing tone for a conference" in a way that can "arouse enthusiasm or promote unity" (OED, 2009).

Thus informed, I found myself with two challenges: finding the key note, that is the leading idea that would set the tone of my presentation, and offering a keynote which would state the main concerns of the conference and arouse enthusiasm for the critical criminology project.

The key note, that is, the leading idea I settled on, is the product of a double borrowing. Drawing from an article I wrote for the first issue of *Critical Criminology,* I propose that the essence of critical criminology is the *critique of domination,* a phrase I originally borrowed from Trent Schroyer's (1973) book of the same name.

The larger keynote I hope to strike, that is, the idea around which I wish to create enthusiasm and unity, is the proposition that the essence of critical criminology's critique of domination is to challenge the epistemological foundations of orthodox criminology—specifically: (1) legal formalism, (2) methodological individualism, (3) ameliorative motivations, and (4) mass-manufactured fears.

Given the complexity of these topics and the need to complete my remarks in a reasonable number of pages, I can only offer a partial elaboration of these concepts. I hope, however, you will find them useful in thinking about the character, purpose, and I would dare to say, the rightness, of our endeavors to transform criminology from a tool of political control to one of human liberation.

The Critique of Domination

Critical criminology is engaged in a critique of domination insofar as it seeks to understand how taken-for-granted systems of control embed, circulate, and reproduce underlying structures and practices of economic, cultural, and political power. This critique of domination is found throughout critical criminology:

- In analyses of class, racial, and ethnic disparities in policing and punishment that reveal the justice system's role in preserving political-economic, racial, and ethnic domination by demonizing the harms available to subaltern classes while ignoring those that can only be perpetrated by elites.
- In studies of laws and justice practices that reveal the state's contribution to validating the domination of men over women and children, and of humans over non-human beings.
- In queer research that reveals how law and justice practices enforce normative heterosexuality.
- In studies that foreground how everyday justice talk reproduces the bio-power of the state and those who most benefit from its discipline of bodies, terrain, and social spaces.
- In the study of discrepancies between the human rights rhetoric of states and their actual human rights practices.
- And in many other criminological inquiries that recognize that law is power; that power is differentially distributed; and that any imbalances of power, whether or not deliberate in their creation, are pernicious in their practice.

The recognition of the centrality of power to all systems of state control, and a desire to reveal its operation lies, I argue, at the very heart of critical criminology. It is this concern that inevitably renders critical criminology a critique of domination. Wherever power operates behind a scrim of ideology, law, and rhetoric that obscures its existence, the not-so-simple act of revealing its presence is an unavoidable critique of the domination that power makes possible—much like revealing the Wizard of Oz or the naked emperor to the populace. Ah! The wisdom of children's stories, those wise narratives we are told to leave behind as part of "growing up."

Because it is fundamentally a critique of domination, critical criminology is inherently a politically marginalized enterprise insofar as it lies outside the dominant consciousness that informs established systems of law and taken-for-granted practices of social control. There are costs to this marginality. Far fewer will be the invitations to sit at the councils of government or to dine at the trough of government-funded research. And even when one is offered a seat or a plate, wise critical criminologists will always query how such benefits might reduce their willingness to critique the dominant authority that is favoring them.

I am not, here, eschewing participation in governmentally supported research or state-authored programs for social change, as might someone more deeply influenced by anarchist politics than myself. In the choice between progressive reform and distant revolution, I am often lured to the side of reform by the voices of immediate suffering. I am suggesting, however, that critical criminologists should remain alert to the contradiction inherent in seeking a political platform from which to make critical change, and remain cautious about the possibilities of the hidden agendas, unintended consequences, and intellectual compromises that lurk in the shadows of participation in governmentality.

Keynote: Mobilizing the Critique of Domination

While the internal keynote of my remarks is the idea that critical criminology is fundamentally a critique of domination, my mobilizing theme is setting out what I think might be a useful framework for recognizing the conceptual barriers to this critique. Those who take a critical stance to criminological inquiry have long recognized that orthodox criminology places relatively little emphasis on the greatest social harms and much on relatively smaller-scale, interpersonal forms of wrongdoing.

Most orthodox criminological inquiries focus on crimes of private greed, rage, or self-destruction. Most murderers, for instance, kill one or two people, with the occasional mass murderer killing ten or twenty. If all the criminological books, articles, and research reports devoted to analyzing these solitary killers were brought together, they would fill miles of library shelves. On the other hand, criminological analyses of political leaders who pursue wars of aggression that kill thousands or even millions of soldiers and civilians *might* fill a small shopping bag or two, if that. The same is true for the corporate and governmental designers of globalized capitalist projects, enterprises that dispossess peoples of land, livelihood, and culture in the name of profitable forms of progress. Most orthodox criminologists would find little reason to analyze the resulting political violence or economic dismemberment. When it comes to studying the dealers of death and misery, Ted Bundy and Wayne Gacy are of much more interest to most criminologists than George W. Bush, Dick Cheney, or even Osama Bin Laden.

Orthodox criminology's primary focus on small-scale crimes arises from four meta-tendencies within the discipline: legal formalism, methodological individualism, ameliorative motivations, and mass-manufactured fear.

1. *Legal formalism.* The legal formalist position holds that "law is a set of rules and principles independent of other political and social institutions" (Garner 1999:913). Within the criminological tradition, legal formalism allows crimes to appear as real, as simple facts separate from the social, political, and economic forces that give rise to the legal system that names them crimes. In Morrison's (1995) terms, "law creates its own ontology." In its extreme, a formalist ethic has been used to argue that only individuals who have been prosecuted and convicted can be appropriately studied by criminologists, for only in these instances has there been a judicial determination that both a crime and a criminal exist (Tappan 1947).

    The long-standing acceptance of legal formalism as the meta-theoretical foundation of criminology places most forms of injury resulting from organizational deviance in pursuit of economic and/or political gain beyond consideration. Insofar as those who determine the content of law are drawn from the same social register as those who manage the economic and political institutions that generate far-reaching forms of organizational deviance, legal formalism shields elites from social inquiry, protects their wrongdoings from condemnation, and clears the pathway for a managerial criminology concerned only with working class varieties of crime.

2. *Methodological individualism.* Methodological individualism is the proposition that crime arises from the private conduct of specific persons acting with a conscious design to cause harm to people or property. As a meta-theoretical assumption, methodological individualism directs the criminological gaze toward individual offenders and victims. This ensures that the focus of criminology will be crimes that can be attributed to the *mens rea* of specific wrongdoers. Harms, crimes, and social injuries rooted in organizational deviance, and I would argue that these are the true sources of the greatest social injuries, are thereby automatically excluded from mainstream criminological inquiry.

3. *Ameliorative motivations.* Historically, the dream of criminology has been to create a knowledge base that leads to the reduction of crime. The positivist promise, that knowing the cause of a problem is tantamount to envisioning its cure, can be deeply seductive to any field of inquiry that hopes to make the world better, and criminology was so seduced. The desire to ameliorate the crime problem led criminological analysts to focus primarily on those crimes they could imagine reducing through the creation of a better informed, more efficient, or fairer justice system that would minimize the common crimes of the least well-off, and/or reform wrongdoers where prevention failed.

While part of the reason for focusing on individuals arises from the tendency for legal formalism to direct criminological inquiry toward crimes of individuals, the desire for ameliorative success, I suggest, exerts an independent pressure against studying the crimes and criminogenic character of large-scale political and economic institutions. Large-scale arrangements are a poor fit with the ameliorative desires of orthodox criminology for two reasons. First, addressing them would require a deep critique of established political-economic and cultural processes, a critique that would appear to violate the canons of value neutrality fundamental to positivist inquiry. Second, the desire for quick, technical fixes wilts in the presence of seemingly unalterable or "natural" social systems. As a result, criminology's ameliorative tendencies have the ironic effect of promoting organizational deviance by normalizing its outcomes as "accidents" or acceptable risks (Perrow 1999; Vaughan 1996).

4. *Mass-mediated fear.* Given its concern with ameliorating recognized criminological problems, the criminological gaze is easily tempted in one direction or another by public fears and mass-mediated crime waves (Altheide 2002). News and entertainment media ubiquitously and continually reinforce narratives about crime and justice organized around discourses of legal formalism and methodological individualism. News and entertainment foreground stories of individual criminals who have "broken the law," naturalizing both the law and the criminal individual. As a cultural process, these communicative systems create a particular "feel for the game" when it comes to the meaning of crime and justice (Bourdieu 1998).[2] This "feel" leaves most elite and organizational deviance outside the frame of "real" crime.

As a cultural project, mass media attention to private crimes is a project of forgetting–forgetting the masses who were or are being victimized in the pursuit of domination. From *Buffalo Bill's Wild West Show* to the contemporarily popular television drama *24*, with its normalization of torture as legitimate investigative strategy, mass communications and mass entertainments have a long history of dehumanizing the victims of elite power and justifying or even celebrating elite crimes. In doing so, they normalize great wrongs such as the aerial bombing of civilians as a tool of war (Kramer 2010) or turning war into a profit center (Whyte 2010)—to the point where they are beyond criminological consciousness.

Frameworks for a Critical Criminology

Creating a criminology that is not constrained by legal formalism and the other pro-power tendencies inherent in the discipline, I suggest, might benefit from theorizing how four characteristics of contemporary bio-power are reflected in whatever specific phenomenon we are analyzing. These are:

1. Political practices are always economic.
2. Economic practices are always political.
3. Both economic and political practices are deeply cultural.
4. The forces of economics, politics, and culture are frequently ill at ease with one another.

When I say political practices are economic, I am not reverting to the instrumentalist elite domination claim that governments are little more than the "executive" of some capitalist or other economic ruling class. State managers serve political constituencies whose perceived goals at any particular moment may, or may not, comfortably coincide with those of capital managers and owners. Thus, at times, as structuralists have noted, states may pursue paths that key sectors of capital would prefer they did not (Jessop 1982; Beirne 1979; Poulantzas 1973). Nevertheless, political practices, even when they are at odds with specific economic interests, are disciplined by the fundamental economic framework of a social order. Thus, managers of capitalist states are able to pursue a relatively wide range of economic policies, but only to the extent that these can be convincingly presented as contributing to the overall goal of ensuring stable capitalist markets, even if some sectors of capital are vigorously opposed to specific reform projects. One need not look beyond the variations on capitalism pursued by both Franklin Roosevelt and Barak Obama, in their efforts to return capitalist markets to stability and growth after significant economic contractions, to recognize the degree to which every state, except a revolutionary state (and only until the revolution is consolidated into a new order), will operate within a distinct band of economic assumptions and possibilities.

The actions of political states, including their laws, cannot be understood independently from the economic arrangements they are designed to facilitate and protect, and upon which they depend for financial support. This does not mean the state is the slavish tool of economic practices. But it does mean that economic considerations are always present in any analysis of political practices, including law making and criminal justice.

When I say that the economic practices are always political, I do not mean to suggest that economic decision-makers are merely the facilitators of less obvious political agendas, as might be the case when economic crises are manufactured and/or used to extend state power via a "shock doctrine" (Klein 2008). Capital is not unitary, cohesive, or self-contained. Nor does it require any particular cultural framework to function (Zizek 2008). Capital, thus, is not exclusive to any particular sociological framework, as evidenced by the ability of capital to coexist with both U.S. neo-liberal democracy and Chinese communist state-capitalism.

While there are often significant overlaps between economic and political agendas, political leaders (at least for the present moment) manage geographically *bounded* states as compared to capital managers who serve the interest of geographically *dispersed* investors, some of whom benefit from particular political designs, and others who may not.

The Iraq war, for instance, advantaged capital sectors associated with the production of military hardware and the provision of military services (O'Reilly 2005). We are only beginning to learn the extent to which profiteering and corruption by military contractors enriched private sector capital (Whyte 2010). The hopes for war profits ensure that some sectors of capital will always support war. Thus, in the United States, representatives of the military-industrial complex have a long history of supporting hawks as political candidates.

At the same time, war or other foreign adventures do not necessarily serve the interests of all capital sectors. In the case of the Iraq war, for instance, the domestic construction sector experienced substantial increases in the cost of material inputs leading to a rise in new home prices that, along with corruption in the mortgage lending sector, may have contributed to the eventual collapse of the housing market and wider destabilization of capitalist profit-making.

For these reasons, any criminological inquiry into economic wrongdoing must always be alert to both the supportive and constraining role of political forces over economic decision-making.

When I say that both economic and political practices are always cultural, I do not mean to suggest that culture—understood here as the material representation and social performance of deeply rooted myths, values, and ideations through speech, ritual action, and routinized daily practices—is either uniform or a simple expression of political and economic forces in any contemporary nation-state. Rather, I suggest that no political or economic action can be understood outside of the cultural frameworks that give meaning to those actions.

Both politics and economics are cultural constructions before they are anything else. Groups with a shared culture must first imagine particular configurations of power or value before these can ever take material form as a government, money, or an economic system. While at the same time, materialized practices exert powerful influences on the construction of cultural products, in a continual dialectic.

Critical analyses of crimes and social injuries must consider how leaders and followers come to believe that practices of domination flow from noble, rather than base motives. They must interrogate how these understandings intersect with culturally constructed historical narratives of a people and their purpose. Foucault's conception of *biopower* and Bourdieu's notion of *habitus* are useful theoretical touchstones for such analyses. However, I feel there is much to be done in applying these to the creation of a culturally sensitive form of critical criminology that neither denies nor overemphasizes the importance of agency in the construction of social life. What I am suggesting here is that critical criminologists need to investigate how domination becomes part of the habitus of societies in ways that enable both elites and large masses of subordinates to become reasonably tolerant of the harms committed by dominant groups, while equivalently outraged at the lesser harms committed by the dominated.

Like David Harvey (2003: 29), I suggest that the logics of capitalism and empire—and to his analyses I would add culture—"frequently tug against each other, sometimes to the point of outright antagonism." In the contemporary moment, neo-liberal capitalism, national geopolitical strategies, and cultural ideations exist in a state of tension. However, they do so with sufficient points of convergence to also make it possible for states to effectively convince large majorities that established justice policies are not strategies to reproduce existing patterns of economic and political domination, but are natural and logical efforts to preserve social order in the interests of all.

Given the tensions among economics, politics, and culture, it is important for critical criminologists to comprehend, not only the convergences among these social forces—but also the fault lines between them. This has two purposes. It is an effective standpoint for understanding apparent anomalies and tensions between law and economics. And, it provides the activist critical criminologist with a clearer understanding of where levers for change might best be inserted.

Beyond Legal Formalism

In a series of articles, Ron Kramer and I argued that the invasion of Iraq and many elements of the subsequent occupation were violations of international law, as designated by the United Nations and Nuremburg charters and the specific treaties and conventions that have evolved from them (Kramer and Michalowski 2005). On reflection, it seems to me that our argument points to several challenges facing efforts to move beyond legal formalist frameworks—that is, frameworks dependant on the claim that somehow the events in question are violations of law.

Our characterization of the invasion and occupation of Iraq as international crimes is not a description of international law in action, but rather our interpretation of how international jurists *might* rule if the Iraq war were to come before them. However, no authoritative international prosecutor or court has yet to rule that these actions are violations of international law. From the standpoint of legal formalism, one which supporters of the war are inclined to embrace, without such a ruling, all claims that the invasion constituted a war crime of aggression are unsupportable. I am not embracing this legalist standpoint. Rather, I use it to note that grounding criminological analyses of, in this case, international wrongdoing, on legalist suppositions of how judges might rule is an analytically vulnerable standpoint.

The appeal to international laws, while certainly a useful guidepost, presents another analytic conundrum. The United Nations, as a framework for creating and applying international law, is itself an expression of geopolitical interests and unequal power relations wherein decisions about the legality of both classes of actions and specific wrongful actions within those classes depend, not upon some routine application of law, but upon the relative strength of geo-political coalitions and the particular interests of powerful members involved in those actions. Any legal system designed so that its most powerful potential violators, that is, the permanent members of the Security Council, can veto enforcement actions directed toward their own violations cannot be reasonably considered a system of law.

The tension between the legalist views of international law and the reality that these laws in action are the expression of existing geo-political balances of power suggests that grounding analyses of crimes of domination on existing international frameworks of human rights as if these frameworks were laws may not be a sound meta-theoretical choice.

One path away from legal formalism is to treat the legal or tolerated wrongdoings of powerful sectors and institutions as forms of deviance. Although The U.N. and Nuremburg Charters, the Universal Declaration of Human Rights, as well as other U.N. covenants and customary international laws lack the primary characteristics of positive law, they nevertheless are significant international norms (Donnelly 2003; Glendon 2002). From this standpoint, one could conclude that acts that appear to contravene these norms are as legitimate a topic for criminological inquiry as any other form of non-criminal deviance.

Criminology has a long history of studying forms of deviance that were either not criminalized, or from the perspective of social activists, not sufficiently penalized. This is certainly true in the areas of civil rights violations, child and woman abuse, hate crimes, and violations of the rights of indigenous peoples. As Dershowitz (2004) argues, legal rights are frequently created out of campaigns against social wrongs. The fact that positive laws do not prohibit many of the social injuries caused by domination does not automatically place these injuries outside the boundaries of criminological inquiry. Many of these harms and social injuries are certainly viewed as deviant by the majority of their victims, and on that basis alone are legitimate topics of inquiry (Green and Ward 2000; 2004).

While there is much to recommend a deviance rather than a legalist model as the meta-theoretical starting point for critical criminological inquiry, doing so relies on *a priori* social constructions of a particular situation or outcome as problematic (Blumer 1971). However, many harmful consequences of domination may not generate even this level of social recognition and approbation, yet they remain injurious nevertheless. To the extent that criminologists identify socially injurious outcomes of domination, these can and should be incorporated within the criminological arena, regardless of their juridical or social movement status.

Some years ago, I had suggested that a possible alternative to legalist and deviance-based approaches to the critique of domination might be the concept of *analogous social injury* (Michalowski 1985). Specifically, analogous social injuries are actions that produce "death, injury, financial loss, fear, emotional distress or deprivation of the rights of political participation that are equivalent or greater in gravity to similar consequences resulting from actions defined as criminal by law" (Michalowski 2007). As a starting point in the conception of our subject matter this approach directs criminologists to actively seek, identify, and analyze social forces that generate individual, collective, and organizational actions whose injurious consequences are equivalent to actions defined as crime by law. It is in this space between accepting and condemning socially injurious actions that states reveal the truth and the contours of domination.

Put simply, murder kills people. War kills people. Thus, why nations commit war and who are its victims ought be at least as central to criminological inquiry as why and whom individuals murder. Similarly, robbery, burglary, and theft use force or guile in ways that make people poorer. Many practices fostered by neo-liberal capitalism also use force or guile to make people poorer (Perkins

2005). Thus, I suggest, it makes little sense, but for the ideology of domination, to claim that robbery, burglary, and theft are legitimate topics of criminological inquiry, but global manipulations of credit, the expropriation of hereditary lands or resources under the guise of development, or mandated "structural adjustments" that impoverish many while benefiting few, are not.

John Braithwaite (1985:18) once suggested that casting such a broad net is an effort to shape criminological inquiry to fit individual moral preferences. However, I suggest that the concept of analogous social injury does just the opposite. It substitutes an analytic measure—degree of injury—for the moral and political preferences inherent in all legal systems. Those attempting to begin their inquiry from an analogous social injury standpoint would, of course, face the challenge of making a compelling factual case that the injuries being studied are indeed analogous in the gravity of injury to criminal acts. Doing this, in itself, however, would play an important role in expanding the horizons of criminological inquiry.

A critical criminology formed around a broad vision of social injury is well suited to the challenge of pursuing social justice in the twenty-first century. The globe has been reshaped into a highly integrated, if fragile, capitalist network, with a class structure arrayed as much across nations as within them. While domination remains to be challenged within the advanced capitalists states, I suggest that the dominion that advanced states exert over those situated lower in the global class structure is an even graver challenge to the ideals of social justice that animate critical criminologies of all flavors. Insofar as many of these injurious actions exist in the "space between laws" created by international structures of dominance and subaltern states, it is imperative that critical criminology transcend legalism and strike out toward a new vision that begins with social injury, not with law.

As we reveal the discrepant choices through which political systems tolerate grave harms while aggressively repressing lesser ones, we contribute to peeling back the many layers of ideological construction that normalize domination. While doing so does not automatically provoke justice or limit domination, it does contribute to the formulation of new understandings and new policy options to be tried when and if the political climate surrounding justice policy undergoes significant change.

Notes

1. Originally presented as the keynote address for the inaugural Critical Criminology and Justice Studies Conference, San Diego, CA, 2009.

2. While Bourdieu was particularly concerned with *habitus* as a class-differentiated phenomenon, and there are identifiable class differences in the "feel for the game" concerning crime and justice, particularly with respect to surplus population groups, I suggest that dominant media outlets represent and reproduce what could be called conventional mass habitus, that is a cultural frame accepted broadly across social classes.

References

Altheide, David. 2002. *Creating Fear: News and the Construction of Crisis.* New York: Aldine de Gruyter.
Austin, James and John Irwin. 2000. *It's About Time: America's Imprisonment Binge.* New York: Wadsworth.
Beirne, Piers. 1979. "Empiricism and the Critique of Marxism on Law and Crime." *Social Problems* 26: 373-385.
Blumer, Herbert. 1971. "Social Problems as Collective Behavior." *Social Problems* 18:298-306.
Bourdieu, Pierre. 1998. *Practical Reason.* Cambridge: Polity Press.
Braithwaite, John. 1985. "White Collar Crime." *Annual Review of Sociology* 11:1-25.
Cohen, Stanley. 1988. *Against Criminology.* New Brunswick, NJ: Transaction.
Dershowitz, Alan. 2004. *Rights from Wrongs: A Secular Theory of the Origins of Rights.* New York: Basic Books.
Donnelley, Jack. 2003. *Universal Human Rights in Theory and Practice.* Cornell, NY: Cornell University Press.
Foucault, Michel. 2003. *Society Must Be Defended.* New York: Picador.
Garner, Bryan A., ed. 1999. *Blacks Law Dictionary.* 7th ed. Egan, MN: West Publishing.
Gibbons, Donald. 1979. *The Criminological Enterprise: Theories and Perspectives.* Englewood Cliffs, NJ: Prentice-Hall.
Glendon, Mary Ann. 2002. *A World Made New: Eleanor Roosevelt and the Universal Declaration of Human Rights.* New York: Random House.
Green, Penny and Tony Ward. 2000. "State Crime, Human Rights, and the Limits of Criminology." *Social Justice* 27:101-115.
Green, Penny and Tony Ward. 2004. *State Crime: Governments, Violence and Corruption.* London, UK: Pluto Press.
Harvey, David. 2003. *The New Imperialism.* New York: Oxford University Press.
Jessop, Bob. 1982. *The Capitalist State.* New York: NYU Press.
Klein, Naomi. 2008. *The Shock Doctrine: The Rise of Disaster Capitalism.* New York: Picador.
Kramer, Ronald C. 2010. "From Guernica to Hiroshima to Baghdad: The Normalization of the Terror Bombing of Civilian Populations." Pp. 118-133 in *State Crime in the Global Age*, edited by W. Chambliss, R. Michalowski and R. Kramer. Uffculme, UK: Willan Publishing.
Kramer, Ronald and Raymond Michalowski. 2005. "War, Aggression, and State Crime: A Criminological Analysis of the Invasion and Occupation of Iraq." *The British Journal of Criminology* 45:446-469.
Michalowski, Raymond. 1985. *Order, Law and Crime.* New York: Random House.
Michalowski, Raymond. 2007. "Who's The Criminal Here: Social Injury and Immigration Politics on the U.S. Mexico Border." Paper presented at the annual meeting of the Western Society of Criminology, February, Phoenix, AZ.
Michalowski Raymond and Ronald Kramer. 2006. *State-Corporate Crime.* New Brunswick, NJ: Rutgers University Press.
Morrison, Wayne. 1995. *Theoretical Criminology: From Modernity to Post-Modernism.* New York: Routledge Cavendish.

O'Reilly, C. 2005. "Security Consultants in Iraq: Private Security in a Transitional State." Paper presented at the annual meeting of the European Group for the Study of Deviance and Control, September, Belfast, Northern Ireland.

OED. 2009. *The Oxford English Dictionary*. Oxford, UK: Oxford University Press.

Patillo, Mary, D. Weiman and B. Western. 2004. *Imprisoning America: The Social Effects of Mass Incarceration*. New York: Russell Sage Foundation.

Perkins, John. 2005. *Confessions of an Economic Hit Man*. New York: Plume.

Perrow, Charles. 1999. *Normal Accidents*. Princeton, NJ: Princeton University Press.

Poulantzas, Nicos. 1973. *Political Power and Social Classes*. London, UK: New Left Books.

Shroyer, Trent. 1973. *Critique of Domination: The Origins and Development of Critical Theory*. New York: G. Braziller.

Sellin, Thorsten. 1939. *Social Conflict and Conduct Norms*. New York: Social Science Research Council.

Tappan, Paul W. 1947. "Who Is the Criminal?" *American Sociological Review* 12:96-102.

Vaughan, Diane. 1996. *The Challenger Launch Decision: Risky Technology, Culture, and Deviance at NASA*. Chicago, IL: University of Chicago Press.

Whyte, David. 2010. "A Fake Law: The 'State of Exception' and *Lex Mercatoria* in Occupied Iraq." Pp.134-151 in *State Crime in the Global Age*, edited by W. Chambliss, R. Michalowski and R. Kramer. Uffculme, UK: Willan Publishing.

Zizek, Slavo. 2008. *Violence*. New York: Picador.

READING 16

Crimes of the State

Richard Quinney

The capitalist system generates its own patterns of crime. For a critical-Marxist understanding of these we begin by examining the capitalist political economy. The class struggle endemic to capitalism is characterized by a dialectic between domination and accommodation. Those who own and control the means of production, the capitalist class, attempt to secure the order by various forms of domination, especially control of crime by the state. Those who do not own and control the means of production, the working class, must accommodate to and resist capitalist domination in many ways.

The contradictions of developing capitalism increase the intensity of class struggle and thereby: (1) the need to dominate by the capitalist class and (2) the need to accommodate and resist by the class exploited by capitalism, the working class. Most of the behavior in response to domination, including the actions of the oppressed that are defined as criminal by the capitalist class, is a product of the capitalist system of production. During capitalist appropriation of labor, for the accumulation of capital, conditions are established calling for behaviors that may be defined as criminal by the capitalist state. These behaviors become eligible for crime control when they disturb or threaten the capitalist order in some way.

But the major crimes in the United States are those which occur during domination. By various schemes and mechanisms, including domination by the state, the capitalist system is reproduced. And in this domination crimes are carried out. It is a contradiction of capitalism that some of its own laws must be violated to secure the system. Not only is this contradiction heightened during times of crisis, making for increased crimes of domination, but the crimes change with the further development of capitalism.

These crimes, committed by the state, the capitalist class, and the agents of the capitalist system, are the crimes of domination. The crimes most characteristic of capitalist domination are those which occur during state control. They include the felonies and misdemeanors that law-enforcement agents, especially the police, carry out in the name of the law, usually against persons accused of other violations. Violence and brutality have become a recognized part of police work. These crimes of control are added to subtler crimes in which agents of the law violate the civil liberties of citizens,

Richard Quinney, Selection from "Crimes of the State," *Criminology*, pp. 163-164, 166-181, 185-188. Little, Brown and Company, 1979.

as in the many forms of surveillance, the use of provocateurs (agents of the law who provoke people into acts that in turn can be dealt with by the law as crimes), and the illegal denial of due process.

Then there are the crimes of the government itself, committed by the elected and appointed officials of the capitalist state. The Watergate crimes, carried out to perpetuate a governmental administration, are the most publicized instances of these crimes. Other offenses too are committed by the state against persons and groups who would seemingly threaten national security. Included here are the crimes of warfare and political assassination of foreign and domestic leaders.

Finally, many social injuries are committed by the capitalist class and the capitalist state that are not usually defined as criminal in the legal code. These systematic actions, involving denial of basic human rights (resulting in sexism, racism, and economic exploitation) are an integral part of capitalism and are important to its survival.

Crimes Against Citizens' Rights

The state commits crimes in numerous areas involving human rights. The civil-rights movement showed how government officials violate the law to keep the system intact. Court decisions and legislative acts have made some of the behaviors illegal, even when committed by officials of the state. We have come to realize that many of our civil liberties are being narrowed by those who are supposed to guarantee these rights. In the name of "law and order," legal agents have slighted laws designed to protect such rights as free speech, assembly, and due process. Federal agents have violated the law in their surveillance and in their quest for evidence usable in criminal prosecution. Local police, too, have been accused of blatantly violating human rights, as well as the conventional laws of murder and assault, in running the affairs of state.[1]

The United States Constitution guaranteed some rights that are not to be infringed upon. Governmental surveillance, according to Supreme Court rulings, is illegal in most situations. Such techniques as unreasonable search and seizure, interrogation, wiretapping, and various forms of electronic surveillance have been declared unconstitutional except in specified cases. Nevertheless, government agents continue to use these forms of surveillance, a fact dramatically brought to public attention by the disclosure that the Army was obtaining information on 18,000 civilians.[2]

It has been disclosed that several governmental agencies, especially the FBI and the CIA, also are heavily engaged in obtaining information about law-abiding citizens by these means.[3] The investigations of the Watergate crimes have uncovered how much citizens are being denied their civil liberties in the name of "national security," and the many criminal techniques (including burglary) the government uses to obtain information. Agencies of the state, including the presidency, may also resort to espionage and sabotage against citizens, obtaining information illegally and even falsifying records and documents. Among the disclosures was the plan approved by President Nixon for gathering domestic intelligence. Blackmail and extortion have been used against individuals and organizations, as in the threat of income-tax prosecutions if funds were not "donated" for campaign and other expenses. Some of these activities, such as burglary by agents of the FBI in gathering information for the presidency, have been going on for many years. These are not only unconstitutional but also violate criminal codes. It is always problematical, however, whether these crimes will be prosecuted, because the government itself would have to do the prosecuting.

A classic strategy used by a state to promote its own security is the criminal law, which it wields against those who appear to threaten the state's existence. The state traditionally responds by establishing a legal system that defines as "criminal" any conduct that threatens it, and denying the citizen's rights of dissent. These "political crimes" form a significant part of legal history, especially in recent years.[4] This use of criminal law is usually illegal; the laws are illegal in formulation and inevitably result in criminal means of enforcement.

In the sixties and seventies the state has gone through many political trials to promote its own interests. Those who objected to war in Southeast Asia were sometimes harassed and prosecuted. "Rioters" in the ghettos, rebelling against the abuses they suffer, have been subjected to laws by the state, which has used many old laws, or created new ones, to control dissent. Law-enforcement agencies and the judiciary have tried to prosecute those who apparently threaten the state. Later, however, trials pending for years, after harassment of the defendants, were thrown out of court because of the means the government used to prosecute them. Charges against such groups as the Chicago Seven, the Harrisburg Seven (the Berrigan case), the Daniel Ellsberg and Anthony J. Russo, Jr. case, and the Gainesville Eight were dropped because the police, the prosecution, or the court used criminal techniques in conducting them.[5]

Yet the extent to which the state has used criminal means to maintain its sense of order continues to be uncovered. Some violations of citizens' rights that have been disclosed indicate that the FBI committed murder in raids against members of the Black Panther Party; that the FBI kidnapped radicals and burglarized their homes and offices; that the FBI has carried out wiretaps and surveillance against citizens at the behest of all six presidents from Franklin D. Roosevelt to Richard M. Nixon; that the CIA has subverted the political process in such countries as Iran and Chile, including assistance in the overthrow and murder of Salvador Allende; and that the FBI and CIA were involved in the attempted assassination of Fidel Castro in Cuba during the administration of John F. Kennedy.[6]

More revelations came out in findings by a ten-month investigation of the intelligence agencies by the Senate Select Committee on Intelligence Activities. These disclosures, so numerous and so complex that they have been likened "to reading the Federal Budget or contemplating the number of stars in the solar system," have been sorted out to include the findings below:

> The Central Intelligence Agency illegally opened 215,000 letters in one of four mail intrusion projects. Totals in the three other projects are not known. The agency,

too, in clear violation of its charter, conducted domestic surveillances, sought data from the National Security Agency and prepared dossiers on Americans.

The National Security Agency scanned virtually every overseas telephone call and cable from 1967 until 1973 to locate communications of 1,680 American citizens involved in political dissent, suspected of being narcotics traffickers or feared to be potential threats to the President.

The Federal Bureau of Investigation has publicly acknowledged that it committed 238 burglaries aimed at domestic dissidents. Bureau officials estimate that 700 others may have been carried out against foreign espionage targets or foreign embassies. The bureau has also acknowledged that, like the CIA, it also opened mail, in eight projects in as many cities. It has not made public how many letters it opened and photographed. In addition, the bureau operated a counterintelligence program against such dissidents as the Ku Klux Klan, the Socialist Workers party and the Black Panthers. Agents used forged letters and made anonymous telephone calls, among other techniques, to harass those they could not charge with a crime.

The Internal Revenue Service set up dossiers on 8,585 political activists and 2,873 political organizations. It traded information with the CIA and the FBI.

Military intelligence units collected political intelligence and spied on domestic dissidents from 1967 until 1970 and prepared dossiers on a broad range of American citizens.[7]

No one knows how many people in the United States, as well as in other countries, have been deprived of their civil rights by these actions. All these and many more, as crimes of domination, have been committed by the state to secure the capitalist system.

Conventional Crimes in Law Enforcement

The police have traditionally been the governmental agents most exposed to opportunities for committing conventional felonies and misdemeanors while enforcing the law. Crimes by the police have been documented throughout the history of law enforcement in American communities. A study of police operations in Washington, Boston, and Chicago reported that "27 percent of all the officers were either observed in misconduct situations or admitted to observers that they had engaged in misconduct."[8] The forms of crime included shaking down traffic violators, accepting payoffs to alter sworn testimony, stealing from burglarized establishments, and planting weapons on suspects. Documented elsewhere are illegal raids against innocent persons, participating in narcotics traffic, and extorting money from the prostitution business.[9] The Knapp Commission of New York City found that well over half the police force in that city are engaged in some form of crime and corruption.[10] The activities range from accepting bribes to selling stolen articles, from selling heroin to tapping telephones illegally, from blackmail to murder.

Violence is part of police work, and brutality is often used in making an arrest. Investigating police abuses in New York City, Paul Chevigny found that the police will make an arrest to cover up an assault committed against the suspect, concealing their own violence by arresting and charging the citizens with some offense.[11]

Crimes by the police can be understood if we look at how the police work. The police recruit, during his training, adopts a very definite outlook on his work and develops a justification for using specific procedures in the line of "duty." He learns an ideology that later affects his work:

> The policeman finds his most pressing problem in his relationships to the public. His is a service occupation but of an incongruous kind, since he must discipline those whom he serves. He regards the public as his enemy, feels his occupation to be in conflict with the community, and regards himself to be a pariah. The experience and the feeling give rise to a collective emphasis on secrecy, an attempt to coerce respect from the public, and a belief that almost any means are legitimate in completing an important arrest. These are for the policeman basic occupational values. They arise from his experience, take precedence over his legal responsibilities, are central to an understanding of his conduct, and form the occupational concepts within which violence gains its meaning.[12]

Many of the illegal activities of the ordinary policeman are prescribed and supported by group norms of rules and expectations of behavior among policemen. Research has shown that criminal practices of police are patterned by an informal "code": "It was found that the new recruits were socialized into 'code' participation by 'old timers' and group acceptance was withheld from those who attempted to remain completely honest and not be implicated. When formal police regulations were in conflict with 'code' demands among its practitioners, the latter took precedence."[13]

In fact, the policeman may give little thought to the legality of his own actions when he is enforcing other laws. The law that is meant to protect the citizen from abuses by government authorities is more likely to be regarded by the policeman as an obstacle to law enforcement. "For him, due process of law is, therefore, not merely a set of constitutional guarantees for the defendant, but also a set of working conditions which, under increasingly liberal opinions by the courts, are likewise becoming increasingly arduous."[14] From the policeman's standpoint, the public's civil liberties impede his performance on the job. That is how the law is sometimes broken by its enforcers.

The opportunity for unlawful behavior among the police is especially acute in the black community and in political protests. Here the police already have their own group norms prescribing some illegal behavior and providing support for it. Several studies have shown that the majority of policemen are hostile and prejudiced toward blacks, which can impair their ability to always keep their behavior lawful.[15] In the ghetto riots of the late sixties, police violence was common.

Police handling of political protesters also has often been violent and illegal. The police response to the demonstrations at the 1968 Democratic National Convention in Chicago has been described as "unrestrained and indiscriminate police violence."[16] These confrontations increase the chances for violence because of the views the police share about protesters. That is, "organized protest tends to be viewed as the conspiratorial product of authoritarian agitators—usually 'Communists'—who mislead otherwise contented people."[17] Such ideas, combined with frustration and anger, provide ready support for harsh police actions. And because the police look on most people they find in these situations as already guilty, they think their own methods of control and apprehension are appropriate—no matter how criminal these methods may be.

Homicides committed by police against citizens have increased in recent years, especially the killing of black men by the police.[18] Police also sometimes kill one another, often because of mistaken identity. All these occurrences are a result of the tendency in law enforcement to employ more sophisticated and deadly weapons. Police departments in several states are adopting soft-headed, hollow-nosed bullets (the "dumdum"). These bullets, wounding more seriously and killing more often, have been banned in some international treaties in an attempt to limit the conduct of war.

Police engaged in enforcing narcotics laws are especially prone to commit crimes in their work. The conventional crimes they commit range from taking illegal bribes to dealing in drugs themselves.[19] Other offenses by narcotics agents include theft of seized property, illegal searches and seizures, and criminal violence in enforcing the law. These violations occur in enforcement of a prohibition (drug use and sale) that is also an integral part of American society. Crime by the enforcers of such a contradictory criminal law are to be expected.

Other agents of the law, such as the officials who guard and "correct" conventional offenders, also violate the law in their work. These crimes correspond closely to the objectives of security and punishment. Prison guards, in particular, are to do whatever is necessary to maintain security in the prison.

These crimes are documented only when a crisis happens. Several crimes committed by correctional workers became known to the public following prison riots in New York City jails.[20] The inmates were responding to the harsh conditions in the jails, including excessive bail, overcrowding, and months of being confined without indictment or trial. After the revolt had been ended peacefully by negotiations between the inmates and the mayor's office, correctional officers systematically beat the prisoners in the courtyard of one of the jails. The beatings were recorded in photographs and eyewitness accounts. A reporter for the *Daily News* described what he saw:

It was a gruesome scene. About 250 prisoners were sitting on the grass. Behind them, 30 Correction Department guards were lined up, all of them holding weapons—ax handles, baseball bats, and night sticks. One inmate was dragged out a doorway onto a loading platform and five guards attacked him with their clubs. They battered his head and blood flowed over his face and body. He was kicked off the platform and several other guards pounded him again with their clubs. His limp form then was lifted off the ground and thrown into a bus as another prisoner was hauled out and belted across the back with a club. Then more clubs rained down on him until he was motionless and bloodsoaked. He too was thrown into the bus. Another man was pushed out, his hands above his head. A bat caught him in the stomach and he doubled over. More clubs came down on his spine. Eight guards were slugging away at one time. A fourth prisoner emerged but the guards seemed to let go of him. He began running but the guards kicked him over and over. Some more prisoners got the same treatment.[21]

As it often turns out with such incidents, three weeks after the beatings the district attorney announced that eight inmates were indicted and all guards exonerated.

The results of crimes committed by agents of the law are usually predictable: the charges are dropped, the defendants are cleared, or, at most, an official may be dismissed. Although three students were killed and several more injured at Orangeburg State College in 1968, the South Carolina highway patrolmen who fired the shots were cleared of wrongdoing. Similar events and results were to occur later at Jackson State College in Mississippi.

Likewise, at Kent State University in 1970, National Guardsmen killed four students, and then were freed of blame. Instead, a state grand jury indicted twenty-five persons in connection with campus protests. The grand jury indicted no guardsmen because they "fired their weapons in the honest and sincere belief and under circumstances which would have logically caused them to believe that they would suffer serious bodily injury had they not done so." (No evidence of the sniper fire that they feared could be found.) The "major responsibility" for the events at Kent State, the grand jury continued, "rests clearly with those persons who are charged with the administration of the university." The university administration, the report asserted, had fostered "an attitude of laxity, overindulgence and permissiveness," and faculty members had placed an "over-emphasis" on "the right to dissent."[22] The idea that the government could be at fault was never entertained by the grand jury.

The September 1971 killings at Attica prison in New York State demonstrate violence by the state; more than forty were killed by state troopers when the prisoners demanded prison reforms.[23] Fearing that the rebellion threatened law and order, Governor Rockefeller ordered in the troopers who fired upon and killed prisoners and their guards. Actions such as these are beginning to be understood by the public; crime by the state is becoming a part of the public consciousness.

Crimes of Provocation

The ideology of the American state promotes the myth that law enforcement is a neutral force intended to maintain the democratic process.

> The history of America contradicts this official image of neutrality and equal justice. The pattern is clear: when women tried to vote and Labor claimed its right to organize, at the beginning of this century, police were used as poll-watchers, as strike-breakers, and as shock troops by those who held industrial power; in the 1950's as black people began a new round in their centuries-old struggle for equal protection, police were once again used to defy the Constitution in the name of states' rights and public order; in the 1960's police again and again were sent in to disperse hundreds of thousands of citizens peacefully exercising their First Amendment rights to protest an unconstitutional war in Southeast Asia. All this time, on a day to day, face to face level the typical law enforcement slogan "to protect and to serve" meant one thing to the powerful or the passive and another to the powerless or the dissident.[24]

The practice in which a law-enforcement agency uses a policeman or an informer to encourage or plan actions that violate the law is itself a crime. Yet, we are now realizing this practice is common. The crime of informers becoming agents provocateurs and encouraging or committing illegal acts is widespread. Instances include these:

> One of the people most involved in encouraging the violence that accompanied the Chicago Democratic Party Convention was actually an undercover police officer; two members of a national peace committee who always tried to push the group into confrontations with the police were both police provocateurs; a young man who provided a bomb to blow up a Seattle U.S. Post Office was an FBI and city police informer; another FBI informer burned buildings at the University of Alabama; police agents tried to incite violence at Yale University during the demonstrations of May 1971; a Chicano activist in Los Angeles who attempted to provoke his group into terrible acts of violence was an informer for the Treasury Department; the Weatherman group in Ohio was infiltrated by an informer who won a position for himself through advocacy of the most extreme forms of violence; the Black Panther Party "Minister of Defense" in Los Angeles, who helped bring about a shootout with the police, was actually a police informer; a New York City undercover police officer tried to convince a veterans' peace group that it should use violent tactics; another police provocateur, who

had vandalized a state college campus, attempted to convert a San Diego peace march into a pitched battle with police; in upstate New York, an informer, who was on the FBI payroll, tried to set up a class to teach students at Hobart University how to make and use bombs; informers working for the FBI and local police set up a bombing attempt in Mississippi in an effort to kill two KKK members; a Chicago police informer provided the false tip which led to the killing of two Panther leaders there; a police informer led an illegal SDS sit-in at an Illinois college and later—claiming he was a Weatherman—helped to hurl the president of the college off the stage; a police informer attempted to force a militant Seattle group into taking on violent activities; two men who had led the shutting of a massive gate at Ohio State University and set off a violent confrontation with the police, were officers of the state highway patrol; and the false report claiming guns were stored in the Black Muslim Temple in Los Angeles came from a paid police informer, who claims he was instructed to make the report so that the police who employed him would have an excuse to raid the temple.[25]

Such accounts appear endless, making us realize that in attempting to protect itself the state systematically engages in acts of provocation. Persons and groups thought to be threats to the system have found themselves harassed by surveillance. Violent criminal acts are committed 'against them in the name of law and order. Law-enforcement agents have raided the homes of blacks, probably in response to acts of provocation by agents provocateurs among the Black Panthers.[26] It was also exposed in the trial of the San Quentin Six that an agent provocateur was involved in the assassination of revolutionary prison organizer George Jackson in an alleged escape from San Quentin prison. The ex-informer from the Los Angeles Police Department was participating in the general plot to infiltrate, disrupt, and destroy black radical organizations.[27] Plans and actions like these are systematically practiced to eliminate any group that does not accept the state's legitimacy; it is, after all, supposed to be guardian of the national interest.

How far will the state go to protect its own interests? Recently revealed plans might have imposed martial law in the United States if a plot involving the 1972 Republican Convention, which was to be held in San Diego, had come off:

> The plan entailed planting a number of agents-provocateurs both inside and outside the 1972 Republican Convention in San Diego. Agents were to infiltrate the groups planning demonstrations against the weir and poverty. At the time of the demonstrations these agents were to provoke street battles with the police surrounding the convention hall; meanwhile, agents inside the convention hall were to have planted explosives, timed to blow up simultaneously with the

"riot in the streets." The result, he [Louis E. Tackwood] claimed, would be to create a nation-wide hysteria that would then provide President Richard M. Nixon with the popular support necessary to declare a state of national emergency; the government could then arrest all "radicals," "militants," and "left-wing revolutionaries."[28]

In the Watergate crimes we recognize the full authoritarian possibilities in the modern state. The break-in at the Democratic National Convention headquarters (in the Watergate apartment complex) was much more than a mere burglary and installation of electronic listening devices. The invading team was discovered putting forged documents *into* the files. They also had incendiary and bomb manufacturing devices and implements.

> One thing was perfectly clear: this espionage mission was involved with far more than eavesdropping. As the investigation of the event unfolded during the 1972 presidential campaign, it became clear that Watergate was but the tip of the iceberg. Hundreds of thousands of dollars and scores of men were revealed as part of a national network for political espionage, sabotage and provocation. The contacts for the provocateurs who were recruited turned out to be men from the White House, some of the President's closest advisors.[29]

Crimes of provocation come from the highest sources.

Crimes of War

Criminologists, content to study criminal acts by individuals against society, have neglected international incidents that are also criminal, in which the state itself or its agents are implicated. One of these is war, today entirely a governmental function. War is, obviously, violence. Many violent acts that are forbidden without question in peacetime are accepted as necessary in wartime. Some acts of this kind, though, go beyond even the laws that nations have accepted as governing their behavior at war. These are crimes of war.

Sociologists, confronted with these acts, conveniently ignore them, suggesting that they are not "crimes" as they define them, that these acts are not a system of behavior, or that only history can determine which acts are crimes. They fail to realize that these acts (1) are covered by the criminal laws, (2) can be systematic, integral parts of a political and economic system, and (3) are crucial in a nation's history. If we do not consider such crimes, we abdicate both our integrity as scholars and our responsibility as human beings.

An elaborate body of international laws covers the crimes of war. The laws of war are of ancient origin, and up to the eighteenth century were mostly preserved by unwritten tradition.[30] Gradually the laws were codified and courts were established to try violations of the laws. In the last hundred years international laws and treaties have firmly codified an international law of war. The United States is party to twelve conventions pertinent to land warfare, including the detailed Geneva Conventions of 1949. The most authoritative and encompassing statement of war crimes is in the chapter of the International Military Tribunal at Nuremberg where war crimes are defined as

> Violations of the laws or customs of war which include, but are not limited to, murder, ill-treatment or deportation to slave-labour or for any other purpose of civilian population of or in occupied territory, murder, or ill-treatment of prisoners of war or persons on the high seas, killing of hostages, plunder of public or private property, wanton destruction of cities, towns or villages, or devastation not justified by military necessity.[31]

"The laws of warfare are part of American law, enforceable in American courts, not only because the United States is party to most of the major multilateral conventions on the conduct of military hostilities but also because the laws of warfare are incorporated in international customary law, which under the Constitution is part of American law."[32] The United States also recognizes that the laws of war apply to us in the Field Manual of the Department of the Army. The Manual makes it clear that the international laws are also "the supreme law of the land," and that "the law of war is binding not only upon States as such but also upon individuals and, in particular, the members of their armed forces."[33] The international laws of war are part of American law, and may be enforced against both civilians and soldiers, by national or international courts.

Now, let us see how international law can be applied to a country that committed monstrous criminal acts in a long war: the United States in Southeast Asia. We assume that the nation and its representatives discussed here are guilty of these crimes. How are they guilty, and how can the international courts prove their guilt and bring the guilty to trial?

At the Nuremberg war crimes trials in Germany after World War II, Chief Prosecutor Justice Jackson of the United States Supreme Court declared: "If certain acts and violations of treaties are crimes, they are crimes whether the United States does them or whether Germany does them. We are not prepared to lay down a rule of criminal conduct against others which we would not be willing to have invoked against us." Years later many believed the United States had put itself in the respondent's position. But those who level the charge of war crimes against the United States are not the obvious victors. The countries in Southeast Asia, though continually advancing their own condition, are not yet in a position to conduct a war crimes trial. And other nations have not been inclined to convene an international trial. Nevertheless, the words of Justice Jackson are coming back to haunt many Americans.

Our century has been dominated by a single view of reality: the liberal view, which may have been the source of both our problems as a nation and our inability to understand these problems. So it is that the war in Southeast Asia and the crimes associated with it may be made understandable by another theory of reality, socialist theory. What did liberals predict about our involvement in Southeast Asia?

> Did they predict that the American government, continuously advised by university professors, would persist for several years in methods of warfare and of pacification that are criminal in international law and custom, and that are modeled on communist methods? Did they predict that the American government, in pursuit of its presumed strategic interests, would prop up, by firepower and money, any puppet, however repressive, provided only that he would not have dealings with Russia and China? Did they anticipate that the principles of the Nuremberg trials and pledges to international order would be brought into contempt so soon and by a democracy?[34]

The liberal theory always held that the Vietnam war was, at most, a mistake. The socialist theory, scoffed at by most intellectuals in the late fifties and early sixties, suggested another meaning. Rather than viewing the war as an accident or miscalculation, an event that would cease with immediate American withdrawal, that theory predicted the United States would extend the war.

What the United States did in Southeast Asia was a logical outcome of policies that have long existed. That the United States has intervened in the affairs of other nations has been taken for granted. Its right to interfere in the development of these countries, including the right to suppress national revolts, has been patently accepted. To overthrow revolutionary governments and to replace them with military dictatorships has been recognized as good foreign policy. Instead of questioning a foreign policy that is guided by corporate capitalism, in which national interests are defined as business interests, liberals have proclaimed this arrangement. And these arrangements and ideas helped bring about the Vietnam war.

The dramatic disclosure of a massacre involving more than 500 civilians in the My Lai #4 hamlet of Son My village raised the first serious consideration of war crimes by the United States in the Vietnam war. That disclosure, not made until several months after the March 16, 1968 massacre, suggested other war crimes over a long time:

> The official policies developed for the pursuit of belligerent objectives in Vietnam appear to violate the same basic and minimum constraints on the conduct of war as were violated at Songmy. B-52 pattern raids against undefended villages

and populated areas, "free bomb zones," forcible removal of civilian populations, defoliation and crop destruction and "search and destroy" missions have been sanctioned as official tactical policies of the United States government. Each of these tactical policies appears to violate the international laws of war binding upon the United States by international treaties ratified by the U.S. government with the advice and consent of the Senate. The overall conduct of the war in Vietnam by the U.S. armed forces involves a refusal to differentiate betweeen combatants and noncombatants and between military and nonmilitary targets.[35]

The implications of Son My are far-reaching. The United States government seems to have pursued official policies of warfare that constitute war crimes: "It would, therefore, be misleading to isolate the awful happening at Songmy from the overall conduct of the war. It is certainly true that the perpetrators of the massacre at Songmy are, if the allegations prove correct, guilty of the commission of war crimes, but it is also true that their responsibility is mitigated to the extent that they were executing superior orders or were even carrying out the general lines of official policy that established a moral climate in which the welfare of Vietnamese civilians is totally disregarded."[36]

Let us, then, examine some of the specific acts by the United States government in Southeast Asia that are defined as criminal in the international laws of war.

Murder and Ill-Treatment of Civilians

The Son My massacre of civilian men, women, and children took place in a standard American military operation. Trying to trap a Vietcong unit, an American brigade (C Company of Task Force Baker) killed almost every villager they could lay hands on, although no opposition or hostile behavior was encountered.[37]

The tragedy of Son My cannot obscure the fact that the killing of civilians by American forces became an every day occurrence in Vietnam. Estimates have suggested that American or South Vietnamese forces killed or wounded ten civilians for every Vietcong.[38] Civilian casualties in South Vietnam ran into the hundreds of thousands. The Kennedy Subcommittee on Refugees estimated that there were about 300,000 casualties in 1968. According to a conservative estimate for the years 1965 to 1969, 1,116,000 South Vietnamese civilians were killed and 2,232,000 were wounded; between a fifth and a quarter of the population was killed or wounded by military operations in the war. Not included in these figures are the unknown number of casualties from disease and malnutrition brought on by the war. Likewise, these figures do not include the casualties suffered by the civilians of North Vietnam, many by massive bombing. Thousands of other civilians were killed as the war was "wound down."

Destruction of Nonmilitary Targets

The United States engaged in heavy aerial bombardment in Vietnam. The bomb tonnage exceeded that delivered in all the allied bombing in Europe and Asia during World War II. By February 1969, 3,200,000 tons of bombs had been dropped on an agricultural country slightly larger than New York State: 180 pounds of bombs for every man, woman, and child in Vietnam, or 25 tons of bombs for every square mile of North and South Vietnam.[39]

The strictly legal question is whether or not these bombs fell on military objectives:

> Under the traditional approach to the war-crimes concept, no legal issue is presented with respect to the bombing of genuinely strategic military targets such as factories, ammunition depots, oil refineries, airports, and—particularly in the Vietnam context—roads, bridges, viaducts, railroad tracks, trucks, trains, tunnels, and any other transportation facilities. Furthermore, we assume that accidental and incidental damage to nonmilitary and nonstrategic targets is not a war crime.[40]

But the kind of bombing carried out by the United States government appears to have been quite different; it is accused of carrying out a deliberate, nonaccidental bombardment of nonmilitary targets. In North Vietnam, B-52 bombers were said to have continuously attacked schools, churches, hospitals, private homes, dikes, and dams.[41]

In South Vietnam, bombing of rural villages was a standard military policy. Any area could be more or less indiscriminately bombed. "While such strategy violates all international law regarding warfare and is inherently genocidal, it also adjusts to the political reality in South Vietnam that the NLF is and can be anywhere and that virtually the entire people is America's enemy."[42] Military policy turned an entire nation into a target.

Murder and Ill-Treatment of Prisoners of War

The laws of war on treatment of prisoners of war are precise: it is a war crime to murder or torture prisoners.

> According to the Nuremberg precedents, captors may not shoot prisoners even though they are in a combat zone, require a guard, consume supplies, slow up troop movements, and appear certain to be set free by their own forces in an imminent invasion. The Hague Conventions of 1907 require that prisoners be humanely treated, and the Geneva Convention of 1949 prohibits "causing death or seriously endangering the health of a prisoner of war." In particular it stipulates that "no physical or mental torture, nor any other form of coercion,

may be inflicted on prisoners of war to secure from them information of any kind whatever."[43]

Yet there are numerous reports of the murder and ill-treatment of prisoners by American military forces as well as by the American trained and supported South Vietnamese Army.[44] Detailed accounts have been given of the beheading and shooting of wounded prisoners and of torture. Instead of incarcerating prisoners, execution is often carried out at the time of capture. Some combat soldiers characterized these actions as "everyday things," "expected" combat behavior, and "standard operating policy." Violations of the international laws of war become an issue of American military policy.

Other Crimes

American armed forces, working with the Army of South Vietnam, sprayed more than 100 million pounds of herbicidal chemicals on about half (5 million acres) of the arable land in South Vietnam. The object was "to defoliate trees affording cover for enemy forces and to kill certain plants, including rice, which furnished food for Vietcong forces and their civilian supporters.[45] In addition, 14 million pounds of CS gas which incapacitates combatants and civilians was used. In other words, the United States relied extensively on chemical warfare in Vietnam and later in Cambodia.

The Geneva Gas Protocol of 1925 states that the "use in war of asphyxiating, poisonous or other gases, and of all analogous liquids, materials, or devices, has been justly condemned by the general opinion of the civilized world," and prohibits the use of such weapons. Even with the most limited interpretation of the protocol, as lethal devices, the liquids and sprays used by the United States in Southeast Asia were in violation of international law.[46] Napalm too was widely used in Vietnam and surrounding countries.

In officially conducting a war against the population of Vietnam, the United States and some of its leaders could be charged with genocide, a crime against humanity, covered by international treaties and for which all but two of the defendants at Nuremberg were convicted.

"The case for these stark accusations is based on the conclusions that both South Vietnam and the United States violated the Geneva Declaration of 1954 by hostile acts against the North, unlawful rearmament, and refusal to carry out the 1965 national elections provided for in the Declaration, and that the United States likewise violated the United Nations Charter by bombing North Vietnam."[47] The United States attempted to legitimize its war by claiming that self-defense measures were required in response to armed attacks.

World Justice

Only a few war-crimes violations have been prosecuted, and these by military courts. Lieutenant William Calley stood a court-martial trial for his part in killing civilians at Son My. It became clear at the trial that Calley was being used as a scapegoat for decisions made by others at higher levels of command. But crucial questions about individual responsibility were raised during the trial.[48] According to the Nuremberg principles and the Army's Field Manual, members of the armed forces are bound to obey only *lawful* orders; orders violating international law are not to be obeyed. Moreover, questions were raised about war crimes by the United States, and according to international law, those who make and administer these policies must be held responsible. In the Tokyo War Crimes Trial, the defendant, General Yamashita, was convicted and executed for failing to restrain his troops from committing crimes against civilians in the Philippines during the closing months of World War II. That trial established for international law that "A leader must take affirmative acts to prevent war crimes or dissociate himself from the Government. If he fails to do one or the other, then by the very act of remaining in a government of a state guilty of war crimes, he becomes a war criminal."[49]

The grounds are considerable, therefore, for regarding policy-makers and those who administer policy as war criminals. One noted legal scholar, Telford Taylor, chief counsel for the prosecution at Nuremberg, suggests that with the precedents in international law, several civilian leaders and military officers could be held criminally responsible for their acts.[50] The political leaders (including Rusk, McNamara, Bundy, and Rostow), as well as the military leaders, such as the Joint Chiefs of Staff (especially General Westmoreland), should have borne responsibility for the war crimes in Southeast Asia.

To invoke the law, if it could be done beyond the manipulations of the regime itself, is probably to expect too much of legal institutions. The war crimes of the United States cannot be probed adequately in a court-martial proceeding when the responsibility lies higher. It seems more critical to develop a moral and political judgment on our recent history.[51]

A national or international board of inquiry may be the most appropriate way to deal with war crimes. The main objective of this approach, as Richard Falk argues, is to achieve a measure of rectitude by *moral clarification*. Moreover:

> Such a focus is not punitive, the idea is not to catch, convict and punish individuals, but to expose, clarify, and repudiate their conduct. Such an enterprise can only be effective if it represents as authoritative a collective judgment of mankind as a whole reached in a proceeding that was fair, but honest. Americans concerned at once with avoiding any deepening polarization at home, and with renouncing crimes committed on their behalf, should join together in calling for an *external* process of inquiry and judgment, perhaps in the form of a specially constituted U.N. Commission of Inquiry. For Americans of conscience this is the time for neither insurgency, nor silence.[52]

In the end, everyone is responsible for the acts of government. It is the responsibility of all peoples of the world to remove the oppression of national empires and to achieve world justice and human liberation.

Notes

1. For documentation on some of these crimes, see Jethro K. Lieberman, *How the Government Breaks the Law* (New York: Stein and Day, 1972); Theodore L. Becker and Vernon G. Murray, eds., *Government Lawlessness in America* (New York: Oxford University Press, 1971).

2. Richard Halloran, "Army Spied on 18,000 Civilians in Two-Year Operation," *The New York Times,* January 18, 1971, pp. 1 and 22.

3. The documentation is extensive. See, for example, reports of the congressional committees, such as the hearings conducted by the Senate Subcommittee on Constitutional Rights and the hearings of the Senate Watergate Committee. Also see daily coverage by *The New York Times.* Analysis is provided in several articles in *Society,* 12 (March-April 1975).

4. See Marshall B. Clinard and Richard Quinney, *Criminal Behavior Systems: A Typology,* 2nd ed. (New York: Holt, Rinehart and Winston, 1973), pp. 154–186.

5. Homer Bigart, "Berrigan Case: A Strategy That Failed," *The New York Times,* April 9, 1972, p. E2; John Kifner, "Court in Chicago Frees 5 in 1968 Convention Case," *The New York Times,* November 23, 1972; "Ellsberg Case: Defendants Freed, Government Convicted," *The New York Times,* May 13, 1973, p. E1; John Kifner, "Eight Acquitted in Gainesville of G.O.P. Convention Plot," *The New York Times,* September 1, 1973, p. 1.

6. John Kifner, "F.B.I. Sought Doom of Panther Party," *The New York Times,* May 9, 1976, p. 1; Nicholas M. Horrock and John M. Crewdson, "F.B.I. Men Linked to 70's Kidnapping of Domestic Radical," *The New York Times,* June 25, 1976, p. 1; Nicholas M. Horrock and John M. Crewdson, "F.B.I. Burglaries Said to Be Sifted by Justice Aides," *The New York Times,* June 24, 1976, p. 1; John M. Crewdson, "Burglaries in '73 Conceded by F.B.I.," *The New York Times,* July 1, 1976, p. 1; Nicholas M. Horrock, "Car Burnings and Assaults on Radicals Linked to F.B.I. Agents in Last 5 Years," *The New York Times,* July 11, 1976, p. 20; Nicholas M. Horrock, "F.B.I. is Accused of Political Acts for 6 Presidents," *The New York Times,* December 4, 1975, p. 1; I. F. Stone, "The Threat to the Republic," *The New York Review of Books,* 23 (May 27, 1976), pp. 3-4; Seymour M. Hersh, "Aides Say Robert Kennedy Told of C.I.A. Castro Plot," *The New York Times,* March 10, 1975, p. 1.

7. Nicholas Horrock, "Public Disclosures of Lost Privacy," *The New York Times,* November 1, 1975, p. E5. Also see John M. Crewdson, "Intelligence Panel Finds F.B.I. and Other Agencies Violated Citizens' Rights," *The New York Times,* April 29, 1976, pp. 1 and 31–33. Further description of the covert and illegal counterintelligence program of the FBI is in Nelson Blackstock, *Cointelpro: The FBI's Secret War*

on Political Freedom (New York: Random House, 1976). Also see Morton H. Halperin, Jerry J. Berman, Robert L. Borosage, and Christine M. Marwick, *The Lawless State: The Crimes of the U.S. Intelligence Agencies* (New York: Penguin Books, 1976); and David Wise, *The American Police State: The Government Against the People* (New York: Random House, 1976).

8. David Burnham, "Misconduct Laid to 27% of Police in Three Cities' Slums," *The New York Times,* July 5, 1968, p. 1.

9. Fred J. Cook, "How Deep Are the Police in Heroin Traffic?" *The New York Times,* April 25, 1971, p. E3; Andrew H. Malcolm, "Violent Drug Raids Against the Innocent Found Widespread," *The New York Times,* June 25, 1973, p. 1; Ralph Blumenthal, "Officer in Albany Says Fellow Police Joined in Thievery," *The New York Times,* September 21, 1973, p. 1; Ralph Blumenthal, "Brothel Boss Tells of Albany Bribes," *The New York Times,* September 25, 1973, p. 39.

10. *The Knapp Commission Report on Police Corruption* (New York: George Braziller, 1972).

11. Paul Chevigny, *Police Power: Police Abuses in New York City* (New York: Random House, 1969), pp. 136–146.

12. William A. Westley, "Violence and the Police," *American Journal of Sociology,* 59 (July 1953), p. 35.

13. Ellwyn R. Stoddard, "The Informal 'Code' of Police Deviancy: A Group Approach to 'Blue-Coat Crime,'" *Journal of Criminal Law, Criminology and Police Science,* 59 (June 1968), p. 212. Also see Barbara Raffel Price, "Police Corruption: Analysis," *Criminology,* 10 (August 1972), pp. 161-176; Julian B. Roebuck and Thomas Barker, "A Typology of Police Corruption," *Social Problems,* 21 (No. 3, 1974), pp. 423-437; and Meyer S. Reed, Jerry Burnette, and Richard R. Troiden, "Wayward Cops: The Function of Deviance in Groups Reconsidered," *Social Problems,* 24 (June 1977), pp. 565-575.

14. Jerome H. Skolnick, *Justice Without Trial: Law Enforcement in Democratic Society* (New York: John Wiley, 1966), p. 202.

15. See Donald J. Black and Albert J. Reiss, Jr., "Patterns of Behavior in Police and Citizen Transactions," in the President's Commission on Law Enforcement and Administration of Justice, *Studies in Crime and Law Enforcement in Major Metropolitan Areas,* vol. 2, Field Surveys III (Washington, D.C.: U.S. Government Printing Office, 1967), pp. 132–139.

16. The Walker Report to the National Commission on the Causes and Prevention of Violence, *Rights in Conflict* (New York: Bantam Books, 1968), p. 1.

17. Jerome H. Skolnick, *The Politics of Protest* (New York: Ballantine Books, 1969). Also see Rodney Stark, *Police Riots* (Belmont, Calif.: Wadsworth, 1972).

18. Paul Takagi, "A Garrison State in 'Democratic' Society," *Crime and Social Justice,* 1 (Spring-Summer 1974), pp. 27–33.

19. Peter K. Manning and Lawrence John Redlinger, "Invitational Edges of Corruption: Some Consequences of Narcotic Law Enforcement," in Paul Rock, ed., *Drugs and Politics* (New York: E. P. Dutton, 1976).

20. Paul L. Montgomery, "Crisis in Prisons Termed Worst Mayor Has Faced," *The New York Times,* October 15, 1970, p. 1.

21. Quoted in Jack Newfield, "The Law is an Outlaw," *The Village Voice,* December 17, 1970, p. 1.

22. John Kifner, "Jury Indicts 25 in Kent Disorder; Guard is Cleared," *The New York Times,* October 17, 1970, p. 1.

23. *Attica,* The Official Report of the New York State Special Commission on Attica (New York: Bantam Books, 1972).

24. Citizens Research and Investigation Committee and Louis E. Tackwood, *The Glass House Tapes* (New York: Avon Books, 1973), p. 259.

25. Paul Jacobs, "Informers, the Enemy Within," *Ramparts,* 12 (August-September, 1973), pp. 53–54.

26. Other cases of provocation against the Black Panthers are presented in Paul Chevigny, *Cops and Rebels: A Study of Provocation* (New York: Random House, 1972). On the sociological implications of provocation, see Gary T. Marx, "Thoughts on a Neglected Category of Social Movement Participant: The Agent Provocateur and the Informant," *American Journal of Sociology,* 80 (September 1974), pp. 402–442.

27. Karen Wald, "Quentin Jury Hears of Plot," *Guardian,* May 5, 1976, p. 5. The full account is in Jo Durden-Smith, *Who Killed George Jackson?* (New York: Alfred A. Knopf, 1976).

28. Citizens Research and Investigation Committee and Louis E. Tackwood, *The Glass House Tapes,* p. 42.

29. Ibid., p. 173.

30. Telford Taylor, *Nuremberg and Vietnam: An American Tragedy* (Chicago: Quadrangle Books, 1970), pp. 19–41.

31. Nuremberg Principle VI, clause b. The full text can be found in *The Nation,* January 26, 1970, p. 78.

32. Anthony A. D'Amato, Harvey L. Gould, and Larry D. Woods, "War Crimes and Vietnam: The 'Nuremberg Defence' and the Military Service Register," *California Law Review, 57* (November 1969), p. 1058.

33. U.S. Department of the Army, *The Law of Land Warfare,* Field Manual No. 27–10, 1956. On the applicability of the international law of warfare to an undeclared war in Vietnam, the Manual clearly states: "As the customary law of war applies to cases of international armed conflict and to the forcible occupation of enemy territory generally as well as to declared war in its strict sense, a declaration of war is not an essential condition of the application of this body of law. Similarly, treaties relating to 'war' may become operative notwithstanding the absence of a formal declaration of war."

34. Stuart Hampshire, "Russell, Radicalism, and Reason," *New York Review of Books,* 15 (October 8, 1970), p. 3. Also see Noam Chomsky, *American Power and the New Mandarins* (New York: Vintage Books, 1969).

35. Richard A. Falk, "War Crimes and Individual Responsibility: A Legal Memorandum," *Trans-action,* 7 January 1970), pp. 33–34.

36. Ibid., p. 34.

37. Richard Hammer, *One Morning in the War: The Tragedy at Son My* (New York: Coward-McCann, 1970). Also see Seymour H. Hersh, *My Lai, 4; A Report on the Massacre and its Aftermath* (New York: Vintage Books, 1970); and Josephy Goldstein, Burke Marshall, and Jack Schwartz, eds., *The My Lai Massacre and Its Cover-Up: Beyond the Reach of Law?* (New York: The Free Press, 1976).

38. Edward S. Herman, *Atrocities in Vietnam: Myths and Realities* (Philadelphia: Pilgrim Press, 1970), pp. 43–45.

39. Ibid., pp. 54–60.

40. D'Amato, Gould, and Woods, "War Crimes and Vietnam," pp. 1081–1082.

41. John Gerassi, *North Vietnam: A Documentary* (Indianapolis: Bobbs-Merrill, 1968).

42. Gabriel Kolko in Erwin Knoll and Judith Nies McFadden, eds., *War Crimes and the American Conscience* (New York: Holt, Rinehart and Winston, 1970), p. 57.

43. D'Amato, Gould, and Woods, "War Crimes and Vietnam," p. 1075.

44. For some of the sources of documentation, see ibid., pp. 1077–1081.

45. Arthur W. Galston in Knoll and McFadden, eds., *War Crimes and the American Conscience,* p. 69.

46. D'Amato, Gould, and Woods, "War and Crimes and Vietnam," pp. 1091–1093.

47. Taylor, *Nuremberg and Vietnam,* pp. 96–97.

48. See *The New York Times,* December 20, 1970, p. 8.

49. Falk, "War Crimes and Individual Responsibility," p. 39.

50. Taylor, *Nuremberg and Vietnam,* pp. 154-207. Also *The New York Times,* January 9, 1971, p. 3.

51. See the Proceedings of the Russell International War Crimes Tribunal, *Against the Crime of Silence* (Flanders, N.J.: O'Hare Books, 1968). Also Bertrand Russell, *War Crimes in Vietnam* (New York: Monthly Review Press, 1967).

52. Richard A. Falk, in *The New York Times Book Review,* December 27, 1970, p. 14.

READING 17

A Suitable Amount of Street Crime and a Suitable Amount of White-collar Crime

Inconvenient Truths about Inequality, Crime and Criminal Justice

Paul Leighton and Jeffrey Reiman

Christie's book, *A Suitable Amount of Crime*, notes that "crime does not exist as a stable entity":

> It is like a sponge. The term can absorb a lot of acts—and people—when external circumstances make that useful. But it can also be brought to reduce its content, whenever suitable for those with a hand on the sponge.

(2004: ix–x)

Acts that can be potentially criminalized are "an unlimited natural resource," although Christie believes that many crimes are genuinely harmful acts that are rightfully defined as crimes (ibid.: 10). The context thus is not moral relativism, but an interest in the volume of acts that become criminalized: "what is the suitable number of officially stigmatized sinners?" And, "is it possible to establish upper, and eventually lower, limits to the amount of punishment that ought to be applied in a modern society?" (ibid.: 101).

The criminalization of drug use is one of many concerns raised in this regard. Oxford's *Crime and Public Policy* notes that there is not moral consensus about whether recreational drug use should be a crime, so "the creation and enforcement of drug laws are seen more as policy decisions rather than as imperatives" (Lynch and Pridemore 2010: 38). The United States chose not just to criminalize recreational drug use but to launch a "war on drugs," which is a substantial source of its prison population. Christie notes that Swedish plans during the 1970s to lower their prison population from 4,000 to 500 were sidetracked when severe punishments became tools in the Swedish war on drugs (2004: 38). Russia seemed to be embracing a drug war as well, so "the lost war against drugs in the West is now dangerously close to being repeated in the East, with predictable results" (ibid.: 110).

Paul Leighton and Jeffrey Reiman, "A Suitable Amount of Street Crime and a Suitable Amount of White-Collar Crime: Inconvenient Truths about Inequality, Crime and Criminal Justice," *The Routledge Handbook of International Crime and Justice Studies*, ed. Bruce A. Arrigo and Heather Y. Bersot, pp. 302-324. Copyright © 2014 by Taylor & Francis Group. Reprinted with permission.

The drug wars, in part because of their failure, keep the criminal justice systems of many nations busy with street criminals. Indeed, beyond the drug war, Christie observes that "if I had the urge to construct a situation for the promotion of crime, then I would have shaped our societies in a form very close to what we find in a great number of modern states" (ibid.: 51). Social and economic policies "encourage unwanted forms of behavior" (ibid.) and again keep the criminal justice systems of many nations busy with lower-class street criminals. The poor, whose behavior has been defined as criminal, become the raw materials of the criminal justice industry (Christie 2000). An increasing number of countries have a prison- or criminal justice-industrial complex, reminiscent of the military-industrial complex that former US President Eisenhower warned about. It is composed of politicians, government bureaucrats, and all the companies who see criminal justice as a lucrative market rather than a burden on taxpayers (Selman and Leighton 2010). With the advent of private prisons—for-profit companies building and/or managing prisons for government—criminals are increasingly "bodies destined for profitable punishment" (quoted in Leighton and Selman 2012).

Thus, we might say that the poor are the object of conspicuous consumption by the criminal justice system. But the wealthy are not consumed. For example, even in the midst of a full-blown drug war in the USA, wealthy college drug dealers are the "anti-targets" of criminal justice agents; they are repelled from entering the system even when they seem to be "deliberately trying to draw attention to themselves or test[ing] social and legal boundaries" (Mohamed and Fritsvold 2010: 11–12). This is not just the "get-out-of-jail-free" card familiar to players of the *Monopoly*™ board game, but a "never-go-to-jail-in-the-first-place" card (ibid.: 132). Further, while those with their hand on the criminal justice sponge suck up shoplifters and vandals, they have decided not to pursue those responsible for the global financial crisis of 2008:

> *Nobody goes to jail.* This is the mantra of the financial-crisis era, one that saw virtually every major bank and financial company on Wall Street embroiled in obscene criminal scandals that impoverished millions and collectively destroyed hundreds of billions, in fact, trillions of dollars of the world's wealth—and nobody went to jail.
>
> (Taibbi 2011, emphasis in original)

While the poor are conspicuously consumed by the criminal justice system, one might be tempted to say the wealthy are conspicuously not consumed because it is well known that prisons are full of poor people. But the class bias in consumption is hidden when the criminal law does not translate the many harms done by the wealthy and by corporations into crimes. And, criminal justice data neither captures information on class (to help assess bias when rich and poor commit the same crime), nor does it report on the prevalence and cost of white-collar crime (even based on the current inadequate level of criminalization of these harms).

The question about a suitable amount of crime, criminalization and penal control, thus needs to be answered not in the aggregate for a society, but asked separately: what is a suitable amount of crime in the street, and what is a suitable amount of crime in the suites? Such an analysis is consistent with Christie's criminological consciousness, and he explicitly notes that class is relevant to an evaluation of criminal justice systems. He believes that "penal systems carry deep meanings" (2004: 101) and a clue to read their meaning is

> the question of *the nature of the receivers* of the intended pain, particularly how representative they are of the population in general with regard to age, gender, race, class, etc. An extremely biased prison population might indicate severe defects somewhere in that system.
>
> (2004: 102, emphasis in original)

Christie's concerns warrant further analysis, especially as applied to neglected issues about economic class, which is among the most important sociological variables. So, our project in this chapter is to start an analysis of the overconsumption of poor people by the criminal justice system, the under-consumption of the rich, and the defects of systems that exhibit such bias. This inquiry is important not just because of the relative neglect of class analysis in criminal justice, but also because many nations have high degrees of economic inequality and "the simple fact is that a criminal justice system cannot be any more just than the society it protects" (Reiman 2001: 17). Further, as Braithwaite (1992: 83) notes, inequality is linked to both the crimes of the poor (by creating unfulfilled needs, either absolute or based on "advertising and dramatization of bourgeois lifestyles") and crimes of the rich (by making them unaccountable and undermining their respect for the dominion (self-determination) of others.

But Christie raises another concern that is not frequently examined: that society is structured to promote street crime—a point Currie also notes in describing America's "pro-crime" policies (1985: 226)—which adds to the consumption of the poor by the criminal justice system. Critical theory and conflict theory generally argue that the function of criminal justice is to control the "dangerous classes," but fail to consider ideological benefits from "crime" being associated with the poor.

Further, while Christie appreciates the role of harm in selecting appropriate conduct of the poor to criminalize, he fails to apply the same analysis to acts of the wealthy, where death, injury and fraud cause real harm but are not criminalized. This largely mirrors the dominant criminological discussion about whether behavior such as drug use and prostitution are "victimless" crimes and thus should be decriminalized, but does not consider that acts of the wealthy also have victims and should be criminalized. Even if the current reality is a global deregulatory race to the bottom, the criminal justice system still should protect people from the worst threats to their lives, health and property, and do so regardless of whether those threats are from the rich or poor. On another level, reflection on harmful conduct and the prohibitions of criminal law is important because crime is defined by a political system. Thus, philosophical reflection on the concept of crime is necessary for criminology to establish its "intellectual independence of the state, which to my mind is equivalent to declaring its status as a social science rather than an agency of social control, as critical rather than servile, as illumination rather than propaganda" (Reiman 2013: 243).

In the first section that follows, "Class, ideology and the failures of criminal justice," we discuss the foundation for this analysis, *The Rich Get Richer and the Poor Get Prison: Ideology, Class and Criminal Justice*, now in its tenth edition (Reiman and Leighton 2013). While the book is a critique of the American criminal justice system, the concerns it raises apply, to varying degrees, to many developed nations. We argue that the criminal justice system was responsible for only a modest amount of the decline in crime in the USA, and question why anti-crime policy does not target a number of sources of crime (like inequality) as well as better fund research-based crime prevention programs. The book also argues that many harmful acts of businesses and corporations should be criminalized because they are done knowingly, recklessly or negligently. Further, it argues that there is class bias in the system when rich and poor commit the same crime. Finally, the book tries to explore how a criminal justice system that neither protects society nor achieves justice is allowed to continue.

The second section, "No wealth of data …," provides a brief overview of data about inequality, including how corporate "persons" factor in. It also critiques the state of criminal justice data about both the class of criminal offenders and white-collar crime. The third section, "Research directions that give justice more class," highlights several strategies to highlight inequality and class that do not depend on changing government policy about data collection. The fourth section, "Policy implications of the inconvenient truths about wealth," reviews recommendations about better criminal justice data before elaborating on the link between inequality and crime. That higher levels of crimes in the suites and crimes on the streets are both linked to higher levels of inequality means that redistribution can reduce all types of crime. The conclusion considers the ideological benefits that accrue to the wealthy and powerful from a system that fails to remedy sources of crime, fails to criminalize harmful acts of the wealthy and that fails to track both class bias and crimes of the wealthy.

Class, Ideology and the Failures of Criminal Justice

The Rich Get Richer (Reiman and Leighton 2013) invites the reader to entertain the idea that the goal of the criminal justice system is not to eliminate crime or to achieve justice, but to project to the American public a credible image of the threat of crime as a threat from the poor. To accomplish this, the justice system must engage in a publicly visible struggle against a sizable population of poor criminals. To do that, it must fail to significantly reduce the level of crimes that poor people commit. Crime may, of course, occasionally decline—but largely because of factors other than criminal justice policies, and never to such an extent that street crime ceases to be a spectacle in the public's consciousness.

This upside-down idea of criminal justice originated 40 years ago in one of Reiman's seminars. The class discussed many systemic problems of the system: arbitrariness in sentencing and treatment in prison; deprivation of dignity, physical violence, and the lack of meaningful rehabilitation or vocational training within prison; the inescapability of the "ex-con" stigma, and the lack of legitimate opportunities for the ex-prisoner. The class kept confronting

> [the] irrationality of a society that builds prisons to prevent crime knowing full well that they do not, and one that does not seriously try to rid its prisons and post-release practices of those features that guarantee a high rate of recidivism, the return to crime by prison alumni.
>
> (Reiman and Leighton 2013: 2–3)

Near the end of the semester, Reiman asked students to design a criminal justice system that would maintain a stable and visible "class" of criminals. He describes the response as "electrifying": "when asked to design a system that would maintain and encourage the existence of a stable and visible 'class of criminals,' the students 'constructed' the American criminal justice system!" (ibid.: 3). Obviously crime is a complex social practice, so there will be areas of improvement and occasional effective programs, but they will be the exceptions and not the beginning of a trend. Indeed, four decades after this seminar, the problem is still recognizable to American students, to Christie, and probably to people in many nations.

The Rich Get Richer notes that the criminal justice system was the cause of *some* of America's dramatic decline in crime. A nation that locks up enough people, and grants police greater power to interfere with liberty and privacy, will prevent some crime. But the cost of criminal justice intervention compared to its effect makes it inefficient at best. For all the hundreds of billions of dollars the USA put into incarceration over the last decades, Zimring suggests that a "best guess of the impact" of incarceration on crime rates "would range from 10% of the decline at the low end to 27% of the decline at the high end" (2007: 131, 55). The effect is modest because prisons have criminogenic (crime-producing) qualities that offset the effects of incarceration. Prisons brutalize the individuals in them rather than rehabilitate and reintegrate them; they also harm the community by undermining the formation of families, having negative effects on the children of incarcerated parents, and eroding informal community social control systems.

To the extent that prisons are criminogenic, they are *sources* of crime that society chooses not to fix. This is part of the first failure of criminal justice, which is the failure to fight crime in ways that can meaningfully reduce it. Other sources of crime—like the easy availability of guns—are unique to the USA. But many nations criminalize drugs and favor incarceration over treatment. And, as is most relevant here, many nations have high levels of inequality and social exclusion that are part of the normal operations of society, not a temporary or abnormal feature (Mooney 2008).

Because policy does not seek to change sources of crime and allows criminogenic environments and practices to persist, it is appropriate to ask readers to look at criminal justice "through the looking glass." This means reversing expectations about criminal justice and inquiring about the benefits of the current system. We call this way of looking at criminal justice policy the *Pyrrhic defeat* theory. A "Pyrrhic victory" is a military victory purchased at such a cost in troops and treasure that it amounts to a defeat. The Pyrrhic defeat theory argues that the failure of the criminal justice system yields such benefits to those in positions of power that it amounts to a victory.

The Pyrrhic defeat theory draws on Erikson's (1966) *Wayward Puritans*, which builds on Durkheim, who "suggested that crime (and by extension other forms of deviation) may actually perform a needed service to society by drawing people together in a common posture of anger and indignation" (quoted in Reiman and Leighton 2013: 43). If deviance and crime promote social solidarity, Erikson wondered whether

> [we can] then assume that [social institutions] are organized in such a way as to promote this resource? Can we assume, in other words, that forces operate in the social structure to recruit offenders and to commit them to long periods of service in the deviant ranks?

> (ibid.)

He answers in the affirmative and notes that

> prisons have done a conspicuously poor job of reforming the convicts placed in their custody; but the very consistency of this failure may have a peculiar logic of its own. Perhaps we find it difficult to change the worst of our penal practices because we expect the prison to harden the inmate's commitment to deviant forms of behavior and draw him more deeply into the deviant ranks.

> (ibid.)

Both Durkheim and Erikson endorse the general proposition that the failure to eliminate deviance promotes social solidarity, and then jump to a specific conclusion: that the form this failure takes in a particular society is explained by the contribution it makes to promoting consensus on shared beliefs and thus feelings of social solidarity. This jump leaves out the important question of how a society forms its particular consensus around one set of shared beliefs (say, fraud by financial institutions) rather than another (say, drug use). Durkheim and Erikson imply that a consensus already exists and social institutions reflect beliefs already in people's heads. But consensus is created, not just reflected, by social institutions—and the failure to stamp out deviance creates a very particular value-laden consensus. The Pyrrhic defeat theory reveals how the failure of criminal justice works to create and reinforce a specific set of beliefs

> about what is dangerous and what is not, and about who is a threat and who is not. This does not merely shore up general feelings of social solidarity; it allows those feelings to be attached to a social order characterized by striking disparities of wealth, power, and privilege, and by considerable injustice.
>
> (Reiman and Leighton 2013: 49)

This analysis has some similarities with Foucault's work, who also suggests that the failure of prisons serves a function for society. *Discipline and Punish* notes that complaints about the failure of prisons to prevent crime and their tendency to promote recidivism have accompanied the prison throughout its history—so much so that Foucault asks, "Is not the supposed failure part of the functioning of the prison?" (1977: 271). The prison "has succeeded extremely well … in producing delinquents, in an apparently marginal, but in fact centrally supervised milieu; in producing the delinquent as a pathologized subject" (ibid.: 277). That is, lawbreakers are transformed into a delinquent in need of correction and treatment, which in turn licenses a permanent policing of the poor "dangerous class." Foucault suggests that the new prison regime was a response to a "new threat" posed by peasants and workers against the "new system of the legal exploitation of labour" (ibid.: 274), by which he means capitalism. This is a class-based explanation of the new prison regime, in which criminality gets identified "almost exclusively" with "the bottom rank of the social order" (ibid.: 275).

In the next section, we note how social theory has become "de-classed," and this phenomenon applies to Foucault's larger theory of modern society—how prison spreads out into a "carceral archipelago" and becomes a whole system of institutions and practices (including disciplines such as psychology and medicine) aimed at "normalization" (ibid.: 296–297). Power in the form of surveillance and self-discipline is everywhere, exercised by everyone on him or herself and on everyone else. But the class-based analysis of power about the origins of the prison system vanishes and Foucault mystifies the exercise of power because "rather than operating along a class axis that might be eliminated, and to serve interests that might be identified and critiqued, power now seems its own goal, a universal fact of modern life" (Reiman and Leighton 2013: 50). Also absent from Foucault's analysis is attention to the difference between those forms of discipline that are necessary for the freedom of each to coexist peacefully with the freedom of the rest and those forms of discipline that simply serve the interests of the rich and powerful.

The second failure of the criminal justice system discussed in *The Rich Get Richer* is to adequately criminalize harms done by the wealthy and thus protect people from serious threats to their lives, health and property. This failure to protect people from the harmful acts of the rich also helps to shape the ideological message that it is (only) the poor who commit crimes and thus should be the focus of criminal justice control. As Quinney argues, crime has a "social reality" rather than an objective reality because crime is "created" by decisions of lawmakers, police, prosecutors, judges and juries. But as Christie notes, rape and murder are acts appropriately called crimes, so the question is whether the label of crime is applied appropriately. We argue that

> the label is applied appropriately when it is used to identify all, or at least the worst, acts that are harmful to society. The label is applied inappropriately when it is attached to harmless acts or when it is not attached to seriously harmful intentional acts.

> (Reiman and Leighton 2013: 74)

Calling crime created points to human actors rather than objective dangers as determining the shape that the reality of crime takes in our society. If the label "crime" is applied consistently to the most dangerous or harmful acts, then it is misleading to highlight the role of human decision-makers in creating reality because "crime" mirrors a reality that already exists. On the other hand, if the label is not applied appropriately, then criminal law is more like a carnival mirror that throws back a distorted image. The image cast back is false because

> large becomes small, and small large; grave becomes minor, and minor grave. Like a carnival mirror, although nothing is reflected that does not exist in the world, the image is more a creation of the mirror [i.e., the legislators and criminal justice system] than a picture of the world.

> (ibid.: 72)

Because our normal intuition about which acts should be crimes is itself shaped by the criminal law,

> criminology must look at crime while staying open to the idea that the legal definitions and, just as crucially, all the righteous beliefs that normally surround the legal enterprise are less than the whole truth, and perhaps even misleading or ideological.

> (Reiman 2013: 247)

Rather than having its central concept—crime—defined by the state, criminology must "seek its own understanding of what crime is" (ibid.) through philosophical reflection about harm and "a moral theory about what human beings owe to their fellows in the way of conduct" (ibid.: 248).

The Rich Get Richer follows up this concern by imagining a conversation with a Defender of the Present Legal Order about the limitations of what is currently defined as crime and the model of interpersonal victimization behind it. While a full review of that argument is beyond the scope of this chapter, we should emphasize that the failure to properly criminalize the harmful acts of the wealthy and corporations do not just make "crime" look like the activity of the poor. More importantly, the failure to criminalize knowing, reckless and negligent acts of corporations means that the criminal justice system fails to protect people from certain losses of life and property, as well as violations of their bodily autonomy. The regulatory system has an important role in trying to prevent these harms, but the criminal law and criminal justice system are necessary to punish and deter serious harm.

The third failure discussed by *The Rich Get Richer* is the failure to remedy class bias in the processing of those who violate the existing criminal law. At each step, from arresting to sentencing, the likelihood of being ignored, released or treated lightly by the system is greater for the wealthy than poor. The US government does not collect data that would verify this claim, and over successive editions of *The Rich Get Richer* the number of studies on class has declined markedly. Nor does the government publish data about the cost and prevalence of white-collar and corporate crime. As we show below, the crime reports of other developed countries do not do this either, with a few minor and woefully incomplete exceptions. First, though, we review the distributions of wealth in several developed nations to remind readers of the significant amount of inequality and the significance of class, which highlights how "the general marginalization of class in much of the social sciences literature is astonishing" (Mooney 2008: 68).

No Wealth of Data …

Mooney notes that while "class remains a primary determinant of social life," most public "discourses about modern society have been largely de-classed" (2008: 68). The neglect of class occurs in a context where "the scale of this inequality is almost beyond comprehension, perhaps not surprisingly as much of it remains hidden from view" (ibid.: 64). In contrast, this section provides an overview of the key concepts used to examine inequality, which usually exclude corporations. The second part of this section reviews the deplorable state of government-published data on class related to criminal offending.

No Wealth of Data about Wealth

Class is less frequently analyzed than race or gender, but it provides an important view of economic inequality and thus social justice. While class can be conceptualized in different ways (Barak *et al.* 2010: 73), we believe primary attention should be placed on income and wealth, because they allow a clear view of inequality in the distribution of economic power and resources. Income is the most straightforward indicator of class. It represents sources of individual revenue such as salary, interest, and the type of items that should be reported on income tax forms. By contrast, wealth is about assets like bank accounts, retirement accounts, houses, cars, and the ownership of stocks, bonds, and businesses; it also takes into account debts such as car loans, student loans, mortgages, and credit card balances. Wealth is what we accumulate over our lives and is about economic security and power. While income is unequally distributed, wealth is more unequal and this inequality is more important.

In the USA, data about household wealth comes from the Survey of Consumer Finances that is completed every three years. The results are reported by staff of the Federal Reserve, the semi-independent US central bank. The latest survey is from 2010 and the main report does not include data about the share of wealth held by certain percentile groups (Bricker *et al.* 2012)—the data that provide direct insight into inequality by revealing the share of wealth controlled by the richest 1 percent, 10 percent, etc. At this point in 2012, the latest available official data is from a 2007 working paper, which reveals that the bottom 50 percent in the USA owned 2.5 percent of the wealth while the top 1 percent owned 33.8 percent of the wealth (Kennickell 2009: 35). Such data is not available in a readily accessible form from the government, such as on the Department of Census website or in the widely used *Statistical Abstract of the United States*.

The United Kingdom publishes statistics on wealth on the website of Her Majesty's Revenue and Customs, which has a page for the "Distribution of Personal Wealth." The data are based on certain identified estates—those requiring a grant of representation to appoint an executor or transfer the estate to probate—and subjected to statistical procedures to make them more representative (see generally HMRC 2011). The data is reported in terms of ownership by decile, in contrast to the USA, where the poor have so little wealth that the ownership of the bottom five deciles is reported in aggregate, and where the rich have so much that the top decile is broken down into three categories (90th–95th percentile, 95th–99th and 99th–100th). Combining data for each country into common categories produces the results in Table 17.1.

Table 17.1 Share of Net Wealth Owned by Percentile Groups in the USA and the UK, 2007

USA (Share Owned by Percentile Group)	Percentile Group	UK (Share Owned by Percentile Group)
2.5	Bottom 50	13
26.0	50 to 90	42
71.5	Top 10	44

Source: Calculated from Kennickell (2009: 35) and HMRC (2011: Table 13.8). UK numbers are based on data from 2005 to 2007.

The USA exhibits the highest degree inequality among the developed nations, a situation made worse by the lack of national health care and some of the social supports that exist in European and the Scandinavian countries. Two economists from the US Federal Reserve note that the lowest levels of inequality "are found in, among others, Australia, Italy, Japan, and Sweden, and intermediate values in Canada, France, and the United Kingdom" (Cagetti and De Nardi 2008: 291). Table 17.2 provides data for (low inequality) Australia and (intermediate inequality) Canada. The report on wealth in Australia is notable for being relatively easy to read, with a section for definitions and the data on share of wealth by percentile group presented early in the report (Australian Bureau of Statistics 2011).

Whether or not law engages in the legal fiction that corporations are "persons," corporations are key players in people's lives as employers, community members, and providers of necessary goods and services. Corporations need to be included in the analysis of economic resources in order to have a full understanding of how inequality relates to crime, justice and equality under a rule of law. The intense concentration of wealth in corporations generates considerable political power, makes accountability increasingly difficult, and increases inequality in a way that is largely invisible to criminological theory.

Using available data on corporate assets and liabilities results in numbers that are not comparable to household wealth, the best comparison is between household income and corporate revenue. In 2010, in the USA, the median *household* income was $49,445 (DeNavas-Walt *et al.* 2011: 5). The smallest company in the Fortune 500 (Seaboard) in 2010 had revenue of $4.3 billion (*Fortune* 2011). If the median household income is represented by the median height in the US, 5'7", then Seaboard would be more than 90 miles tall. The biggest company in the Fortune 500 (Wal-Mart) has revenue of $421.8 billion—which would be over 9,000 miles tall.

Another way to problematize the size of corporate personhood is to compare the revenue of a corporation against the gross domestic product (GDP) of a country. (GDP is a measure of the value of all goods and services produced by a country.) This process results in a list of the largest economies

Table 17.2 Share of Net Worth by Quintile, Canada and Australia

Australia 2009–10		Canada 2005
0.9	Lowest quintile (bottom 20%)	0.1
5.4	Second quintile	2.3
11.9	Third quintile	8.4
20.0	Fourth quintile	20.2
61.8	Highest quintile (top 20%)	69.2

Source: Statistics Canada (2005: 9) and Australian Bureau of Statistics (2011: 31).

in the world and is presented in Table 17.3. That 34 corporations are in the top 100 largest economies highlights some of the problems that governments can have holding big corporations accountable. Corporations can effectively dominate the social control apparatus of many nations—including many developed nations (Alvesalo *et al.* 2006). Given that corporations hold massive economic resources, it would be surprising if there were no class-based dynamic to Foucault's analysis of surveillance and disciplinary power.

Table 17.3 World's Largest Economies GDP and Fortune 500 Revenue, 2010

Overall Rank	Country Rank	Company Rank	Country/Company	GDP/Revenue (in Billions of US$)
1	1		United States	15,064.8
2	2		China	6,988.5
3	3		Japan	5,855.4
7	7		United Kingdom	2,481.0
11	11		Canada	1,758.7
15	15		Australia	1,507.4
21	21		Saudi Arabia	560.3
29	29		South Africa	422.0
30		1	Wal-Mart Stores	421.8
31	30		United Arab Emirates	358.1
32		2	Exxon Mobil	354.6
50	48		Pakistan	204.1
51		3	Chevron	196.3
52	49		Romania	185.3
53		4	ConocoPhillips	184.9
57	53		Kuwait	171.1
61		5	Fannie Mae	153.8
62		6	General Electric	151.6
63	57		Hungary	147.9
64		7	Berkshire Hathaway	136.1
65		8	General Motors	135.6

66		9	Bank of America Corp.	134.2
67		10	Ford Motor	128.9
68		11	Hewlett-Packard	126.0
69		12	AT&T	124.6
70	58		Vietnam	121.6
71		13	J.P. Morgan Chase & Co.	115.5
72	59		Bangladesh	115.0
73		14	Citigroup	111.1
75	60		Iraq	108.6
76		16	Verizon Communications	106.5
77		17	AIG	104.4
78	61		Morocco	101.8
79		18	IBM	99.8
82		20	Freddie Mac	98.4
83	63		Slovak Republic	97.2
84		21	CVS Caremark	96.4
85		22	United Health Group	94.2
86		23	Wells Fargo	93.2
89		26	Procter & Gamble	79.7
91		28	Costco Wholesale	77.9
92	64		Azerbaijan	68.5
93		29	Marathon Oil	68.4
94		30	Home Depot	68.0
95		31	Pfizer	67.8
96		32	Walgreen	67.4
97		33	Target	67.4
100	66		Ecuador	65.3
101		35	Apple	65.2

Source: Fortune 500 from http://money.cnn.com/magazines/fortune/fortune500/2011/full_list International Monetary Fund, World Economic Outlook Database, September 2011. Gross domestic product is expressed in current (2011) US dollars. http://www.imf.org/external/pubs/ft/weo/2011/02/weodata/index.aspx.

No Wealth of Data About Class and Criminal Justice

Official government data is important in shaping the perception of the "crime problem" by news media, the public, and policy-makers, not to mention criminology books and academic research. To the extent that government data about crime is "de-classed," then readers of that data will not develop a consciousness about the relationships between class, criminal behavior and social control. Our aim, then, is to explore two issues related to class and criminal justice data. First, to what extent do nations provide data on class, income or wealth, as they do with gender and race? Government data on gender and race do not answer all questions about bias in criminal justice processing, but their existence reminds people that the variables are important and facilitates accountability by allowing researchers to start probing problematic decision points to help uncover injustice. Second, nations have one or two regular seminal reports on crime and victimization, and to what extent do those contain reporting on white-collar and corporate crime?

Developed nations share a commitment to a rule of law that includes equality before the law, so similar cases should not have different outcomes merely because one defendant is poor and another is rich. While nations that (rightly or wrongly) believe themselves to be homogeneous may not publish criminal justice statistics about race or ethnicity, developed nations have significant levels of inequality (as reviewed earlier). To ensure that the criminal justice system does not reflect and recreate excessive levels of inequality, governments should publish data about the class of criminal offenders and their movement through—or their removal from—the criminal justice system. Without data, accountability for class bias becomes substantially more challenging and there is a risk that criminal justice becomes "de-classed" at a time when it is providing law and order for a morally unjust economic system.

Developed nations have a victimization survey, but it is not well suited to identifying the income or wealth level of perpetrators, so our focus will be on publications reporting crimes known to the police. We do note, however, that some developed countries are willing to ask victims about their level of income, suggesting an awareness that class is important to under-standing and responding to victimization. But even those nations do not ask offenders the same question.

Because the USA has the highest crime rates of any developed nation, it has more detailed reporting of crime than other developed nations. Both the National Crime Victimization Survey (NCVS) and reports on crimes known to the police (Federal Bureau of Investigation 2011) do include important information on gender and race/ethnicity, but the NCVS has only one table about the income of victims. Until 2004, the victimization survey reported on violent and property victimizations by income, but only the data on property crime victimization remains (Barak *et al.* 2010: 161–162). The most likely reason for the disappearance of this data is budget cuts that have reduced the sample size and thus made estimates of violent crime unstable because they occur less frequently than property crime. Still, officials made a conscious decision that retaining this limited data about class was not important enough to justify the expense. Developed nations have the resources, but choose not to collect data about the inconvenient truth of class bias, which leads to larger discussions about the inconvenient truth of inequality.

Australia reports on adult detainees' education level (Australian Institute of Criminology 2012a: 85) and *source of income* (full- or part-time job, welfare, friends/family, savings, sex work, drug dealing, shoplifting, other crime) (ibid.: 86–7). But there is no data about actual income or assets. The sections on criminal courts and corrections also contain nothing about income or wealth, in contrast with the numerous figures about age and gender. (Indigenous status is occasionally reported in this publication.) Given the detailed, thoughtful and systematic presentation of wealth data in Australia (Australian Bureau of Statistics 2011), it is disappointing that criminal justice data on class is absent.

British crime and victimization data are based on both the Crime Survey for England and Wales (CSEW) and crimes known to the police, neither of which contains data about class, race or gender. The survey reports on the number of offenses, but not the characteristics of victims or offenders, with the exception of a section on crime experienced by children aged 10–15 (Office for National Statistics 2012a). For some offenses, especially fraud, data is supplemented with other reports, but still do not cover the victim's or offender's race, citizenship, class or gender. The report on crimes known to the police focuses on whether a known crime is "detected" or "cleared-up" by the identification of a suspect, and whether there is a sanction (which can range from a warning to being charged) (Home Office 2012). The tables break down the percentage of outcomes for various crimes and the changes over time. But the data do not allow for an analysis of, say, whether class influences the decisions about which drug offenders get a warning and which are charged.

In Canada, the report on crimes known to police mostly breaks down the level of known offenses by geography (province/territory and city) and by year, with a few tables on the "characteristics of accused persons" containing gender and age (Statistics Canada 2012a). Data from the General Social Survey reports only limited information on the income levels of those experiencing property and violent victimization (Statistics Canada 2010: 22–3, 26), without a similar interest in the income of the offender. The publication *Adult Criminal Court Statistics in Canada* describes the volume of different crimes, age, sex, geography, outcome, and time-to-disposition of the case—but does not provide information on wealth or income (Statistics Canada 2012b).

The second important issue is whether the main reports on crime include crime in the suites as well as crime on the streets. A national report supposedly summarizing "crime" that does not include white-collar and corporate crime sends the message that street crime is "real" crime; it trivializes the serious harm done by the wealthy even as it presents great detail on even the minor wrongdoing of the lower classes. The point is not to have a report on "crime" and a separate one on white-collar and corporate crime, but to integrate the violations of law by rich and poor into a report that is a useful tool because it presents comprehensive information about criminal harms and the threats citizens face.

The NCVS in the USA does not have any questions about white-collar crime, even though the National White Collar Crime Center completed large-scale surveys in 1999 and 2005—and found that half of the households were aware of experiencing a white-collar victimization (Friedrichs 2010: 47). The Federal Bureau of Investigation (FBI) publishes data about offenses known to local police departments, which do not tend to be involved with white-collar crimes. The section on property crime includes the offenses of burglary, larceny-theft, motor vehicle theft, and arson. Larceny-theft excludes embezzlement, con games and fraud. The FBI does note that in 2010 there were about 78,000 arrests for forgery and counterfeiting, 188,000 for fraud, and almost 17,000 for embezzlement (Federal Bureau of Investigation 2011: Table 29). While many of these arrests are for small-scale scams and cons that are not central to the study of white-collar crime, the exclusion of these categories from the main body of a report on crime removes white-collar crimes from the public consciousness. As a result, during the collapse of Enron and other companies in 2001—when accounting fraud cost investors 70–90 percent of their money and top officials of those companies "were getting immensely, extraordinarily, obscenely wealthy" (in Reiman and Leighton 2013: 146)—the Department of Justice reported that "property crimes had continued their downward trend and fallen to an all-time low" (cited in Barak 2012: 73).

Following the corporate scandals that began with Enron (Reiman and Leighton 2013: 146), then-President Bush launched the Corporate Fraud Task Force. They issued reports on corporate fraud in 2003 and 2004, but they were lists of cases and settlements, with no effort to summarize data, discuss larger problems, make policy recommendations, etc. After 2004, the task force did not issue another report until early 2008, which included a substantial number of cases from the 2003 and 2004 reports. Although this report was issued right before the financial crisis, it did not detect or note any patterns that forewarned an imminent global crisis. There were no reports after the financial crisis and the website address for the task force contains the word "archive" (Corporate Fraud Task Force [no date]), implying—in the face of massive evidence to the contrary (Barak 2012)—that the time for a focus on corporate fraud has passed.

The Australian Capital Territory passed an industrial manslaughter act in 2003 to facilitate the prosecution of corporate bodies responsible for employee deaths, but the rest of the country follows the *Criminal Code Act* of 1995 that clarified how the overall criminal code applies to corporations. Australian crime statistics (Australian Institute of Criminology 2012a) do not indicate how frequently these provisions are applied, if ever. A detailed look at homicide does not address whether "employer" could be a victim–offender relationship or whether "workplace" contains any health and safety crimes (Australian Institute of Criminology 2008).

Australian reports on fraud do include fraudulent trade practices, in addition to the expected acts of forgery, counterfeiting, credit card fraud and other deceptive practices (Australian Institute of Criminology 2012a: 36). They also present minimal information on cybercrime, including malware (malicious software), compromised web sites, and scams (ibid.: 58), many of which are considered white-collar crime. The victimization survey does not ask about fraud, however, the Australasian Consumer Fraud Task Force conducts a yearly consumer fraud survey to assess the prevalence of consumer scams, which they define as attempts "designed to obtain someone's personal information or money or otherwise to obtain a financial benefit by deceptive means" (Australian Institute of Criminology 2012b: 1). Although this definition could include acts by businesses and financial institutions, reporting is limited to scams involving notices about advance fee scams, alleged lottery winnings, inheritance, financial advice, work from home, phishing (attempts to get personal information for activities like identity theft), dating, etc. The median 2010 loss was $700, and respondents also reported emotional trauma, loss of confidence in people and/or marital or relationship problems because of the victimization. Thus, these incidents are more serious than a range of acts frequently reported in regular crime statistics, like petty theft and most vandalism.

The British victimization survey (CSEW) contains information on offense types like "wounding" – and changes have increased the reporting of violent crimes without injuries (Office for National Statistics 2012a)—but wounding by defective consumer products or criminal health and safety violations are not asked about. Theft includes "bicycle theft and shoplifting" and "pick-pocketing" among the common forms of the offense (ibid.: 4, 42) as well as "opportunistic" incidents like the "theft of garden furniture" outside the house (ibid.: 43). But it neglects more serious crimes because "unauthorized taking" offenses do not apply to the behavior of financial institutions or business that try to impose inappropriate fees, penalties or charges to people's accounts.

According to the report, fraud is "often targeted at organisations rather than individuals" (ibid.: 56), but fraud targeted at individuals by institutions is not mentioned. Fraud data is supplemented by "non-National Statistics" from the National Fraud Intelligence Bureau about some white-collar crimes and scams involving charities, corporate employees, computer misuse, investment, insurance-related, advance fee, corporate procurement, telecommunications industry, banking/payment, and business trading (ibid.: 58). However, business trading is only about ("illegitimate") businesses set up to commit scams, not the scams of "legitimate" businesses. Telecommunications industry fraud refers to mobile phone fraud by individuals directed at telecom companies, not the behavior of the companies or telemarketing firms. The banking and payment fraud largely involves check/cheque fraud and (credit and debit) "plastic card" fraud, which means unauthorized purchases rather than financial institutions' wrongdoing. The corporate employee fraud refers to "an employee making a fraudulent claim for travel or subsistence" (Office for National Statistics 2012b: 35) rather than the behavior of executives perpetrating frauds on their employees, shareholders, customers, or the government. In these cases, police work with powerful institutions (e.g., the UK Cards Association) to prevent losses perpetrated by individuals, with no effort even to recognize that individuals are victimized by institutions. The British are starting a survey about the victimization of business establishments that will be incorporated into future releases of the regular CSEW survey reports (Office for National Statistics 2012a: 79), but there is no consideration of expanding the survey to include more victimizations of consumers, employees and communities by business establishments.

The British report on crimes known to the police helpfully includes under the "theft" category: "fraud by a company director" (207 offenses in 2010/11 and 45 in 2011/12), false accounting (108 offenses in 2010/11 and 75 in 2011/12) and fraud by abuse of position (1,033 offenses in 2010/11 and 1,170 in 2011/12) (Home Office 2012: 19). Further, homicide does include acts charged under the Corporate Manslaughter and Corporate Homicide Act 2007, under which an organization is guilty "if the way in which its activities are managed or organised causes a death and amounts to a gross breach of a relevant duty of care to the deceased" (Ministry of Justice 2008).The detailed table for violent crime reports that, in 2010/11, there was one such offense with no sanctions, and in 2011/12, there were two offenses and two sanctions (Home Office 2012: 16). Observers can then ask whether that level is too high, too low or seems consistent with the prevalence of the harm.

Every five years in Canada the General Social Survey collects information on a limited range of criminal offenses: "sexual assault, robbery, physical assault, break and enter, motor vehicle/parts theft, theft of household property, vandalism and theft of personal property" (Statistics Canada 2010: 6). Theft does not include consumer fraud, scams or white-collar financial fraud—harms that are typically more serious than vandalism. Violent victimization also excludes consumer products and workplace safety issues. The perceptions of personal safety asks about acts like walking alone or using public transportation after dark (ibid.: 18, 30), but not the behavior of corporations.

The section on property crimes known to Canadian police is part of a write-up on nonviolent crime that is two pages long, mostly about breaking and entering and motor vehicle theft (Statistics Canada 2012a: 17–18). It provides no detail about fraud, which occurs at a similar rate to auto theft. Property crime does include fraud and identity theft, but it seems not to include frauds by financial institutions, especially those preying on the general public (ibid.: 30–31). Consumer fraud and fraudulent trade practices also are not considered.

In 2004, Bill C-45 modernized Canada's criminal code to clarify how it applied to increasingly complex organizations (Department of Justice (Canada) 2012). However, any crime reported under this law is not counted in a way that would allow the reader to see how frequently it is applied. Indeed, the first time criminal negligence was applied to a corporation was after four workers died from falling 13 stories when scaffolding collapsed on Christmas Eve in 2009. Thus, charges are unusual, but it is unclear if even these figures are reflected in the homicide reports, which include manslaughter (Statistics Canada 2011: 17) and thus ought to cover negligence. But data breakdowns on method (number of "other" offenses) (ibid.: 27) and relationship ("business relationship (legal)") (ibid.: 31) do not seem to include these four deaths for either 2009 or 2010.

Research Directions that Give Justice More Class

We suggest two avenues to help "re-class" data: one about general inequality in developed nations, and the other about white-collar and corporate crime. (The collection of data about an offender's income is important, but that is a policy issue requiring government action rather than being an existing research strategy.) The first avenue collects people's beliefs about the ideal distribution of wealth and their knowledge of current actual distributions. The results can start a conversation about the injustice of current distributions and provide insight into the effects of ideology. The second avenue works around omission of white-collar and corporate crime in official data by advocating that researchers use additional existing data sources to compile alternative or shadow statistics that paint a more realistic picture of crime. But data is still scarce where corporations victimize—sometimes on a mass scale—workers, consumers or communities, and this category of wrongdoing especially needs more original research on behalf of the public interest.

In his classic theory of justice, Rawls suggests evaluating society based on the preferences people would have if choosing from behind a veil of ignorance: decide what society should look like without knowledge of race, sex, class, religion, disability, etc. Norton and Ariely (2011) tried a simplified version of this by asking 5,500 adults to choose from three distributions, which, unknown to the subject, represented the distribution in Sweden, the USA and an equal distribution. Americans overwhelmingly chose Sweden, with very low levels of inequality.

In Rawls' writing, the veil of ignorance exercise includes specified information and thus constraints on what can be rationally agreed to. This yields the principle that justice requires the least inequality necessary to maximize the share of the worst off. We believe that inequality in the USA clearly is far greater than what would be necessary to increase the well-being of those at the bottom of the spectrum (Reiman and Leighton 2013: 205, n. 60). Subjects in Norton and Ariely's (2011) survey did not have the full information available in Rawls' exercise, but chose distributions of wealth far more equal than what exists in reality. The researchers did not just compare this "ideal" to the actual distribution of wealth, but they asked people what they believed the distribution of wealth to be. The full results are available in Table 17.4, which indicates that Americans believed the top 20 percent owned 59 percent of the wealth, when it was really 84 percent and people believe it should be 32 percent. This has profound implications for the amount of wealth distributed at the bottom: the ideal distribution for the poorest 60 percent would involve them owning about 45 percent of the wealth, compared to a perceived ownership of 20 percent of the wealth and an actual ownership of less than 5 percent.

Table 17.4 Actual, Perceived, and Ideal Distributions of Wealth in the United States

Wealth of Poorest 60% as a Percentage		Wealth of Richest 20% as a Percentage
5	Actual amount of wealth	84
20	Perceived amount of wealth	59
45	Ideal amount of wealth	32

Source: Calculated from Norton and Ariely (2011).

People collectively underestimate inequality by a substantial amount, and mistakes about economic facts support the unequal status quo. When ideas—whether intentionally or not—"distort reality in a way that justifies the prevailing distribution of power and wealth, hides society's injustices, and thus secures uncritical allegiance to the existing social order, we have what Marx called ideology" (Reiman and Leighton 2013: 195). Those with little far outnumber the top few percentage who have plenty. Thus, "the have-nots and the have-littles could have more if they decided to take it from the have-plenties. This, in turn, means that the have-plenties need the cooperation of the have-nots and the have-littles" (ibid.: 196). This cooperation must be voluntary, and so "the have-nots and the have-littles must believe it would not be right or reasonable to take away what the have-plenties have" (ibid.)—that the system is legitimate.

Replicating Norton and Ariely's work (2011) in other developed nations would help develop data on questions about social justice and ideology. Evidence that the existing society violates citizens' expectations for fairness is a powerful tool to motivate deeper investigation about what social arrangements should look like—and how to advocate for change. Also, the discrepancy between the actual distribution of wealth and what people believe it to be is important data for the study of ideology. Random error would be evenly distributed in a way that was equally likely to over- and under-estimate inequality, with the average being close to the correct value. But error that consistently underestimates inequality is the result of systematic forces and constitutes evidence of the effect of ideology, which refers to what is necessarily deceptive. Some writers use ideology to refer to a "belief system" or "worldview." But this "moral neutralization of the concept of 'ideology' dulls an instrument that thinkers such as Marx and others have sharpened into an effective tool for cutting through the illusions that dog our political life" (Reiman and Leighton 2013: 196).

"Systematic forces" does not mean that ideology is conscious deception. Marx wrote that "the ideas of the ruling class are in every epoch the ruling ideas ... The class which has the means of material production at its disposal, has control at the same time over the means of mental production" (in Reiman and Leighton 2013: 194). Those who have economic power own newspapers, endow universities, finance the publication of books and journals, and control television, radio and other electronic media. The controllers of the "means of mental production" broadcast a picture of reality that they believe to be accurate, and which will be largely the picture of reality that fills the heads of the readers and viewers of the mass media. What people take to be "common sense" or conventional wisdom is nevertheless based on a distorted consensus. And an important question this research helps us understand is how distorted people's pictures of reality are, and whether nations with higher levels of inequality have more distortion.

The second research direction involves putting class back into data about crime so it includes white-collar and corporate crime. Even though the existing law needs to further criminalize white-collar and corporate crime to mirror the harmful acts, crime reports should reflect all the threats to people's lives, health and property as currently defined by law, not merely compile data on the wrongdoing of the poor. Broader inclusion of data on white-collar and corporate crime in government reports requires policy changes, but researchers can still compile data from alternative sources to create de-classed crime reports (e.g. ibid.: 95). The goal would be to include fraud by a company director and corporate manslaughter (as the British do) or fraudulent trade practices (as Australia does). These alternative, or shadow, government statistics are explicit about their methodology, assumptions, and data sources—just like any transparent and useful data source.

However, this strategy has some important limitations because data increasingly comes from industries that study their own losses and victimization, usually by the poor and middle class. But there's little data—and little money to study—victimization perpetrated by corporations and industries. The discussion above noted that Britain worked with the trade association for credit and debit cards to gather more information on fraud—fraud against financial institutions, which pay for charges on lost and stolen cards. To the extent that abuses of consumers by card issuers are criminalized, no one collects data on the types of crimes, their frequency or aggregate cost to the public. A publication by the British National Fraud Authority (NFA)—an executive agency within the Home Office—has estimates of fraud *against* insurance companies and mortgage lenders (National Fraud Authority 2012: 17), but not corresponding estimates of fraud done *by* these industries against the public to boost profits. For example, in the USA—and most likely Britain too—"paying out less to victims of catastrophes has helped produce record profits," according to Bloomberg News (Dietz and Preston 2007). The investigative report did not put a total dollar amount on such losses, but noted:

> The insurance companies routinely refuse to pay market prices for homes and replacement contents, they use computer programs to cut payouts, they change policy coverage with no clear explanation, they ignore or alter engineering reports, and they sometimes ask their adjusters to lie to customers, court records and interviews with former employees and state regulators show.

Discussions of problems like fraud contain language that obscures the very existence of crimes by financial institutions. The NFA's discussion of fraud against individuals included "mass marketing fraud," which means unsolicited communications for money (National Fraud Authority 2012: 8–9) rather than false advertising or deceptive trade practices. "Insider-enabled fraud" is "staff fraud" and "employee fraud" (ibid.: 24), but not control fraud, which is perpetrated by executive-level insiders. Executives who control a company create fictitious profits to turn corporate assets into personal assets (through stock bonuses, etc.) and ultimately defraud a variety of people, like shareholders. Businesses "report sensational profits, followed by catastrophic failure" (in Barak 2012: 73)—a pattern that should be immediately recognizable to the British and citizens of every developed nation. Yet an Australian government report on fraud noted:

> Fraud affects all sectors of the community, extending from individuals who have responded to online offers to make 'quick money', to large companies and government departments that have suffered fraud at the hands of their employees or members of the public.
>
> (Australian Institute of Criminology 2012c: ix)

Certainly businesses and corporations in Australia have enough of a history of perpetrating fraud that they should be included as part of the basic description of the fraud problem.

In general, the missing data are about the crimes of the powerful that protect and advance the accumulation of capital (Barak *et al.* 2010: 11). Crime reports can retain data on minor theft, but they also need to recognize that

> the most consequential white-collar crimes—in terms of their scope, impact and cost in dollars—appear to require for their commission, that their perpetrators operate in an environment that provides access to both money and the organization through which money moves.
>
> (Braithwaite 1992: 86)

Financial and corporate interests make sure that acquisitive activities they perpetrate against people are not criminalized, and if criminalized, not prosecuted, counted or conceived of as "real" crime. Instead, wealthy industries produce data about their own victimization, including white-collar crimes like fraud by middle managers and card fraud. But the key to future research is to examine the direction of the victimization and explore the areas where the wealthiest and most powerful are the perpetrators, because those are the uncounted harms—and if left uncounted, the harms they represent will disappear from consciousness.

Policy Implications of the Inconvenient Truths about Wealth

The problem of inequality is the primary policy implication, but several smaller policy issues are worth noting briefly. First, the development of better data is necessary where a criminal justice system produces minimal data on class and is thus not accountable for bias. In the USA, for-profit probation companies are growing rapidly—with a debt collection business model and "onerous 'user fees'" (Bronner 2012)—so collection of data about income and wealth needs to be done in a way that does not lead to criminal justice becoming (more) complicit in legal extortion for private gain.

Second, policies need to promote the systematic collection and regular dissemination of data about white-collar and corporate harm, preferably in existing reports on the nation's crime problem. The inclusiveness of German crime data makes it a possible model in terms of what should be presented. For example, it includes economic crime, which captures criminal violations of the patent, trademark and copyright acts; the Act Against Unfair Competition, Act on the Financial Statements of Certain Enterprises and Groups, Insurance Industry Supervision Act, Securities Trading Act, and Economic Offenses Act of 1954; and, among others, criminal offenses according to the Wine Act and food products legislation (Bundeskriminalamt 2011: 8).

Third, existing laws regulating the conduct of the poor need to be applied equally to corporations or repealed for all. For example, the British crime data reports 2.7 million Antisocial Behavior Orders (ASBOs) (Office for National Statistics 2012a: 70). An ASBO is recorded using three simplified categories. As relevant here, *nuisance* includes "where an act, condition, thing or person causes trouble, annoyance, irritation, inconvenience, offence or suffering to the local community in general rather than to individual victims." And, *environmental* "captures incidents where individuals and groups have an impact on their surroundings, including natural, built and social environments" (ibid.: 71). ASBOs are described over a number of pages in the crime report that details noisy neighbors, drunk or rowdy behavior, litter, drug use/dealing, teenagers loitering, vandalism/graffiti, and abandoned/burnt-out cars (ibid.). But neither the law nor the concept applies to corporations, even though economic theory and legal structures drive it to focus narrowly on self-interest, thus maximizing the likelihood of inconsiderate behavior that damages others. Corporate behavior may not fit this law as it was written, but the question remains why nuisance behaviors of individuals are worth sanctioning and counting (and studying), but the nuisance behaviors of corporations are not. If the ASBO has merit—a debatable proposition (Prior 2009)—then it should also apply to "nuisance" and "environmental" impacts of corporate behavior that pollutes communities, economically exploits workers, cuts corners with workers' health and safety, commits unfair trade practices, produces dangerous products, defrauds consumers, etc. Some of these behaviors are already against the law, but an ASBO could fill in where the behavior is a nuisance that needs to be officially recognized but other systems do not have the resources for a full investigation and prosecution.

Attending to the recommendations above and other concerns raised by this chapter requires policies to combat inequality. Braithwaite nicely summarizes the problem by explaining that inequality "worsens both crimes of poverty motivated by *need* for goods for use and crimes of wealth motivated by *greed* enabled by goods for exchange" (1992: 81). For Braithwaite, "need" is culturally constructed and based on community norms, expectations and advertising. In general, then, "the more unequal the class structure, the more scarce national wealth is devoted to gratifying greed among people whose needs are satisfied, the less is devoted to satisfying unmet needs" (ibid.: 83). As suggested by opportunity theory, where legitimate means to achieving such needs are blocked, illegitimate and criminal means for satisfying needs become more likely.

Even when the rich have their needs met, additional dollars still have value to them and they pursue additional wealth "to signify their worth by conspicuous consumption, to prove success to themselves, to build an empire, to leave an inheritance" (ibid.: 84). If legitimate means are blocked, the rich can pursue existing illegitimate means—or create new types of illegitimate means. The limitation on traditional opportunity theory is that it is not applied to the wealthy, and, notes Braithwaite, "if they are powerful enough, criminals can actively constitute illegitimate opportunities" (ibid.: 86). Further, these novel illegitimate strategies "excel because they cannot be contemplated by those who are not wealthy" (ibid.: 88), and at times they cannot be contemplated even by regulatory agencies.

One of the greatest advantages of the wealthy and corporations is to prevent their actions from becoming criminal in the first place. They can also use their resources to frustrate regulation and thus remain unaccountable for their wrongdoing and the harm they have caused to others. Braithwaite notes: "power corrupts and unaccountable power corrupts with impunity" (ibid.: 89). This analysis dovetails with Christie's concern about weak states, which is supported by a quote from Bauman: "weak, quasi-states can be easily reduced to the (useful) role of legal police precincts, securing a modicum of order required for the conduct of business, but need not be feared as effective brakes on the global companies' freedom" (Christie 2004: 36). Even though the USA is the largest global economy, Ritholtz—the CEO of a financial research firm and author of *Bailout Nation*—believes that the Securities and Exchange Commission is "defective by design" (in Reiman and Leighton 2013: 159). Meanwhile, the "janitors of the suitably weakened states" need to prove their worth, so fighting street crime "becomes indispensable in creating legitimacy" (Christie 2004: 37).

Inequality thus extends crime through the power of the wealthy and undermines the effectiveness of guardians who should protect the vulnerable from motivated offenders (Alvesalo *et al.* 2006). Braithwaite further argues that inequality reduces the respect the powerful have for the dominion of others, especially the poorest.

> [Dominion] includes the sphere of control citizens properly enjoy over their persons, their property and the province. To enjoy dominion, a citizen must live in a social world where other citizens respect his or her liberty and where mutual respect is socially assured and generally recognized.
>
> (Braithwaite 1992: 80)

The idea that greater levels of inequality lead to crime via contempt for the citizenship rights of the weak is an important complement to concerns that inequality and social exclusion lead the poor to commit crimes because they have little respect for the law (Reiman and Leighton 2013: 33, 186).

Further, inequality plays a role in violent crime as well. Braithwaite draws on Katz and others who have developed theories about the role of humiliation, which can turn into righteous rage and violent acts. While Katz focused on the immediate transformation of emotions and denied the relevance of background and material factors, Braithwaite integrates it:

> *[I]negalitarian societies are structurally humiliating.* When parents cannot supply the most basic needs to their children, when they are assailed by the ostentatious consumption of the affluent, this is structurally humiliating for the poor. Where inequality is great, the rich humiliate the poor through conspicuous consumption and the poor are humiliated as failures for being poor. Both sides of this equation are important. The propensity to feel powerless and exploited among the poor and the propensity of the rich to see exploiting as legitimate, both ... enable crime.
>
> (1992: 94, emphasis in original)

Currie's analysis is similar and emphasizes not just poverty or "the simple absence of material goods, but rather the deeper attitudes of hopelessness and alienation produced by inequalities that are unjust" (1985: 162). Simply put, "violence results 'not so much from lack of advantages as from being taken advantage of'" (ibid.).

Redressing inequality—and especially the alienation, exclusion and hopelessness—is important for social justice and crime prevention. This conclusion is not new, although it is an(other) inconvenient truth about inequality. As Braithwaite summarizes:

> If crime in the suites arises from the fact that certain people have great wealth and power, and if crime in the streets arises from the fact certain other people have very little wealth or power, then policies to redistribute wealth and power may simultaneously relieve both types of crime problems.
>
> (1992: 90)

Currie fills out this prescription by adding that "we must build a society that is less unequal, less depriving, less insecure, less disruptive of family and community ties, less corrosive of cooperative values" (1985: 225).

Conclusion

An issue raised in this chapter's Introduction was Christie's observation that prison populations biased in terms of the identity of the receivers of the intended pain can "indicate severe defects somewhere in that system" (2004: 102). In our view, there is bias, with the poor being (conspicuously) over-consumed by the criminal justice system and the rich being (inconspicuously) under-consumed. Based on *The Rich Get Richer and the Poor Get Prison*, we suggest that three separate defects contribute to this phenomenon. First, society does not deal with root causes of crime—especially inequality—and may enact policies that promote criminogenic conditions for the poor. Second, legislatures do not adequately criminalize real harms of business that create real victims of workers, consumers, investors and communities. Third, the criminal justice system operates with class bias, although it is hidden by both not collecting income data on criminal offenders and not including white-collar crimes in annual government reports on "crime."

This analysis has important implications because the moral legitimacy of a legal system hinges on whether coercion is being used in the interests of all equally, or whether it promotes some people's interests at the expense of others. Criminals and occupying troops use force to subject some people to the interests of others, while legal systems claim moral superiority because they are supposed to use force to protect equally the interests and rights of all and to punish equally all who endanger these interests or who violate these rights. This adds up to something that should be obvious but is not: A criminal justice system is criminal to the extent that it is not truly a system of justice (Reiman and Leighton 2013: 207).

Because the system protects certain interests does not mean that it is the result of a conspiracy. The focus on one-on-one (rather than corporate) harm reflects the main ways in which people harmed each other in the days before large-scale industrialization. The Pyrrhic defeat theory suggests that current failed criminal justice policies persist because they fail in a way that does not give rise to an effective demand for change. First, this failing system provides benefits for those with the power to make changes, while it imposes costs on those without such power. The wealthy experience low rates of victimization from street crime, generally profit from the opportunity to expose workers or consumers to extra risk, and benefit from class bias in processing offenders. Second, because the criminal justice system shapes the public's conception of what is dangerous, it creates the impression that the harms it is fighting are the real threats to society. Thus, even when people continue to experience "fear of crime," they only demand a continuation or escalation of the same policies: more police, more prisons, longer prison sentences, and so on.

Consider first the benefits that the system provides for those with wealth and power. The failure of criminal justice policy diverts attention from the harmful noncriminal acts of the well-off and focuses people's attention on a real threat of theft and violence on the street, and a large and visible population of poor criminals in the courts and prisons. This conveys a vivid image—supported by the crime reports that lack white-collar and corporate crime data—that the real threat to people's lives and limbs is from the poor. The media, criminal justice textbooks and public policy reports amplify this message by reproducing the statistics and dramatizing the interpersonal acts in the crime reports. This image of crime provides benefits to the rich and powerful through an ideological message that the threat to law-abiding Middle America comes from below them on the economic ladder, not above them. It creates (or reinforces) fear of, and hostility toward, the poor. It leads people to ignore the ways in which they are injured and robbed by the acts of the affluent, and thus it points toward a *conservative* defense of society's disparities of wealth, power, and opportunity—and leads them away from a *progressive* demand for equality and a more equitable distribution of wealth and power (Reiman and Leighton 2013: 180).

References

Alvesalo, A., Tombs, S., Virta, E. and Whyte, D. (2006). "Re-Imagining Crime Prevention: Controlling Corporate Crime?" *Crime, Law and Social Change*, 45: 1–25.

Australian Bureau of Statistics (2011). *Household Wealth and Wealth Distribution, 2009–10*, Canberra: Australian Bureau of Statistics, available at: http://www.ausstats.abs.gov.au/Ausstats/subscriber.nsf/0/51342DFD-54324472CA257928001107B4/$File/65540_2009-10.pdf (accessed 27 August 2012).

Australian Institute of Criminology (2008). *Homicide in Australia: 2006–07 National Homicide Monitoring Program Annual Report*, Canberra: Australian Institute of Criminology, available at: http://www.aic.gov.au/ documents/F/F/B/%7BFFB9E49F-160F-43FC-B98D-6BC510DC2AFD%7Dmr01.pdf (accessed 27 August 2012).

Australian Institute of Criminology (2012a). *Australian Crime: Facts and Figures 2011*, Canberra: Australian Institute of Criminology, available at: http://www.aic.gov.au/documents/0/B/6/%7B0B619F44-B18B-47B4-9B59-F87BA643CBAA%7Dfacts11.pdf (accessed 27 August 2012).

Australian Institute of Criminology (2012b). *Australasian Consumer Fraud Taskforce: Results of the 2010 and 2011 Online Consumer Fraud Surveys*, Canberra: Australian Institute of Criminology, available at: http://www.aic.gov.au/documents/7/C/F/%7B7CF8C691-F02E-41EA-8DB4-74922AEEDDAF%7Dtbp50.pdf (accessed 27 August 2012).

Australian Institute of Criminology (2012c). *Fraud against the Commonwealth 2009–10 Annual Report to Government*, Canberra: Australian Institute of Criminology, available at: http://www.aic.gov.au/documents/B/5/1/%7BB514C8BC-4578-4D7F-A9C8-475FF1269004%7DMR18.pdf (accessed 27 August 2012).

Barak, G. (2012). *Theft of a Nation: Wall Street Looting and Federal Regulatory Colluding*, Lanham, MD: Rowman and Littlefield.

Barak, G., Leighton, P. and Flavin, J. (2010). *Class, Race, Gender and Crime*, 3rd edn, Lanham, MD: Rowman and Littlefield.

Braithwaite, J. (1992). "Poverty, Power, and White-Collar Crime," in K. Schlegel and D. Weisburd (eds.) *White-Collar Crime Reconsidered*, Boston: Northeastern University Press.

Bricker, J., Kennickell, A., Moore, K. and Sabelhaus, J. (2012). "Changes in U.S. Family Finances from 2007 to 2010: Evidence from the Survey of Consumer Finances," *Federal Reserve Bulletin*, 98(2): 1–80, available at: http://www.federalreserve.gov/pubs/bulletin/2012/pdf/scf12.pdf (accessed 27 August 2012).

Bronner, E. (2012). "Poor Land in Jail as Companies Add Huge Fees for Probation," *New York Times*, 2 July, available at: http://www.nytimes.com/2012/07/03/us/probation-fees-multiply-as-companies-profit.html (accessed 27 August 2012).

Bucks, B., Kennickell, A., Mach, T. and Moore, K. (2009). "Changes in U.S. Family Finances from 2004 to 2007: Evidence from the Survey of Consumer Finances," *Federal Reserve Bulletin*, 95: A1–A55, available at: http://www.federalreserve.gov/econresdata/scf/files/2007_scf09.pdf (accessed 27 August 2012).

Bundeskriminalamt (2011). *Police Crime Statistics, 2010*, Wiesbaden: Federal Criminal Police Office, available at: http://www.bka.de/nn_194552/EN/Publications/PoliceCrimeStatistics/policeCrime Statistics_node.html?_nnn=true (accessed 27 August 2012).

Cagetti, M. and De Nardi, M. (2008). "Wealth Inequality: Data and Models," *Macroeconomic Dynamics*, 12 (Supplement 2): 285–313.

Christie, N. (2000). *Crime Control as Industry*, 3rd edn, London: Routledge.

Christie, N. (2004). *A Suitable Amount of Crime*, London: Routledge.

Corporate Fraud Task Force (n.d.) "The President's Corporate Fraud Task Force," Washington, DC: Department of Justice, available at: http://www.justice.gov/archive/dag/cftf/ (accessed 27 August 2012). Currie, E. (1985) *Confronting Crime*, New York: Pantheon.

DeNavas-Walt, C., Proctor, B. and Smith, J. (2011). *Income, Poverty, and Health Insurance Coverage in the United States: 2010*, U.S. Census Bureau, Current Population Reports, P60-239. U.S. Washington, DC: Government Printing Office, available at: http://www.census.gov/prod/2011pubs/p60-239.pdf (accessed 27 August 2012).

Department of Justice (Canada) (2012). *A Plain Language Guide Bill C-45—Amendments to the Criminal Code Affecting the Criminal Liability of Organizations*, Ottawa: Department of Justice, available at: http://www.justice.gc.ca/eng/dept-min/pub/c45/p02.html#sec2 (accessed 27 August 2012).

Dietz, D. and Preston, D. (2007). "Home Insurers' Secret Tactics Cheat Fire Victims, Hike Profits," *Bloomberg News*, August 3, available at: http://www.bloomberg.com/apps/news?pid=newsarchive&sid=aIOpZROwhvNI.

Erikson, K. (1966) *Wayward Puritans*, New York: Macmillan.

Federal Bureau of Investigation (2011). *Crime in the U.S., 2010*, available at: http://www.fbi.gov/about-us/cjis/ucr/crime-in-the.u.s/2010/crime-in-the.u.s.-2010 (accessed 27 August 2012).

Foucault, M. (1977). *Discipline and Punish: The Birth of the Prison*, trans. A. Sheridan, London: Allen Lane.

Friedrichs, D. (2010). *Trusted Criminals*, Belmont, CA: Wadsworth/Cengage.

HMRC (Her Majesty's Revenue and Customs) (2011). "Table 13.8 Identified personal wealth," *Personal Wealth Statistics, 2001 to 03 and 2005 to 07*, available at: http://www.hmrc.gov.uk/stats/personal_wealth/intro-personal-wealth.pdf (accessed 27 August 2012).

Home Office (2012). *Crimes Detected in England and Wales 2011/12*, London: Home Office, available at: http://www.homeoffice.gov.uk/publications/science-research-statistics/research-statistics/crime-research/hosb0812/hosb0812?view=Binary (accessed 27 August 2012).

Kennickell, A. (2009). "Ponds and Streams: Wealth and Income in the U.S., 1989 to 2007," Federal Reserve Board, available at: http://www.federalreserve.gov/pubs/feds/2009/200913/200913pap.pdf (accessed 27 August 2012).

Leighton, P. and Selman, D. (2012). "Private Prisons, the Criminal Justice-Industrial Complex and Bodies Destined for Profitable Punishment," in W. DeKeserdy and M. Dragiewicz (eds) *Routledge Handbook of Critical Criminology*, New York: Routledge.

Lynch, J. and Pridemore, W. (2010). "Crime in International Perspective," in J. Q. Wilson and J. Petersilia (eds.) *Crime and Public Policy*, Oxford: Oxford University Press.

Ministry of Justice (2008). "Corporate Manslaughter and Corporate Homicide Act 2007," available at: http://www.justice.gov.uk/downloads/legislation/bills-acts/circulars/moj/corporate-manslaughter-act-2007-circular-9-feb-08.pdf (accessed 27 August 2012).

Mohamed, A. R. and Fritsvold, E. (2010). *Dorm Room Dealers*, Boulder, CO: Lynne Rienner.

Mooney, G. (2008). "Explaining Poverty, Social Exclusion and Inequality," in T. Ridge and S. Wright (eds.) *Understanding Inequality, Poverty and Wealth*, Bristol: Policy Press.

National Fraud Authority (2012). *Annual Fraud Indicator*, London: Home Office, available at: http://www.homeoffice.gov.uk/publications/agencies-public-bodies/nfa/annual-fraud-indicator/annual-fraud-indicator-2012?view=Binary (accessed 27 August 2012).

Norton, M. and Ariely, D. (2011). "Building a Better America—One Wealth Quintile at a Time," *Perspectives on Psychological Science*, 6(1): 9–12.

Office for National Statistics (2012a). *Crime in England and Wales, Quarterly First Release to March 2012*, London: Office of National Statistics, available at: http://www.ons.gov.uk/ons/dcp171778_273169.pdf (accessed 27 August 2012).

Office for National Statistics (2012b). *User Guide to Crime Statistics for England and Wales*, London: Office of National Statistics, available at: http://www.ons.gov.uk/ons/guide-method/method-quality/specific/crime-statistics-methodology/user-guide-to-crime-statistics.pdf (accessed 27 August 2012).

Prior, D. (2009). "The 'Problem' Of Anti-Social Behaviour And The Policy Knowledge Base," *Critical Social Policy* 29(1): 5–23.

Reiman, J. (2001). "Criminal Justice Ethics," in P. Leighton and J. Reiman (eds.) *Criminal Justice Ethics*, Upper Saddle River, NJ: Prentice Hall.

Reiman, J. (2013). Appendix II: "Between Philosophy and Criminology," in J. Reiman and P. Leighton *The Rich Get Richer and the Poor Get Prison*, 10th edn, Boston: Allyn & Bacon/Pearson.

Reiman, J. and Leighton, P. (2013). *The Rich Get Richer and the Poor Get Prison*, 10th edn, Boston: Allyn & Bacon/Pearson.

Selman, D. and Leighton, P. (2010). *Punishment for Sale*, Lanham, MD: Rowman and Littlefield.

Statistics Canada (2005). *The Wealth of Canadians*, Ottawa: Statistics Canada, available at: http://www.statcan.gc.ca/pub/13f0026m/13f0026m2006001-eng.pdf (accessed 27 August 2012).

Statistics Canada (2010). *Criminal Victimization in Canada, 2009*, Ottawa: Statistics Canada, available at: http://www.statcan.gc.ca/pub/85-002-x/2010002/article/11340-eng.pdf (accessed 27 August 2012).

Statistics Canada (2011). *Homicide in Canada, 2010*, Ottawa: Statistics Canada, available at: http://www.statcan.gc.ca/pub/85-002-x/2011001/article/11561-eng.pdf (accessed 27 August 2012).

Statistics Canada (2012a). *Police-Reported Crime Statistics in Canada, 2011*, Ottawa: Statistics Canada, available at: http://www.statcan.gc.ca/pub/85-002-x/2012001/article/11692-eng.pdf (accessed 27 August 2012).

Statistics Canada (2012b). *Adult Criminal Court Statistics in Canada, 2010/2011*, Ottawa: Statistics Canada, available at: http://www.statcan.gc.ca/pub/85-002-x/2012001/article/11646-eng.pdf (accessed 27 August 2012).

Taibbi, M. (2011). "Why Isn't Wall Street in jail?" *Rolling Stone*, 3 March, available at: http://www.rollingstone.com/politics/news/why-isnt-wall-street-in-jail-20110216 (accessed 27 August 2012).

Zimring, F. (2007). *The Great American Crime Decline*, New York: Oxford University Press.